T0398286

# Institutional Reforms and Peacebuilding

This book deals with the question of how institutional reform can contribute to peacebuilding in post-war and divided societies.

In the context of armed conflict and widespread violence, two important questions shape political agendas inside and outside the affected societies: How can we stop the violence? And how can we prevent its recurrence? Comprehensive negotiated war terminations and peace accords recommend a set of mechanisms to bring an end to war and establish peace, including institutional reforms that promote democratization and state building. Although the role of institutions is widely recognized, their specific effects are highly contested in research as well as in practice. This book highlights the necessity to include path-dependency, pre-conflict institutions and societal divisions to understand the patterns of institutional change in post-war societies and the ongoing risk of civil war recurrence. It focuses on the general question of how institutional reform contributes to the establishment of peace in post-war societies. This book comprises three separate but interrelated parts on the relation between institutions and societal divisions, on the path dependency of institutional reform and on security sector reform. The chapters contribute to the understanding of the relationship between societal cleavages, pre-conflict institutions, path dependency and institutional reform.

This book will be of much interest to students of peacebuilding, conflict resolution, development studies, security studies and international relations.

**Nadine Ansorg** is a Research Fellow at the GIGA German Institute of Global and Area Studies, Germany, and a Post-Doctoral Research Fellow at the University of Kent, UK.

**Sabine Kurtenbach** is a Political Scientist and Senior Research Fellow at the GIGA German Institute of Global Area Studies, Germany.

**Series: Studies in Conflict, Development and Peacebuilding**
Series Editors: Keith Krause, Thomas J. Biersteker and Riccardo
Bocco, Graduate Institute of International and Development
Studies, Geneva

This series publishes innovative research into the connections between insecurity
and under-development in fragile states, and into situations of violence and
insecurity more generally.

It adopts a multidisciplinary approach to the study of a variety of issues,
including the changing nature of contemporary armed violence (*conflict*), efforts
to foster the conditions that prevent the outbreak or recurrence of such violence
(*development*), and strategies to promote peaceful relations on the communal,
societal and international level (*peacebuilding*).

**The Political Economy of
Peacemaking**
*Achim Wennmann*

**The Peace In Between**
Post-war violence and peacebuilding
*Edited by Mats Berdal and Astri
Suhrke*

**Local and Global Dynamics of
Peacebuilding**
Postconflict reconstruction in Sierra
Leone
*Christine Cubitt*

**Peacebuilding, Memory and
Reconciliation**
Bridging top-down and bottom-up
approaches
*Bruno Charbonneau and Geneviève
Parent*

**Peacebuilding and Local Ownership**
Post-conflict consensus-building
*Timothy Donais*

**Stabilization Operations, Security
and Development**
States of fragility
*Edited by Robert Muggah*

**Controlling Small Arms**
Consolidation, innovation and
relevance in research and policy
*Edited by Peter Batchelor and Kai
Michael Kenkel*

**An Ethnographic Approach to
Peacebuilding**
Understanding local experiences in
transitional states
*Gearoid Millar*

**Peacebuilding and Ex-Combatants**
Political reintegration in Liberia
*Johanna Söderström*

**Local Ownership in International
Peacebuilding**
Key theoretical and practical issues
*Edited by Sung Yong Lee and Alpaslan
Özerdem*

**Institutional Reforms and
Peacebuilding**
Change, path-dependency and societal
divisions in post-war communities
*Edited by Nadine Ansorg and Sabine
Kurtenbach*

# Institutional Reforms and Peacebuilding

Change, path-dependency and societal divisions in post-war communities

Edited by Nadine Ansorg and
Sabine Kurtenbach

LONDON AND NEW YORK

First published 2017
by Routledge
2 Park Square, Milton Park, Abingdon, Oxon OX14 4RN

and by Routledge
711 Third Avenue, New York, NY 10017

*Routledge is an imprint of the Taylor & Francis Group, an informa business*

*British Library Cataloguing-in-Publication Data*
A catalogue record for this book is available from the British Library

*Library of Congress Cataloging-in-Publication Data*
Names: Ansorg, Nadine, editor. | Kurtenbach, Sabine, editor.
Title: Institutional reforms and peacebuilding : change, path-dependency and societal divisions in post-war communities / edited by Nadine Ansorg and Sabine Kurtenbach.
Description: New York, NY : Routledge, 2016. | Series: Studies in conflict, development and peacebuilding | Includes bibliographical references and index.
Identifiers: LCCN 2016013417| ISBN 9781138682306 (hardback) | ISBN 9781315545219 (ebook)
Subjects: LCSH: Nation-building. | Peace-building. | Postwar reconstruction.
Classification: LCC JZ6300 .I55 2016 | DDC 303.6/6--dc23LC record available at https://lccn.loc.gov/2016013417

ISBN: 978-1-138-68230-6 (hbk)
ISBN: 978-1-315-54521-9 (ebk)

Typeset in Times New Roman
by Saxon Graphics Ltd, Derby

# Contents

# Tables

# Figures

# Contributors

**Nadine Ansorg** is a Post-Doctoral Research Fellow at the University of Kent and Research Fellow at the GIGA German Institute of Global and Area Studies. Her current research interests include institutional reforms in post-conflict countries, security sector reform and UN peacekeeping. Her current research project (with Sabine Kurtenbach and Julia Strasheim) is on security sector reform, funded by the German Research Foundation.

**Matthias Basedau** is Lead Research Fellow at the GIGA German Institute of Global and Area Studies in Hamburg, adjunct Professor at Hamburg University and also affiliated to the Peace Research Institute Oslo (PRIO). His research focuses on the role of ethnicity, political institutions, natural resources and religion as determinants of conflict.

**Volker Boege** is a peace researcher and historian, and a Research Fellow at the School of Political Science and International Studies at the University of Queensland, Brisbane, Australia. His fields of work include peacebuilding and state formation; non-Western approaches to conflict transformation; and environmental degradation and conflict. His main regional area of expertise is Oceania. He has published numerous articles, papers and books on peace research and contemporary history.

**Artak Galyan** is a Ph.D. candidate at the Doctoral School of Political Science, Public Policy and International Relations at Central European University in Budapest, Hungary. His research interests lie at the nexus between constitutional design, democratization and social peace, with a focus on divided and post-conflict societies.

**Brian Ganson** is Head of the Africa Centre for Dispute Settlement, an extraordinary associate professor at the University of Stellenbosch Business School, Cape Town, South Africa, and a research associate with the Centre on Conflict, Development and Peacebuilding (CCDP) of the Graduate Institute of International and Development Studies in Geneva, Switzerland.

**Felix Haaß** holds an MA in Peace Research and International Politics from the University of Tübingen. He is a Research Fellow at the Arnold Bergstraesser Institute, Freiburg, and the GIGA German Institute of Global and Area Studies and a Ph.D. candidate at the University of Greifswald. His current research interests include political economy of power sharing, foreign aid and UN peacekeeping.

**Sabine Kurtenbach** is a political scientist and Senior Research Fellow at the GIGA German Institute of Global Area Studies. She is working on peace processes and postwar societies with a specific focus on postwar violence, institutional reforms and youth. Her current project (with Nadine Ansorg and Julia Strasheim) is on security sector reform.

**Esteban Ramírez González** is a career diplomat and a Ph.D. candidate in International Relations and Political Science at the Graduate Institute of International and Development Studies, Geneva (IHEID). He has previously served as security adviser to CARE International's Secretariat and officer at the United Nations in Geneva.

**Roland Schmidt** is a Ph.D. candidate in Comparative Political Science at the Central European University, Budapest, Hungary. In his work he explores the long-term consequences of post-conflict power-sharing agreements and focuses on the incompatibilities between the short-term necessities of external peacemaking and the long-term requirements for the emergence of a self-sustaining peace.

**Gerald Schneider** is Professor of International Politics at the Department of Politics and Public Administration and the Graduate School of Decision Sciences at the University of Konstanz. He is also a former President of the European Political Science Association and a past Vice President of the International Studies Association.

**Julia Strasheim** holds a MSSc. in Peace and Conflict Research from Uppsala University. She is a Research Fellow at the GIGA German Institute of Global and Area Studies and a Ph.D. candidate at the University of Heidelberg. Her current research interests include interim governments, post-conflict peace processes and security sector reform.

**Achim Wennmann** is a senior researcher at the Centre on Conflict, Development and Peacebuilding of the Graduate Institute of International and Development Studies in Geneva. His research focuses on the political economy of violent conflict, conflict resolution and peacebuilding, and includes *The Political Economy of Peacemaking* (London: Routledge, 2011).

# Introduction

## Institutional reforms and peacebuilding[1]

*Nadine Ansorg and Sabine Kurtenbach*

In the context of armed conflict and widespread violence, two important questions shape political agendas inside and outside the affected societies: How can we stop the violence? And how can we prevent its recurrence? The answers to these questions depend on a complex interplay of actors with diverging interests and allies as well as on these actors' power and capabilities. The Syrian war and the postwar situations in Afghanistan and Iraq are recent showcases of the complexity of peacebuilding. International peacebuilders like the United Nations, the World Bank and bilateral donors have become increasingly engaged in institutional reforms designed to foster the nonviolent management of conflict and to prevent a renewed outbreak of violence. Institutions may be seen as those rules and procedures that regulate social behaviour and embed conflict in nonviolent borders (cf. Coser 1956; North 1990). Comprehensive negotiated war terminations and peace accords recommend a set of mechanisms to bring an end to war and establish peace. These include institutional reforms that promote democratization and state building (e.g. interim governments, power sharing, a substantial increase in political participation, and an accountable and democratically controlled security sector). Although the role of institutions is widely recognized, their specific features – namely their formal or informal character, their relations to state and society, and their effects on societal conflicts and divisions – are highly contested in research as well as in practice.

However, the institutional reform recipe is not always successful in postwar countries, as evidenced by the highly volatile situations in Iraq and Afghanistan. Practitioners and researchers alike often use an external or global lens to identify and analyse societal divisions, which cause them to miss out on the real power relations on the ground. For instance, the underlying assumption of the 2001 Bonn Process on Afghanistan was that the different ethnic and social groups were going to cooperate during an interim phase to develop a democratic constitution leading to sustainable peace. However, some of these groups had a rather specific agenda of increasing their political and economic shares. Because of this miscalculation, the Afghan state's influence continues to be limited to the area around Kabul, while the dynamics in the rest of the country have followed very distinct paths (Simonsen 2004; Suhrke *et al.* 2002). As the lead interventionist force, the United States expelled most Baath Party members from the Iraqi state apparatus due to their relationship with former dictator Saddam Hussein. In doing so, the United States disregarded the fact that (1) most of these people were necessary to ensure the minimum functioning of the state; and (2) they were all Sunni Muslims. As a result, this approach destroyed existing institutional arrangements and deepened divisions between the Shiite, Sunni and Kurd groups in the country. Today, Iraq qualifies as a fragile state (if not a failed state), in which various armed groups control specific regions (Kalyvas and Kocher 2007).

These examples are part of a large body of evidence which reveals that international approaches to dealing with local violent conflict often follow a logic that is at odds with the realities on the ground. It highlights the difficulty in finding the right balance between the need for the international community to play an active supporting role in negotiations and the implementation of peace agreements, on the one hand, and the need for local communities to take ownership of any peace process, on the other. A majority of actors inside and outside the affected societies agree that third-party guarantees and support are sometimes necessary, and that we should not 'give war a chance' (Luttwak 1999) – the continuing war in Syria is a very strong case in point here. However, the question of how much support international interveners should provide and which strategies they should employ remain unanswered. Furthermore, these as well as other examples show that postwar peacebuilding and institutional reform do not happen in a vacuum; rather they occur within specific historical, social and political contexts which need to be taken into account. Nevertheless, international organizations often implement large-scale peacebuilding missions that are heavily driven by global 'best practices' and international supply instead of the needs of conflict-affected populations.

This book aims to understand the patterns of institutional change in postwar societies and the ongoing risk of civil war recurrence. It focuses on the general question of how institutional reform contributes to the establishment of peace in postwar societies. The main argument of this book rests on the assumption that for institutional reform to successfully prevent violence from recurring, interveners need to take into account the relationship between societal cleavages, pre-conflict institutional settings, and institutional reform in the aftermath of war. Up until now, this relationship has been both under-theorized and empirically under-investigated.

## Institutions and sustainable peace

The role of institutions in peacebuilding, as well as in democratization and state building, has been increasingly discussed in recent years. While these debates overlap in certain respects, they differ significantly in terms of academic focus and policy implications. And even though they touch upon the diverse challenges of institutional reform and postwar peace building, they have not yet found a final answer to the question of how institutional reform can contribute to the establishment of peace in postwar societies. In the following section we discuss the findings from and gaps in previous research on postwar reforms.

Theoretically, institutions can channel social, political and economic conflicts at different levels of a society. Most of the institutions intended to build peace in divided postwar societies are rooted in the historical experience of Western democracies.[2] However, there is a significant lack of systematic comparative research on the context-specific conditions that may enable or hinder these reforms' effects on peace. If the effect of a specific institution depends on or is shaped by the context, it will have no causal effect on peace, democracy or state building (Przeworski 2004). Although academic debates increasingly acknowledge these challenges, most policy approaches promote institutional engineering based on best practice or a one-size-fits-all perspective.

Nevertheless, the content, sequencing and priorities of reform should differ depending on the aims and specific context. For instance, the peacebuilding approaches prioritize preventing the recurrence of war and armed conflict; other manifestations of violence are rarely addressed. Thus institutional arrangements between the former warring actors via power sharing or other elite bargains dominate the agenda, while the lack of broader participation or long-term costs due to the missing flexibility of these arrangements are recognized as necessary trade-offs (Mac Ginty and Richmond 2013; Richmond and Mitchell 2011). In contrast, democratization approaches seek to increase the political representation and participation of the various social groups via free and fair elections, offer greater protection of minority rights, and introduce checks and balances so that governments can be held accountable. As a result, institutions are (or should be) designed to manage conflicts through nonviolent means.

Because democratization is a highly conflictive process, postwar societies are unlikely candidates for success (Hartzell and Hoddie 2015; Jarstad and Sisk 2008; Paris 2004; Zürcher *et al.* 2013). Meanwhile, state-building approaches look to enhance the stability and capacity of formal state institutions. Therefore, democratic control, the participation of the population and an efficient security sector are considered paramount for the long-term viability and legitimization of a postwar state (Fukuyama 2005; Paris and Sisk 2009). The political economy approach focuses on international interventions in post-conflict countries and the impact thereof on countries' political and economic dynamics and structures, as well as state–society relations (Anten *et al.* 2012; Berdal and Zaum 2012). Political economy studies point to the tensions that arise from the competing interests and values of different interveners and local actors, and also to the salience of economic and political violence in state-building processes and war-to-peace transition.

Like the debates on peacebuilding, state building and democratization, the theoretical debate on institutional reform relies heavily on concepts based on empirical developments in Western industrialized democracies; societies from the Global South have only recently been included in these debates (cf. Alexander 2008; Croissant 2004; Geddes 1999; Mahoney and Thelen 2010). While we recognize the challenges of institution building in postwar societies, we know little about the causes, patterns and consequences of institutional reform in violence-ridden societies. The failure of research to provide a final answer to the question of how institutional reform can contribute to the establishment of peace in postwar societies is due to three major gaps in the study of institutional reform.

First, although there is extensive research on institutional reform that focuses on Western countries and those that experience democratization from authoritarian to more open regimes (e.g. Mahoney and Thelen 2010), it is still unclear under what conditions what types of institutional change occur in postwar settings. Many studies that deal with institutional change mainly focus on institutional reforms during peaceful times (cf. Greif and Laitin 2004; Moe 2005). Scholars often point to exogenous shocks that bring about radical institutional reform, such as waves of democratization or international economic constraints (cf. Mahoney and Thelen 2010, 2). Others explain incremental change by the appearance of opportunities in the political context (e.g. a changed regional environment) and certain agents of change (e.g. strong advocates of a municipality-based system) (cf. Falleti 2010; Mahoney and Thelen 2010; Onoma 2010) without explicitly dealing with the complex and specific conditions that apply to postwar countries.

Second, those studies that deal with institutions in postwar societies often assume institutional design on a tabula rasa and fail to acknowledge the continuity or adaptation of prewar institutional arrangements. This perspective assumes that armed conflict destroys all existing local institutions and that new Western institutions need to be built once the violence comes to an end. For instance, Guttieri and Piombo study the role of interim institutions in postwar societies under the premise that these institutions are put in place to create a 'government from scratch' (2007, 13). There is a large body of literature on liberal peacebuilding that deals with the introduction of democratic institutions such as parliaments, political parties and power-sharing institutions in conflict societies (cf. Hartzell 2007; Paris 2004; Reilly 2006). Based on the experiences of post-World War II Europe, the 'ingredients' of successful peacebuilding and state-building often contain democratic institutions, an effective security sector and economic reconstruction (cf. Bächler 2004; Brinkerhoff 2005). The link to local societal structures and theoretically sound explanations of the specific patterns of institutional reform in postwar societies in the non-OECD world are often missing; research especially neglects the connection between prewar and postwar institutional settings.

Third, the interdependence of institutions and the structure of a society (e.g. divisions between groups and institutional design) are generally under-theorized and empirically under-investigated. If designed to support sustainable peace, institutional change needs to account for the specific characteristics of societal divisions (cf. Mehler 2013; see also Basedau, Chapter 1, this volume). Even if war ends, postwar societies remain characterized by major cleavages between, for example, ethnic or religious groups. These are often a source of continued tension in the aftermath of war and can contribute to a recurrence of war. Hence, a major challenge in postwar societies is to address these cleavages and to re-embed violent conflict into nonviolent institutional settings. Further, the experience of severe violence perpetrated by members of specific societal groups during a war can also have a major influence on the postwar decisions of institutional change. Thus, research needs to take into account societal divisions that very likely will have an impact on the choice of institutional arrangements and the chances of postwar peace.

This book seeks to build bridges between the different approaches and methodologies that deal with the challenges posed by institutional reform and peacebuilding. It offers new insights into the conditions of successful institutional reform by exploring the specific context conditions of postwar societies – that is, societal context conditions as well as prewar experiences with specific institutions – that have a major impact on the outcome of postwar institutional reform. What connects the contributions to this volume is the inclusion of path dependency, as well as the societal context, as an important factor shaping the patterns and outcome of institutional reforms. We state that the current debates on the possibility and viability of peacebuilding, state building and democratization after the end of war could be much more constructive if a historical and global dimension were systematically included (Newman 2013). At the same time, political economy approaches to postwar transformations show how important it is to frame the relationship between local contexts and globalized influences during and after civil war. Even in contexts where external actors may not have played a direct role in war and war termination, economic, political and social relations will be affected by global developments and interactions. Resources that finance rebels or governments are an example, as are human rights activists who monitor violence and armed conflict even in remote areas of the globe. The chapters in this book thus pay particular attention to institution building while linking their research to democratization, state-building and peacebuilding debates and acknowledging existing structures (the local) and specific patterns in the respective post-war society.

## Specific challenges of institutional reform in postwar societies

A postwar society is a country that has suffered from intense and severe armed conflict (Rausch and Banar 2006; World Bank 2012). The war would have ended as the result of a negotiated peace accord, the military victory by one party, the intervention by a third party, or armed conflict activity dropping below a noticeable threshold for an extended time period (cf. Kreutz 2010; Licklider 2001; Sambanis 2004). However, the terms 'postwar society' and 'post-conflict society' do not mean that all violence has ended and that there is sustainable peace; rather, they merely signify an absence of war and collective violence. For instance, women often face a greater threat of violence in postwar periods than during war itself (*Human Security Report 2012*). However, violence in postwar periods may be different from violence during war. Two cases in point are El Salvador and Guatemala, where criminal groups and youth gangs without a political agenda have become the main perpetrators of violence in these countries' postwar periods. Nevertheless, these states' responses resemble the repressive counterinsurgency strategies from the past (Cruz 2011).

In these environments institution building is often understood as the (initial) creation or reform of formal state institutions (e.g. constitutions, (electoral) laws, property rights, the government system, the judiciary and the security sector (Helmke and Levitsky 2004; North 1990) in a way that promotes nonviolent conflict management between social and political groups. 'Desirable' outcomes are typically related to the prevention of the recurrence of war or armed conflict and may therefore include the implementation of democracy or equal representation of politically salient groups, especially in deeply divided societies (cf. Reilly 2001; Wolff 2010). On the contrary, informal institutions (e.g. culture, sanctions, taboos, customs, traditions, codes of conduct) are often not integrated into institution-building efforts in postwar societies – a fact that is highlighted by critical peacebuilding theories (cf. Heathershaw 2008; Mac Ginty 2011; Ottaway 2002).

When studying institutional reform, the specific context characteristics of postwar societies need to be taken into account. First, postwar societies are characterized by the large-scale destruction of political, social and economic structures. The state is weak, meaning that there is a lack of social cohesion and popular legitimacy towards authorities. These authorities furthermore often do not have the capacity – or willingness – to perform basic tasks such as providing security and the rule of law. Second, many postwar societies also experience a large degree of international involvement and the presence of hundreds of international organizations. This could lead local relevant actors to simply accept the practices proposed by international organizations at the expense of more suitable peace-establishing institutional reforms that correspond to existing prewar institutions. However, large-scale institutional reform programmes often do not provide solutions to actual problems of postwar situations (cf. Ottaway 2002, 1004), such as the compatibility of formal and informal institutions or the lack of funding for or local trust in important reforms. Instead, 'what external agents do is set up organizations, not institutions' (Ottaway 2002, 1004). International organizations are then not accepted by important local actors, as they do not provide rules or procedures that correspond with their daily realities or are rooted in their historical traditions and norms. In some cases, the international community assumes responsibility and control over most of the postwar reforms, thus greatly limiting local ownership of the process and creating massive aid dependencies, such as in Kosovo, Bosnia, Liberia and Afghanistan.

Third, a 'shadow of conflict and violence' is persistent in every postwar society (cf. Schlichte 2009). The threat of organized intergroup violence and past experience of large-scale violence affect the behaviours and motives of local actors. As the failed peace agreements in Liberia, Angola and Sudan show, the risk of renewed violence remains high. Research on micro-level developments during wartime shows high variation in the adaptation or change of local institutions with regard to different types of armed actors (Arjona 2014; Staniland 2012). Justino (2013) similarly argues that 'institutional change takes place in particular when different actors contest and sometimes win over existing state institutions in certain areas, or over the whole country, transforming social, economic and political structures, organizations and norms'. As a consequence, micro-level developments can support or undermine institutional reform at the national level. For instance, Duncan (2005) shows how the local paramilitary networks in Colombia were able to transfer their rural-based power to the cities and increase their influence in national politics.

Thus, institutional change in postwar societies is highly dependent on the context characteristics of postwar societies; that is, the presence and interests of external peacebuilders and international donors, the destruction of or changes to existing institutions due to war, the ongoing threat of organized intergroup violence, and the conflicting interests of former warring parties.

## Conceptual framework: institutional reform in the context of violence

How can institutional reform contribute to the establishment of peace in postwar societies? In the context of the above-outlined specific conditions of postwar societies, we assume that the ability of institutional reform to promote a stable postwar peace is dependent on two interrelated aspects: the connection of reforms to pre-conflict institutions and the societal cleavages that affect the choice of postwar institutional settings.

### *Pre-conflict institutions*

Institutional reform is highly dependent on the prewar institutional settings and follows the logic of path dependency. After all, prewar institutions often do not cease to exist with the outbreak of violence but continue to function during conflict and postwar times. For instance, even though the 1991 Paris Peace Agreement for Cambodia created the United Nations Transitional Administration in Cambodia and a domestic power-sharing council for the interim period leading up to the 1993 elections, the bureaucracy of the prewar communist government was largely left intact to manage civil administration also in the immediate postwar period, which impeded the transitional administration's ability to transform corrupt and authoritarian state structures (Doyle and Suntharalingam 1994). New institutional arrangements thus complement former institutional experiences. Different reform strategies towards pre-conflict institutions may account for different success stories among postwar institutions. For example, though in South Africa it was deemed necessary to turn the whole political system upside down after the end of apartheid, constitutional practice in Chad has remained the same despite decades of ongoing conflict and several peace agreements. In other contexts democratization of the political systems and related institutional change may occur in the midst of war and before an armed conflict has been ended, as happened in Central America (Kurtenbach 2013).

In postwar countries in particular, there is an increased need to change pre-conflict institutions. Rebel groups that engage in peace negotiations may call for postwar institutional reform that grants them political recognition, political rights and political power. Opening up the political system and 'rebel-to-party' transformations are major ingredients of most peace accords. In addition, the more former opponents are respected and integrated into the political system, the less likely they are to take up arms again and the less likely violence is to recur (Walter 2002). In those cases where prewar institutions proved to be dysfunctional and have been replaced by more democratic institutions, a recurrence of violence may be less likely. Central America underwent a significant process of political opening and democratization in the midst and after war, which was central to reducing collective political violence. However, the region is now characterized by high levels of criminal violence and, to a lesser degree, selective state repression (Cruz 2011).

In those cases where certain institutions were already in place before war broke out, it may be assumed that they failed to prevent the outbreak of violence. Hence, if the 'defective' pre-conflict institutional system is not reformed in the aftermath of violence, it is unlikely to be able to resolve the problems between ethnic or identity groups after the war, in which case a recurrence of armed conflict is more likely.

Moreover, if institutions become more authoritarian rather than more democratic, we can also expect an increased likelihood of postwar violence. For example, Rwanda's history of genocide and military victory in 1994 is said to have determined the decision to opt for a strong presidency, prohibit the creation of ethnic parties, allow the government to strictly control party activities and reject power-sharing between ethnic groups. Although Rwanda's institutions are designed to prevent ethnicization of the political system, it has failed to ease the ongoing tensions between Hutus and Tutsis in the country. In fact, these tensions have spilled over into the neighbouring Democratic Republic of Congo, from where Hutu rebels continue to attack Rwanda (Autesserre 2010; Straus 2008). Furthermore, Rwanda's institutional arrangement has paved the way for an authoritarian system, which is controlled by the leading Rwandan Patriotic Front.

The central question is whether and how institutional reforms interact with existing institutions. Do they transform the very substance of institutions? Or are such changes merely superficial? In Nicaragua, for example, a new civilian police force was established with high levels of legitimacy following the Sandinista revolution; however, support for the police has dropped due to high levels of police corruption and victimization (Cruz 2015).

### Societal divisions

The cleavages between societal groups, particularly in postwar societies, are very deep, and mistrust and violence persist. Hence, institutional reforms are highly dependent on societal cleavages and the question of how to mitigate societal conflict in the aftermath of war. In Guatemala, for example, institutional reforms were heavily undermined by the dominance of status quo-oriented actors. While a set of new 'peace institutions' (the peace secretariat and the new civilian police force) were established and aided by international cooperation, they were underfunded and bypassed by the ministries that were controlled by the traditional, status quo-oriented elites. With the new civilian police force unable to tackle the crime wave, the government sent in the military; this in turn undermined the division of labour between the police (internal security) and the armed forces (external security) that had been established in the peace accords (Kurtenbach 2013). As postwar societies are always characterized by major cleavages between societal groups, such as ethnic or religious groups, a central challenge is to address these cleavages and to re-embed conflict into nonviolent institutional settings. A lack of social cohesion can hamper institution-building and peacebuilding efforts in the aftermath of war. Following the formal end of war by a peace agreement, formerly warring groups are often forced to continue living together in a shared, though invariably contested, state (Cox *et al.* 2015). In Lebanon, for example, constitutionally prescribed quotas for Christians, Muslims and Druzes led to an imbalance in societal representation and eventually to the outbreak of war in 1975. This sectarian system of governance deeply constrained efforts to foster cross-cutting social engagement and to reconfigure state–society relationships even after the termination of war (Aoun and Zahar 2015). Therefore, one major task faced by both local and international actors is to promote and foster cohesion between formerly warring parties as a condition to help prevent a renewed outbreak of violence.

There are various strategies of societal inclusion, but the research cannot yet definitively tell us what works and what does not. While advocates of consociations see power-sharing features in peace agreements as one way to ensure cooperation and accommodation across ethnic divides (Hartzell and Hoddie 2007; Lijphart 1977; McGarry and O'Leary 2006), others are far less optimistic about the peace-enhancing functions of these features (Reilly 2006; Mehler 2009; Tull and Mehler 2005). For the latter, power-sharing agreements are often not flexible enough for fast-changing postwar environments; thus an agreement that may be effective in bringing warring parties to the negotiating table may become undemocratic some months or years later (cf. also Durant and Weintraub 2014). Further, peripheral visible groups and civil society are often left out of these elite arrangements.

However, it may not be the strategy that prevents the establishment of societal peace, but rather the context conditions or the process itself. As Cox *et al.* (2015) state in their project report, 'social cohesion is advanced when political systems are fully inclusive of all major groups, yet there are often practical and normative barriers to full inclusion, in part as a consequence of radicalization and extremism'. Moreover, Levitsky and Murillo (2009) emphasize the necessity to analyse the conditions of enforcement and activation of new institutional arrangements. Hence, we need to study potential barriers or triggers of institutional reform – such as the level of societal destruction, the scope of external interventions, missing economic investment and the continued risk of a recurrence of violence – to reach reliable conclusions on which institutional reform strategies do and do not work in postwar societies.

The main question is how societal divisions relate to postwar peace. To what degree do conflict resolution and the strategy of institutional reform matter? The following chapters provide some insights and seek to forward a research agenda which goes beyond the simple normative statement that reform needs to be shaped according to Western experiences. Empirical evidence using comparative methods and including a historical dimension provides new avenues.

In sum, the ability to create stable peace through institutional reform is dependent on pre-conflict institutions and societal cleavages. The causal relation between these aspects is twofold. First, in those cases where pre-conflict institutions are not able to prevent a major outbreak of violence, they need to be reformed in order to re-embed conflict within the nonviolent borders of institutions and to reduce societal cleavages. In Bosnia-Herzegovina, for instance, there was an urgent need to reform prewar institutional settings to accommodate all three major groups in the political system and to increase societal cohesion after the devastating violence the country had experienced (Chandler 2000). Hence, the Dayton Agreement specified a very detailed consociational design that established not only a government shared between Bosnian, Croat and Serb groups and a three-member presidency that rotates every eight months, but also a party-list proportional representation electoral system and group autonomy in the form of a two-entity federation (i.e. the Federation of Bosnia and Herzegovina and the Republika Srpska). While some observers may consider this system complicated and inflexible, it is hard to deny the fact that it has prevented a recurrence of violence in Bosnia, especially given that societal tensions still persist among the three groups.

Second, societal cleavages and a lack of social cohesion can hamper reform efforts and thus must be taken into account when reforming pre-conflict institutions: doing so can increase the effectiveness of reform in fostering peace. In Liberia, for instance, all key societal groups (from warlords to civil society organizations) participated in the postwar interim government. During that period, the pre-conflict institutional system – which was considered as unjust by some parts of the society – was reformed.

Figure 0.1 shows the interaction between the different concepts we analyse.

The contributions to this book will test the above-outlined assumptions with regard to the relationship between pre-conflict institutions and the societal cleavages, on the one hand, and the ability of institutional reform to promote stable postwar peace based on diverse theoretical, methodological and regional backgrounds, on the other.

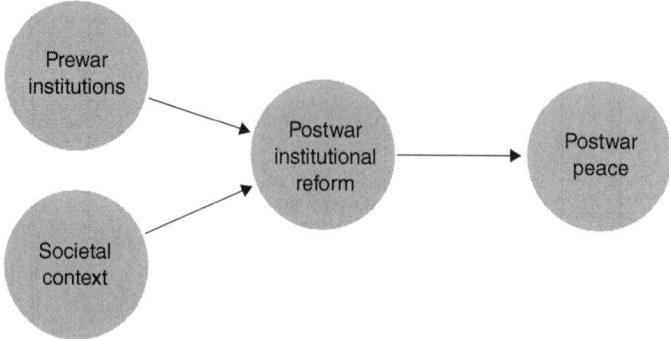

*Figure 0.1*  Interaction between institutional reform, prewar institutions, societal context and postwar peace.

## Contributions to this book

This book comprises three separate parts that contribute to the overall aim of the book, namely the understanding of the relationship between societal cleavages, pre-conflict institutions, path dependency and institutional reform. Part I investigates the relationship between societal divisions and institutional design with a focus on their ability to channel or mitigate conflicts. Part II focuses on the path dependency of institutions and the effect war has on their capabilities to manage conflict and mitigate societal divisions. Part III examines the security sector, as reforms here are crucial in all postwar societies. Despite the differences in approaches to security, there is a rather broad consensus that a minimum level of physical security for the population is a key condition for postwar political, economic and social development. At the same time security sector reform is a policy field where external actors have been very much involved either by monitoring or implementing the demobilization of former combatants or by providing resources and advice for the restructuring of the armed forces and the police.

Part I deals with the relationship between existing divisions, societal cleavages and institutional designs and their impact on the success of institutional reform in the aftermath of large-scale violence. It comprises chapters by Matthias Basedau, Gerald Schneider and Artak Galyan. Basedau argues that the success of institutional engineering is conditional upon the depth of divisions. He develops an innovative measure of the depth of divisions and tests its conditional effect on ethnic conflict in 34 African countries that have undergone major institutional reform since 1990. He finds that the levels of depth of divisions are related to the inclusiveness of institutions: where divisions are deeper, inclusiveness seems to work; where divisions are absent, inclusiveness levels appear to be irrelevant.

Schneider explores the determinants of power sharing and power-sharing reforms. He argues that divided societies can escape the ills of diversity ex ante through inclusive policy making. However, short-term considerations of politicians who want to stay in power often prevent fractionalized and polarized states from the farsighted adoption of adequate conflict-management strategies. His statistical analysis shows that countries often do not escape the 'shadow of the past', which manifests itself in previous choices on how to govern a country and the adoption of the legal tradition of the former colonial power. Moreover, Schneider's analysis shows that – in line with theoretical expectations – highly diverse or polarized societies, as well as war-torn societies, often have fewer chances to adopt power sharing than more homogeneous societies. His contribution demonstrates that institutional reformers rarely preventively adapt constitutions and informal power arrangements to address the ills of diversity.

Galyan explores a conjunctural institutional framework that integrates insights into the impact of separate institutions and forms of ethnic diversity into a more holistic framework. His framework conceptualizes the effects of institutions as being nested in the socio-institutional context while their impact upon social peace is dependent on the degree of congruence between the institutional configurations on the one hand and social structure on the other. He applies this framework to the case of Sri Lanka, which experienced three cycles of institutional change with three different socio-institutional combinations between 1948 and 2010. Galyan attributes the escalation of interethnic relations and intergroup violence to the incongruence between Sri Lanka's political institutions and social structure.

Part II analyses the path dependency of institutional designs as well as the influence of war and violence on reforms and eventually on the establishment of post-conflict peace. It includes contributions by Sabine Kurtenbach, Roland Schmidt and Artak Galyan, and Brian Ganson and Achim Wennmann. Taking Colombia as an example, Kurtenbach assesses the particular challenges of introducing institutional reforms in the midst of war. She argues that such reforms can influence the dynamics of conflict and in some cases reduce violence or even help bring war to an end; however, they also run the risk of exacerbating existing cleavages and thus reproducing violence. Because reforms implemented in the midst of war are only done so gradually, they are likely to produce fewer fractures than fundamental reforms, which are only possible once a war has ended. Still, these gradual reforms can open windows of opportunity for non-armed actors, which may serve to build confidence between actors and help end the war. The specific effects of institutional reform on peacebuilding in Colombia mirror the changing power relations among the state, armed actors and civil society.

Schmidt and Galyan examine the temporal constraints upon power-sharing arrangements, namely sunset clauses. This mechanism has so far received little scholarly attention. In their qualitative analysis on ten peace agreements with sunset clauses, Schmidt and Galyan trace the dynamics of the periods before and after the sunset clauses were triggered and identify the factors that help explain why in some cases the removal of safeguards prompted by a triggered sunset clause leads to a resurgence of violence and in others it constitutes a further significant step towards the consolidation of peace.

Ganson and Wennmann's private sector perspective focuses specifically on the role of large-scale investments in institutional change in postwar states. They explore how struggles by a variety of formal and informal actors for power and authority over business activities can frustrate mainstream 'good governance' initiatives and result in a series of unintended outcomes, ranging from elite entrenchment, to greater conflicts risk, and to the weakening of state and traditional institutions. Ganson and Wennmann argue that by acknowledging that business becomes part of the hybrid political order, new opportunities for institutional reform emerge through bottom-up multi-stakeholder process designs. According to this view, international business can actively foster institutional reform from the bottom up by using its power to support cross-sectoral, multilevel and locally owned governance processes in hybrid political orders. The authors show that such approaches can also increase the sustainability of institutional reform and support the development of legitimate government institutions that are more strongly rooted in their own context.

Part III focuses on a key reform that occurs in all postwar societies – namely security sector reform – and assesses to what degree the extent of international intervention, prewar institutional settings and societal context conditions influence the security sector. It contains chapters by Felix Haaß, Julia Strasheim and Nadine Ansorg, Esteban Ramirez Gonzalez and Volker Böge. Haass, Strasheim and Ansorg analyse the influence international peacebuilders have on the successful implementation of post-conflict police reform. They argue that external peacebuilders possess two characteristics that are associated with the postwar implementation of police reform: the volume of resources they bring and the extensiveness of their mandate. They test their hypotheses using cases where two types of police reform have been implemented: (1) provisions on political control of the police force achieved through strengthening accountability structures; and (2) provisions that regulate the composition of police forces, such as the mode of representation of identity groups, women and former warring parties. Using new data on police reform implementation for their logistical regression analysis, they reveal that international financing for security sector reform is indeed correlated with a higher likelihood of implementing political control reforms, but does not affect the likelihood of implementing reforms that regulate the composition of a police force. They also show that peace operations are positively associated with a higher likelihood of implementing political control aspects of police reform.

Esteban Ramirez Gonzalez identifies the predominant models for the organization of armed force in nineteenth-century Mexico and traces their impact on the reproduction of wartime actors and local governance mechanisms in post-conflict settings. He makes the case for placing the organizational and historical dimensions of armed actor dynamics at the centre of questions about post-conflict reform. He then reflects on the paradoxical patterns of institutional change driven by armed actors in settings – such as in present-day Latin America – where armed disorder and low-intensity violence, rather than peace or outright conflict, remain the norm.

Volker Boege argues that the mainstream liberal peacebuilding approach, with its focus on building and reforming state institutions, overlooks the institutional complexity and fluidity of post-conflict societies. Instead, he finds that informal, customary, local 'illiberal' institutions and actors play important roles in maintaining peace and order in postwar situations. Their relations and interactions with state institutions lead to the emergence of complex hybrid institutional arrangements that elude technocratic attempts of institution building and institutional reform. Institutional reform is but one element in the ongoing hybridization of peace, order, security and governance, which blurs and makes porous the boundaries between the formal and the informal, the state and the non-state, the liberal and the local, and the external and the internal.

The book concludes with a summary of the previous chapters' main findings on institutional reforms in the context of violence. In doing so, it answers that guiding question of how institutional reform can contribute to the establishment of peace in postwar societies. The findings here take into consideration the path dependency of institutions and societal context and are thus able to account for the effects and conditions caused by societal cleavages and both pre-conflict and wartime institutions. Where possible, the results produced here are generalized and used to highlight potential avenues for future research.

## Notes

1　This book project is the final outcome of the Institutions for Sustainable Peace project, which ran from 2012 to 2016 at the German Institute of Global and Area Studies and was funded by the Leibniz Association. We thank Felix Haaß and Julia Strasheim, as well as the two anonymous reviewers, for their valuable comments on earlier versions of this introduction.

2　In recent years research on institutional approaches towards divided societies has been strongly influenced by the debate on Lijphart's (1977) concept of consociationalism based on grand coalitions, mutual veto, proportional representation electoral systems and group autonomy. Critics such as Horowitz (1985) claim that this perpetuates group identities and that centralist institutions may be better suited to mitigating and preventing violent conflict.

## References

Alexander, M. 2008. 'Democratization and Hybrid Regimes: Comparative Evidence from Southeast Europe'. *East European Politics and Societies* 22(4): 928–954. doi:10.1177/0888325408327634.

Anten, Louise, Ivan Briscoe and Marco Mezzera. 2012. 'The Political Economy of State-building in Situations of Fragility and Conflict: From Analysis to Strategy. A Synthesis Paper Based on Studies of Afghanistan, Democratic Republic of Congo, Guatemala, Kosovo and Pakistan'. Conflict Research Unit, Netherlands Institute of International Relations 'Clingendael'.

Aoun, Joy and Marie-Joelle Zahar. 2015. 'Confessionalism, Consociationalism, and Social Cohesion in Lebanon'. Available at: www.du.edu/korbel/sie/media/documents/faculty_pubs/sisk/religion-and-social-cohesion-reports/lebanon.pdf.

Arjona, Ana. 2014. 'Wartime Institutions: A Research Agenda'. *Journal of Conflict Resolution* 58(8): 1360–1389. doi:10.1177/0022002714547904.

Autesserre, Séverine. 2010. *The Trouble with the Congo: Local Violence and the Failure of International Peacebuilding*. Cambridge Studies in International Relations 115. Cambridge; New York: Cambridge University Press.

Bächler, Günter. 2004. 'Conflict Transformation through State Reform'. Berlin: Berghof Research Center for Constructive Conflict Management. Available at: www.berghof-handbook.net.

Berdal, Mats R. and Dominik Zaum. 2012. *Political Economy of Statebuilding: Power after Peace*. New York: Routledge.

Brinkerhoff, Derick W. 2005. 'Rebuilding Governance in Failed States and Post-conflict Societies: Core Concepts and Cross-cutting Themes'. *Public Administration and Development* 25(1): 3–14. doi:10.1002/pad.352.

Chandler, David. 2000. *Bosnia: Faking Democracy after Dayton*, 2nd edn. London: Pluto Press.

Coser, Lewis A. 1956. *The Functions of Social Conflict*. London: Routledge & Kegan Paul.

Cox, Fletcher D., Catherine R. Orsborn and Timothy D. Sisk. 2015. 'Religion, Peacebuilding, and Social Cohesion in Conflict-affected Countries'. Available at: www.du.edu/korbel/sie/media/documents/faculty_pubs/sisk/religion-and-social-cohesion-reports/rsc-researchreport.pdf.

Croissant, Aurel. 2004. 'From Transition to Defective Democracy: Mapping Asian Democratization'. *Democratization* 11(5): 156–178. doi:10.1080/13510340412331304633.

Cruz, José Miguel. 2011. 'Criminal Violence and Democratization in Central America: The Survival of the Violent State'. *Latin American Politics and Society* 53(4): 1–33. doi:10.1111/j.1548-2456.2011.00132.x.

Cruz, José Miguel. 2015. 'Police Misconduct and Political Legitimacy in Central America'. *Journal of Latin American Studies* 47(2): 251–283. doi:10.1017/S0022216X15000085.

Doyle, Michael W. and Nishkala Suntharalingam. 1994. 'The UN in Cambodia: Lessons for Complex Peacekeeping'. *International Peacekeeping* 1(2): 117–147. doi:10.1080/13533319408413498.

Duncan, Gustavo. 2005. *Del Campo a La Ciudad En Colombia: La Infiltración Urbana de Los Señores de La Guerra*. University de los Andes. Available at: www.plataformademocratica.org/Publicacoes/3652.pdf.

Durant, T.C. and M. Weintraub. 2014. 'How to Make Democracy Self-enforcing after Civil War: Enabling Credible yet Adaptable Elite Pacts'. *Conflict Management and Peace Science* 31(5): 521–540. doi:10.1177/0738894213520372.

Falleti, Tulia G. 2010. 'Infiltrating the State: The Evolution of Health Care Reforms in Brazil, 1964–1988'. In *Explaining Institutional Change*, edited by James Mahoney and Kathleen Thelen, 38–62. Cambridge: Cambridge University Press. Available at: http://ebooks.cambridge.org/ref/id/CBO9780511806414A011.

Fukuyama, Francis. 2005. '"Stateness" First'. *Journal of Democracy* 16(1): 84–88.

Geddes, Barbara. 1999. 'Authoritarian Breakdown: Empiricial Test of a Game Theoretic Argument'. Paper Prepared for Presentation at the Annual Meeting of the American Political Science Association, September. Available at: www.uvm.edu/~cbeer/geddes/tp.pdf.

Greif, Avner and David D. Laitin. 2004. 'A Theory of Endogenous Institutional Change'. *American Political Science Review* 98(4): 633–652.doi:10.1017/S0003055404041395.

Guttieri, Karen and Jessica Piombo. 2007. *Interim Governments: Institutional Bridges to Peace and Democracy?* Washington, DC: United States Institute of Peace Press.

Hartzell, Caroline A. and Matthew Hoddie. 2007. *Crafting Peace: Power-sharing Institutions and the Negotiated Settlement of Civil Wars*. University Park, PA.: Pennsylvania State University Press. Available at: http://search.ebscohost.com/login.aspx?direct=true&scope=site&db=nlebk&db=nlabk&AN=228471.

Hartzell, Caroline A., and Matthew Hoddie. 2015. 'The Art of the Possible: Power Sharing and Post-Civil War Democracy'. *World Politics* 67(1): 37–71. doi:10.1017/S0043887114000306.

Heathershaw, J. 2008. 'Unpacking the Liberal Peace: The Dividing and Merging of Peacebuilding Discourses'. *Millennium – Journal of International Studies* 36(3): 597–621. doi:10.1177/03058298080360031101.

Helmke, Gretchen and Steven Levitsky. 2004. 'Informal Institutions and Comparative Politics: A Research Agenda'. *Perspectives on Politics* 2(4): 725—740. doi:10.1017/S1537592704040472.

Horowitz, Donald L. 1985. *Ethnic Groups in Conflict*. Berkeley: University of California Press.

Human Security Report. 2012. *Sexual Violence, Education, and War* [S.l.]. Vancouver, Canada: Human Security Press.

Jarstad, Anna K. and Timothy D. Sisk. 2008. *From War to Democracy: Dilemmas of Peacebuilding*. Cambridge: Cambridge University Press.

Justino, Patricia. 2013. 'Research and Policy Implications from a Micro-level Perspective on the Dynamics of Conflict, Violence, and Development'. HiCN Working Paper 139, Brighton: The Institute of Development Studies at the University of Sussex.

Kalyvas, S.N. and M.A. Kocher. 2007. 'Ethnic Cleavages and Irregular War: Iraq and Vietnam'. *Politics and Society* 35(2): 183–223. doi:10.1177/0032329207302403.

Kreutz, Joakim. 2010. 'How and When Armed Conflicts End: Introducing the UCDP Conflict Termination Dataset'. *Journal of Peace Research* 47(2): 243–250.

Kurtenbach, Sabine. 2013. 'The "Happy Outcomes" May Not Come at All – Postwar Violence in Central America'. *Civil Wars* 15(supp.1): 105–122. doi:10.1080/13698249 .2013.850884.

Levitsky, Steven and María Victoria Murillo. 2009. 'Variation in Institutional Strength'. *Annual Review of Political Science* 12(1): 115–133. doi:10.1146/annurev. polisci.11.091106.121756.

Licklider, Roy. 2001. 'Obstacles to Peace Settlements'. In *Turbulent Peace: The Challenges of Managing International Conflict*, edited by Chester A. Crocker, Fen Osler and Pamela Aall. Washington, DC: United States Institute of Peace Press.

Lijphart, Arend. 1977. *Democracy in Plural Societies: A Comparative Exploration*. New Haven, CT: Yale University Press.

Luttwak, Edward N. 1999. 'Give War a Chance'. *Foreign Affairs*, July/August.

Mac Ginty, Roger. 2011. *International Peacebuilding and Local Resistance: Hybrid Forms of Peace*. New York: Palgrave Macmillan.

Mac Ginty, Roger and Oliver P. Richmond. 2013. 'The Local Turn in Peace Building: A Critical Agenda for Peace'. *Third World Quarterly* 34(5): 763–783. doi:10.1080/01436 597.2013.800750.

Mahoney, James and Kathleen Thelen. 2010. 'A Theory of Gradual Institutional Change'. In *Explaining Institutional Change*, edited by James Mahoney and Kathleen Thelen, 1–37. Cambridge: Cambridge University Press. Available at: http://ebooks.cambridge. org/ref/id/CBO9780511806414A010.

McGarry, John and Brendan O'Leary. 2006. 'Consociational Theory, Northern Ireland's Conflict, and Its Agreement. Part 1: What Consociationalists Can Learn from Northern Ireland'. *Government and Opposition* 41(1): 43–63. doi:10.1111/j.1477-7053.2006. 00170.x.

Mehler, Andreas. 2009. 'Peace and Power Sharing in Africa: A Not So Obvious Relationship'. *African Affairs* 108(432): 453–473. doi:10.1093/afraf/adp038.

Mehler, Andreas. 2013. 'Consociationalism for Weaklings, Autocracy for Muscle Men? Determinants of Constitutional Reform in Divided Societies'. *Civil Wars* 15(supp.1): 21–43. doi:10.1080/13698249.2013.850874.

Moe, Terry M. 2005. 'Power and Political Institutions'. *Perspectives on Politics* 3(2). doi:10.1017/S1537592705050176.

Newman, Edward. 2013. 'The Violence of Statebuilding in Historical Perspective: Implications for Peacebuilding'. *Peacebuilding* 1(1): 141–157. doi:10.1080/21647259. 2013.756281.

North, Douglas C. 1990. *Institutions, Institutional Change and Economic Performance*. Cambridge: Cambridge University Press.

Onoma, Ato Kwamena. 2010. 'The Contradictory Potential of Institutions: The Rise and Decline of Land Documentation in Kenya'. In *Explaining Institutional Change*, edited by James Mahoney, Kathleen Thelen, 63–93. Cambridge: Cambridge University Press. Available at: http://ebooks.cambridge.org/ref/id/CBO9780511806414A012.

Ottaway, Marina. 2002. 'Rebuilding State Institutions in Collapsed States'. *Development and Change* 33(5): 1001–1023. doi:10.1111/1467-7660.t01-1-00258.

Paffenholz, Thanja. 2010. 'Civil Society and Peacebuilding'. In *Civil Society and Peacebuilding : A Critical Assessment*, edited by Thanja Paffenholz, 43–63. Boulder, CO: Lynne Rienner.

Paris, Roland. 2004. *At War's End. Building Peace After Civil Conflict.* Cambridge: Cambridge University Press.

Paris, Roland and Timothy D. Sisk, eds. 2009. *The Dilemmas of Statebuilding: Confronting the Contradictions of Postwar Peace Operations*, 1st edn. London and New York: Routledge.

Przeworski, Adam. 2004. 'Institutions Matter?' *Government and Opposition* 39(4): 527–540.

Rausch, Colette and Elaine Banar. 2006. *Combating Serious Crimes in Postconflict Societies: A Handbook for Policymakers and Practitioners.* Washington, DC: United States Institute of Peace Press.

Reilly, Benjamin. 2001. *Democracy in Divided Societies: Electoral Engineering for Conflict Management.* Cambridge; New York: Cambridge University Press. Available at: http://dx.doi.org/10.1017/CBO9780511491108.

Reilly, Benjamin. 2006. 'Political Engineering and Party Politics in Conflict-prone Societies'. *Democratization* 13(5): 811–827.

Richmond, Oliver P. 2011. *A Post-liberal Peace.* Routledge Studies in Peace and Conflict Resolution. Abingdon, Oxon ; New York: Routledge.

Richmond, Oliver P. and Audra Mitchell, eds. 2011. *Hybrid Forms of Peace: From Everyday Agency to Post-liberalism.* Basinkstoke: Palgrave Macmillan.

Sambanis, Nicholas. 2004. 'What Is Civil War? Conceptual and Empirical Complexities of an Operational Definition'. *The Journal of Conflict Resolution* 48(6): 814–858.

Schlichte, Klaus. 2009. *In the Shadow of Violence: The Politics of Armed Groups.* Frankfurt: Campus Verlag.

Simonsen, Sven Gunnar. 2004. 'Ethnicising Afghanistan?: Inclusion and Exclusion in Post-Bonn Institution Building'. *Third World Quarterly* 25(4): 707–729. doi:10.1080/0 1436590410001678942.

Staniland, Paul. 2012. 'States, Insurgents, and Wartime Political Orders'. *Perspectives on Politics* 10(2): 243–264. doi:10.1017/S1537592712000655.

Straus, Scott. 2008. *The Order of Genocide: Race, Power, and War in Rwanda.* Ithaca, NY: Cornell University Press.

Suhrke, Astri, Kristian Berg Harpviken and Arne Strand. 2002. 'After Bonn: Conflictual Peace Building'. *Third World Quarterly* 23(5): 875–891.

Tull, Denis M. and Andreas Mehler. 2005. 'The Hidden Costs of Power-sharing: Reproducing Insurgent Violence in Africa'. *African Affairs* 104(416): 375–398. doi:10.1093/afraf/adi034.

Walter, Barbara. 2002. *Committing to Peace: The Successful Settlement of Civil Wars.* Princeton, NJ: Princeton University Press.

Wolff, Stefan. 2010. 'Consociationalism, Power Sharing, and Politics at the Center'. In *The International Studies Encyclopedia*, edited by Robert A. Denemark. New York: Wiley-Blackwell.

World Bank. 2012. 'Definitions of Fragility and Conflict'. World Bank. Available at: http://web.worldbank.org/WBSITE/EXTERNAL/PROJECTS/STRATEGIES/EXT LICUS/0,,contentMDK:22230573~pagePK:64171531~menuPK:4448982~piPK:641715 07~theSitePK:511778,00.html.

Zürcher, Christoph, Carrie Manning, Kristie Evenson, Rachel Hayman, Sarah Riese and Nora Roehner. 2013. *Costly Democracy: Peacebuilding and Democratization After War.* Stanford, CA: Stanford University Press.

# Part I

# Divisions, societal cleavages and institutional reforms in the aftermath of war

# 1  Does the success of institutional reform depend on the depth of divisions?

## A pilot study on 34 African countries

*Matthias Basedau*

### Introduction[1]

The debate on institutional or constitutional engineering (Lijphart 1977; 2008; Horowitz 1985; Sisk 1996; Reilly 2002; Bogaards 2003a; Kurtenbach and Mehler 2013) has led to a number of ideas on how to make formal state institutions work for peace and democracy. However, thus far, comparative empirical research has found only limited evidence that institutional engineering can actually help in the management of ethnic conflict (see e.g. Selway and Templeman 2012; Wimmer 2012). This chapter argues that this may be because the success of institutional engineering in multiparty systems depends on the depth of divisions. According to the late Robert A. Dahl (1996), the relationship between institutional arrangements and democracy is nonlinear: institutions may be largely irrelevant when conditions are very favourable or extremely bad; however, 'in-between' institutions may make the difference. This chapter thus asks: Does the depth of divisions condition the impact of (inclusive) institutions on ethnic conflict?

Investigating this question, this chapter first briefly reviews the empirical literature and outlines related challenges in research. Subsequently, a theoretical section attempts to make the case that (inclusive) institutions are not equally important in all countries.

Methodologically, the chapter exploits the introduction by almost all African countries of multiparty institutions in the wake of the third wave of democratization in the early 1990s. The new setup of institutions differs in terms of the levels of inclusiveness, as does the depth of divisions before the reforms and the levels of ethnic conflict afterwards. Employing cross-tabulation and bivariate statistics to 34 African countries, the chapter finds evidence that a newly created index of 'depth of divisions' predicts ethnic conflict far better than does any measure of inclusiveness of institutions or ethnic diversity. Taking the depth of divisions into account, I find substantial initial evidence to suggest that the inclusiveness of institutions reduces ethnic conflict risks when divisions are deeper. An analysis of countries deviating from general trends reveals that the intensity and peripheral character of ethnic conflict may matter. The final section discusses implications for future research.

## Previous research

The debate on institutional engineering has led to the development of a number of conceptualizations of how ethnic conflict may be avoided through (formal) political state institutions. Bogaards (2007) develops a typology of 'blocking','translation' or 'aggregation'. Wolff (2011) discusses the three most influential approaches: 'consociationalism' (Lijphart 1977, 2008), 'centripetalism/integrationism' (Horowitz 1985; Sisk 1996; Reilly 2001; Bogaards 2003a) and "power dividing" (Roeder 2005). In essence, these three concepts differ with regard to whether ethnic diversity is accepted as a source of political mobilization and how it should consequently be dealt with institutionally. These concepts are discussed at length in the Introduction to this book by Sabine Kurtenbach and Nadine Ansorg, and the interested reader might turn to that chapter or other summaries (e.g. Basedau 2011).

Aside from principal conceptualizations, the 'menu of institutional engineering' offers many options (see e.g. Wolff 2011).[2] However, it usually comprises the design of formal state institutions in multiparty systems (or at least formal democracies) such as the territorial state structure, the legislative (or other) electoral system and other regulations of the party systems, as well as the form of government (parliamentary vs. presidential). Other conceptualizations of institutional set-ups exceed the sheer formal design laid down in constitutions and other laws and take into account how inclusive institutions actually perform. The level of democratization, the fragmentation and other traits of the party system may be classified as institutions that capture actual rather than formal inclusiveness.

Turning to the results of empirical studies on the subject matter, the scope of this chapter does not allow for an extensive review of the empirical literature – which constitutes a research programme in its own right – but the results of major quantitative and comparative studies on the key (formal) institutions may be summarized as follows (see also Table 1.9 in the Supplementary Appendix).

Regarding *theoretical expectations* of the institutions under investigation, almost all of the measures are theoretically ambivalent when it comes to their effects on ethnic conflict. For instance, proportional representation (PR) electoral systems will allow a more adequate representation of all ethnic groups than will plurality systems; thus grievances are avoided. However, it may also be argued that PR encourages ethnic headcounts, opening an 'ethnic Pandora's box', as many observers of African politics expected in the early 1990s. While possibly helping to reduce grievances, PR boosts the *opportunity* for ethnic groups to mobilize.

In line with the theoretical ambivalence, empirical results are almost always mixed, if not sketchy or altogether absent. Institutional engineering has apparently worked in some circumstances but not in others. As demonstrated in Table 1.9 in the Supplementary Appendix, results almost consistently lack robustness and findings are often confined to certain geographically or politically defined groups of cases such as African or democratic countries (see Moroff and Basedau 2010 on Africa; Brancati 2006 on democratic countries).

In most of the studies, key variables remain underspecified. Most studies investigate armed or other violent conflict in general rather than specifically the ethnic character of conflict. Frequently, if not mostly, the dependent variable is democracy rather than (ethnic) conflict (e.g. Lijphart 1999; Linder and Bächtiger 2005).

Regarding the crucial independent variables, a number of the more sophisticated institutional options have remained widely untested. Typically, single institutions are tested but not the concert of institutions, and if several institutions are taken into account (Brancati 2006; Schneider and Wiesehomeier 2008) they are tested one by one, rather than in terms of their interaction. Power-sharing institutions were aggregated in only one study (see Selway and Templeman 2012). Whether we look at the formal design of institutions or at an institution's effective inclusiveness in the form of how many ethnic groups are actually included in a given institutional setting has also been only rarely addressed.

Some results on the impact of federalism/decentralization and (post-conflict) power-sharing arrangements (e.g. Brancati 2006; Hoddie and Hartzell 2003) suggest that the effectiveness of institutions depends on the exact nature of the institutional set-up. For instance, Hartzell and Hoddie (2007) find evidence for a 'the more, the better hypothesis': the more areas (political, military, territorial, economic) included in a power-sharing peace agreement, the higher the likelihood that peace holds.

With few exceptions (e.g. Schneider and Wiesehomeier 2008; see also Selway and Templeman 2012), little effort has been made to test the effectiveness of institutions vis-à-vis the character of ethnic diversity, let alone the 'depth' of divisions or other qualities of interethnic relations.[3] Schneider and Wiesehomeier (2008) find that conflict risk varies according to levels of democratization and the ethnodemographic constellation. Some findings on ethnic party bans and post-conflict power-sharing agreements strongly underscore that effectiveness is dependent on contextual conditions, particularly with regard to ethnicity and the respective institutions (e.g. Basedau and Moroff 2011). In sum, the initial question may be wrongly formulated. The question is not whether an institution is effective, but *under what conditions* and *how* it is effective. The following section will discuss the idea that the depth of divisions makes the difference in that regard.

## Why the depth of divisions matters for the effectiveness of institutions

In theory, it has been widely accepted that the success of institutional engineering is not independent from the specific character of the ethnic diversity and the particular conditions of the country in question (see e.g. Wolff 2011; Reilly 2003; Horowitz 1985, 2000). When we look at divided societies, obviously, it is the character and depth of divisions, and possibly other qualities, that matter in that regard. This section will discuss how ethnic divisions can be conceptualized, and how institutions, divisions and conflict are interrelated. The section concludes with three main hypotheses for the empirical analysis.

### Conceptualizing the 'depth' of ethnic divisions

Not all divisions are created equal. Divisions are multidimensional (see e.g. Horowitz 2000, 3–54) and comprise aspects such as numerical constellations, salience and hierarchies, as well as a number of less frequently discussed issues such as intensity, severity and depth, as well as space and dynamics.

The classical characteristic widely discussed in the theoretical and, in particular, the empirical literature is the *numerical constellation of ethnic diversity*, which refers to the number and relative size of ethnic groups (e.g. Bussmann *et al.* 2009; Esteban and Schneider 2008). Scholars and results differ regarding the constellation deemed most risky. While some argue that high fractionalization increases the risk of conflict, others maintain that either polarization – that is, the presence of a few large groups, which makes ethnic differences more salient and easier to mobilize – or the dominance of one ethnic group creates more conflict-prone situations.

Empirical results are mixed (Bussmann *et al.* 2009, 15–18; Fearon 2010), and indicators have been criticized for a variety of reasons, one being that numerical constellations tell us little about the actual salience of ethnic diversity. It is obvious that diversity and divisions are not identical. Divisions, at the very least, require that diversity be politically salient. For instance, in highly ethnically diverse countries such as Tanzania, ethnicity is said to be only marginally salient at best. Accordingly, alternative measures of ethnic diversity such as the index of Politically Relevant Ethnic Groups (PREG) by Posner (2004) calculate diversity only on the basis of ethnic groups that are politically important.

The issue of *salience* is also reflected in contributions that deal with how ethnic identities relate to *other cultural differences*. There is reason to believe that overlaps between ethnic and other identities reinforce the salience of diversity and make it more prone to conflict (Stewart 2009). Some empirical studies support the idea that conflict is more likely when ethnic and religious identities run parallel (e.g. Basedau *et al.* 2011). In contrast, cross-cutting cleavages[4] may have an alleviating effect on existing differences (Gubler and Selway 2012).

The concepts of 'ranks' (Horowitz 1985), relative deprivation (Gurr 1970) and horizontal inequalities (Stewart 2009) among ethnic groups suggest that inequalities or *hierarchies between ethnic groups* will result in grievances and thus make conflict more likely. Hierarchies can take different shapes, but the most important ones are economic and political. Available data to engage in a systematic test of such hierarchies include that of the Minorities at Risk (MAR) project, concentrating on ethnic and other minorities, and the Ethnic Power Relation (EPR) dataset (Cederman *et al.* 2009), which systematically assesses which groups are politically relevant and to what extent they are excluded from power in the central government. Using EPR as well as its georeferenced variant (Wucherpfennig *et al.* 2011), recent analyses provide evidence that political and economic ethnic hierarchies do indeed increase ethnic conflict risks (e.g. Cederman *et al.* 2010, 2011) (see Table 1.1).

There are more dimensions of potential relevance. An important dimension refers to the level of hostility of relations. A classical measure of the confrontational

*Table 1.1* Dimensions of ethnic divisions

| Dimension of diversity/division | Operationalization |
|---|---|
| Numerical constellation of diversity (or divisions) | Number of relative size of ethnic groups |
| Principal salience of diversity | Yes/no; more or less; political or other |
| Reinforcing parallel cultural differences | Overlaps with religious, linguistic and other cultural differences, and number thereof |
| Hierarchy of intergroup relations | Political, economic or other inequalities/ranks between groups, and intensity thereof |
| Hostility of intergroup relations | Degree and frequency of interethnic violence |
| Geography of divisions ('locus') | Central or peripheral |
| Number of divisions | Single dyadic or multiple (dyadic) |
| Dynamics of divisions | Stable/increasing/decreasing |

Source: Author's compilation.

level of Inter-ethnic relations is the intermarriage ratio. The intensity of prior interethnic violence represents an alternative and more readily available indicator. Further dimensions include number, geography and time. There can be multiple divisions in a given country. Horowitz (2000) argues that divisions at the centre of the political system may have different implications from divisions at the periphery, or divisions in which groups at the centre confront (small) groups in peripheral regions. Last but not least, the 'map' of divisions is not static, but may be subject to multiple dynamics.

This chapter will delve into what may be called the *depth of divisions*. By 'deep' divisions I mean salient ethnic differences that have resulted in hierarchical and hostile relations between major ethnic groups in the past. A country suffers from deep (ethnic) divisions when ethnic differences are politically salient, when there is a record of the political exclusion of ethnic groups, and when interethnic violence occurred previously.

### How do deep divisions condition the effect of institutions?

It is obvious that deep divisions will make ethnic conflict more likely –and probably more than other properties of ethnicity. As noted above, empirical works have confirmed that more salient differences between ethnic groups, the exclusion of groups and prior (ethnic) conflict increase conflict risks (e.g. Gubler and Selway 2012; Cederman *et al.* 2011). Institutional engineering seems appealing, particularly when working on exclusion. When institutions are sufficiently inclusive to overcome (perceived) marginalization and hence reduce grievances, violence will not occur. Consequently, inclusive institutions such as PR electoral systems, decentralized or federal state structures and parliamentary systems can work for peace.

Why are empirical studies unable to support this straightforward hypothesis? One reason may be that almost all studies fail to consider the conditioning effect of divisions and their depth. This is probably a serious flaw, both methodologically and conceptually. Conceptually, the late Robert A. Dahl (1996), who sought to explain the stability of democratic regimes, argued that the exact institutional set-up of a country matters for that stability, but only when other conditions for democracy are neither extremely bad nor highly favourable. Institutions matter for the cases 'in between'. Applied to our research question, one might expect that the inclusiveness of institutions is unimportant in cases without divisions (or when divisions are extremely severe). As almost all studies throw countries with and without divisions into the same basket, any effect of institutions becomes invisible as it only materializes for the countries with divisions.

An additional likely reason why studies fail to identify effects is the endogeneity of the inclusiveness of institutions (see e.g. Wucherpfennig 2011). Countries with deeper divisions will tend to introduce more inclusive institutions as a reaction to their problems. As a result, the countries with more inclusive institutions will also evince deeper divisions. Deep divisions in turn negatively impact upon the chances that ethnic conflict will be avoided compared to countries without deep divisions. The latter countries will have less inclusive institutions on average, as they do not need them: they will not suffer from conflict anyway. As a result, the effect of inclusive institutions will be masked and underestimated in empirical studies.

## Hypotheses

Given the endogeneity of institutions and the conditional effect of the depth of divisions, I do not expect inclusive institutions to have an independent effect on peace or conflict:

> Hypothesis 1: Inclusive institutions do not have an independent effect on the likelihood of an onset of ethnic conflict.

In contrast, the depth of divisions will have an independent impact on ethnic conflict onset, namely salient ethnic cleavages, exclusion of ethnic groups and hostile previous interethnic relations:

> Hypothesis 2: The deeper the divisions in a given country, the more likely it will experience an onset of ethnic conflict.

Finally, it is likely that institutions impact upon the likelihood of the onset of ethnic conflict once we take into account how they relate to the depth of ethnic divisions:

> Hypothesis 3: The depth of ethnic divisions conditions the impact of institutions. With shallow or absent (or very deep) divisions, inclusiveness is largely irrelevant, but countries with deeper divisions will benefit from more inclusive institutions.

## Empirical strategy

Hypotheses are investigated with a medium-N sample of African countries that have engaged in varying institutional reforms since the early 1990s. This section will present first the sampling strategy and then the operationalization of the key variables before turning to the method employed to infer causality.

### *Sample*

The sweeping introduction of multiparty elections in sub-Saharan Africa in the wake of the third wave of democratization offers an excellent opportunity to test the hypotheses, as countries had different degrees of divisions before the political openings and introduced institutions with varying degrees of inclusiveness afterwards; some countries suffered ethnic conflict thereafter, others did not. I used the following selection criteria (see Tables 1.5 and Table 1.5):

- Generally, I include all countries that introduced multiparty institutions between 1980 and 2000 by holding founding multiparty elections in this period.[5] Consequently, countries that have not yet introduced multipartyism (Eritrea, Somalia and Swaziland) and countries that introduced multipartyism later (i.e. after 2000, e.g. Rwanda, Uganda and the Democratic Republic of the Congo) were excluded.[6]
- The sample is limited to all countries for which sufficient data for ethnic divisions, conflict and state institutions are available, which excludes six relatively small countries, most of which are island states.[7]
- Finally, all countries that experienced long-lasting nationwide state collapse following the introduction of multiparty institutions (e.g. Sierra Leone) were also excluded.

The sampling procedure results in 34 cases; it should be stressed that this study looks at country periods and not at country years. The period after the introduction of –more or less inclusive – state institutions until 2010 or a possible onset of ethnic conflict constitutes one case.

### *Dates and period(s) under investigation*

The primary period under investigation is the time span after the multiparty founding elections in the early 1990s. The date of these elections was identified for every single country. The earliest date is Zimbabwe, with founding elections in 1980, and the latest is Nigeria, with founding elections in 1999.[8] Botswana is the only case with continuous multiparty elections between 1990 and 2010 and before. The period under investigations for all 'successful cases' without ethnic conflict onset ends in 2010; in all cases in which ethnic conflict broke out, the period under investigation runs from the date of the founding elections until the onset of ethnic conflict. For instance, in Nigeria, founding elections were held in

1999, while ethnic conflict broke out in 2001. In other cases, this period is substantially longer. In a few cases, such as Burundi, the year of the founding elections is identical to that of the onset of ethnic violence. In this case, the period under investigation is 1993. An overview of all country periods is listed in Table 1.8 in the Appendix.

### Dependent variable: ethnic conflict onset

Generally, two different dependent variables are employed, both of which conceptualize the failure of ethnic conflict management as the onset of ethnic conflict. The first dependent variable uses the Ethnic Armed Conflict (EAC) dataset by Cederman *et al.* (2009), which is built on UCDP/PRIO armed conflict data but additionally assesses whether warring factions and rebel groups recruited along ethnic lines or 'ethnic aims', such as a better representation of a group's interest, can be observed. If an armed conflict shows at least one of these features, it is coded as *ethnic armed conflict*.

Since this database does not include substantial nonstate ethnic violence, such as in Kenya after the 2007 elections, it seems imperative to add all cases in which such massive ethnic, nonstate violence occurred. It would be difficult to defend the categorization of such cases as 'cases of success'. Nonstate ethnic violence is recorded in the MEPV dataset, and this information adds another three cases with ethnic violence following the introduction of multiparty politics (Kenya, Ghana and Zimbabwe[9]). According to this operationalization, our sample comprises 16 cases with and 18 without ethnic conflict (see Table 1.5). In order to check for robustness, we also look at the results of the EAC data exclusively, which represents our second dependent variable.

### Independent variables

The independent variables include several measures for institutions and divisions (as well as a number of key surrounding conditions). The variables for institutions as well as divisions will be presented below, but all elements of the indices are tested individually. The values for the variables on institutions are calculated for the period after the multiparty elections,[10] and the values for 'divisions' for the period before. Surrounding conditions include the 'usual suspects' (see e.g. Hegre and Sambanis 2006) such as population size, income level, regime stability, as well as status as an oil-producing country.

### Inclusive institutions

This chapter tests the 'inclusiveness' of institutions. This is not the same as consociationalism, although it is not completely different from it. Given the specific meaning of consociationalism, which comprises four specific features (segmental autonomy, mutual veto, proportional representation and a grand coalition), a full-blown test of all the classical features of consociationalism would require time-consuming data collection and is thus beyond the scope of this chapter. According to my understanding, inclusiveness embraces all formal state institutions that allow or aim to allow the inclusion of different ethnic groups into state institutions. Conventional choices of institution include the territorial state structure, the electoral system (for the legislature) and the form of government (see Lijphart 1999; Linder and Bächtiger 2005; Selway and Templeman 2012): a more decentralized or federal state structure is more inclusive than a unitary state structure. As already mentioned above, a PR electoral system, rather than a majoritarian system, is usually recommended for divided societies, given PR's ability to include more and smaller groups. In addition, parliamentary systems of government are also inclusive – at least less exclusive than presidential systems of government, with their (alleged) winner-takes-all logic (e.g. Linz 1990a, 1990b).

Looking at these three institutions, a relatively simple additive index of (formal political) institutional inclusiveness – similar to Selway and Templeman's index of power sharing (2012) – may be constructed. The index comprises three elements (see Table 1.2) and all indicators are assessed on a 3-point scale (1–3) in which the value 3 represents the highest degree of inclusiveness, while 1 indicates the lowest level of inclusiveness. The highest possible value for the index is, accordingly, 9.

The values are assigned according to strict coding rules. For instance, majoritarian electoral systems all receive a 1, while proportional electoral systems with medium and large multimember districts are considered very inclusive and are assigned a value of 3. Mixed electoral systems are rated as 2. For the operationalization of all variables and their sources, please refer to the Supplementary Appendix, Table A2 (see n. 1); for the country scores, please consult Table 1.8.

### Depth of divisions

Based on the theoretical considerations above, I construct an innovative index that captures how deep divisions are in a given country. This index may be called the 'depth of divisions index'. The index does not claim to comprehensively capture all dimensions of ethnic divisions discussed above, but consists of three dimensions, all of which seem theoretically highly relevant and can be principally present independently of each other (Table 1.3).

First, the index includes the relationship between ethnic diversity and other cultural differences, in this case religious differences, for which data are available (Basedau *et al.* 2011). The more ethnic and religious boundaries run parallel, the more one can argue that ethnic divisions are reinforced, thus prone to mobilization

*Table 1.2* Index of (overall) inclusiveness of state institutions

| *Subindex 1: Inclusiveness of state institutions* |
| --- |
| Territorial state structure (most inclusive: strong decentralization) |
| Legislative electoral system (proportional representation) |
| Form of government (parliamentary) |

For details, see the Supplementary Appendix, Table 1.10, and main text.

in conflict, and can be considered deeper. Second, the index captures the hierarchical relations of the groups; that is, whether we are dealing with a 'ranked system'. As comprehensive data on economic differences between ethnic groups are not readily available,[11] this chapter concentrates on political inequalities, using EPR in order to assess to what extent ethnic groups are excluded from central power. Finally, the index captures the degree of confrontation of divisions or intergroup hostility by looking at past interethnic violence using the EAC dataset.

Corresponding to the indices on inclusiveness of institutions, all indicators are assessed on a 3-point scale (1–3), in which the value 3 represents the highest degree of depth, while 1 indicates the lowest level of depth, actually indicating that ethnic divisions are largely absent. The highest possible value for the index is, accordingly, 9, and signals a deeply divided society. The values are assigned according to strict coding rules. For instance, if the population share of politically excluded ethnic groups exceeds 10 per cent, the highest score of depth (3) is assigned. No exclusion at all earns the lowest value (1), while a value in between is rated 2. All assessments refer to the last time period before the introduction of the reforms. For the operationalization of all variables and sources, please refer to the Supplementary Appendix, Table 1.10 (see n. 1). Country scores are available in Table 1.8 in the Appendix at the end of this chapter.

### *Methods of causal inference*

Methodologically, this chapter exploits the secular institutional changes in sub-Saharan Africa at the beginning of the 1990s. Countries had to deal with varying levels of the depth of divisions before the institutional reforms. They introduced institutional set-ups with varying degrees of inclusiveness, and some experienced ethnic conflict while others did not. While this design may not exactly represent a natural experiment, it is not extremely far from it; it can also partially address endogeneity issues, as divisions are measured before the introduction of the institutional reforms. A sample with a relatively small N of only 34 cases, however, makes conventional regression techniques rather unpromising as the major form of methodology. The chapter thus makes use of a multimethod approach and employs a number of different techniques. First, I look at the simple bivariate correlations of our dependent variables to our independent variables on institutions and divisions, particularly the newly developed indices, as well as a number of control variables. Second, the analysis will engage in cross-tabulation, particularly regarding the test of Hypothesis 3, in which we want to test the relative impact of institutions vis-à-vis the depth of divisions. I dichotomize all variables and employ

*Table 1.3* Depth of Divisions Index

| |
|---|
| Parallel cultural differences: Overlap of ethnic and religious identities (most divisive: mostly) |
| Hierarchy of groups: Exclusion of groups (more than 10 per cent of the population) |
| Hostility between groups: Prior ethnic violence (ethnic war) |

For details, see the Supplementary Appendix, Table A1.2, and main text.

2×2 contingency tables; significance is tested by using chi-squares with the Yates correction, the test usually applied when the N is between 20 and 60. Finally, the chosen method has the advantage of keeping single cases identifiable and facilitates a qualitative assessment of individual cases that are chosen according to their status as outliers from general relationships. Generally, having relatively few cases makes even bivariate analysis extremely vulnerable to the coding of single cases. While this is not ideally suited to detect 'finer' relationships, it may also be interpreted as a hard test, as only really strong links will prove significant.

## Results

In the following, the results of the hypotheses are presented one by one before we turn to the pertinent country cases. Hypothesis 1 expects that neither the index of inclusiveness of institutions nor its constituent institutions significantly impact upon (or reduce) the onset of ethnic conflict. On a descriptive note, generally, institutions do not seem very inclusive in the 34 African states under investigation. On a scale from 3 to 9, the mean is a mere 3.82 (6 would be the mean; see Appendix, Table 1.8).[12] Bivariate statistics and cross-tabulation lend no evidence to support the assumption that the inclusiveness of all institutions matters for ethnic conflict onset, either for the index or for any single inclusive institution. All measures of inclusiveness remain insignificant for both dependent variables in all instances. As we expected this, Hypothesis 1 is confirmed.

Hypothesis 2 assumes that deeper divisions increase the likelihood of ethnic conflict onset. In order to test this hypothesis, we assessed all countries' divisions for the period before multiparty institutions were introduced (most around 1990). Generally, results show that divisions were relatively deep before the introduction of multiparty institutions, as the mean of 2.47 on a scale of 0 to 6 reveals. It also turns out that the index and almost all of its elements can predict fairly well whether subsequent ethnic conflict occurs. Deeper divisions apparently greatly increase the ethnic conflict risk. The correlation coefficients of the index stand at 0.67 for both dependent variables and are highly significant. This also holds true when we engage in cross-tabulation. Chi-squares indicate strong significance (see Table 1.4).

Table 1.5 illustrates how strong the relationship is. An index value of 3, indicating no divisions, sufficiently explains peace. If the index has a value of 6 or more, only four out of 18 countries deviate from the expectation that ethnic conflict will occur. Altogether, 28 out of 34 cases (82 per cent) are explained by the index of deep divisions. Almost all elements of the index prove robustly significant, in particular the substantial exclusion of ethnic groups. Only parallel religious cleavages and prior ethnic conflict are not significant for all dependent variables in the cross-tabulation (see Table 1.4). Exclusion of ethnic groups comes close to the explanatory power of the index in general, though it is somewhat weaker for the second dependent variable and at lower levels of significance.

Table 1.4 Relations between institutions, divisions and ethnic conflict

| | Bivariate correlation coefficients | | Chi-square test with Yates' corrections for dichotomized IV (p-values, two-tailed)[a] | |
|---|---|---|---|---|
| | DV I: Ethnic violence | DV II: Ethnic armed conflict | DV I: Ethnic violence | DV II: Ethnic armed conflict |
| *(Formal) inclusiveness of state institutions* | | | | |
| Decentralization | −0.077 | 0.020 | 0.951 | 0.541 |
| Proportional electoral system | 0.023 | 0.214 | 0.760 | 0.541 |
| Parliamentary form of government (vs. presidential) | −0.053 | −0.133 | 0.803 | 0.878 |
| Index of inclusiveness | −0.057 | 0.064 | 0.4770 | 0.724 |
| *Ethnic divisions (before introduction of multiparty politics)* | | | | |
| Reinforcing parallel cultural differences (overlaps with religious boundaries) | 0.353** | 0.526*** | 0.303 | 0.034 |
| Hierarchy: Exclusion of ethnic groups[b] | 0.656*** | 0.627*** | 0.014 | 0.006 |
| Hostility: Prior ethnic conflict | 0.522*** | 0.418** | 0.017 | 0.092 |
| Index of depth of divisions | 0.676*** | 0.676*** | 0.002 | 0.001 |
| *Other measures of ethnicity* | | | | |
| Fractionalization (Alesina et al.) | 0.078 | 0.165 | – | – |
| Fractionalization (Fearon) | −0.009 | 0.037 | – | – |

| | Bivariate correlation coefficients | | Chi-square test with Yates' corrections for dichotomized IV (p-values, two-tailed)[a] | |
| --- | --- | --- | --- | --- |
| | DV I: Ethnic violence | DV II: Ethnic armed conflict | DV I: Ethnic violence | DV II: Ethnic armed conflict |
| Cultural fractionalization (Fearon) | 0.244 | 0.315* | – | – |
| Fractionalization (PREG, Posner) | 0.198 | 0.132 | – | – |
| Polarization (Montalvo and Reynal-Querol) | 0.099 | 0.070 | – | – |
| 'Compensation' Index I (inclusiveness/ divisions) | –0.484*** | –0.393** | 0.002 | 0.049 |
| *Surrounding conditions* | | | | |
| Population size | 0.255 | 0.241 | – | – |
| Regime stability | –0.338* | –0.304* | – | – |
| Oil-producing country | 0.249 | 0.348** | 0.306 | 0.112 |
| Income per capita | –0.239 | –0.204 | – | – |

Notes

* $p<0.10$. ** $p<0.05$, *** $p<0.01$, **** $p<0.001$; bold figures denote statistical significance, italics denote p-values close to significance; a all variables were dichotomized using thresholds, see the Supplementary Appendix, Table A1.2, only for variables with an originally ordinal scale level, not for continuous variables; b refers to ordinal scale 0–2, not the continuous values of percentages, see the Supplementary Appendix, Table A1.2.

*Table 1.5* Depth of divisions and ethnic conflict onset after introduction of multiparty politics

| | *Ethnic conflict* | *No ethnic conflict* |
|---|---|---|
| Deep divisions (index value 6 or more) | Angola<br>Burundi<br>Central African Republic<br>Chad<br>Congo, Rep.<br>Côte d'Ivoire<br>Ethiopia<br>Kenya*<br>Liberia<br>Mali<br>Niger<br>Nigeria<br>Sudan<br>Zimbabwe* | Guinea<br>Mozambique<br>South Africa<br>Togo |
| Moderate divisions (index value 4–5) | Ghana*<br>Senegal | Benin<br>Botswana<br>Cameroon<br>Guinea-Bissau<br>Namibia<br>Tanzania |
| No divisions (index value 3) | | Burkina Faso<br>Gabon<br>Gambia<br>Lesotho<br>Madagascar<br>Malawi<br>Mauritania<br>Zambia |

Note
* Only ethnic conflict with dependent variable I; 82 per cent explained cases.

The index of deep divisions is clearly superior to all other classical measures of ethnic diversity, including conventional indicators of ethnic diversity such as ethnic fractionalization (e.g. Fearon 2003) or polarization, but also fragmentation, according to Posner's index of Politically Relevant Ethnic Groups (PREG). It is only Fearon's index of cultural fractionalization that proves significant, but only for the second dependent variable in bivariate statistics. Out of the surrounding conditions, only regime stability robustly affects the likelihood of ethnic conflict. To sum up, Hypothesis 2 receives strong support.

Hypothesis 3 is the most important hypothesis but is more difficult to test, as it assumes that the impact of institutions on ethnic conflict depends on how deep divisions are. More divided societies will tend to choose more inclusive institutions, making it difficult to assess the impact of institutions. In fact, there is a positive, though not overly strong relationship between the depth of divisions and the inclusiveness of divisions for our sample. The depth of divisions and the institutional inclusiveness, driven mainly by decentralization and more proportional electoral systems, is correlated by 0.3 and is significant at the 10 per cent level.

The main question is whether the depth of divisions makes a difference with regard to the ethnic conflict management potential of inclusive institutions. For this purpose, this chapter engages in two different types of tests. First, the sample was divided into three groups according to their level of divisions, and tests were carried out to determine whether the conflict rate decreases when more inclusive institutions are applied (see Table 1.6).

In the group of eight countries at the bottom of Table 1.6, we find those cases in which no divisions were detected. Not unexpectedly, no ethnic conflict occurred in this group and thus the institutional set-up is apparently irrelevant. Countries without divisions can afford to employ less inclusive institutions, and most did.

In a second group of another eight cases we find moderate divisions indicated by divisions index values of 4 or 5, meaning that divisions reach the highest score in only one element of the depth of divisions index or a medium score in two out of three. In this group, inclusiveness makes a difference. Less inclusive institutions are connected with a 33 per-cent risk of ethnic conflict while the risk is 0 per cent for more inclusive setups.

A pacifying effect of institutions is also confirmed when we look at the countries with deep divisions – those that show values of 6 or more on the index of deep divisions. Generally, the conflict rate is high, but it decreases substantially, from 81 per cent to 57 per cent, when institutions are more inclusive. The maximum of depth of divisions (value = 6) is also a strong predictor of ethnic conflict. Both cases, namely Nigeria and Sudan, have suffered from ethnic conflict. Unfortunately,

*Table 1.6* Pacifying effect of inclusive institutions relative to depth of divisions*

| | Conflict rate baseline | Levels of inclusiveness | |
|---|---|---|---|
| N = 34 | 47% | Less inclusive (index < 3) | More inclusive (at least 3) |
| Deep divisions (index score 6 or more); N = 18 | 78% | 81% (N = 11) | 57% (N = 7) |
| Moderate divisions (4–5); N = 8 | 25% | 33% (N = 6) | 0% (N = 2) |
| Absent divisions (3); N = 8 | 0% | 0% (N = 7) | 0% (N = 1) |
| % = conflict | 47% | 50% (N = 24) | 40% (N = 10) |

Note
* Refers to dependent variable I (ethnic conflict, including nonstate conflict); relationship also works for individual institutions; see the Supplementary Appendix, Matrix A1.1.

we cannot tell whether inclusiveness would have made a difference, as both cases have quite exclusive institutions according to our index.[13] When all cases with a depth of divisions' value of at least 8 are included, the conflict risk with more inclusive cases stands at 60 per cent, which is lower than the 100 per cent conflict risk associated with rather exclusive institutions.

The results of this cross-tabulation are perhaps not entirely reliable, as the number of countries is low (sometimes just one case in one box) and results may also depend on the use of thresholds. Thus, we make use of further options to test whether institutions have the potential to compensate for deep divisions. First, I repeat the exercise with the individual institutions. As shown (only) in Matrix A1.1 in the Supplementary Appendix (see n. 1), the results are identical for all three institutions. Second, I dichotomize the levels of inclusiveness and depth of divisions in a 2 × 2 table and compare the (ethnic) conflict risk levels. With deeper divisions, inclusiveness reduces the conflict rate from 83 per cent to 33 per cent. With lower divisions, the risk decreases from 15 per cent to 0 per cent.

*Table 1.7* Compensatory potential of inclusive institutions relative to depth of divisions*

|  | *Ethnic conflict* | *No ethnic conflict* |
|---|---|---|
| No 'compensation' (index value < 1) | Angola<br>Burundi<br>Central African Republic<br>Chad<br>Congo, Rep.<br>Côte d'Ivoire<br>Ethiopia<br>Kenya**<br>Liberia<br>Mali<br>Nigeria<br>Sudan<br>Zimbabwe** | Cameroon<br>Guinea<br>Tanzania<br>Togo |
| 'Compensation' (index value 1 or above) | Ghana**<br>Niger<br>Senegal | Benin<br>Botswana<br>*Burkina Faso*<br>*Gabon*<br>*Gambia*<br>Guinea-Bissau<br>*Lesotho*<br>*Madagascar*<br>*Malawi*<br>*Mauritania*<br>Mozambique<br>Namibia<br>South Africa<br>*Zambia* |

Note
* 'Compensation' means that deep divisions are offset through high inclusiveness (or low divisions through lower levels of inclusiveness) ** Only ethnic conflict with dependent variable I. Countries in italics are cases with absent divisions.

A third, additional test relates the two indices to each other and constructs a simple index of 'compensatory potential' in which the inclusiveness values are divided by the divisions score. A value of 1 or more suggests that inclusive institutions fully 'compensate' for the divisions, while values below 1 imply that this compensation has not been achieved.[14] Although we may not have a perfect measure of compensation, this index at least captures the relation between inclusiveness and divisions.

Table 1.7 shows how the country cases distribute regarding 'compensation' of divisions through inclusive (formal) institutions and ethnic conflict. Only seven cases deviate from the expectation that full compensation results in ethnic peace. It is not that compensation just reflects shallow or absent divisions. The group of 'compensating' cases includes deeply divided societies like Mozambique and South Africa.

A total of 79 per cent of all cases may be explained by this compensatory index. The bivariate correlation stands at a highly significant -0.48 and the chi-square test with Yates corrections for dichotomized variables is also highly significant. Results are similarly strong for the alternative dependent variable (–0.38, explained cases: 76 per cent). The 'compensation index' is also statistically significant in preliminary multiple regressions, though for dependent variable I (ethnic violence) only.

Summing up, Hypothesis 3 receives quite a lot of support; there is a substantial initial indication that institutions with a more inclusive design work, but the effect depends on how deep divisions are. If divisions are absent institutions are irrelevant, but many more seriously divided societies can apparently increase their chances of maintaining ethnic peace by employing more inclusive institutions.

### *A closer look at critical cases: outliers*

Thus far, this study has looked at the aggregate rather than individual cases. This section exploits the fact that we are dealing with a relatively small sample and looks more closely at pertinent country cases and how they relate to the findings thus far. Obviously, it is impossible to consider all 34 countries, but one can make an informed choice of a smaller number of cases.

The first option is to look at outliers that maintained *ethnic peace despite deep divisions*: the countries that avoided ethnic conflict after the introduction of multiparty institutions despite having had deep divisions before – according to our expectations, institutional choices might explain this finding. Four countries demonstrate this pattern: Guinea, Mozambique, South Africa and Togo.

At first glance we have only limited evidence that the success of ethnic conflict management can be explained by the inclusiveness of state institutions. It works for South Africa – the most inclusive country in all respects – but institutions in Mozambique, Togo and Guinea have not been particularly inclusive, receiving respective values of 6 and 5 out of a maximum of 9. Taking into account the compensation index, it may be argued that Mozambique at least compensates for the country's (not so) deep divisions, which also holds true for South Africa. But even for South Africa we cannot exclude that a third variable accounts for both inclusive institutions and ethnic peace. It may have been the spirit of responsible leaders that both created peace and more inclusive institutions.[15]

However, what the four cases have in common is their having been governed by dominant parties, with the (partial) exception of Guinea, where the dominant party system broke down following the death of the long-standing autocrat Lansane Conté in 2008.[16] It is also remarkable that another set of outliers, those cases that are peaceful despite an unfavourable value on the compensation index (besides Guinea and Togo, these are Cameroon and Tanzania), also display dominant party systems. It may well be that dominant parties have intraparty integrative mechanisms. This is certainly very plausible for the ANC in South Africa (Bogaards 2003b). Alternatively, dominance may reflect an effective authoritarian regime (Cameroon and Togo, and Guinea until 2008). The ethnic conflict management potential of dominant parties should not be overstated – conflict-ridden cases such as Angola, Chad and Ethiopia also show dominant party systems – but it would be worthwhile to research the potentially integrative character of dominant parties and authoritarian regimes in more detail in the future.

Another group of outliers shows *ethnic conflict despite relatively high inclusiveness*. According to the concept of 'compensation' and the main findings from this study, highly inclusive countries should be associated with peace. These deviant cases are Ghana, Senegal and Niger (see Matrix 1.3). In these cases, a closer look at the character of ethnic conflict may help explain why they deviate. In all three countries, the underlying conflict is not very intense and is both geographically and politically at the periphery of the political system. In Ghana we saw an intercommunal conflict between Dagombas and Gonjas in 1994, which was largely unrelated to the (ethnic) power struggles at the centre (see Lund 2003). In Niger, the Tuareg insurgency recurred in 2007 after having been settled in the late 1990s. The Tuareg, who make up less than 10 per cent of the population, reside in the sparsely populated north; the central ethnic groups in the Southern center are the Djerma-Songhai and the Hausa (see Lawel 2010). Likewise, the conflict in the Senegalese province Casamance is also a peripheral conflict. Djoula in the province south of Gambia (the state and the river) fight for autonomy. Politics in the capital, Dakar, are largely unrelated to this conflict (see Marut 2010).

This finding suggests that peripheral ethnic conflict requires institutional responses other than those for ethnic conflicts over central government. Effective decentralization may count more than the form of government or even the electoral system.[17] Looking at the respective characters of conflicts in the other cases of ethnic conflict lends additional preliminary support to this idea. Many (but not all) of the conflict cases feature central conflicts (Angola, Burundi, Chad, Côte d'Ivoire, Republic of the Congo, Kenya, Liberia, Sudan); some feature multiple peripheral conflicts (Chad, Ethiopia, Nigeria) or a combination thereof. Few cases (Mali, possibly Niger) show violence at the periphery only. It is of course too early to draw conclusions from these patterns, but the 'locus' of conflict (Horowitz

1985) – that is, the peripheral or central character of (not necessarily violent) ethnic conflict, or the number of such conflicts – should certainly be studied more thoroughly in the future.

## Conclusion, discussion and future work

This study has argued that the success of institutional ethnic conflict management depends on the depth of divisions, an assumption thus far widely neglected in systematic empirical research. In an attempt to contribute to filling this gap, this chapter has developed an innovative measure for the depth of divisions and has engaged in a preliminary empirical test of whether the depth of divisions conditions the relationship between institutions and ethnic conflict in 34 African countries that introduced more or less inclusive multiparty institutions in the third wave of democratization. As these countries also differ regarding their divisions before these reforms and the occurrence of ethnic conflict thereafter, they offer a good opportunity to explore this relationship.

Given endogeneity issues, this chapter did not expect to find a simple relationship between more inclusive institutions and ethnic conflict, and this hypothesis was confirmed. Yet, depth of divisions matters, and if the inclusiveness of institutions is related to the depth of divisions – looking at subsamples with comparably deep divisions and an index capturing the compensation for divisions through inclusive institutions – we find some evidence that inclusiveness indeed has the potential to reduce conflict in more deeply divided societies; absent divisions make institutions largely irrelevant. A look at outliers suggests that in cases such as South Africa it may be argued that institutional engineering was indeed successful; in others, repression may have worked for peace. Cases like Ghana, Niger and Senegal suggest that the geographically peripheral character of divisions is not easily dealt with by the classical set of state institutions.

In essence, the preliminary analysis lends substantial support to the theory that the character of divisions greatly matters and provides evidence to at least suggest that the potential for institutions to help manage conflict is dependent on the depth of divisions. This finding supports the idea – outlined in the introduction – that institutional reforms must be adapted to local conditions and that blueprint solutions will not do the trick. At the same time, we can be cautiously confident that more inclusion in institutions helps, especially in postwar societies.

Nevertheless, many challenges for future research persist, and these challenges also confirm (and partly exceed) the introductory notes by Ansorg and Kurtenbach. In terms of theory, we must further refine the conceptualization of institutions and the multidimensional character of divisions, and determine how to relate them to each other. First, existing theories beyond consociationalism – and the related concept of inclusiveness – such as *centripetalism, integrationism* and *power-dividing* institutions should be related systematically to divisions. Such theorizing should include other possibly division-alleviating institutions such as integrative measures of presidential electoral systems (territorial quota requirements, three-term limits, regionally or ethnically balanced cabinets), the regulation of the party system, and features of the security sector and the judiciary, to mention just a few. We should look more closely at the extent to which actual inclusion is achieved (not only at the formal institutions designed to allow for inclusion), the fragmentation of party systems, the size and composition of cabinets, and the actual levels of democracy.[18]

Second, we need to think about how to conceptualize dimensions of divisions beyond 'depth' and how to integrate them into an aggregate concept. Such dimensions are the peripheral or central character of the conflict (geography), the number of conflicts in a given country or region, and the relative size of groups involved, including conceptualizations such as polarization, dominance and fractionalization.

Third, it is necessary to develop a set of hypotheses on how different institutional conceptualizations relate to the depth of divisions. What incentives do particular institutions offer for what groups? How is bargaining between groups affected by particular rules and arrangements? How do such institutions impact upon the motivation and the opportunity of groups to act collectively and cross the line of taking up arms? Are unintended side effects possible? What exact properties of institutions, divisions and conflict have to be taken into account?

Beyond the hypotheses of this study, additional hypotheses may include that peripheral minority problems demand special designs to ensure the accommodation of the minority's interest rather than classical inclusive state institutions such as the form of government. Another hypothesis may be that presidentialism is less exclusive when it is amended by territorial requirements, ethnic balancing in government, or informal alternation such as in Nigeria or Kenya (Theuerkauf 2013).

In terms of methodological issues, a number of related challenges derive directly from the theoretical challenges outlined above. We need to develop more refined measures of institutions and divisions and to compile data for larger samples exceeding sub-Saharan Africa. We should also look at country years or the group level. Larger samples will be more suitable for employing multivariate quantitative methodologies that better capture the competing or conditioning effect of divisions on institutions as well as surrounding conditions.[19] Last but not least, carefully selected case studies and thoroughly crafted small-N comparisons, such as the preliminary outlier analysis in this chapter, can help further refine theoretical arguments and identify variables that should be tested in larger samples.

## Notes

1   I would like to thank Don Horowitz and Ben Reilly for their very useful comments on an earlier draft of this chapter. I would also like to thank Sebastian Prediger for helping out with statistics. A supplementary appendix is available from the author upon request (matthias.basedau@giga-hamburg.de). The usual caveat applies.

2   I do not claim to come anywhere near to being exhaustive with regard to empirical and theoretically possible options, even if we limit ourselves to multiparty set-ups. In particular, institutional options in the fields of justice and the security sector certainly deserve more attention.

3   To the best of my knowledge, just one paper has done so: Andreas Wimmer (2012).

4  Using the term 'cleavages' in this context helps us keep in mind that the terms 'divisions' and 'cleavages' are used interchangeably in this chapter. However, in order to avoid confusion I prefer 'divisions'.

5  All countries that did so before and continued to uphold this form of government (Botswana, Mauritius) are also included.

6  These countries are not better off regarding the onset of ethnic conflict after 1990. Except for Somalia (only nonethnic conflict) and Swaziland, all experienced ethnic conflict.

7  These cases are Cape Verde, Comoros, Djibouti, Mauritius, São Tomé and Príncipe, and the Seychelles. All of these countries were apparently spared from ethnic conflict. An exception may be Mauritius, in which low-level ethnic violence occurred in 1999/2000.

8  An alternative date would have been 1992 or 1993, when legislative and presidential elections were held for Nigeria. However, the presidential election results were annulled and thus there was no complete transition.

9  In Zimbabwe, the conflict in the Ndebele area that broke out in 1980 is not recorded in the EAC dataset, although it was certainly an (ethnic) armed conflict.

10  We have to concede that data for decentralization (DPI 2009) are questionable as we have a number of missing data for single elements of the decentralization index, which forced us to use the average value of available indicators. This number of available indicators differs. In a few cases, just one out of four is available.

11  Cederman *et al.* (2011) have created a dataset on horizontal economic inequalities that is confined to the year 1990 and does not include all African cases under investigation in this study.

12  A more intuitive scaling from 0 to 6 returns a mean of 1.82.

13  Nigeria has tried some alternative measures, such as informal proportionality regarding the posts of president and vice president, alternation between northerners and southerners in the presidency, territorial quotas, positive party bans, etc. (see e.g. Theuerkauf 2013). These features are not captured by the index and follow a more centripetalist logic.

14  The logic of this index might be questionable from a number of angles. We can question the compatibility of two scales. In any case, however, it makes sense to relate the phenomena to each other.

15  It should be noted that both in Guinea and Mozambique more or less ethnic violence occurred or recurred after the end of the period under investigation in 2010.

16  One might also argue that, in fact, ethnic violence occurred in the turmoil after the death of Conté. However, MEPV does not code ethnic violence or war until 2012.

17  It may be no coincidence that all three cases, particularly Niger, had no pronounced decentralized state structure.

18  Exclusion of ethnic groups (after introduction of multiparty systems), levels of democracy, and the type of party system were tested as robustness checks. There is no evidence that they impact ethnic conflict whatsoever.

19  In fact, preliminary probit regressions were already calculated and confirm the strong impact of the "depth of divisions."

# References

Basedau, Matthias (2011) 'Managing Ethnic Conflict. The Menu of Institutional Engineering'. *GIGA Working Paper* 171, Hamburg: GIGA.

Basedau, Matthias and Anika Moroff (2011) 'Parties in Chains – Do Ethnic Party Bans in Africa Promote Peace?' *Party Politics* 17(2): 205–225.

Basedau, Matthias, Georg Strüver, Johannes Vüllers and Tim Wegenast (2011) 'Do Religious Factors Impact Armed Conflict? Empirical Evidence from Sub-Saharan Africa'. *Terrorism and Political Violence* 23(5): 752–779.

Bogaards, Matthijs (2003a) 'Electoral Choices for Divided Societies: Multiethnic Parties and Constituency Pooling in Africa'. *Journal of Commonwealth and Comparative Politics* 41(3): 59–80.

Bogaards, Matthijs *(*2003b*)* 'Powersharing'. In Südafrika*: Ist der* ANC *eine* Konkordanzpartei? *Afrika Spectrum* 38(1, S): 49–70.

Bogaards, Matthijs (2007) 'Electoral Systems, Party Systems, and Ethnicity in Africa'. In Matthias Basedau, Gero Erdmann and Andreas Mehler (eds), *Votes, Money and Violence. Political Parties and Elections in Africa.* Uppsala: Nordic Africa Institute, 168–193.

Brancati, Dawn (2006) 'Decentralization: Fueling the Fire or Dampening the Flames of Ethnic Conflict'. *International Organization* 60: 651–685.

Bussmann, Margit, Andreas Hasenclever and Gerald Schneider (2009) Identität, Institutionen und Ökonomie: Ursachen und Scheinursachen innenpolitischer Gewalt, Bussmann, Margit, Andreas Hasenclever and Gerald Schneider, eds, Identität, Institutionen und Ökonomie. Ursachen innenpolitischer Gewalt, Wiesbaden, 9–38.

Cederman, Lars-Erik, Brian Min and Andreas Wimmer (2009), 'Ethnic Armed Conflict dataset'. Available at: http://hdl.handle.net/1902.1/11797 V1 [Version 1,0].

Cederman, Lars-Erik, Brian Min and Andreas Wimmer (2010) 'Why Do Ethnic Groups Rebel? New Data and Analysis'. *World Politics* 62(1) (January): 87–119.

Cederman, Lars-Erik, Nils B. Weidmann and Kristian Skrede Gleditsch (2011) 'Horizontal Inequalities and Ethnonationalist Civil War: A Global Comparison'. *American Political Science Review* 105(3): 478–495.

Dahl, Robert A. (1996) 'Thinking about Democratic Constitutions: Conclusions from Democratic Experience, I'. In I. Shaoiro and R. Hardin (eds), *Political Order.* New York: Nomos, 175–206.

Esteban, Joan and Gerald Schneider (2008) 'Polarization and Conflict: Theoretical and Empirical Issues'. *Journal of Peace Research* 45: 131–141.

Fearon, James D. (2003) 'Ethnic and Cultural Diversity by Country'. *Journal of Economic Growth* 8(2): 195–222.

Fearon, James, D. (2010) 'Governance and Civil War Onset'. World Development Report, Background Paper, 31 August 31. Washington, DC: the World Bank

Gubler, Joshua and Joel Sawat Selway (2012) 'Horizontal Inequality, Crosscutting Cleavages, and Civil War'. *Journal of Conflict Resolution* 56(2): 206–232.

Gurr, Ted R. (1970) *Why Men Rebel.* Princeton, NJ: Princeton University Press.

Hartzell, Caroline and Matthew Hoddie (2007) *Crafting Peace: Power-sharing Institutions and the Negotiated Settlement of Civil Wars.* Philadelphia: the Pennsylvania State University Press.

Hegre, Håvard and Nicholas Sambanis (2006) 'Sensitivity Analysis of Empirical Results on Civil War Onset'. *Journal of Conflict Resolution* 50: 508–535.

Hoddie, Matthew and Caroline Hartzell (2003) 'Civil War Settlements and the Implementation of Military Power-Sharing Arrangements'. *Journal of Peace Research* 40(3): 303–320.

Horowitz, Donald (1985) *Ethnic Groups in Conflict.* Berkeley: University of California Press.

Horowitz, Donald L. (2000) *Ethnic Groups in Conflict,* 2nd edn. Berkeley: University of California Press.

Horowitz, Donald (2013) 'Ethnic Power Sharing: Three Big Problems'. *Journal of Democracy* 25(2): 5–20.

Kurtenbach, Sabine and Andreas Mehler (eds) (2013) 'Institutions for Sustainable Peace'. Special Issue *Civil Wars*, November.

Lawel, Chekou Koré (2010) *La rébellion touareg au Niger: raisons de persistance et tentatives de solutions*. Paris: L'Harmattan.

Lijphart, Arendt (1977) *Democracy in Plural Societies*. New Haven, CT: Yale University Press.

Lijphart, Arendt (1999) *Patterns of Democracy: Government Forms and Performance in Thirty-Six Countries*. New Haven, CT: Yale University Press.

Lijphart, Arendt (2008) *Thinking about Democracy. Power Sharing and Majority Rule in Theory and Practice*. London: Routledge.

Linder, Wolf and Andre Bächtiger (2005) 'What Drives Democratization in Asia and Africa?' *European Journal of Political Research* 44(6): 861–880.

Linz, Juan J. (1990a) 'The Perils of Presidentialism'. *Journal of Democracy* 1(1): 51–69.

Linz, Juan J. (1990b) 'The Virtues of Parliamentarism'. *Journal of Democracy* 1(4): 84–91.

Lund, Christian (2003) ' "Bawku is Still Volatile": Ethno-political Conflict and State Recognition in Northern Ghana'. *The Journal of Modern African Studies* 41(4): S. 587–610.

Marut, Jean-Claude (2010) *Le conflit de Casamance : ce que disent les armes*. Paris: Karthala.

Mehler, Andreas (2009) 'Peace and Power Sharing in Africa: A Not So Obvious Relationship'. *African Affairs* 108(432): 453–473.

MEPV (Major Episodes of Political Violence) Available at: www.systemicpeace.org/warlist.htm (accessed 5 January 2011).

Montalvo, José G. and Marta Reynal-Querol (2005) 'Ethnic Polarization, Potential Conflict, and Civil Wars'. *American Economic Review* 95(3): 796–813.

Moroff, Anika and Matthias Basedau (2010) 'An Effective Measure of Institutional Engineering? Ethnic Party Bans in Africa'. *Democratization* 17(4): 666–686.

North, Douglas C. (1990) *Institutions, Institutional Change and Economic Performance*. Cambridge: Cambridge University Press.

Posner, Daniel (2004) 'Measuring Ethnic Fractionalization in Africa'. *American Journal of Political Science* 48: 849–863.

Reilly, Ben (2001) *Democracy in Divided Societies: Electoral Engineering for Conflict Management*. Cambridge: Cambridge University Press.

Reilly, Ben (2002) 'Electoral Systems for Divided Societies'. *Journal of Democracy* 13(2): 156–170.

Roeder, Philip G. (2005) 'Power Dividing as an Alternative to Power Sharing'. In Philip G. Roeder and Donald Rothchild (eds), *Sustainable Peace: Power and Democracy after Civil Wars,* Ithaka, NY: Cornell University Press, 51–82.

Schneider, Gerald and Nina Wiesehomeier (2008) 'Rules That Matter: Political Institutions and the Diversity–Conflict Nexus'. *Journal of Peace Research* 45(2): 183–203.

Selway, Joel Sawat and Kharis Templeman (2012) 'The Myth of Consociationalism? Conflict Reduction in Divided Societies'. *Comparative Political Studies* 45(12): 1542–1571.

Sisk, Timothy D. (1996) *Power Sharing and International Mediation in Ethnic Conflict*. Washington, DC: United States Institute of Peace Press.

Stewart, Frances (2009) 'Religion versus Ethnicity as a Source of Mobilisation. Are There Differences?' MICROCON Research Working Paper 18.

Theuerkauf, Ulrike G. (2013) 'Presidentialism and the Risk of Ethnic Violence'. *Ethnopolitics* 12(1): 72–81.

Wimmer, A. (2012) 'Can Peace Be Engineered? Institutions, Political Inclusion and Ethnic Conflict'. *Comparative Democratization* 10(2): 4–23.

Wolff, Stefan (2011) 'Managing Ethno-national Conflict: Towards an Analytical Framework'. *Commonwealth and Comparative Politics* 49(2): 162–195.

Wucherpfennig, Julian (2011) 'Endogenizing Power-sharing after Ethnonationalist Civil War'. Paper prepared for presentation at the AFK Kolloquium in Haus Villigst, Germany, April.

Wucherpfennig, Julian, Nils B.Weidmann, Luc Girardin, Lars-Erik Cederman and Andreas Wimmer (2011) 'Politically Relevant Ethnic Groups Across Space and Time: Introducing the GeoEPR Dataset'. *Conflict Management and Peace Science* 28: 423–437.

*Table 1.8* Countries and key dates and indicators

| Country | Date of first multiparty election | Date of onset of ethnic conflict | Formal inclusiveness index | Depth of divisions index | Compensation index I |
|---|---|---|---|---|---|
| | – | – | 0–6 (max) | 0–6 (max) | Ratio of inclusiveness index/ depth of divisions index |
| Period(s) | Year | Year | Post-multiparty election (MPE) period | Pre-MPE period | Pre-MPE period (divisions)/ post-MPE period |
| Status | – | DV (I) | IV | IV | IV |
| Source | – | Ethnic armed conflict dataset, MEPV | GIGA | GIGA | GIGA |
| Angola | 1992 | 1994 | 6 | 8 | 0.75 |
| Benin | 1991 | | 6 | 3 | 2 |
| Botswana | 1989* | | 6 | 4 | 1.5 |
| Burkina Faso | 1992 | | 5 | 3 | 1.7 |
| Burundi | 1993 | 1993 | 6 | 7 | 0.86 |
| Cameroon | 1992 | | 4 | 5 | 0.8 |
| Central African Republic | 1992 | 2001 | 4 | 6 | 0.67 |
| Chad | 1996 | 1998 | 4 | 8 | 0.5 |
| Congo, Rep. | 1992 | 1993 | 5 | 6 | 0.83 |
| Côte d'Ivoire | 1990 | 2002 | 4 | 7 | 0.57 |
| Ethiopia | 1994 | 1996 | 6 | 8 | 0.75 |
| Gabon | 1993 | | 4 | 3 | 1.33 |
| Gambia | 1996 | | 4 | 3 | 1.33 |
| Ghana | 1992 | 1994** | 4 | 4 | 1 |
| Guinea | 1993 | | 5 | 6 | 0.83 |
| Guinea-Bissau | 1994 | | 5 | 4 | 1.25 |
| Kenya | 1992 | 2007** | 3 | 6 | 0.5 |
| Lesotho | 1993 | | 6 | 3 | 2 |
| Liberia | 1997 | 2000 | 5 | 8 | 0.625 |
| Madagascar | 1993 | | 4 | 3 | 1.33 |
| Malawi | 1994 | | 3 | 3 | 1 |
| Mali | 1993 | 2006 | 5 | 6 | 0.83 |
| Mauritania | 1992 | | 3 | 3 | 1 |
| Mozambique | 1994 | | 6 | 6 | 1 |

| Country | Date of first multiparty election | Date of onset of ethnic conflict | Formal inclusiveness index | Depth of divisions index | Compensation index I |
|---|---|---|---|---|---|
| Namibia | 1989 | | 5 | 4 | 1.25 |
| Niger | 1993 | 1996 | 6 | 6 | 1 |
| Nigeria | 1999 | 2001 | 4 | 9 | 0.44 |
| Senegal | 1983 | 1990 | 5 | 5 | 1 |
| South Africa | 1994 | | 9 | 8 | 1.125 |
| Sudan | 1986 | 2003 | 4 | 9 | 0.44 |
| Tanzania | 1994 | | 3 | 4 | 0.75 |
| Togo | 1994 | | 6 | 7 | 0.86 |
| Zambia | 1991 | | 4 | 3 | 1.33 |
| Zimbabwe | 1980 | 1981** | 5 | 7 | 0.71 |
| mean | | | 4,823529412 | 5,470588235 | – |

Notes
* First multiparty election in 1966, but in this study 1989 election is used as reference date; ** Only (nonstate) ethnic conflict with MEPV.

## Supplementary Appendix to Article Basedau: Does the Success of Institutional Reform Depend on the Depth of Divisions? A Pilot Study on Thirty-Four African Countries in: Ansorg and Kurtenbach

*Table 1.9* Political Institutions and Management of Ethnic Conflict: Logic and Evidence

| Measure | Logic of how measure institution may work on ethnic conflict* | Major quantitative and comparative studies | Empirical evidence |
|---|---|---|---|
| **1. Political system as a whole** | | | |
| Democracy vs. Autocracy | Rather consociational: Allowing fair competition of ethnic groups | e.g., Hegre et al. 2001; Schneider and Wiesehomeier 2008 | Mixed: hybrid regimes rather conflict-prone; democracies deal better with ethnic polarization; autocracies deal better with fractionalization and dominance |
| **2. State structure** | | | |
| Federalist/decentralized states vs. unitary states | Consociational: Allowing autonomy for regional groups thus avoiding marginalization of ethnic groups | e.g., Brancati 2006; Siegle and Mahony 2007; Schneider and Wiesehomeier 2008; Selway and Templeman 2012; Wimmer 2012 | Mixed: Some specific arrangements may promote peace others violence |
| **3. Electoral system** | | | |
| PR vs. majoritarian systems | Consociational: PR systems avoid marginalization of ethnic groups | Brancati 2006; Schneider and Wiesehomeier 2008; Selway and Templeman 2012; Wimmer 2012 | Limited evidence at best that PR systems are less conflict-prone |
| Compensatory systems (e.g., "best loser") | Consociational: After allocation of seats through "regular" electoral system, underrepresented groups get compensatory seats | – | Rare and only tested for few cases (e.g., Mauritius) |
| Preferential voting systems (e.g., AV and STV) | Centripetalist/ integrationist: voters express ranking of preferences, candidates with many second (and third etc.) preferences enjoy advantage. Appeal to other communities pays off | Reilly 2002 | Rare and only tested for few cases with mixed results (e.g., Fiji vs. Papua New Guinea) |

| Measure | Logic of how measure institution may work on ethnic conflict* | Major quantitative and comparative studies | Empirical evidence |
|---|---|---|---|
| Constituency pooling | Centripetalist/ integrationist: Constituencies from different parts of the country, successful candidates have to draw support from different parts of the country | Bogaards 2003 | Never put into practice |
| Distribution requirements in presidential elections | Centripetalist/ integrationist: Successful candidates have to meet certain quotas of nationwide support (e.g.,25% of vote share in two-thirds of federal states in Nigeria) | Theuerkauf 2013 | Rare (e.g., Nigeria, Kenya) and thus not systematically tested |
| **4. Party system** | | | |
| Party bans | Rather centripetalist / integrationist: Banning ethnic parties or proscribing national representation blocks ethnicity from politics thus decreasing ethnic conflict | e.g., Moroff and Basedau 2010; Basedau and Moroff 2011; Bogaards, Elischer, and Becher forthcoming | Only tested for Africa, unsupported; no evidence that bans are generally effective, used as part of the "menu of manipulation" in some cases |
| **5. Form of government** | | | |
| Presidential vs. parliamentary systems | Rather consociational: Presidentialism follows winner-takes-all logic thus potentially excluding ethnic groups | e.g., Brancati 2006; Schneider and Wiesehomeier 2008; Selway and Templeman 2012;Wimmer 2012 | No evidence that presidentialism is harmful in divided societies |
| Power sharing agreements (after civil war) | Consociational: Including all relevant ethnic groups in government ensures cooperation | e.g., Binningsbø 2006; Walter 2002; Hoddie and Hartzell 2005; Jarstad and Nilsson 2008; Derouen et al. 2009; Mehler 2009; Binningsbø et al. 2012 | Inconclusive: some specific arrangements may foster peace |
| **6. Combined approaches** | | | |
| Consociational Democracy | Consociational: Accepting ethnicity and promoting incentives for representation and cooperation (Grand coalition, proportional representation, mutual veto and segmental autonomy) | e.g., Lijphart 1999; Linder and Baechtiger 2005; Norris 2008, Roeder 2005; Selway and Tempelman 2012 | Only partly tested, mainly regarding democracy, limited evidence at best that consociational democracies are less conflict-prone |

* For further details, particularly counterarguments, see Basedau 2011.

Table 1.10 Codebook of Variables

| Variable | Description | Period under investigation | Source | Range of values, threshold for cross tabulation | Index values (if applicable) | | |
|---|---|---|---|---|---|---|---|
| | | | | | Low (1) | Medium (2) | Strong (3) |
| **Dependent variables** | | | | | | | |
| Ethnic violence onset (DV I) | onset of ethnic conflict (ethnic armed conflict and large-scale nonstate ethnic violence) after the introduction of multiparty elections | period after introduction of multiparty elections until 2010 | Cederman et al., Ethnic armed conflict data set, supplemented by MEPV (nonstate ethnic violence) | no (0), yes (1) | No | n/a | yes, onset |
| Ethnic armed conflict onset (DV II) | onset of ethnic armed conflict (ethnic war/ conflict) after the introduction of multiparty elections | period after introduction of multiparty elections until 2010 | Cederman et al. Ethnic war dataset (only) | no (0), yes (1) | No | n/a | yes, onset |
| **Independent variables and controls** | | | | | | | |
| **Formal state institutions** | | | | | | | |
| Decentralization | degree of decentralization of the territorial state structure, composite index of four decentral elements according to DPI: AUTON, MUNI, STATE, AUTHOR, calculated per indicator due to many missing variables | from year after introduction of multiparty elections until end of period / first onset of ethnic violence | DPI 2009 (Beck et al.) | no elements (1) to strong decentralization (3), threshold: 2 (more inclusive) | no decentral elements (1) | some decentral elements (<1 per available indicator) | stronger decentral elements (> 1 per available indicator) |

| Variable | Description | Period under investigation | Source | Range of values, threshold for cross tabulation | Index values (if applicable) | | |
|---|---|---|---|---|---|---|---|
| | | | | | Low (1) | Medium (2) | Strong (3) |
| Proportional electoral system | theoretical (dis) proportionality of legislative electoral system | dto. | Erdmann and Basedau 2007 on the basis of Hartmann 2007 | plurality (0) to pure PR (2), threshold: 1 (more inclusive) | FPTP, plurality in two round system | mixed electoral systems, PR in small districts | PR in medium and large districts |
| Parliamentary form of government | Degree of winner-takes-all logic in form of government | dto. | EPB 2007 | pure presidential government (1) to parliamentary government (3), threshold: 1 (more inclusive) | Presidential (chief executive independent from parliament) | semi-presidential (chief executive shared or partly dependent on parliament) | parliamentary (chief executive fully dependent on parliament) |
| Formal Inclusiveness of Institutions Index | aggregates inclusiveness by adding values of decentralization, electoral system and form of government | dto. | GIGA | 3–9,, threshold: 6 (more inclusive) | n/a | n/a | n/a |
| **Ethnic divisions** | | | | | | | |
| Reinforcing parallel cultural differences: Parallel religious boundaries | describes whether and to what extent ethnic cleavages run parallel to religious differences | dto. | RCDC (GIGA) | no (1) to largely parallel (3) to religious cleavages, threshold: 2 (deeper) | no, religion cross-cutting | significant but partly parallel to religious cleavages | significant and largely parallel to religious cleavages |

Table 1.10 Continued

| Variable | Description | Period under investigation | Source | Range of values, threshold for cross tabulation | Index values (if applicable) | | |
|---|---|---|---|---|---|---|---|
| | | | | | Low (1) | Medium (2) | Strong (3) |
| Hierarchy: Exclusion of ethnic groups | describes whether and to what extent ethnic groups are excluded from central political power | dto. | EPR, exclusion meaning: either "discriminated" or "powerless" | no exclusion (1) to exclusion of large parts of the population (3), threshold: 2 (deeper) | no excluded groups | small minorities (< 10% of the population) excluded | at least substantial minorities (> 10%) excluded |
| Hostility: prior ethnic conflict | describes to what extent interethnic violence occurred before advent of multiparty politics | dto. | Cederman et al., Ethnic conflict data set, complemented by MEPV | no to ethnic war/ large-scale interethnic violence, threshold: 2 (deeper) | No | low-intensity ethnic conflict (> 1,000 battle deaths) | ethnic war or large-scale interethnic violence (> more than |
| Depth of divisions index | aggregates dimensions of divisions by adding values of parallel religious cleavages, hierarchy and prior ethnic conflict | dto. | GIGA | 3–9, threshold: 6 (deeper) | n/a | n/a | n/a |

| Variable | Description | Period under investigation | Source | Range of values, threshold for cross tabulation | Index values (if applicable) | | |
|---|---|---|---|---|---|---|---|
| | | | | | Low (1) | Medium (2) | Strong (3) |
| Compensation index 1 | measures to what extent inclusiveness compensates for divisions by dividing value of inclusiveness of institutions by depth of divisions; values below 1 considered noncompensatory | divisions: before multiparty elections; inclusiveness: after multiparty elections | GIGA | 3 to 0.33; threshold: 1 | n/a | n/a | n/a |

**Alternative measures of ethnicity**

| Variable | Description | Period under investigation | Source | Range of values, threshold for cross tabulation | Index values (if applicable) | | |
|---|---|---|---|---|---|---|---|
| | | | | | Low (1) | Medium (2) | Strong (3) |
| Fractional-ization (Alesina et al.) | describes the probability that two randomly drawn individuals are from a different group | static variable | Alesina et al. 2003 | 0–1 | n/a | n/a | n/a |
| Fractional-ization (Fearon) | dto. | static variable | Fearon 2003 | 0–1 | n/a | n/a | n/a |
| Cultural fractional-ization (Fearon) | dto. | static variable | Fearon 2003 | 0–1 | n/a | n/a | n/a |

Continued overleaf

Table 1.10 Continued

| Variable | Description | Period under investigation | Source | Range of values, threshold for cross tabulation | Index values (if applicable) | | |
|---|---|---|---|---|---|---|---|
| | | | | | Low (1) | Medium (2) | Strong (3) |
| Fractional-ization (PREG) | Dto., refers to politically relevant groups only | static variable | Posner 2004 | 0–1 | n/a | n/a | n/a |
| Polarization | describes to what extent the distribution of ethnic groups is close to a 50:50 situation | static variable | Montalvo and Reynal-Querol 2004 | 0–1 | n/a | n/a | n/a |
| **Controls/ surrounding conditions** | | | | | | | |
| Population size | number of inhabitants in millions | 1990 | Africa Year Book | Principally open | n/a | n/a | n/a |
| Income level | GDP p.c. in US$ 1990 | 1990 | African development indicators | Dto. | n/a | n/a | n/a |
| Regime stability | number of years since last regime change | 1990 | African Elections data base | Dto. | n/a | n/a | n/a |
| Oil-producing country | yes/no | period after introduction of multiparty elections until 2010/ethnic violence onset | GIGA | 0/1 | n/a | n/a | n/a |

*Table 1.11* Summary Descriptive Statistics

| Variable | Obs | Mean | Std. dev. | Min | Max | Type |
|---|---|---|---|---|---|---|
| Ethnic violence (dv1) | 34 | 0.47 | 0.51 | 0 | 1 | Dummy |
| Ethnic armed conflict (dv2) | 34 | 0.38 | 0.49 | 0 | 1 | Dummy |
| Decentralization | 34 | 0.68 | 0.64 | 0 | 2 | Ordinal/binary |
| Proportional electoral system | 34 | 0.79 | 0.77 | 0 | 2 | Ordinal/binary |
| Government form | 34 | 0.35 | 0.73 | 0 | 2 | Ordinal/binary |
| Parallel religious boundaries | 34 | 0.62 | 0.697 | 0 | 2 | Ordinal/binary |
| Exclusion of ethnic groups | 34 | 1.09 | 0.97 | 0 | 2 | Ordinal/binary |
| Prior ethnic conflict | 34 | 0.77 | 0.89 | 0 | 2 | Ordinal/binary |
| Index of depth of divisions | 34 | 2.47 | 1.99 | 0 | 6 | Ordinal/binary |
| Ethnic fractionalization (Alesina) | 34 | 0.71 | 0.16 | 0.26 | 0.91 | Continous |
| Ethnic fractionalization (Fearon) | 34 | 0.73 | 0.17 | 0.26 | 0.95 | Continous |
| Cultural fractionalization (Fearon) | 34 | 0.45 | 0.197 | 0.04 | 0.73 | Continous |
| Fractionalization (PREG, Posner) | 33 | 0.39 | 0.23 | 0 | 0.71 | Continous |
| Polarization (Montalvo and Reynal-Querol) | 32 | 0.55 | 0.17 | 0.02 | 0.84 | Continous |
| "Compensation" Index I (inclusiveness/divisions) | 34 | 0.58 | 0.73 | 0 | 3 | Ordinal/binary |
| "Compensation" Index II (inclusiveness/divisions) | 34 | 0.29 | 0.21 | 0 | 1 | Ordinal/binary |
| Population size | 34 | 12.6 | 20.00 | 0.82 | 110 | Continous |
| Regime stability | 34 | 11.4 | 10.0 | 0 | 42 | Continous |
| Oil-producing country | 34 | 0.21 | 0.41 | 0 | 1 | Dummy |
| Income per capita | 33 | 625.97 | 710.1 | 80 | 3330 | Continous |

*Matrix 1.1* Pacifying Effect of Inclusive Institutions Relative to Depth of Divisions*

| DV I: Ethnic violence | Ethnic conflict rate baseline | Level of decentralization | | Proportionality of electoral system | | System of government (presidential vs. parliamentary | |
|---|---|---|---|---|---|---|---|
| N = 34 | 47% | Less decentralized (< 2) | Strongly decentralized (2) | Less proportional (> 2) | Strongly proportional | (semi) presidential (> 2) | parliamentary (2) |
| Deep divisions (6 and more) N = 18 | 78% | 88% | 0% | 83% | 67% | 80% | 67% |
| Moderate divisions (4–5) N = 8 | 25% | 29% | 0% | 29% | 0% | 29% | 0% |
| Absent divisions (3) N = 8 | 0% | 0% | 0% | 0% | 0% | 0% | 0% |

* Refers to dependent variable I (ethnic conflict, including nonstate conflict). Please note that with moderate or deep divisions conflict rates are consistently lower with all three forms of more inclusive institutions.

*Matrix 1.2* Contingency Table with Conflict Risks according to Higher/Lower Levels of Inclusiveness and Depth of Divisions.

| Divisions/inclusiveness | Lower: < 6 | Higher: 6 or more |
|---|---|---|
| Higher: 6 or more | 83% (N = 12) | 33% (N = 6) |
| Lower: < 6 | 15% (N = 13) | 0% (N = 3) |

Note: Percentages refer to conflict risks; the distribution of percentages is statistically significant according to chi square test (two-tailed) with Yates* corrections.

# 2 Matches and misfits
## Divided societies and the adoption of power sharing

*Gerald Schneider*

## Acknowledgements

Previous versions of this chapter were presented at the Annual Convention of the International Studies Association, 18–21 February 2015, New Orleans, Louisiana, and the third Institutions for Sustainable Peace (ISP) Network Conference, Geneva, 29–30 May 2014. I would like to thank the participants and especially Joakim Kreutz for their helpful comments. I also gratefully acknowledge Marlon Brandt's research assistance.

## Introduction

Power sharing is one of the most frequently advocated conflict management tools, regardless of whether it manifests itself formally through inclusive institutions or informally through the empowerment of previously excluded groups. However, the evidence in support of the peace-through-power-sharing proposition, commonly traced back to Lehmbruch's (1967) and Lijphart's (1968, 1977, 1984, 1996) studies of consociationalism and consensus democracy, is less clear-cut than these policy prescriptions would lead us to expect. While Norris (2008) and Cammett and Malesky (2012), for instance, link one important institutional facet of formal power sharing, proportional representation, to a decreased risk of conflict, others are more sceptical, offering evidence that qualifies or contradicts the hope of advocates of the traditional inclusive approach. Critics of the power-sharing approach particularly fear that the co-optation of other political groups into the political system through inclusive institutions or informal rules will politicize ethnic groups even more (Horowitz 1985, 1991; but see Huber 2012). As Esteban and Ray (2008) theorize and Schneider and Wiesehomeier demonstrate empirically (2008; see also Basedau, Chapter 1, this volume), formal power-sharing instruments only bring about peace in societies with a specific diversity profile. What is more, power sharing, whether formal or informal, is largely endogenous to the conflict outcome and becomes more likely if the conflict ended inconclusively (Pospieszna and Schneider 2013; Hartzell and Hoodie 2015). In line with the rich literature on institutional reform (e.g. Rokkan 1970; Elster 1993), this regularity suggests that ruling elites only co-opt competing groups into the power structures of their country if they cannot prevent it or if they believe they can consolidate their long-term grip on decision-making power in this way.

This chapter argues that the limited prevalence of both formal and informal power sharing in exactly those societies where it would, according to the advocates of the concept, be most needed is a consequence of sunk costs of past decisions. To put it metaphorically, a 'shadow of the past' in the form of initial decisions on inclusive rules frequently limits the possibility of opting for specific arrangements that would better suit a society and would enlarge its 'shadow of the future'. In particular, the constitutional legacy of a country limits the scope of attempts to appease divided societies through the preventive co-optation of real or potential challengers to the incumbent government. Pospieszna and Schneider (2013) show, for instance, that 90 per cent of post-conflict parliamentary elections employed the same electoral system as the one in place before the war. If a society does decide to change the rules of the game, it often follows the international community's standard recommendation of inclusive decision making. According to Bogaards (2013), proportional representation has become the fallback option in the aftermath of conflict, and many policy makers have recommended decentralization as an instrument through which peace can be restored in war-torn societies. For instance, US Senator Joe Biden stated in 2007, in this vein, that 'federalism is Iraq's best possible future' (quoted in Brancati 2009, 4).

The chapter therefore examines the conditions under which countries opt in favour of inclusive formal and informal institutions. Using longitudinal regression models, it clearly establishes that the 'shadow of the past' limits the scope for preventive conflict management. Countries that have already opted for a particular set of rules continue to employ them. The influence of a colonial past, in the form of the legal tradition on which a country relies, also hinders countries from embarking on a more inclusive path. A legal system of English origin reduces the chance that countries will adopt proportional representation, but slightly increases the chance of horizontal power sharing. In addition, ethnic diversity in the form of ethnic fractionalization and the marginalization of relevant ethnic groups reduces the chance that a country will adopt formal power-sharing rules. Ethnic fractionalization also limits the chance of informal, inclusive power sharing. The experience of war, from which one would expect an increased chance of inclusive policy making, is only positively associated with regional autonomy and thus one aspect of informal power sharing. This means, in other words, that countries which may be in particular need of power-sharing institutions or arrangements do not adopt them ex ante or ex post.

## Choosing power-sharing institutions and arrangements

One of the perennial questions of the social sciences is what rules a particular society should adopt to govern its domestic affairs. This governance discussion gained new impetus in the 1960s, when continental European political scientists observed a high degree of variance between the pluralism of the Anglo-Saxon hemisphere and neo-corporatism or consociationalism in the rest of the developed world (Lehmbruch 1967; Lijphart 1968). The interpretations shared the conviction that some of the linguistically, religiously or ideologically divided societies had established quite inclusive policy-making processes to appease powerful minorities, and with them the entire nation. This recognition led to the recommendation that what would come to be known as 'power sharing' could also be helpful outside the orbit of the industrialized countries.[1]

In its ideal-typical form, power-sharing forces contending political groups to decide by consensus or at least through a qualified majority what course a country should take. Such practices become theoretically inevitable if a single group is unable to control the central government or at least one region without the approval of a competing political force. Power sharing thus has a horizontal and a vertical dimension. The resulting 'consensus democracies', to use Lijphart's (1984, 1999) catchphrase, are characterized by grand coalitions, a system of mutual veto power, proportionality in political representation, and the granting of partial regional autonomy to strong minorities.

Power sharing can rely on both formal and informal rules. In line with Pospieszna and Schneider (2013), this chapter distinguishes between de jure and de facto power sharing. While the former includes *power-sharing institutions* such as proportional representation and constitutional provisions for a federal structure, the latter includes *power-sharing arrangements* such as the voluntary co-optation of a group into central government or the granting of political autonomy to a regionally powerful group.

While power sharing was initially conceived of primarily as a preventive tool in divided societies, it has in recent years been seen as a key conflict management tool for war-torn societies. Yet the effects of power sharing as either an ex ante or an ex post prescription for conflicts in divided societies remain the subject of debate. Norris (2008) and others contend that political power sharing between governments and insurgents generally lowers the risk of war in ethnically or religiously diverse societies. This is in line with Lijphart's recommendation that divided societies rely on consensual practices in order to avoid conflict. Extensions of this vision to post-conflict situations often rely on a broader understanding of power sharing, taking, for instance, the design of peace agreements and the military or economic disparities between contending groups into account. Hartzell and Hoodie (2007) argue that all-encompassing power-sharing agreements that strengthen previously marginalized groups politically, economically, territorially and militarily are the most effective.

According to Walter (2002), territorial and political power-sharing pacts particularly boost the chance that warring parties will sign and implement a peace agreement. Jarstad and Nilsson (2008) establish furthermore that power sharing in the military and the empowerment of regional groups make such treaties endure, while political pacts do not possess this positive effect. In an individual-level analysis of the case of Burundi, Samii (2013) shows how ethnic integration in the form of quotas for different groups within the military reduces prejudice. These results are in line with those of a general evaluation by Hartzell and Hoodie, who establish that multiple forms of power sharing increase the chance that a country will democratize following a civil war (Hartzell and Hoodie 2015).

Such findings on the peace-inducing effects of inclusive policy making are often in stark contrast to the pessimism of power-sharing sceptics. Horowitz (1985, 2005) in particular argues that a key component of de jure horizontal power sharing, proportional representation, increases the risk of ethnic divisions and of electoral competition taking place along the ethnic faultlines of a society. He favours the alternative-vote system, which in his view encourages voters to elect politicians from another ethnicity as it stimulates coalition building among minorities to gain political representation. Selway and Templeman (2012) demonstrate in empirical studies that power sharing is dysfunctional and endangers the stability of divided societies.

The effect of decentralization, another key component of power sharing, is similarly controversial. Chapman and Roeder (2007) advocate partition as a solution to territorial demands made by regionally concentrated groups over unitarism or regional autonomy. Brancati (2009), by contrast, qualifies this argument, arguing that it depends largely on the party systems. If statewide parties dominate the political landscape and regional demands have to be channelled through them, the empowerment of regional elites might serve the purpose that proponents of power sharing attribute to multilevel policy making. Cederman *et al.* (2015), conversely, demonstrate that many extant studies suffer from endogeneity bias and that territorial autonomy can pacify states.

Other findings occupy a middle ground between these two opposing camps, showing that the conflict-mitigating effect of power sharing depends heavily on the ethnic structure of a country (Schneider and Wiesehomeier 2008). In both ethnically fractionalized and polarized democracies, proportional representation reduces the risk of conflict, while federalism has the same effect only in highly fractionalized states. This is in line with theoretical work by Esteban and Ray (2008), whose rent-seeking contest model suggests that high levels of polarization act as a deterrent to competing groups up to a certain threshold, but that once hostilities have become lethal, the violence in such societies is especially violent. Basedau (Chapter 1, this volume) also shows that the depth of the divisions is key to understanding the success of the institutional reforms.

The contrasting findings point out, in line with the general premise of this volume, that institutions can be both part of the solution and part of the problem. Power sharing can only be successful if it responds to the pertinent cleavages of a society and if its design is comprehensive. Structurally, the discrepant results can have many causes, such as varying definitions and operationalizations of power sharing or differences in the cases that are examined.[2] In other words, what has been lacking so far is a meta-study that comparatively tests the robustness of the various claims. Yet there may also be theoretical reasons for the difficulties in coming up with conclusive evidence on the power-sharing thesis. I argue below that the interests of the ruling elite and the sunk costs of past decision making frequently create a misfit between the ethnic or religious makeup of a country and the formal and informal institutions that regulate how power is shared among competing groups. Assuming that inclusive policy making has the desired conflict-reduction effects, this chapter accordingly examines the possible incongruence between the need for power sharing and the actual adoption of this conflict management tool. I contend, in other words, that we need to understand the roots of power sharing and of its absence before we can grasp the possibly beneficial externalities of inclusive policy making.

While the effects of power sharing have, as indicated above, been well studied in recent years, fewer studies have explored the origins of power sharing. Differentiating between de jure and de facto power sharing along both horizontal and vertical lines, the following discussion distinguishes between four key facets of inclusive decision making: (1) electoral rules, (2) federalism, (3) grand coalitions, and (4) regional autonomy (Pospieszna and Schneider 2013). To start with, most of these explanations see the adoption of power-sharing rules as an attempt by the ruling elite to preserve or further consolidate its power. Obviously, such choices, especially constitutional ones, in favour of inclusive policy making take place behind a Rawlsian veil of ignorance and do not exclude the possibility that the incumbent government will miscalculate its future influence (Elster 1993). This perspective, however, emphasizes that short-run considerations – and not the wish to bring long-term peace to a society – typically characterize the introduction of power-sharing institutions and arrangements. The difficulty of amending constitutions in favour of excluded groups also plays into the hands of the status quo-oriented rulers. Most democracies rely on qualified majority hurdles to change the rules of the game, rendering it extremely difficult for minorities to change the constitutional status quo.

### *Horizontal power sharing*

Democracies use a variety of rules to regulate the competition between contending social interests. Proponents of the power-sharing approach have largely focused on proportional representation, as this electoral rule leads, at least in the Duvergerian logic, to a multiparty system. This in turn increases the likelihood of shifting coalitions and opens up the chance for minorities to participate in the government of the country at some point. Lijphart (1984) argues that proportional representation is ideal for fragmented societies because it eases party formation and does not force groups to build large but less representative parties. In his view, the relative peacefulness of India's domestic politics is largely due to its success in establishing power-sharing mechanisms (Lijphart 1996). Powell (1981) similarly points out that entry thresholds for new parties are lower in proportional systems than in majoritarian ones and that multiparty systems are less prone to mass violence. The international community of conflict managers seems to have adopted these lessons. Bogaards (2013, 72) describes proportional representation (PR) systems as the standard choice in the aftermath of war and writes: 'when peace agreements specify the electoral system for national parliamentary elections, this always involves PR.'

Most contributions to the literature on the origins of proportional representation stand in the shadow of Rokkan (1970), who famously argued that electoral rules do not develop in a vacuum. According to his pioneering study, governing parties supported the introduction of proportional representation out of fear of an impending loss of power due to the disproportional growth in the electoral appeal of the challenging party or due to the disproportionality of the translation of seats to votes. Subsequent studies have extended the scope of these two explanations, showing that they complement each other (Leeman and Mares 2014) or that they are more likely under majority rule with run-off elections than under plurality rule (Blais *et al.* 2005).

In some countries, minorities are co-opted into the government without constitutional provisions that make inclusive policy making more or less inevitable. Grand coalitions are, according to this literature, more likely to emerge in times of crisis. In their criticism of Rokkan (1970) and the tradition of his landmark thesis on the origins of proportional representation, Cusack *et al.* (2007, 328) add a political economy alternative to the adoption of grand coalitions. According to them, consociationalist decision making began with the start of industrialization, when countries began to invest to different degrees in skills. The emergence of proportional representation was thus one of the manifestations of both employers' and workers organizations' certitude that they needed 'consensus decision making in the regulatory areas that concern them'.

This alternative perspective suggests that the ruling elite may decide, in the context of broader economic and social developments, to opt for inclusive policy making. Hence, the anticipation of increased social conflict may be a reason why governments preventively co-opt strong minorities, either directly (via grand coalitions) or indirectly (through the introduction of rules such as proportional representation). This suggests that power-sharing rules are to some extent endogenous to the social fabric surrounding them. It has been noted for quite some time that the installation of a majoritarian system is more probable in homogeneous societies. Lijphart (1992) has, for instance, found considerable support for this conjecture in a comparative analysis of the democratization processes in Czechoslovakia, Hungary and Poland. Boix (1999), examining the determining factors for electoral system choice in advanced democracies, concludes that ethnic and religious fractionalization promotes the adoption of proportional representation. Although Brambor *et al.* (2006) reject this result, I explore the influence of anticipated changes to the diversity constellation on the adoption of power sharing and contrast their influence with that of constitutional traditions and the outcomes of war.

### *Vertical power sharing*

According to Riker's (1964) classical perspective, granting de facto or de jure autonomy to a region is, similarly to the introduction of proportional representation, a sign of weakness. Politicians who cannot expand their territory or who feel threatened opt for what he termed the 'bargain of federalism'. Calle (2015) employs a similar argument, but turns the perspective inward towards the calculations of the ruling elites. He argues that regional territorial conflicts that escalate into civil wars may largely be explained by the presence of regional power holders who fear losing their grip on the population and federal governments that are unresponsive to demands from a substate.

Organizing regional opposition requires, however, a cohesive identity within the region where the discontent is located. This is why increased diversity fuels the wish for regional autonomy. Fractionalized societies and countries with substantial minorities should therefore exhibit an increased chance of certain regionally concentrated groups obtaining power (Marks *et al.* 2008; Hooghe *et al.* 2010). The diversity of a country is largely a function of its size. Such diversity increases the chance that certain groups will entertain other preferences regarding the distribution of public goods than those of the majority of the country. According to Alesina and Spolaore (2003), the wish for disintegration is further fuelled by democracy and economic integration. The first claim finds support in the literature. Hooghe *et al.* (2008, 178) even predict that democracy and autocracy will bring about diverse developments: 'Countries that become democracies will experience a shift in the causality of regionalization that will, on average, lead to higher levels of regional authority, whereas countries that become non-democracies will, on average, face absolute declines." The claim, however, that economic integration is linked to regional authority is more controversial. The model by Alesina and Spolaore (2003) indicates that the provision of public goods becomes less important the more a country is integrated into the world economy. Globalization would thus enable regions to harvest the gains that free trade arrangements create and to disregard the much smaller advantages associated with belonging to a large state. Brancati (2014, 91) re-examines this claim systematically and writes: 'While EU integration has a weakly significant effect on the percentage of votes won by separatist parties in general, neither bilateral trade nor foreign direct investment has a significant effect on the vote for separatist parties.' This means that only the size of the state should be linked to vertical forms of power sharing, while the 'shadow of the past' and the ruling elite's wish to stay in power should reduce the chance that diverse countries will experience this form of inclusive governance. It is thus not surprising that Pospieszna and Schneider (2013) have found that countries that had opted for centralized decision-making institutions and arrangements also demonstrated considerable resistance to territorial concessions, even after a war.

In sum, power sharing may be used as both an ex ante and an ex post mechanism to resolve internal conflicts. However, constitutional engineering to reduce the escalatory potential within a divided society endangers the power base of the ruling elite, which will only give in to the co-optation of a minority into the central or regional government if it cannot avoid it. Ideally, highly diverse countries or war-torn societies that have experienced a civil war should be the prime candidates for the adoption of power-sharing institutions or arrangements. However, the shadow of the past, in the form of institutional stickiness and the interests of the ruling elite, makes such reforms highly unlikely.

## Research design

To empirically evaluate the origins of power-sharing institutions and arrangements, I examine a global sample of countries for the period between 1946 and 2010. As the institutional variables hardly change over time, I have chosen the country half-decade as the unit of analysis. This conservative strategy helps me to avoid comparing nearly identical country years against each other, which would introduce a 'disaggregation bias' to the study (Schneider 2015). I run longitudinal population-averaged models to test the hypotheses on the origins of power sharing. This econometric model is 'most appropriate for assessing the effects of cluster-level covariates' (Neuhaus 1992, 251), which is the case for this comparison between countries. Note that the inclusion of constant or nearly constant explanatory variables prevented me from using fixed-effect models, while the less conservative random-effect models provided almost identical results to the population-averaged approach.

### *Outcome variables*

This chapter differentiates between *horizontal* and *vertical* power-sharing institutions and arrangements. This double categorization entails four outcome variables: *proportional representation* and *federalism* as the two key components of de jure forms of power sharing, and *grand coalition* and *regional autonomy* as indicators of the corresponding de facto forms. The study of power-sharing institutions refers to democracies only. I employ the minimalist definition of democracy introduced by Przeworski *et al.* (2000), according to which (1) the chief executive is elected, (2) the legislature is elected, (3) there is more than one party competing in elections, and (4) an alternation under identical electoral rules has taken place.

*Proportional representation* is a dummy variable which indicates with a value of 1 that a country uses a proportional electoral formula with either single or multiple electoral tiers, and with a value of 0 that it does otherwise. The measure is based on the Democratic Electoral Systems around the World (1946–2011) dataset collected by Bormann and Golder (2013). In order to measure whether a country grants its subunits some de jure autonomy, I have relied on the Institutions and Election Project (IAEP) dataset. *Federalism* is 1 in the event that a country is either a confederation or a federal system; the variable takes a value of 0 for unitary systems.

*Grand coalition* stands for horizontal power-sharing arrangements. The variable is based on the natural logarithm of the share of the population excluded relative to the ethnopolitically relevant population in a country (Wimmer *et al.* 2009) and is taken from the Ethnic Power Relations (EPR) Core Dataset 2014 (Vogt 2014). I calculated this indicator of inclusiveness by mirroring it and by adding a value of 4.6, which is the maximum for the original indicator. Finally, *regional autonomy* refers to the World Bank Dataset of Political Institutions and codes a region as 1 if 'a source explicitly mentions a region, area, or district that is autonomous or self-governing' (Teorell *et al.* 2016, 159).

### Explanatory variables

To estimate the impact of the 'shadow of the past', I use the lag of the power-sharing-outcome indicators in some model specification. As the inclusion of such an autoregressive model is linked to a considerable loss of cases, I then contrast these models without the lagged dependent variable. I also assume that the legal tradition of a country affects the chance that power sharing will occur. *English legal origin*, which is taken from La Porta *et al.* (1999), measures dichotomously whether or not a country follows the English common law tradition. In many countries, the particular legal tradition indicates which colonial power was at the helm before independence.

I use *ethnic fractionalization* and *ethnic fractionalization squared* to gauge the influence of various forms of diversity. The multiplicative term is used to determine whether polarized countries also have an independent influence. As the results with the squared term are inconclusive for power-sharing institutions, I have only employed it to establish a possible impact for power-sharing arrangements. I obtained the fractionalization data from Fearon (2003). *Ethnic discrimination* measures the size of the excluded population relative to the total population in a logarithmic version. As a similar variable is used as a proxy for the size of the grand coalition, this variable, which is taken from the EPR dataset, is only used for the analysis of the correlates of power-sharing institutions. The variable allows me to test the thesis that rulers who exclude a significant part of the population do not have an interest in introducing inclusive rules.

Finally, I have used the Uppsala war termination dataset to establish whether a country experienced a *war end* in the past five years. The empirical basis is the dataset v.2010-1 (Kreutz 2010).[3] I have also controlled for the sociodemographic attributes of a country, namely its development level and population variables. I have used the natural logarithm for both the GDP per capita and population. The results obtained with these variables, which stem from the World Bank, did not, however, alter the results and are not reported below.

## Results

This chapter examines the origins of power sharing across the world, arguing that inclusive policy making is not necessarily established within the societies that need it according to the normative postulations of consociationalism. The empirical analysis proceeds in two steps. Table 2.1 reports the findings for power-sharing institutions that pertain to democratic countries only. Table 2.2 includes the equivalent findings for power-sharing arrangements.

### Power-sharing institutions

Slightly fewer than half of the cases examined here exhibited *proportional representation*, and about one-third *federalism*; 152 country half-decades, approximately one-fifth of the cases included for this part of the analysis, relied on

Table 2.1 Determinants of power-sharing institutions (half-decades)

| | Proportional representation | | | | Federalism | | | |
|---|---|---|---|---|---|---|---|---|
| | 1 | 2 | 3 | 4 | 5 | 6 | 7 | 8 |
| Lag power-sharing inst. | 0.35* | | 0.35* | | 5.52*** | | 5.56*** | |
| | (0.19) | | (0.19) | | (0.28) | | (0.28) | |
| English legal origin | -1.26* | -2.05*** | -1.88*** | -2.03*** | -0.30 | 0.03 | -0.17 | 0.08 |
| | (0.67) | (0.55) | (0.72) | (0.51) | (0.31) | (0.33) | (0.31) | (0.33) |
| Ethnic fractionalization | -1.77* | -1.15 | | | 0.32 | -0.35 | | |
| | (1.04) | (0.88) | | | (0.54) | (0.57) | | |
| Ethnic discrimination | | | -0.08 | -0.23*** | | | 0.04 | 0.09* |
| | | | (0.10) | (0.06) | | | (0.09) | (0.06) |
| War end last five years | -0.14 | -0.05 | -0.13 | -0.03 | -0.37 | -0.11 | -0.34 | -0.09 |
| | (0.13) | (0.10) | (0.12) | (0.11) | (0.35) | (0.12) | (0.35) | (0.11) |
| Constant | 0.93* | 1.03** | 0.35 | 0.97*** | -2.89*** | -0.47 | -2.82*** | -0.81*** |
| | (0.53) | (0.53) | (0.35) | (0.26) | (0.31) | (0.29) | (0.27) | (0.21) |
| Observations | 397 | 873 | 382 | 856 | 950 | 1105 | 899 | 1046 |
| No. of cluster | 63 | 98 | 59 | 95 | 154 | 154 | 146 | 146 |
| Wald chi-2 | 11.89** | 18.83*** | 10.17** | 24.89*** | 390.95*** | 1.31 | 376.64*** | 3.34 |

Notes

The models are longitudinal population-averaged logit models. Standard errors in parentheses. *** $p<0.01$, ** $p<0.05$, * $p<0.1$.

Table 2.2 Determinants of power-sharing arrangements (half-decades)

| | Grand coalition | | | | Regional autonomy | | | |
|---|---|---|---|---|---|---|---|---|
| | 1 | 2 | 3 | 4 | 5 | 6 | 7 | 8 |
| Lag power-sharing arrang. | 0.77*** | | 0.77*** | | 9.32*** | | 9.87*** | |
| | (0.01) | | (0.01) | | (0.93) | | (1.04) | |
| English legal origin | 0.11* | 0.51** | 0.09 | 0.43* | -0.57 | -0.51 | -0.54 | -0.55 |
| | (0.07) | (0.24) | (0.06) | (0.23) | (0.73) | (0.52) | (0.73) | (0.51) |
| Ethnic fractionalization | -0.46*** | -2.00*** | -2.10*** | -8.42*** | -1.65 | -1.37* | -6.76* | 2.37 |
| | (0.11) | (0.40) | (0.39) | (1.45) | (1.17) | (0.82) | (3.94) | (3.17) |
| Ethnic fract. squared | | | 1.78*** | 6.85*** | | | 5.64 | -4.34 |
| | | | (0.40) | (1.50) | | | (4.12) | (3.59) |
| War end last five years | -0.06 | -0.15*** | -0.05 | -0.15*** | 1.92*** | 0.24* | 2.05*** | 0.26* |
| | (0.04) | (0.06) | (0.04) | (0.06) | (0.63) | (0.13) | (0.65) | (0.14) |
| Constant | 0.83*** | 3.55*** | 1.07*** | 4.60*** | -4.20*** | -1.02*** | -3.60*** | -1.57*** |
| | (0.08) | (0.21) | (0.10) | (0.30) | (0.08) | (0.38) | (0.71) | (0.60) |
| Observations | 1541 | 1630 | 1541 | 1630 | 989 | 1143 | 989 | 1143 |
| No. of cluster | 145 | 145 | 145 | 145 | 154 | 154 | 154 | 154 |
| Wald chi-2 | 3103.61*** | 33.37*** | 3651.03*** | 58.28*** | 100.31*** | 7.62* | 92.46*** | 8.47* |

Notes
The models are longitudinal population-averaged linear regression (models 1–4) and logit models (models 5–8), respectively. Standard errors in parentheses.
*** p<0.01, ** p<0.05, * p<0.1.

both power-sharing institutions simultaneously. The results show clearly that there is considerable path dependency within the states. The longitudinal models establish that countries which exhibited proportional representation or federalism in the past half-decade have a high chance of relying on the same rules again. Models 1, 3, 5 and 7 in Table 2.1 report the corresponding results. The relationships are particularly strong for federalism. This suggests that the shadow of the past is particularly strong for decentralized decision making, despite the trend towards strengthened regional authority (Hooghe *et al.* 2010; Marks *et al.* 2008). A second factor that indicates the institutional legacy is *English legal origin*. It consistently reduces the chance of the introduction of proportional representation, but does not exert a systematic impact on the introduction of federalism. The analysis further shows that the institutional setting does not respond to ethnic diversity. On the contrary, in model 1 *ethnic fractionalization* reduces the chance of proportional representation. While *ethnic discrimination* limits the chance of horizontal power sharing, it marginally increases the chance of federalism. Both results suggest that countries which should be prime candidates for power sharing do not necessarily opt for institutions that would increase the chance of minority participation. Note also that wars do not influence the probability of power sharing. This means, all in all, that de jure power sharing is used neither ex ante nor ex post in a systematic fashion.

### *Power-sharing arrangements*

The shadow of the past not only reduces the chance of formal power sharing but also decreases the possibility that regional autonomy is granted or that grand coalitions emerge. Models 1, 3, 5 and 7 in Table 2.2 show that countries that have had large ruling coalitions have also relied on inclusive forms of policy making in the next half-decade. The impact of past decision making on regional autonomy is even stronger. Interestingly, countries with an English common law tradition tend to have larger ruling coalitions. The impact of *ethnic fractionalization* and its squared term is u-shaped. This indicates that both more homogeneous and more heterogeneous countries are more inclusive, while countries with a medium level of diversity tend to exclude important minorities. The latter group of societies includes highly polarized states where steps towards creating a more inclusive setting are linked to an increased risk of losing power. This result is in line with the argument outlined in the theoretical section that politicians will only opt for power sharing if they cannot avoid it or if they believe that a new arrangement may benefit them. It is thus also not surprising that countries in which a civil war has ended within the past five years have an increased tendency to grant regional autonomy but generally have smaller coalitions in domestic politics. While decentralization is not linked to a loss of influence within the power centre of a country, enlarging the coalition in the capital endangers the survival of the ruling elite. The results generally show that countries do not adopt informal power sharing in a preventive fashion and that ethnic diversity hinders rather than encourages inclusive policy making.

# Conclusion

This chapter has examined the origins of power sharing across the world. The absence of conclusive evidence that inclusive policy making renders divided societies more peaceful could be due to a mismatch between the need for power sharing and its actual supply. The theoretical framework suggests that only changes in the incentives for the ruling elite can help a country overcome the gap between its ethnic fabric and its institutional setting. Hence, a government is only willing to co-opt powerful groups into central or regional power arrangements and thus to move out of the shadow of past decisions if it fears that it will lose influence in the long run without power-sharing compromises.

Distinguishing between the presence of power sharing and reforms working towards such arrangements, I have shown, with the help of longitudinal models, that diversity only increases the chance of informal power sharing through grand coalitions. More polarized states are less likely to implement inclusive decision making, while homogeneous or highly fractionalized states are more likely to establish grand coalitions. This demonstrates, in line with Schneider and Wiesehomeier (2008), that power sharing is a partial response to the social diversity within a country, but not a perfect one. Concessions are somewhat more likely following a civil war, but this is only the case for regional autonomy. Note, however, that such cessations of war often lead to a very fragile peace in which the long-term success of power sharing is far from being guaranteed (Pospieszna and Schneider 2013).

The analysis clearly shows that we need to study the origins of power sharing more intensively before we can fully comprehend its potential peace-inducing effects. This chapter has examined these origins quantitatively. This means that it has not evaluated the quality of power sharing or whether the inclusion of previously excluded groups in policy making has improved the economic and social situation of these groups. The evidence assembled in the other studies of this volume clearly shows that the design of power-sharing arrangements in a post-conflict society can clearly make a difference in some cases, despite the initial wishes of the political leaders, who may have hoped to save some time by signing such a treaty but were not necessarily trying to bring peace to the state. Future studies should undertake in-depth examinations of how such provisions appear on the negotiating table and which implementation strategies render them successful.

# Notes

1   One of the first instances where 'power sharing' was discussed in a critical fashion was Puntambekar's (1949, 66) critical discussion of the Indian secular state. Many of the early conceptualizations, however, only employ it as a synonym for a system of checks and balances. The history of power sharing as an idea goes back much further. O'Leary (2005, 3), for instance, traces it to the sixteenth-century Protestant philosopher Althusisus, and Lehmbruch (1996) considers the term 'Amicabilis composition' (amicable settlement) of the Peace of Westphalia to be an early manifestation of consociationalism. This principle, which was later adopted by the German Reichstag, prevented majoritarian decisions in religious matters.

2   Binningsbø (2013) offers a comprehensive review of the effects of power sharing.
3   Earlier research by the author suggests that some countries that have experienced civil wars 'self-select' themselves into the set of countries that are likely to adopt power sharing. These countries have experienced civil wars that ended inconclusively or with a peace agreement (Pospieszna and Schneider 2013). The empirical analysis, however, does not support this thesis, perhaps due to the relatively small number of such cases. These findings are not reported below.

# References

Alesina, Albert and Enrico Spolaore. 2003. *The Size of Nations*. Cambridge, MA: MIT Press.

Binningsbø, Helga Malmin. 2013. 'Power Sharing, Peace and Democracy: Still an Uneasy Relationship?' *International Area Studies Review* 16(1): 89–112.

Blais, Andre, Agnieszka Dobrzynska and Indridi H. Indridason. 2005. 'To Adopt or not to Adopt Proportional Representation: The Politics of Institutional Choice'. *British Journal of Political Science* 35(1): 182–190.

Bogaards, Matthijs. 2013. 'The Choice for Proportional Representation: Electoral System Design in Peace Agreements'. *Civil Wars* 15(S1): 71–87.

Boix, Charles. 1999. 'Setting the Rules of the Game: The Choice of Electoral Systems in Advanced Democracies'. *American Political Science Review* 93(3): 609–624.

Bormann, Nils-Christian and Matt Golder. 2013. 'Democratic Electoral Systems Around the World, 1946–2011'. *Electoral Studies* 32(2): 360–369.

Brambor, Thomas, Clark, William and Golder, Matt. 2006. 'Understanding Interaction Models: Improving Empirical Analyses'. *Political Analysis* 14(1): 63–82.

Brancati, Dawn. 2009. *Peace by Design. Managing Intrastate Conflict through Decentralization*. Oxford: Oxford University Press.

Brancati, Dawn. 2014. 'Another Great Illusion: The Advancement of Separatism through Economic Integration'. *Political Science Research and Methods* 2(1): 69–95.

Calle, Luis de la. 2015. *Nationalist Violence in Postwar Europe*. Cambridge: Cambridge University Press.

Cammett, Melani and Malesky, Edmund. 2012. 'Power Sharing in Postconflict Societies: Implications for Peace and Governance'. *Journal of Conflict Resolution* 56(6): 982–1016.

Cederman, Lars-Erik, Simon Hug, Andreas Schädel and Julian Wucherpfennig. 2015. 'Territorial Autonomy in the Shadow of Conflict: Too Little, Too Late?' *American Political Science Review* 109(2): 354–370.

Chapman, Thomas and Philip G. Roeder. 2007. 'Partition as a Solution to Wars of Nationalism: The Importance of Institutions'. *American Political Science Review* 101(4): 677—691.

Cusack, Thomas R., Torben Iversen and David Soskice. 2007. 'Economic Interests and the Origins of Electoral Systems'. *American Political Science Review* 101(3): 331–391.

Elster, Jon. 1993. 'Constitution Making in Eastern Europe: Rebuilding the Boat in the Open Sea'. *Public Administration* 71(1–2): 169–217.

Esteban, Joan and Debraj Ray. 2008. 'Polarization, Fractionalization and Conflict'. *Journal of Peace Research* 45(2): 163–182.

Fearon, James D. 2003. 'Ethnic and Cultural Diversity by Country'. *Journal of Economic Growth* 8(2): 195–222.

Hartzell, Caroline and Matthew Hoddie. 2003. 'Institutionalizing Peace: Power Sharing and Post-civil Conflict Management'. *American Journal of Political Science* 47(2): 318–332.

Hartzell, Caroline and Matthew Hoddie. 2007. *Crafting Peace: Power-sharing Institutions and the Negotiated Settlement of Civil Wars.* University Park: Pennsylvania State University Press.

Hartzell, Caroline and Matthew Hoddie. 2015. 'The Art of the Possible: Power Sharing and Post-Civil War Democracy'. *World Politics* 67(1): 37–71.

Hooghe, Liesbet, Gary Marks and Arjan H. Schakel. 2010. *The Rise of Regional Authority. A Comparative Study of 42 Democracies.* Abingdon: Routledge.

Horowitz, Donald L. 1985. *Ethnic Groups in Conflict.* Berkeley: University of California Press.

Horowitz, Donald L. 1991. *A Democratic South Africa? Constitutional Engineering in a Divided Society.* Berkeley: University of California Press.

Huber, John D. 2012. 'Measuring Ethnic Voting: Do Proportional Electoral Laws Politicize Ethnicity?' *American Journal of Political Science* 56(4): 986–1001.

Jarstad, Anna K. and Desiree Nilsson. 2008. 'From Words to Deeds: The Implementation of Power-sharing Pacts in Peace Accords'. *Conflict Management and Peace Science* 25(3): 206–223.

Kreutz, Joakim. 2010. 'How and When Armed Conflicts End: Introducing the UCDP Conflict Termination Dataset'. *Journal of Peace Research* 47(2): 243–250.

La Porta, Rafael, Florencio Lopez-de-Silanes, Andrei Shleifer and Robert Vishny. 1999. 'The Quality of Government'. *Journal of Law, Economics and Organization* 15(1): 222–279.

Leemann, Lucas and Isabela Mares. 2014. 'The Adoption of Proportional Representation'. *Journal of Politics* 76(2): 461–478.

Lehmbruch, Gerhard. 1967. *Proporzdemokratie. Politisches System und politische Kultur in der Schweiz und in Österreich.* Tübingen: Mohr Siebeck.

Lehmbruch, Gerhard. 1996. 'Die korporative Verhandlungsdemokratie in Westmitteleuropa'. *Swiss Political Science Review* 2(4): 1–41.

Lijphart, Arend. 1968. *The Politics of Accommodation. Pluralism and Democracy in the Netherlands.* Berkeley: University of California Press.

Lijphart, Arend. 1977. *Democracy in Plural Societies: A Comparative Exploration.* New Haven, CT: Yale University Press.

Lijphart, Arend. 1984. *Democracies: Patterns of Majoritarian and Consensus Government in Twenty-one Democracies.* New Haven, CT: Yale University Press.

Lijphart, Arend 1992. 'Democratization and Constitutional Choices in Czecho-Slovakia, Hungary and Poland, 1989–91'. *Journal of Theoretical Politics* 4(2): 207–223.

Lijphart, Arend. 1996. 'The Puzzle of Indian Democracy: A Consociational Interpretation'. *American Political Science Review* 90: 258–268.

Lijphart, Arend. 1999. *Patterns of Democracy: Government Forms and Performance in Thirty-six Countries.* New Haven, CT/London: Yale University Press.

Marks, Gary, Liesbet Hooghe and Arjan H. Schakel. 2008. 'Patterns of Regional Authority'. *Regional and Federal Studies* 18(2–3): 167–181.

Neuhaus, John M. 1992. Statistical Methods for Longitudinal and Clustered Designs with Binary Responses. *Statistical Methods in Medical Research* 1: 249–273.

Norris, Pippa. 2008. *Driving Democracy: Do Power-sharing Institutions Work?* New York: Cambridge University Press.

O'Leary, Brendan. 2005. 'Debating Consociational Politics: Normative and Explanatory Arguments'. In Sid Noel (ed.), *From Power Sharing to Democracy: Post-conflict Institutions in Ethnically Divided Societies*. Montreal: McGill-Queen's Press. pp. 3–43.

Pospieszna, Paulina and Gerald Schneider. 2013. 'The Illusion of "Peace Through Power-sharing": Constitutional Choice in the Shadow of Civil War'. *Civil Wars* 15(S1): 44–70.

Powell, G. Bingham. 1981. 'Party Systems and Political System Performance: Voting Participation, Government Stability and Mass Violence in Contemporary Democracies'. *American Political Science Review* 75(4): 861–879.

Przeworski, Adam, Michael E. Alvarez, José A. Cheibub and Fernando Limongi, 2000. *Democracy and Development: Political Institutions and Well-being in the World, 1950–1990*. Cambridge: Cambridge University Press.

Puntambekar, S.V. 1949. 'The Secular State: A Critique'. *Indian Journal of Political Science* 10(1–2): 58–72.

Riker, William. 1964. *Federalism: Origin, Operation, Significance*. Boston, MA: Little Brown.

Rokkan, Stein. 1970. *Citizens, Elections, Parties: Approaches to the Comparative Study of the Process of Development*. Oslo: Universiteesforlaget.

Samii, Cyrus. 2013. 'Perils or Promise of Ethnic Integration? Evidence from a Hard Case in Burundi'. *American Political Science Review* 107(3): 558–573.

Schneider, Gerald. 2015. 'Von Makro zu Mikro: Grundlagen und Perspektiven der Bürgerkriegsforschung'. *Zeitschrift für Friedens- und Konfliktforschung* 4(2): 308–329.

Schneider, Gerald and Nina Wiesehomeier, 2008. 'Rules that Matter: Political Institutions and the Diversity–Conflict Nexus'. *Journal of Peace Research* 45(2): 183–203.

Selway, Joel and Kharis A. Templeman. 2012. 'The Myth of Consociationalism'. *Comparative Political Studies* 45(12): 1542–1571.

Teorell, Jan, Stefan Dahlberg, Sören Holmberg, Bo Rothstein, Felix Hartmann and Richard Svensson. 2016. The Quality of Government Standard Dataset, version Jan15. University of Gothenburg: The Quality of Government Institute, www.qog.pol.gu.se.

Vogt, Manual. 2014. 'The Ethnic Power Relations (EPR) Core Dataset 2014'. Codebook. Mimeo, ETHZ.

Walter, Barbara. 2002. *Committing to Peace: The Successful Settlement of Civil Wars*. Princeton, NJ: Princeton University Press.

Wimmer, Andreas, Lars-Erik Cederman and Brian Min. 2009. 'Ethnic Politics and Armed Conflict: A Configurational Analysis'. *American Sociological Review* 74(2): 316–337.

# 3 Socio-institutional congruence and social peace in divided and post-conflict societies

*Artak Galyan*

## Introduction

The question of how to establish sustainable peace in divided and post-conflict societies has been the focus of much scholarly and practitioner attention for several decades. The end of the Cold War saw many multiethnic authoritarian regimes open and embark on a thorny road to democracy. Many of the civil wars that had their geneses in Cold War rivalries came to an end as the new post-conflict societies built institutional structures that would help avoid renewed conflict. In their attempts to resolve intrastate conflicts and to consolidate democracy, many of the world's post-conflict and divided societies have implemented consecutive reforms of their political institutions in recent decades. As a result, the topic of institutional reform has grown from a purely academic subfield into an issue of considerable policy importance, with numerous international and regional organizations and governments having a strong interest in the subject.

One of the main challenges faced by reformists has been to design macro-political institutions that are capable of managing ethnic tensions and conflicts and of enhancing the consolidation of democracy. Debates between proponents and opponents of ideal models of institutional design have resulted in the emergence of a voluminous literature that identifies both the advantages and disadvantages of using separate political institutions to achieve social peace and democracy in divided and post-conflict societies. However, the empirical literature has tended to isolate the impact of institutions by looking at their net effects, thus detaching the impact of separate institutions from institutional configurations and the social structures in which institutions are embedded. Both of these trends have led to a lack of understanding about the impact configurations of political institutions.

This chapter highlights some of the pitfalls of the literature on institutional design in divided societies by following a different path and exploring an alternative conjunctural institutional framework, which integrates insights into the impact of separate institutions and social structures into a unified framework. This framework conceptualizes the effects of institutions as being nested in the socioinstitutional context and their impact on social peace as being dependent on the degree of congruence between institutional configurations, on the one hand,

and social structure, on the other. This framework is applied to the case of Sri Lanka, which experienced several cycles of institutional reform with three different socioinstitutional combinations between 1948 and 2010. I show how socioinstitutional incongruence contributed to the escalation of intergroup conflict and, eventually, a long and bloody civil war.

The success of institutional reform in preventing the emergence or recurrence of intrastate conflicts largely depends on the degree to which the reformed institutional framework responds to the needs of society. By explicitly linking the effect of political institutions to social structure, the conjunctural institutional framework outlined in this chapter allows us to evaluate the degree of congruence between a country's political institutions and its social structure. This parsimonious framework can offer new insights into the successes and failures of past instances of institutional reforms in divided and post-conflict societies. The framework could also inform future institutional reform attempts that aim to tailor the adoption of political institutions to the social structure and specific needs of a country.

The chapter is structured as follows. The second section discusses the two main theoretical approaches to institutional design, the major trends of the empirical literature, and emphasizes the importance of studying the impact of institutions not in isolation but in conjuncture with other institutions and sociodemographic conditions. The third section outlines the conjunctural institutional framework and details the socioinstitutional configurations that could provide ethnic groups access to political power. The fourth section presents the case of institutional design in Sri Lanka to illustrate the conjunctural effects of political institutions and sociodemographic conditions.

## Institutions and social peace in divided societies

### Theoretical approaches

The literature on institutional design in divided societies has evolved out of the debate on the advantages and disadvantages of two ideal models: consociational and centripetal. The consociational model stems from the work of Arendt Lijphart (1968, 1969, 1977, 1991, 2004) and is based on the idea that in deeply divided societies[1] cleavage groups should be empowered by inclusion in government through explicit recognition of the social cleavages. Extensive inclusion of groups along the lines of salient social cleavages is expected to create mutual constraints against the usurpation of power by any segment of the divided society. The creation of constraints is based on four main principles: grand coalition, proportional representation (PR), segmental autonomy and mutual veto power. Achieving these principles depends on the presence of a PR electoral system, a parliamentary executive and a federal system with ethnically defined federal units. An important part in the Lijphartian approach is that the desired effect of institutions is expected to be achieved through the implementation of this institutional prescription as a unified package (Lijphart 1969).

An alternative approach to designing institutions for social peace is centripetalism, which is most prominently associated with the work of Donald

Horowitz (1985, 1990, 1993, 2008). Centripetalism sees the creation of incentives for intergroup cooperation and moderation as the key to managing interethnic relations. According to this perspective, constraints – which are established from the outset – are unproductive because their binding force is not based on current interests. Constraints can corrode as the interests and power balance of parties change (Horowitz 2014, 8–11). Incentives, however, are not bound to a given point in time when institutions are established but persist and change as preferences, identities and, most importantly, the balance of power change. The crucial distinction of the centripetal approach is its preference for vote-pooling electoral systems, a presidential executive elected by vote pooling or qualified majority systems, and federalism with ethnically heterogeneous units.

Paradoxically, both Lijphart (2004, 99) and Horowitz (1990, 2008, 2014) recognized that most empirical instances of institutional design divert from these ideal models despite presenting their respective approaches as ready-made packages of institutional design. Real-world instances of institutional design divert from ideal models, since negotiation over and the adoption of institutions is a complex process. It is rather unlikely that all actors' preferences converge around one single template. Countries' institutional choices are influenced by path dependence on colonial heritage, constitutional diffusion, international and regional organizations, and individual countries advocating their domestic institutions as models (see e.g. Reilly and Reynolds 1999; Elgie 2011; Bogaards 2013). In this context consociational and centripetal approaches contain a contradiction: they both promote institutional packages while simultaneously acknowledging that such packages are unlikely to be adopted.

### *Empirical literature*

The empirical literature provides valuable insights into the capacity of separate institutions to achieve sustainable peace in divided societies. Small-N studies have focused on the impact of individual institutions as well as constellations of institutions in a wide variety of individual countries and regions. Despite its obvious merits and important contributions, case study research has not generally strived and lacks the capacity for generalization. Unlike the small-N studies, the booming large-N literature has sought to identify general trends that hold in various settings and has been able to produce generalizable findings on the effect of political institutions. The goal of this stream of literature has thus been to find, *ceteris paribus*, which institution is better able to reduce intrastate violence in divided and post-conflict societies. Most of the large-N research has come to a consensus that proportional electoral systems, federalism and, to a lesser degree, parliamentarianism, are better equipped to do so.

However, by just looking at the net effects of separate institutional variables, a considerable amount of conflict activity remains unexplained. Furthermore, even though statistically significant, the differences in these net effects are not so big in absolute terms. Even in cases where the conflict-reducing net effect is established for a given institution, there is still considerable conflict within many instances of these conflict-reducing institutions. We then do not know under what circumstances some of the countries with a proportional electoral system, federal structures or parliamentary forms of government experience various degrees of intrastate conflicts. Similarly, we cannot explain why some countries with conflict-exacerbating majoritarian institutions do not experience conflict.

### Relevance of a conjunctural institutional approach

Along with the focus on the net effects of institutions, there is also a growing understanding that political institutions' effect can be conditioned by a variety of institutional and sociodemographic factors. Reilly and Reynolds (1999) have so far given the most elaborate overview of the contextual factors that can determine the effect of political institutions and electoral systems in particular. They identify the nature of the societal cleavage, the number and geographical distribution of groups, and the intensity of conflict. The authors argue, for example, that centripetalism will fail in countries where cleavages run deep and which have experienced protracted civil wars with gross human rights violations, making vote pooling based on a level of intergroup trust and moderation impossible (Reilly and Reynolds 1999, 48).

More recent empirical research has shed light on the (mostly two-way) interactive effects among institutions with a variety of contextual conditions. Brancati (2006, 2009) shows that the peace-enhancing capacity of territorial devolution is strongly conditioned by the nature of the party system. Relying on the 'state in society framework', Bakke and Wibbels (2006) and Bakke (2009) look at the conditions for the peace-preserving impact of federalism. Schneider and Wiesehomeier (2008) analyse the interactive effects of the degree of ethnic fragmentation, polarization and ethnic dominance in autocratic and democratic regimes, as well political institutions such as PR electoral systems, presidentialism, federalism, party systems and district magnitude. Theuerkauf (2012) examines the interactive effect of ethnic diversity with presidentialism and majoritarian electoral systems. Neudorfer and Theuerkauf (2014) look at the impact of electoral systems in resource-rich countries.

This tendency to look at institutions' interactive effects relates to the argument put forward by various scholars that no institution is bad or good in its own right. Institutions acquire qualities and produce outcomes depending on the environments in which they are embedded. Sisk (1996) argues that debating which institutional model is the best is an unfruitful enterprise, as none of the models or separate institutions is universally good or bad. Institutional design scholars should rather investigate the conditions under which any one model or hybrid combination of institutions is more likely to mitigate the negative consequences of segmental divisions. According to Sisk (1996, 47–48), the goal is not to develop a unified theory of institutional design but rather a menu of choices from which the most suitable option may be chosen for the requirements of a specific conflict.

The case for studying the impact of institutional configurations rather than separate institutions is also made by Belmont *et al.* (2002, 3–4), who argue that there is no 'uniform institutional design that should be applied in all divided societies [.] [S]ome mechanisms of power-sharing, are important in most divided societies. The "best" way of achieving power-sharing may vary across cases.' They further emphasize that 'political institutions interact in complex ways; such interactions are not fully recognized by studies that address more specific and delimited themes' (Belmont *et al.* 2002, 3–4). The importance of studying the effects of institutions by looking at their empirical configurations is that institutions are mutually connected and reinforce or modify each other's effect. Mixing two or three institutions with different institutional logics and incentives will completely change the expected effects of the separate institutions and the entire configurations in which they are built.

The importance of a conjunctural perspective on both the effects of institutions and on the influence of social conditions is that the latter can have a dramatic impact on the effects of institutions. Social conditions can turn even the most inclusive institutions and institutional configurations into the least inclusive, with destructive conditions for a society. Social conditions can reinforce, decrease or completely change the logic embedded in political institutions. A misfit among institutional elements and social conditions can lead to unexpected and often disastrous impacts on the stability of a divided society.

## Conjunctural institutional framework

The provision of access to central- and subnational-level political power to all segments of a society and civil war belligerents is one of the primary institutional reform mechanisms for addressing deep segmental cleavages and preventing intrastate conflict in divided and post-conflict societies. By 'access to political power', I mean the ability of ethnic groups to influence central and subnational executive governments and legislatures, and thus make state policies congruent with, or at least not contradictory to, groups' interests. When groups are excluded from power, central and subnational state institutions can adopt policies contrary to their interests without obstacle, explicitly or implicitly discriminating against the excluded groups.

Recent research has shown that the exclusion of politically relevant groups from political power leads to intrastate conflict (Cederman *et al.* 2010, 2011, 2013; Wucherpfennig *et al.* 2011; Buhaug *et al.* 2014). The crucial element of the conjunctural institutional framework presented in this chapter is that access to and exclusion from political power are not provided by any single institution or sociodemographic condition, but by conjunctures of different political institutions and sociodemographic conditions. These different conjunctures have different mechanisms of access to and exclusion from political power. I distinguish between two categories of institutions (i.e. power concentrating and power dispersing), two categories of social structures (i.e. socially fragmented and socially polarized), and two different modes of access to political power (indirect and direct), which are provided by specific conjunctures of institutions and social structures.

### Power concentration versus power dispersion in institutions and social structures

Central to the understanding of the role of political institutions is the question of how and to what extent political institutions concentrate or disperse power among social groups. This distinction between power-dispersing and power-concentrating political institutions has been most prominently discussed by Lijphart (1999; see also Lijphart 1977, 1991, 1994) and more recently by Schneider (2009) in his research on the consolidation of democracy and by Mine *et al.* (2013) in their work on conflict management in Africa.

Power-concentrating institutions – such as majoritarian electoral systems, presidential executives and unitary state structures – provide fewer social groups with access to political power. By doing so, these institutions introduce a centripetal incentive that aims to make it more beneficial for social groups to move closer to the centre of the political spectrum and refrain from ethnic outbidding. It is assumed that by moving towards the centre, ethnic groups will moderate their positions and become more open to cooperation across group lines. A majoritarian 'winner-takes-all' logic of these institutions clearly demarcates the winners and losers in political competition. The stakes of competition are therefore high given the high rewards for cooperation and costs of noncooperation.

By contrast, power-dispersing institutions – such as proportional electoral systems, parliamentary executives and federal or decentralized territorial structures – distribute power among a greater number of state agencies and social groups that are competing for political power at both horizontal and vertical levels. Through their ability to disperse power among a higher number of social groups, these institutions introduce a centrifugal incentive that encourages social groups to seek political power by relying only on their own electoral base. This is because the centrifugal aspect means that all social groups can, theoretically, gain access to political power in one branch or at one level of power without having to cooperate with each other in order to do so.

Similar to institutions, social structures may also be argued to have a certain predisposition towards either power concentration or power dispersion; that is, they introduce incentives for either power concentration or power dispersion. In this context, I differentiate between *socially fragmented* and *socially polarized* social structures.

*Socially fragmented* societies are characterized by a high number, usually more than four politically relevant,[2] small groups competing for power at the central level. This creates an incentive to concentrate power within a few institutions and among fewer political parties. In socially fragmented societies there is less polarization among groups, the nature of competition is not zero-sum and elites are more accommodative. Due to this, cooperation among groups is not only possible but even necessary in instances where groups want to achieve power through democratic means. Countries like Benin, Cameroon, Ghana and Zambia are examples of socially fragmented societies. In each of these countries multiple politically relevant, relatively small groups compete for power – none of which is capable of solely dominating state institutions in the context of democratic government.

*Socially polarized* societies have fewer ethnic groups (usually no more than four), which are of equal demographic size and strength and are big enough or strong enough to present a (real or perceived) threat to the sheer existence of other groups. The balance of size and capabilities between the groups makes it a highly polarized society. Thus, politics in these societies is adversarial and zero-sum. Because of the underlying polarization, ethnic groups are highly sensitive to any actual or perceived restriction of their access to political power. The demographic size of the groups gives them both legitimacy and capability to lay a strong claim to a significant role in state institutions. To ignore such claims or grievances can be very costly because of their insurgency-fuelling capability. Countries like Bosnia and Herzegovina, Burundi, Fiji and Sri Lanka are typical cases of socially polarized societies.

The different categories of political institutions and social structures employ different mechanisms to provide ethnic groups with either *indirect* or *direct* access to political power. Indirect access refers to a group's ability to influence state policy through broad-based catchall political organizations that articulate, mobilize and organize the interests of several segments in a plural society[3] and which also recruit cadres (a multiethnic task given that cadres are not necessarily members of the segments they represent). Such organizations do not directly represent any of the societal segments, but rather indirectly represent a number of – if not most – segments in a plural society.

Indirect access is characteristic of power-concentrating institutions, which through their majoritarian logic and integrative incentives contribute to the emergence of broad political organizations that cut across several segments of a divided society. Indirect access is also more characteristic of socially fragmented societies, where the emergence of social organizations with support in a single segment is unlikely since they are demographically too weak to win majorities on their own. In addition, the absence of polarization makes intergroup cooperation, vote pooling and multiethnic recruitment possible. In the context of democratic government, political organizations in such societies will necessarily have to appeal to several ethnic groups.

Direct access refers to a group's ability to influence state policy through political organizations that explicitly or implicitly articulate, mobilize and organize the interests of a single segment of a society and that recruit cadres who are also members of the respective segment. The support base of such organizations is somewhat rigid and comprises a specific segment. Direct access is more characteristic of power-dispersing institutions – which distribute power to multiple ethnic groups – and polarized societies, where segments are demographically big enough to have competitive political organizations even when support is limited to their narrow segment. The support base of such organizations is restricted to a single segment since ethnic polarization makes intergroup cooperation, vote pooling and multiethnic recruitment difficult.

### Socioinstitutional (in)congruence: access to and exclusion from political power across political institutions and social structures

The conjunctural institutional framework rests on the argument that access to political power is an outcome of the specific conjunctural combination of institutions and social structures. More specifically, access to political power is an outcome of congruence between the logical predisposition of institutions, on the one hand, and the social structure, on the other. Access to political power is possible when the logic and incentives of political institutions are congruent with the logic and incentives of social structure. Accordingly, access to political power is restricted or completely absent when the logic and incentives of institutions are incongruent with the logic and incentives of the social structure.

In his book on democracy and social peace in Norway, Eckstein (1966) claims that stability in a state depends on the congruence between state institutions and society. In particular, Eckstein argued that 'democracies [.] tend to be stable if governmental and social authority patterns are highly congruent – if they involve considerable resemblances and thus have a certain fit' (1966, 186). The congruence between social structure and political institutions discussed in this section resembles the mechanism of congruence elaborated by Eckstein. Socioinstitutional congruence exists where the component social structure and political institutions resemble each other. More specifically, socioinstitutional congruence exists when both the social structure and institutions embedded in them follow the same pattern of power distribution; that is, both are either predisposed to concentrating power or dispersing it. In contrast, socioinstitutional incongruence occurs when political institutions and social structure have different or contradictory patterns of power distribution.

Table 3.1 shows the different modes of access to political power as a function of the (in)congruence between conjunctures of institutions and social structures. There are two instances of socioinstitutional congruence when access to political

*Table 3.1*  Access to political power as an outcome of in(congruence) of institutions and social structures

| | | Social fragmentation | Social polarization |
|---|---|---|---|
| **Institutions** | Concentration | Indirect access to political power | Exclusion from political power |
| | Dispersion | Exclusion from political power | Direct access to political power |
| | | **Social structure** | |

power is present. First, when power-concentrating institutions are nested in socially fragmented societies; second, when power-dispersing institutions are nested in socially polarized societies. The opposite of the previous two scenarios are the instances of socioinstitutional incongruence that impede or completely restrict access to political power. The first instance of incongruence is when power-dispersing institutions are nested in socially fragmented societies. The second scenario of incongruence occurs when power-concentrating institutions are nested in socially polarized societies.

In socially fragmented societies groups can achieve political power through the indirect mode. Social fragmentation tends to lead to centripetal politics, making ethnic groups move towards moderation and more centralized state institutions. In such a social structure a corresponding institutional logic introduced through centripetal institutions will provide society with what it needs to sustain the democratic political system. Centripetal institutions in such a social structure will concentrate power in a few state institutions and provide groups with indirect access to political power through broad multiethnic parties, centralized executives dependent on the support of intergroup coalitions, and centralized or decentralized forms of governance. Following this logic, indirect access to political power is present when there is congruence between power concentrating-institutions and social fragmentation.

The fragmentation of socially fragmented societies makes power dispersion and direct access to political power unfit, for three reasons. First, power-dispersing institutions in such societies will produce highly fragmented and unmanageable governments with an excessive number of veto players. Second, despite their ability to disperse power among multiple ethnic groups, these institutions will nevertheless exclude certain groups simply because of the multiplicity of groups and the restrictions on how fragmented a manageable government can be. Third, power-dispersing institutions that are based on explicit recognition and political mobilization of existing social cleavages will increase polarization among groups.

The small number of groups, their considerable demographic size and intergroup polarization make socially polarized societies predisposed to power dispersion. Due to their considerable demographic size, groups in such a society can achieve power independently of each other. Cooperation is difficult because of ethnic polarization and ensuing intergroup distrust and animosity. The high capabilities of groups along with societal polarization create a predisposition to power-dispersing institutions that facilitate the maintenance of independent pockets of power created by the demographic structure of society. Because of the predisposition to power-dispersing institutions, direct access to political power is possible in socially polarized societies.

In socially polarized societies any institutional structure that concentrates rather than disperses power will create instability, since power concentration will inevitably lead to the exclusion of certain powerful and polarized groups. The underlying polarization and distrust also mean that groups will only be satisfied with direct access to political power, since they will find it difficult to trust politicians who hail from a different group. Exclusion from political power is consequently a key source of intrastate conflict, since groups are both capable and antagonized.

## Socioinstitutional congruence and social peace in Sri Lanka

Postcolonial Sri Lanka has experienced three distinct institutional configurations, making it an illustrative case for a conjunctural institutional framework. This section discusses Sri Lanka's social structure and its three different institutional configurations. It shows that institutional configurations on their own contain contradictions. In addition, recurrent incongruence between the country's institutional configurations and social structure has further undermined the ability of institutions to provide minorities with access to political power. The continuous political exclusion of Tamils both at the central and subnational levels has allowed the majority to adopt discriminatory policies, which has gradually marginalized and radicalized the minority and led to a long and bloody civil war.

Sri Lanka is a deeply divided society. The chief cleavage is between the two main groups: the Buddhist Sinhala-speaking Sinhalese and the Hindu Tamil-speaking Sri Lanka Tamils. At the time of independence Sinhalese constituted 69 per cent of the population, Sri Lanka Tamils constituted 11 per cent of the population, while Indian Tamils comprised almost 12 per cent of the population, although as of the 1981 census their share of population decreased to 5 per cent.[4] Other minorities constituted almost 8 per cent of the overall population.

Sri Lanka features three demographic characteristics that are associated with increased risk of intercommunal violence. First, it is an ethnically bipolar society that features competition between two main groups (i.e. the Tamils and Sinhalese). Second, there is a component of ethnic dominance (Collier and Hoeffler 2004), since the Buddhist Sinhalese constitute an overwhelming majority of around 70 per cent. Third, there is also an element of geographical concentration, since a large portion of Sri Lankan Tamils live in the north and northeast of the country, while Indian Tamils are concentrated in the central mountainous region of the country. In addition, Tamils have a kin state, since many Tamils live in southern India, primarily in the state of Tamil Nadu. Tamils have a sizeable politically active and economically capable diaspora. The combination of ethnic polarization, ethnic dominance and a geographically concentrated minority makes Sri Lanka a socially polarized society.

According to the conjunctural framework presented above, power-concentrating institutional configurations are ill-advised for a society like Sri Lanka, as they are likely to prevent a sizeable and powerful minority with territorial sanctuary from gaining access to political power. Given the high intergroup polarization, broad multiethnic coalitions are unlikely to emerge in such a society, and integrative majoritarian institutions will thus be unable to provide a degree of intergroup support. Consequently, the only feasible mode of group access to political power in Sri Lanka is direct access, which can only emerge if Sri Lanka adopts power-dispersing political institutions. To date, however, socially polarized Sri Lanka has been governed by some of the most power-concentrating institutional configurations in the world.

Upon gaining independence in 1948 Sri Lanka inherited a Westminster system of government, which combined a first-past-the-post (FPTP) plurality electoral system, a parliamentary executive and a unitary territorial organization.[5] In 1972 Sri Lanka adopted its first republican constitution with the governor general becoming a ceremonial president and head of state. However, the 1972 Constitution did not alter its government structure, and the Westminster system persisted. In 1978 Sri Lanka adopted a new constitution which formally established a semi-presidential executive with sweeping presidential powers and a government that was essentially only accountable to the president (de Silva 1979; Reilly 2001, 115).[6] The president was elected by supplementary vote (SV), a non-mandatory preferential electoral system. Parliamentary elections were scheduled for 1982 and were to be conducted according to PR as introduced by the 1978 Constitution. However, the life of Parliament elected in 1977 was extended and elections were postponed. It was thus not until 1989 that Sri Lanka saw its first PR-elected Parliament. In 1987 Sri Lanka attempted to formally, though only slightly, change its territorial organization, which fell short of granting full-scale devolution.

There are several instances of incongruence with regard to the institutional configurations of Sri Lanka. There is incongruence between the social structure and the institutional configurations. With a polarized social structure, Sri Lanka was governed for the first 30 years of independence under a highly power-concentrating Westminster institutional combination. The majoritarian electoral system saw minorities underrepresented in the legislature, thus depriving them of leverages to affect and prevent government policies that were harmful to their interests. Combined with a FPTP electoral system, the otherwise consensual and inclusive parliamentary executive became very exclusive. Between 1956 and 1978 a Sri Lankan Tamil party was only once represented in the Cabinet, occupying the post of minister of local government (1965–1968).[7] In addition, the unitary state structure inherited from the colonial period left regionally concentrated Tamils without any degree of political power at the subnational level either. As such, the Tamils had no access to any branch of government at either national or subnational level for nearly 30 years.

The electoral system contributed to the formation of a two-party system dominated by the United National Party and the Sri Lanka Freedom Party. Smaller and primarily ethnic parties of Tamil and Muslim communities had no bargaining or veto power. The electoral system enabled a high level of disproportionality in the vote-seat share, with the winning party gaining a disproportionally higher share of seats than votes (Reilly 2001, 116). As Horowitz points out, parties gained an absolute majority of parliamentary seats by winning only 35 per cent – 40 percent of the vote (Horowitz 1989, 23). Finally, the electoral system translated small swings in popular votes into large swings of seats (Horowitz 1989, 23). Thus, prior to 1978, incumbents always lost the election. This resulted in a robust two-party system and regular government turnover, on the one hand, and increased intra-Sinhalese party competition, which encouraged outbidding on ethnic issues, on the other (Reilly 2001, 116; Horowitz 1989, 23; de Silva 1997, 100).[8]

It was during the Westminster institutional configuration that the government of Sri Lanka adopted policies explicitly discriminating against minority Tamils. The Citizenship Act of 1948 deprived Indian Tamils of their citizenship and franchise, while the 1956 Sinhala-Only Act declared Sinhala as the only state language.[9] The state also initiated a higher education 'standardization' policy that restricted Tamils' admission to universities. The 1972 Constitution established Buddhism as the state religion, explicitly alienating the overwhelmingly Hindu Tamils. Sri Lankan Tamils vigorously opposed all these policies, but without any effective leverage on the executive they were not able to veto any of them. Although some of these policies were later overturned (e.g. Tamil was later made a national language[10]), such episodic concessions were always too little, too late and unable to compensate for decades of underrepresentation and exclusion. As a consequence, the Tamil community gradually became unwilling to engage in institutional and electoral politics.

The next institutional configuration (1979–1989) came about as a result of the change from a parliamentary executive to a presidential executive and the extension of Parliament's life in 1982. This configuration combined the three most exclusive political institutions: Parliament elected through FPTP, a president with full executive authority, and a unitary form of government (de Silva 1997). Within this highly power-concentrating arrangement Tamils were again deprived of any power or opportunity to engage with the state at any level, which resulted in grievances that arose under the previous institutional configuration remaining unaddressed.

The presidential executive and its incongruence with the electoral systems and the social structure warrant further elaboration. The president was elected under a SV electoral system. Unlike in the alternative vote system, the marking of preferences is optional in the SV system. The voluntary marking of preferences was the first major obstacle to producing moderating outcomes for the preferential system. Preferential electoral systems have been shown to be effective in terms of vote pooling and moderation in fragmented societies with at least four to five groups (Reilly and Reynolds 1999, 50; Reilly 2001, 186). However, such a system was destined to be highly ineffective in Sri Lanka's highly polarized, essentially bipolar society. Finally, moderation and vote pooling are very unlikely to occur in the course or aftermath of a civil war (Reilly 2001, 186). Given that ethnic violence in Sri Lanka was already widespread at the time and immediately following the adoption of an SV-elected presidency, their chances of success were very low from the beginning.

The incongruence of the executive format and the social structure is also evident if we consider the demographic size of Sri Lanka's cleavage groups. Due to the dominant demographic position of the Sinhalese, a Tamil candidate could not hope to be elected as president ahead of a Sinhalese candidate. Vote pooling could only occur in one direction: a Sinhalese candidate attempting to attract second- and third-preference votes from Tamils, but not the other way round (Reilly 2001, 124). Because the Sinhalese were demographically bigger, a Sinhalese candidate could also be elected by maximizing the Sinhala votes; for example, by engaging in ethnic outbidding, which has been an effective electoral strategy ever since the adoption of the divisive language policy in 1956.[11] The electoral system only allowed second and third preferences to be counted if no candidate had won an absolute majority (de Silva 1979, 199). This is what actually happened in the presidential elections of 1982, 1988 and 1994, when the winning candidates won absolute majorities of mostly Sinhalese votes, and second- and third-preference votes were never counted.[12] The demographic structure of society thus put considerable limits on moderation becoming a viable incentive and election strategy.

With FPTP being replaced by PR in legislature elections in 1989, another potential incongruence came to the fore. The combination of a PR electoral system for the election of the legislature and presidential executive has been cited as one of the most troublesome institutional configurations (Mainwaring 1993) due to the fact that a PR system is likely to fragment a legislature and thus make it difficult for a president to secure a stable parliamentary majority. This was the case in Sri Lanka, where the inability of successive governments to secure effective majorities in the legislature had a negative impact on attempts to find a settlement to the ongoing conflict (Reilly 2001, 124). Such executive–legislative conflicts can lead a president to invoke emergency powers and rule by decree in an attempt to assert dominance over a hostile majority in a parliament.[13] In the case of Sri Lanka, an additional aspect of incongruence was that the SV-elected president was expected to moderate positions in the hope of securing second- and third-preference votes from minorities. At the same time, there would have been no moderation incentives for either Sinhalese or Tamil political parties running for election to Parliament under the PR system. As a result, politicians and parties running in parliamentary and presidential elections were provided with contradicting incentives. This latter aspect of incongruence is, however, only theoretical and speculative, since Tamils typically boycotted elections.

Territorial autonomy was only formally introduced in 1987 with the Thirteenth Amendment to the Constitution, which came after the signing of the Indo–Sri Lanka Peace Agreement. The amendment provided for a legal framework for the establishment of a system of elected provincial councils that would function as provincial legislatures, a chief minister, and provincial governments with executive powers. These provincial authorities were to administer a number of policy areas, such as education, health, housing and social services. However, the central government retained its authority in crucial policy spheres, such as land settlement and law and order (Shastri 1992, 735; Bose 2002, 641). In addition, the framework of territorial devolution preserved the position of the province governor, who was appointed by the president and endowed with substantive executive powers and the responsibility to oversee and supervise the work of the provincial councils and chief ministers (Bose 2002, 641). The provincial councils had no independent fiscal powers, could not command an independent source of revenue and depended on the central government for allocation of financial resources (Bose 2002, 641).

Leaving aside the shortcomings of the formal devolution framework, extremely poor implementation of the provisions of the peace agreement and the Thirteenth

Amendment (Bose 2002) represented an even bigger impediment to effective devolution. The Liberation Tigers of Tamil Eelam viewed devolution as too little too late and refused to embrace the process (Shastri 1992, 735). A wide spectrum of Sinhalese political forces, including the internal opposition within the ruling United National Party, its main opposition the Sri Lanka Freedom Party and the more radical Janatha Vimukthi Peramuna opposed the peace agreement and the resulting framework for territorial devolution (Shastri 1992, 726; Oberst 1990, 192). Implementation stalled because of actors' unwillingness to implement the provisions and logistical difficulties, as the two factions who most opposed the devolution framework (the Liberation Tigers of Tamil Eelam and the Janatha Vimukthi Peramuna) launched insurgencies in the North and South, respectively (Oberst 1990, 192; Bose 2002).

It took 40 years for the Sinhalese majority to formally recognize Tamil calls for territorial autonomy. When a degree of territorial devolution was finally introduced, it fell very short of the Tamils' expectations. As such, Tamil demands and Sinhala concessions were never synchronized. As a result, each subsequent concession was consequently deemed irrelevant and rejected by the Tamils, whose demands and grievances had become further radicalized. Horowitz (2002, 25) has argued that the crucial intervening condition in the effectiveness of federalism is the timing. Whereas generous early devolution is unproblematic, late devolution will create problems, since the combination of accumulated grievances and greater capacity is likely to incite secessionist tendencies among the minority and fear among the majority.

A socially polarized society, Sri Lanka was governed by some of the most power-concentrating institutional configurations, which left the Sri Lanka Tamils without any meaningful access to political power or opportunities to influence state policies. The result of this mismatch was a gradual escalation of intergroup conflict over three decades. Over the years, incongruent socioinstitutional configurations have eliminated any incentives for moderation on both sides; that is, there are no incentives for the majority to accommodate minority grievances and no incentives for minorities to comply with the unavoidable dominance of the Sinhala majority. This impasse eventually exploded into a full-fledged civil war that lasted until the Liberation Tigers of Tamil Eelam were militarily defeated.

## Conclusion

In this chapter I have sought to account for the conjunctural effects of political institutions in divided societies. Acknowledging the immense contribution of the literature to ideal models, I highlight the inherent contradiction of theorizing the impact of ideal models of institutional design while at the same time acknowledging that ideal models are unlikely to be implemented in their pure form. I briefly identify the two main streams of empirical research on the impact of separate institutions and point out that the focus on institutions' net effects leaves considerable variation on the effect of institutions unexplained. The institutions that the literature finds to be conducive to peace are also found to have experienced episodes of violence, while institutions that are argued to be dangerous have experienced peace under certain circumstances.

Highlighting the shortcomings of the theoretical and empirical literature, I argue for a more complex approach to the study of the effects of political institutions. It is particularly necessary to understand the impact of institutions in configurations that depart from any of the ideal models of institutional design. In this context it is essential to conceptualize the interactive effects among institutions, on the one hand, and institutional configuration and social structure, on the other.

In this chapter I suggest conceptualizing the conjunctural impact of political institutions and social structure. Using congruence theory as developed by Eckstein, I argue that political institutions can be effective in divided societies by providing ethnic groups and civil war belligerents with access to political power if these institutions and social structures follow the same pattern of power distribution. For the purpose of theory development, I recommend not only differentiating between power-concentrating and power-dispersing institutions and socially fragmented and socially polarized societies, but also distinguishing between direct and indirect access to political power.

The conjunctural institutional framework developed here suggests that access to political power is present in two instances. First, when power-dispersing institutions are implemented in socially polarized societies. Second, when power-concentrating institutions are embedded in socially fragmented societies. However, access to political power is restricted in two other instances. First, when power-concentrating institutions are imbedded in socially polarized societies. Second, when power-dispersing institutions are embedded in socially fragmented societies. When applied to the case of Sri Lanka, the framework reveals that consecutive institutional configurations were incongruent with the social structure in which they were embedded and gradually led to interethnic conflict which resulted in a long and bloody civil war.

## Notes

\*   I am grateful to the reviewers and the editors of this volume for their useful comments and suggestions.
1   Where political divisions very closely follow and especially concern lines of objective social cleavages, such as ethnicity, religion, language, race, region of origin and so on (Lijphart 1977).
2   The threshold of four or more politically relevant groups for a society to be considered as socially fragmented is informed by the insights of Lijphart (1977, 56), Reilly and Reynolds (1999, 50) and Reilly (2001, 186). They argue that the minimum number of groups for intergroup moderation to work is four to five and that the prospects increase as the number of groups increases and the stakes of political competition and intergroup polarization decrease, thus making moderation and cooperation not only possible but necessary. For consociational accommodation to take place, a country should have three to four groups and the prospect for consociationalism should get progressively worse as the number of groups increases.
3   For more on such political organizations, see Bogaards (2014).
4   The Sri Lankan Tamils and Indian Tamils (sometimes also called Estate, Hill and Upcountry Tamils) are distinct communities. The former group has been living in Sri

Lanka for over 1,000 years. Indian Tamils are descendants of migrant labourers who came to Sri Lanka from India from the nineteenth century onward to work on tea plantations located in the central highlands on the island.

5   For an extensive discussion of the Westminster system in Sri Lanka, see Kumarasingham (2013, 114–201).

6   Sri Lanka formally has a semi-presidential system, since the president has the discretion to appoint cabinet members and the prime minister. However, Parliament can also dissolve the cabinet through a vote of no-confidence with a two-thirds majority. Despite the no-confidence vote, the president can reappoint the prime minister and other cabinet members. Consequently, the president has disproportionally greater control over cabinet formation than Parliament. Sri Lanka experienced intra-executive cohabitation only once between 2001 and 2004 during the period of cohabitation between the representatives of the two major parties: President Kumaratunga of the Sri Lanka Freedom Party and Prime Minister Wickremesinghe of the United National Party.

7   Sri Lanka Tamil parties were represented in the first three governments from 1948 to 1955.

8   The frequent government turnover was also one of the reasons for the emergence a gradual consensus among the Sinhalese political elite for the adoption of a proportional electoral system and a change to an executive presidency (Reilly 2001, 116; de Silva 1997, 101–102).

9   For more on the language issue, see Choudhry (2009, 598–600). For the divisive role of the 1948 Citizenship Act and the disenfranchisement of Indian Tamils, see Shastri (1999).

10   Sri Lanka still preserved Sinhala as the only 'official' language, while Sinhala, Tamil and English had a status of 'national' languages.

11   For a discussion on the structural conditions that made ethnic outbidding, rather than interethnic moderation, a profitable electoral strategy, see Horowitz (1989, 21–26), Devotta (2005) and Shastri (1999).

12   A few qualifications about specific elections are necessary. The first president, Jayewardene, was elected in 1978 by Parliament and not through direct election. In 1982 the main rival of the incumbent Jayewardene, Sirimavo Bandaranaike, was disqualified from the campaign; hence the competiveness of 1982 elections was limited. In 1994 a series of suicide bomb attacks by the Liberation Tigers of Tamil Eelam killed several top United National Party politicians; thus the party was unable to present a strong candidate at the elections. Therefore, the competitiveness of the 1994 elections was also limited. In all of these elections Tamil parties disengaged from electoral politics, refusing to put forward any candidate and effectively mobilizing their constituency to boycott elections.

13   This scenario materialized in Sri Lanka in 2004 during a period of cohabitation between a president and a prime minister from the two main rival parties. President Kumaratunga of the Sri Lanka Freedom Party accused Prime Minister Wickremesinghe of the United National Party and the government of conceding too much power to the Liberation Tigers of Tamil Eelam during the negotiation process. As a result, the President used executive powers to dissolve Parliament, assumed three key ministerial positions and called new elections. Subsequently, her party could form a coalition government with the more radical Janatha Vimukthi Peramuna (Kelegama 2015, 243).

## Bibliography

Bakke, K.M., 2009. 'State, Society and Separatism in Punjab'. *Regional and Federal Studies* 19(2): 291–308.

Bakke, K.M. and Wibbels, E., 2006. 'Diversity, Disparity, and Civil Conflict in Federal States'. *World Politics* 59(1): 1–50.

Belmont, K., Mainwaring, S. and Reynolds, A., 2002. 'Institutional Design, Conflict Management, and Democracy'. In A. Reynolds, ed., *The Architecture of Democracy : Constitutional Design, Conflict Management, and Democracy.* Oxford: Oxford University Press, pp. 1–14.

Bogaards, M., 2013. 'The Choice for Proportional Representation: Electoral System Design in Peace Agreements'. *Civil Wars* 15(supp.1): 71–87.

Bogaards, M., 2014. *Democracy and Social Peace in Divided Societies: Exploring Consociational Parties.* Basingstoke: Palgrave Macmillan.

Bose, S., 2002. 'Flawed Mediation, Chaotic Implementation: The 1987 Indo–Sri Lanka Peace Agreement'. In S.J. Stedman, D. Rothchild and E.M. Cousens, eds, *Ending Civil Wars: The Implementation of Peace Agreements.* Boulder, CO: Lynne Rienner Publishers, pp. 631–659.

Brancati, D., 2006. 'Decentralization: Fueling the Fire or Dampening the Flames of Ethnic Conflict and Secessionism?' *International Organization* 60(3): 691–685.

Brancati, D., 2009. *Peace by Design: Managing Intrastate Conflict through Decentralization.* Oxford: Oxford University Press.

Buhaug, H., Cederman, L.E. and Gleditsch, K.S., 2014. 'Square Pegs in Round Holes: Inequalities, Grievances, and Civil War'. *International Studies Quarterly* 58(2): 418–431.

Cederman, L-E., Gleditsch, K.S. and Buhaug, H., 2013. *Inequality, Grievances, and Civil War.* Cambridge: Cambridge University Press.

Cederman, L-E., Weidmann, N.B. and Gleditsch, K.S., 2011. 'Horizontal Inequalities and Ethnonationalist Civil War: A Global Comparison'. *American Political Science Review* 105(3): 478–495.

Cederman, L-E., Wimmer, A. and Min, B., 2010. 'Why Do Ethnic Groups Rebel? New Data and Analysis'. *World Politics* 62(1): 87–119.

Choudhry, S., 2009. 'Managing Linguistic Nationalism through Constitutional Design: Lessons from South Asia'. *International Journal of Constitutional Law* 7(4): 577–618.

Collier, P. and Hoeffler, A., 2004. 'Greed and Grievance in Civil War'. *Oxford Economic Papers* 56: 563–595.

de Silva, C.R., 1979. 'The Constitution of the Second Republic of Sri Lanka (1978) and its Significance'. *Commonwealth and Comparative Politics* 17(2): 192–209.

de Silva, K.M., 1997. 'Sri Lanka: Surviving Ethnic Strife'. *Journal of Democracy* 8(1): 97–111.

Devotta, N., 2005. 'From Ethnic Outbidding to Ethnic Conflict: The Institutional Bases for Sri Lanka's Separatist War'. *Nations and Nationalism* 11(1): 141–159.

Eckstein, H., 1966. *Division and Cohesion in Democracy: A Study of Norway.* Princeton, NJ: Princeton University Press.

Elgie, R., 2011. 'Exogenous Political Institutions? Constitutional Choice in Postindependence Francophone Sub-Saharan Africa'. *Political Research Quarterly*: 771–783.

Horowitz, D.L., 1985. *Ethnic Groups in Conflict.* Berkeley: University of California Press.

Horowitz, D.L., 1989. 'Incentives and Behaviour in the Ethnic Politics of Sri Lanka and Malaysia'. *Third World Quarterly* 11: 18–35.

Horowitz, D.L., 1990. 'Comparing Democratic Systems'. *Journal of Democracy* 1(4): 73–79.

Horowitz, D.L., 1993. 'Democracy in Divided Societies'. *Journal of Democracy* 4(4): 18–38.

Horowitz, D.L., 2002. 'Constitutional Design: Proposals Versus Processes'. In A. Reynolds, ed., *The Architecture of Democracy: Constitutional Design, Conflict Management, and Democracy*. Oxford: Oxford University Press, pp. 15–36.

Horowitz, D.L., 2008. 'Conciliatory Institutions and Constitutional Processes in Post-conflict States'. *William and Mary Law Review* 49(4): 1213–1248.

Horowitz, D.L., 2014. 'Ethnic Power Sharing: Three Big Problems'. *Journal of Democracy* 25(2): 5–20.

Kelegama, T., 2015. 'Impossible Devolution? The Failure of Power-sharing Attempts in Sri Lanka'. *Strategic Analysis* 39(3): 237–253.

Kumarasingham, H., 2013. *A Political Legacy of the British Empire: Power and Parliamentary System in Post-colonial India and Sri Lanka*. London: I.B. Tauris.

Lijphart, A., 1968. *The Politics of Accommodation: Pluralism and Democracy in the Netherlands*. Berkeley: University of California Press.

Lijphart, A., 1969. 'Consociational Democracy'. *World Politics* 21(2): 207–225.

Lijphart, A., 1977. *Democracy in Plural Societies*. New Haven, CT: Yale University Press.

Lijphart, A., 1991. 'Constitutional Choices for New Democracies'. *Journal of Democracy* 2(1): 72–84.

Lijphart, A., 1994. 'Democracies: Forms, Performance, and Constitutional Engineering'. *European Journal of Political Research* 25(1): 1–17.

Lijphart, A., 1999. *Patterns of Democracy: Government Forms and Democracy in Thirty Six Countries*. New Haven, CT: Yale University Press.

Lijphart, A., 2004. 'Constitutional Design for Divided Societies'. *Journal of Democracy* 15(2): 96–109.

Mainwaring, S., 1993. 'Presidentialism, Multipartism and Democracy. The Difficult Combination'. *Comparative Political Studies* 26(2): 198–228.

Mine, J., Stewart, F., Fukuda-Parr, S. and Mkandawire T., 2013. *Preventing Violent Conflict in Africa: Inequalities, Perceptions and Institutions*. Basingstoke: Palgrave Macmillan.

Neudorfer, N.S. and Theuerkauf, U.G., 2014. 'Who Controls the Wealth? Electoral System Design and Ethnic War in Resource-Rich Countries'. *Electoral Studies* 35: 171–187.

Oberst, R.C., 1990. 'Federalism and Ethnic Conflict in Sri Lanka'. *Publius* 20(3): 1–17.

Reilly, B., 2001. *Democracy in Divided Societies: Electoral Engineering and Conflict Management*. Cambridge: Cambridge University Press.

Reilly, B. and Reynolds, A., 1999. *Electoral Systems and Conflict in Divided Societies*. London: National Academies Press.

Schneider, C.Q., 2009. *The Consolidation of Democracy: Comparing Europe and Latin America*. New York and Abingdon: Routledge.

Schneider, G. and Wiesehomeier, N., 2008. 'Rules That Matter: Political Institutions and the Diversity–Conflict Nexus'. *Journal of Peace Research* 45(2): 183–203.

Shastri, A., 1992. 'Sri Lanka's Provincial Council System: A Solution to the Ethnic Problem?' *Asian Survey* 32(8): 723–743.

Shastri, A., 1999. 'Estate Tamils, The Ceylon Citizenship Act of 1948 and Sri Lankan Politics'. *Contemporary South Asia* 8(1): 65–86.

Sisk, T.D., 1996. *Power Sharing and International Mediation in Ethnic Conflicts*. United States Institute of Peace.

Theuerkauf, U.G., 2012. *Ethno-embedded Institutionalism: The Impact of Institutional Repertoires on Ethnic Violence*. London: London School of Economics and Political Science.

Wucherpfennig, J., Metternich, N.W., Cederman, L-E. and Gleditsch, K.S., 2011. 'Ethnicity, the State, and the Duration of Civil War'. *World Politics* 64(1): 79–115.

# Part II

# Path dependency of institutional designs during and after war

# 4 The challenges of institutional reforms in the midst of war

## Lessons from Colombia

*Sabine Kurtenbach*

## Introduction

The main prescription for sustainable peace in current postwar societies is either institutional reconstruction or institutional reform with a major emphasis on the state and its agencies (Sisk 2013). The underlying assumption is that institutions provide mechanisms with which to manage conflicts without resorting to violence, support the accountability of state actors through rules, and sanction the illegitimate use of violence (e.g. Walter 2014). As external actors such as the United Nations or donors are important drivers of institutional reform in current postwar societies, there is much debate about the necessity to anchor institutions in local contexts in order to enhance their legitimacy (e.g. MacGinty and Richmond 2013). While this debate focuses on postwar reforms, we know little about the determinants and the effects of reform processes in the midst of war.[1] Nevertheless, many countries introduce reforms in the midst of war, largely in the expectation that such measures will either de-escalate violence or have an impact on the outcome of their conflicts. Elections are a case in point, as many regimes seek to enhance their legitimation by holding (often flawed) elections despite there being an ongoing war. The question is whether institutional reforms can reduce violence and pave the way towards the end of war or whether they simply promote path-dependent superficial changes.

Theoretically, the argument can be made both ways. On the one hand, reforms introduced in the midst of war may be rather superficial and merely perpetuate the interests of the controlling elite. Institutions not only have a certain historical trajectory but are also part of societal conflicts.[2] On the other hand, they may open windows of opportunity for nonarmed actors, serving as confidence-building measures and helping to 're-embed' conflicts in institutions (Koehler and Zuercher 2003). In these circumstances levels of armed conflict may be reduced over time, and peace will be a rather incremental process shaped by the dynamics of ongoing violence. The analysis of reforms in the midst of war is important for theory development as well as for policy implications. It goes beyond the common 'war termination first, reforms later' sequence and allows for a more nuanced approach by including the interaction between violence and institutional reform. This approach contributes to the conceptual frame of this book by analysing the interaction between violence and institutional reforms aiming to mitigate societal divisions. Employing this perspective can provide important evidence for policies based on incremental peacebuilding, where partial reforms and the reduction of armed violence go hand in hand.

The first section of this chapter develops the conceptual framework, linking the literature on institutions as a means to manage conflict and violence with the debate on institutional reform. Following Elwert (2004) and Zuercher (2004), I assume that armed conflict may be perceived as a result of the failure of existing institutions to process societal conflicts. Institutional reforms aimed at 're-embedding' conflicts in reformed or new institutions should thus help reduce violence (or bring an end to war). However, this is a nonlinear process, and the experience of violence as well as the prevailing patterns of collective violence will influence the scope and content of institutions and their reforms (Arjona 2014).

The second section presents the main features of the Colombian case study. Colombia is an important case for this topic due to its long history of internal war and phases of political stability since independence (Mazzuca and Robinson 2009). Following an extremely violent civil war in the mid-twentieth century – the so-called *La Violencia*, which resulted in over 200,000 deaths – Colombia's elites agreed to a power-sharing arrangement in 1958. The National Front was one of the few non-European cases of consociational democracy and was relatively stable for nearly two decades (Dix 1980). However, the arrangement was unable to accommodate the demands of a growing number of social and political actors (Berquist *et al.* 1992). Although violence was limited to certain rural regions and only occasionally affected national politics up until the 1980s, a process of disembedding conflicts from institutions may be observed. The main societal divisions were related to land access in rural Colombia and political participation opportunities in urban areas.

Aware of civil wars and mediation processes in neighbouring Central America, successive Colombian governments initiated negotiations with different armed groups and a series of institutional reforms. These reforms, however, overwhelmingly addressed the political system (specifically decentralization, the constitution, the judiciary and the security sector) while only indirectly dealing with the question of access to land.

The third section analyses the scope of these reforms and their implications for Colombia's war. The reforms that addressed underlying grievances helped 're-embed' conflict into new or reformed institutions, while those that sought to increase representation and participation among the urban population helped demobilize and disarm smaller guerrilla groups and transform them into political actors. At the same time, these reforms threatened the power of the rurally based elites, who either openly resisted or tried to undermine any significant changes by adapting to the new rules of the game. This changed the dynamics of violence as many of these actors captured local institutions. Overall, the results of more than two decades of institutional reform mirror the underlying military and political power relations.

The final section summarizes this chapter's findings and draws some conclusions about the possibilities of ending war through a process of institutional reform.

## Institutions, conflict and reform

The role of formal and informal institutions in the management of societal conflicts is a recurring topic throughout various strands of the social sciences. The escalation of organized violence into armed conflict and war is a very complex phenomenon that may be perceived as the result of institutional failure independent of a specific concept of 'institutions'. Formal and informal institutions 'embed' conflicts; that is, they provide rules and procedures for their management (cf. Koehler and Zuercher 2003, 25; Elwert 2004; Zuercher 2004). The process of disembedding conflict from institutions may be the result of rapid institutional (or more general societal) change that weakens or even destroys established hierarchies and a state's capacity to sanction the use of violence. Koehler and Zuercher (2003) identify four markers that indicate a weak institutional design even before the outbreak of collective and widespread violence: (1) institutions have lost their binding power; (2) the state has lost its monopoly on force; (3) the organizers of violence have access to resources (e.g. finances, weapons and combatants), and (4) the organizers of violence have replaced the state at least partially in, for example, the provision of security at the subnational level or for specific groups.

Following this perspective, institutional reform designed to end war (or to prevent war from recurring after its formal termination) needs to re-embed conflict either by reconstructing or reforming existing institutions or by establishing new institutions. In the context of war the specific patterns of reform, reconstruction or renewal will depend on the military, political, economic and social power relations among the different actors who shape, promote or spoil these processes. Should one party to the conflict achieve a military victory, this would produce different institutional arrangements than would a peace accord.[3] However, as Koehler and Zuercher (2003, 258) observe,

> the problem of institutionalising peace is usually not regarded as a dynamic social process in its own right, separate from the departure of violence. It is either treated as a problem of society after conflict, detaching the question of peace from the dynamics that ruled conflict before, or peace is simply treated as the absence of war.

Under such conditions it is necessary to develop an analytical framework of institutional reform that links institutions to the causes and dynamics of the relevant conflicts (e.g. underlying grievances, opportunities, mobilization, actors) and the effects of violence on these conflicts. Violence can destroy existing institutions and establish new ones.[4] The nature of these institutions (at both the national and the local level) will differ depending on the relationship between armed actors and local constituencies. Arjona (2014) distinguishes between an 'aliocracy' and a 'rebelocracy' based on the scope of armed-group interventions in civilian affairs (broad versus narrow). In an 'aliocracy' nonstate armed groups generally only provide security and leave other issues to the existing authorities, whereas in a 'rebelocracy' the armed group becomes a de facto ruler, providing more than just security. Even after the formal termination of war, these institutions shape further developments and can even 'transform state-building trajectories' (Arjona 2014, 24). These considerations are directly linked to the debate on incremental institutional change, although here the focus is on a context of nonviolent change and not on one of widespread violence and war. Nevertheless, Thelen and Mahoney (2010, 4) argue 'that institutional change often occurs precisely when problems of rule interpretation and enforcement open up space for actors to implement existing rules in new ways'. Collective violence and war are clearly indicators of 'problems of rule' and may thus be regarded as drivers of change. However, the specific outcomes of these reforms and their impact on violence are not predetermined given that they depend on military and political power relations as well as on the conflicts at stake.[5]

The different modes of institutional change offered by Thelen and Mahoney (2010, 14–18) are suitable for showing how conflict can be re-embedded into socially accepted and nonviolent institutions. Their central indicator for distinguishing between displacement, layering, drift and conversion is based on the relationships among existing institutions and the changes made during the reform process to re-establish nonviolent conflict management. In the context of war the outcome of reforms may be characterized by one of the following four processes.

### Displacement

'Displacement' refers to the replacement of existing rules either through an abrupt change or through a gradual change in the context of competing new and old institutions. Actors that are 'losers' under the existing system often introduce displacement. In the context of war displacement is a common outcome after a rebel military victory given that the winning side has ample possibilities to define and enforce rules, and their opponents will likely have very limited veto power in cases of abrupt displacement. Territorial control provides a basis in which abrupt displacement typically occurs, as groups (usually rebel groups) that have gained control over an area look to establish new institutions. Gradual displacement is more often the result of peace agreements or of wartime reforms that seek to re-embed conflict. Of course, in the latter context opponents (armed actors in particular) have far greater veto opportunities.

### Layering

'Layering' refers to the attachment of new rules to an existing body of rules. Here the capacities to change the whole institution are limited and only gradual reform is possible. However, such reform can lead to significant change in the long term. Government initiatives to re-embed conflict in the midst of war may be interpreted as processes of layering, as they add new rules to existing ones – a case in point being elections that offer new, or formerly excluded, actors the possibility to participate in the political system changing the relevance of elections and making a nonviolent change in government possible. At the same time, armed actors have significant electoral veto power (e.g. boycott or obstruction) in the midst of war.

### Drifting

'Drifting' means that institutions remain formally in place but their impact changes due to a lack of response to external factors such as social change. In the context of armed conflict, drifting can be a result of the disembedding process. Institutions that are no longer able to process conflicts may become delegitimized if they remain in place. Again, elections provide a good example of drifting. For instance, if armed actors and their political allies are prevented from participating, elections will be a rather meaningless mechanism.

### Conversion

'Conversion' refers to the process whereby rules continue to exist, but their interpretations change. Institutional innovators may try to adapt existing institutions to new problems (or conflicts) or to exploit these institutions' ambiguities. In the context of war, conversion resembles reform processes where displacement is not viable due either to the power of antireform actors or to the necessity of adapting institutional reforms to specific local and cultural contexts. The necessity to include warlords' in state-building processes due to de facto power relations on the ground is an example of conversion; political parties based on clientelistic relations instead of programmes is another.

Thelen and Mahoney (2010, 10–14) also emphasize that compliance with new institutions is essential for the 'positive outcome' of reform processes and that it is necessary to go beyond the dichotomy of 'winners' and 'losers' of institutional reform. Nonetheless, the possibility for reform and the reform process in the midst of war will be different, as armed actors can seriously impede reforms. At the same time, reform can open up space for nonviolent actions and change the relationship between violent and nonviolent actors. The following section will analyse how societal conflicts were disembedded and violence escalated into war in Colombia.

## From power sharing as the solution to power sharing as the problem

Colombia has had a long history of civil war since its independence from Spain in the early nineteenth century. The country has high levels of regional diversity regarding population distribution, geography and natural resources. The main societal divisions in Colombia are related to social disparities and those between rural regions and urban regions. Rural Colombia is shaped by different natural resources and the respective export cycles (e.g. gold during colonial times, tobacco in the nineteenth century and coffee in the twentieth century). Social relations are overwhelmingly based on clientelistic relationships between large landowners, traders and small-scale peasants. For most of the nineteenth and the first decades of the twentieth century landless peasants were able to migrate and further push the agricultural frontier. While Colombian labour started to organize in the aftermath of the Great Depression, peasant movements remained fragmented. At the same time, local conflicts over land access increased as public land was privatized. Labour organizations in commercial agriculture began to organize and demand increased wages and improved living conditions. The state responded to these demands primarily with repression and some rather formal reforms. The Land Law of 1936, for example, generally strengthened the property rights of large landowners (cf. Berquist 1986; Zamosc 1986).

In the nineteenth century regional elites organized politically under the banner of the Liberal and Conservative Parties, whose only point of difference was on the relationship between the Catholic Church and the state. While the Liberals favoured a secular state, the Conservatives preferred close cooperation with the Catholic Church. Most of Colombia's civil wars during the nineteenth and early twentieth century were between different elite factions, even though the boundaries between the political parties were fluid and regional elites changed their affiliation according to their interest. Colombian elites have a long history of intra-elite accommodation via institutional reform and power-sharing arrangements, so-called gentlemen's agreements (Mazzuca and Robinson 2009). At the same time, regional elites never ceded their economic or coercive power to the central state. As a consequence, the Colombian state never secured a monopoly on the means of violence or taxes. Urban growth in the 1930s and 1940s changed the political landscape (Berquist *et al.* 1992; Safford and Palacios 2002; González 2014).

During *La Violencia* (1948–1957), rural and urban conflicts escalated into war and resulted in over 200,000 deaths. The first phase resembled an intra-elite war, but the patterns of conflict began to change during the second phase (1953–1957), when factions of the Liberal Party and communist guerrillas started to demand more radical land reform. A brief military government headed by Gustavo Rojas Pinilla ended the war and laid the foundations for a power-sharing regime between the Conservatives and Liberals. The agreement ensured that the presidency was rotated and that all other positions in the administration and the political system were equally distributed between the two parties. Elections were only employed to determine the share of influence of different political tendencies within the two parties (Oquist 1978; Dix 1980; Hartlyn 1988). In the decades that followed, the existing institutions lost their capacities to mitigate conflict as they were unable to adapt to social change. Colombia has experienced a civil war with changing levels of violence and a multitude of armed actors since the 1960s. The following section shows that all four of Koehler and Zuercher's (2003) markers of disembedding conflict are present: the loss of binding power of state institutions, the absence of a state monopoly on violence, armed actors with access to resources, and the substitution of the state.

### First marker: state institutions lose their binding power

Rural conflicts remained a major issue with peasants being displaced by larger landowners promoting industrialized agriculture, though there is a high level of regional variation. During the 1960s various reform initiatives were announced but rarely implemented, thus raising expectations and radicalizing protests. According to Grindle (1986, 152–153),

> The peasant mobilization that had provided an impulse to redistribution in the late 1960s and early 1970s was increasingly subjected to repression and co-optation [.] rural areas were heavily militarized and peasant organizational activities were more firmly repressed. [.] The expansion of large-scale capitalist agriculture was championed as a rational means to achieve national development.

Due to the growing pressure on small-scale farmers and the landless, armed groups began to spread.

In the political system the limits of the conflict-management capacities of the National Front – the power-sharing arrangement established after *La Violencia* in 1958 – became visible.[6] Although formal democratic mechanisms of political participation were in place, the electoral system became increasingly dysfunctional. The fixed quotas of the National Front were inflexible and did not allow political actors beyond the two traditional parties to stand for election. Even after the National Front formally ended, the electoral system was unable to adapt to demographic and social changes. The electoral system favoured rural constituencies and personalistic voting, leading to 'pork and patronage' (Nielson and Shugart 1999, 317) voting rather than voting for programmatic agendas concerning national policy. Political programmes were more important in the presidential vote that was cast in a single national district. This produced a disconnect between the executive and the legislative as well as a lack of acknowledgement of the increasing percentage of urban voters (Nielson and Shugart 1999). The blockade between the main political institutions, the uneven patterns of political representation and the lack of reforms were a major driver of the growing discontent among the expanding urban middle classes across the country.

### Second marker: the absence of a state monopoly on force

The Colombian state never had a monopoly on force, as regional elites always had their official or nonofficial armed groups or militias. During the second half of the twentieth century, however, new actors entered into the conflict and various groups took up arms.[7]

- *Reorganized peasant self-defence forces.* Established as a means to fight the displacement of subsistence peasants during *La Violencia*, they allied with the Communist Party in order to demand a more equal distribution of land. In

1964 these groups came together to establish the Revolutionary Armed Forces of Colombia: the People's Army (FARC – EP or FARC).

- *Student organizations*. Consisting of members of the urban intelligentsia who were influenced by the Cuban Revolution, the Chinese Civil War and other global developments, these groups advocated greater political and social participation for marginalized rural groups. The National Liberation Army (ELN) and the Popular Liberation Army (EPL) emerged in this context.
- *The 19 April Movement (M-19)*. This guerrilla group emerged out of the urban conflict that followed the fraudulent elections of 1974, when former (military) president Rojas Pinilla tried to be elected under a bipartisan popular flag. M-19 carried out a series of highly symbolic, though not necessarily violent, actions (such as stealing Simon Bolívar's sword), which brought the topic of armed conflict back into the spotlight of the national and international media.
- *Quintin Lamé Armed Movement (MAQL)*. Named after Quintin Lamé, an indigenous leader who tried in vain to establish an indigenous republic, this indigenous guerrilla group took up arms in 1984 in order to protect indigenous reservations from large landowners. They operated in the department of Cauca, where the population is 40 per cent indigenous.

Nevertheless, the armed conflict did not destabilize Colombia until the 1980s, when access to resources (related primarily to the drug economy) changed the dynamics of the violence.

### Third marker: armed actors' access to resources

From the 1970s onward Colombia's economy experienced profound changes. Employment opportunities in the declining peasant-dominated coffee sector were replaced by those in the growing coca industry providing employment opportunities and income especially for young people (production of cocaine first, growing coca leafs later). At the same time, the formal termination of the National Front as well as the introduction of austerity policies brought an end to employment possibilities within the state administration, which was once a central pillar of the clientele system. The illicit economy served as a substitute, since the coca bonanza profited all actors in Colombia. Regional elites used it to uphold and renew their clientelistic relationships and to finance private paramilitary groups. Armed actors, especially the FARC, taxed the production and trade of coca leaves and cocaine to finance their war activities. In addition, the central government received an increasing flow of military aid from the United States to combat drug trafficking (cf. Richani 2002; Thoumi 2003; Romero 2003).

Thus the growth of the drug trade and drug production formed the basis of 'war systems' (Richani 2002). As the drug industry became a central pillar of the economy, other types of criminal enterprise also flourished (such as kidnapping, extortion and illegal mining), which enabled criminals to secure political influence and control. At the same time, there was a proliferation in the number of armed actors. Colombia's armed forces personnel increased from 60,000 in 1980 to 144,000 in 1999 and 285,000 in 2010. The number of FARC combatants escalated from around 8,000 in 1980 to 20,000 in 2002 (though it had dropped back down to 8,000 in 2010). The manpower of private militias grew from around 100 in 1986 to over 8,000 in 2000.[8]

### *Fourth marker: substitution of the state*

Although the FARC only controlled remote rural areas until the 1980s, access to economic resources increased their influence and allowed the FARC in some regions to replace the state at the subnational level. In fact, the Colombian state is not, and has rarely been, present in the country's rural areas, which has seen armed groups fulfil state functions such as taxation, protection and rule enforcement. Patterns of territorial control were shaped by the presence and dynamics of the confrontation between the Colombian state, paramilitaries and other guerrilla groups (cf. Richani 2002; González *et al.* 2003; Berquist *et al.* 2001; Romero 2003). Levels of violence increased where competing actors fought over access to resources and territorial control; though once a nonstate armed group established territorial control, the levels of violence decreased. Developments in the regions of the Atlantic coast provide empirical evidence of changing levels of violence. After paramilitary groups secured control via the displacement of local populations and rival armed groups, the levels of indiscriminate violence diminished but selective political violence was common (targeting independent journalists, human rights defenders and so on) (García and Aramburu 2011).

The following section examines whether and how Colombia's reforms helped re-embed the main Colombian conflicts (i.e. access to land and political participation) in institutions. The focus will be on formal state institutions, namely the territorial structure, the government system, the electoral system, the security sector and the justice system. The reforms will be classified according to Thelen and Mahoney's differentiation (introduced above). Subsequently, the influence of these reforms on the ongoing civil war will be investigated.

## Partial reforms and the quest for peace

Starting in the early 1980s, various Colombian governments tried to end the war by reforming state institutions to mitigate and/or re-embed conflicts by increasing the state's capacities and legitimacy. These reforms had a clear focus on the political conflicts but did not directly address conflicts regarding access to land. The major reforms were as follows:

- decentralization of the political system and the devolution of economic resources to local administrations (territorial structure and government);
- a new constitution (which revamped the electoral and the justice system);
- reorganization of the security sector, namely the armed forces and the police.

### *Territorial reform: bringing the state to the regions*

When civil war spread across neighbouring Central America and threatened to escalate into a regional war, Colombian president Belisario Betancur (1982–1986) participated in a regional mediation effort (Contadora Group). Domestically, the Colombian state initiated a peace process with a comprehensive agenda that included a series of institutional reforms (cf. Ramírez and Restrepo 1989; Chernick 2001; Kurtenbach 2006). Even though the peace process failed, its central political reform project was implemented, which led to the decentralization of the Colombian government and the democratization of local politics. As a result, Colombian municipalities received more financial resources and administrative competencies after 1983. Moreover, after a 1986 amendment to the constitution, mayors were elected by popular vote from 1988 onwards.[9] Betancur also designed the National Rehabilitation Plan for the country's rural areas to alleviate the 'objective causes of violence'; that is, the lack of access to land and to sustainable rural livelihoods.

These reforms may be classified as a process of 'layering' as new rules were attached to existing institutional frameworks (municipalities), providing them with more rights and competencies. The various reforms interacted with the armed conflict in different ways. The decentralization process relocated financial resources and administrative capacities from the central state to the municipalities. This increased the importance for all political actors to control local processes, independent of their specific political and economic goals.

Following the signature of a peace accord between the government and several guerrilla groups in 1984, demobilized FARC members founded the Patriotic Union (UP), a left-wing political party whose presidential candidate went on to secure around 5 per cent of the vote in 1986. In the first municipal elections in 1988 16 UP candidates were successfully elected as mayors and 256 as councillors. Fearing a loss of power, economic, military and political elites began to resist and to sabotage the reforms and their implementation. Within this context UP representatives, members and candidates became the preferred targets of political violence by both the armed forces and the myriad private armies under the control of regional elites. Over 3,000 members and representatives of the UP were murdered, the most prominent politician being its presidential candidate Bernardo Jaramillo, who was shot in 1990 at Bogotá airport.[10]

While the reforms managed to bring the state to the municipalities, they rather failed to re-embed conflict. During the 1990s the war became decentralized and took on different dynamics in Colombia's regions.[11] This development affected the national political system, as many paramilitary 'warlords' were elected as congressmen in regions under their control (Duncan 2005). Unsurprisingly, they had a major interest in maintaining the status quo and not in institutional reform or in strengthening the central state.

### The new constitution: changing the rules of the game

Even though Betancur's peace process failed, it paved the way for new initiatives to end the war. Subsequent negotiations had a narrow focus on the demobilization of armed groups and not on substantial institutional reforms. They rather resembled traditional 'gentlemen's agreements' that granted amnesty and thus allowed militarily weak or defeated armed actors to transform into political parties. During the administrations of Virgilio Barco (1986–1990) and César Gaviria (1990–1994), the M-19 and some smaller groups demobilized. Despite its limited approach, the peace process helped different civil society actors mobilize in favour of political reforms. Before the 1990 general election a student organization advocated for a 'seventh ballot' (in addition to those for president, Congress, mayors, municipal councils and departmental assemblies) for a constitutional assembly. The initiative received more than 2.5 million supporting votes (out of 14 million registered voters and a turnout of 7 million).[12]

Changing the constitution had been on the political agenda of most presidents between 1974 and 1990, but Congress – which has the sole right to amend or change the Colombian Constitution by absolute majority only – refused to support any of these initiatives. To overcome this impasse, President Barco and his successor Cesar Gaviria issued presidential decrees under state of siege provisions. In May 1990 an 'official' vote on a constitutional assembly was held alongside the presidential election. At the same time, the members of the assembly were elected in a single nationwide district (Nielson and Shugart 1999). This change to the electoral rules and the extremely high abstention rate in assembly elections (67 per cent) weakened the influence of the traditional rural elites within the assembly. As a result, representatives on different lists of the Liberal Party and the former M-19 guerrillas dominated the assembly. The traditional regional elites neither mobilized their clientele to vote nor adapted their traditional networks to the new electoral system. In 1991 Colombia passed one of Latin America's most progressive constitutions, which included important provisions on a series of institutional reforms:

- *Territory*: democratization of the departmental level through general elections for each departmental assembly and governor, acknowledgement of 'indigenous territories' and specific rights for the indigenous population.
- *Justice*: strengthening political and civil rights through a series of legal reforms such as the right to constitutional complaint (*tutela legal*) and the creation of new institutions (Constitutional Court and the Ombudsman's Office).
- *Electoral system*: guarantee of freedom to create and affiliate with political parties, recognition of legal status and financing of electoral campaigns for those with more than 50,000 votes (since 2004 for those achieving at least 3 per cent of the votes), and the introduction of a single nationwide district for the Senate.

Because some provisions of the 1886 Constitution remained while new provisions were added, and others were deleted or changed, the constitutional reform of 1991 resembles a 'layering' process. For instance, the rules for the Senate elections were changed, but those for the House of Representatives remained the same. A similar partial reform occurred regarding state of siege provisions. Up until 1991 Colombia was almost permanently ruled by decree, which significantly limited recourse to and the enactment of civil rights. However, the new constitution restricted the use of state of siege declarations and also established new institutions such as the Constitutional Court. These reforms had two important effects on political participation and representation.

First, the constitution opened and secured space for civil society participation by strengthening the rule of law and civil rights. Key to this was the introduction of constitutional complaint *(tutela legal)*, a mechanism that guarantees fundamental rights by allowing individuals to appeal to the Constitutional Court. It also provided the basis for a variety of legal mechanisms for indigenous communities such as information on resource extraction and at least a small share of the revenues.[13] These rights-based reforms empowered nonviolent actors and opened significant spaces at the local and national levels for a debate on alternatives to violence, such as local peace communities or national peace NGOs. Hence, the new constitution played an important role in strengthening nonarmed political participation and re-embedding the conflicts into nonviolent institutional frameworks. At the same time, as no broad political consensus on these reforms existed, the reforms provoked conflicts. Various governments tried to use old rules, while civil society actors (i.e. reform-oriented change agents) contested this legally. The judiciary became a central player in the reforms. However, as Uprimny (2003, 62) observes, 'The court's active intervention in developing the progressive components of this constitution would not have been necessary if the political forces themselves had taken on this task'.

Second, the reforms introduced important changes to the electoral system by reducing the number of seats in the House of Representatives as well as by increasing the number of senators now elected in a single nationwide district. These measures were designed to reduce the influence of clientelistic and personalistic politics and to increase the importance of nationwide policy issues. Nevertheless, a process of party fragmentation occurred during the following elections with the two traditional parties (the Liberal and Conservative Parties) organizing myriad lists around regional elites (or *caziques*), modernizing or adapting the prevalent political clientelism thanks to the fiscal decentralization (González 2014; Gutiérrez Sanín 2007). This thus increased the crisis of political representation (Shugart *et al.* 2007) and saw these two parties lose their joint monopoly.

Regarding the war, a nonintended result of these reforms during the 1990s was that representatives of civil society organizations advocating nonarmed institutional change became the targets of various state and nonstate violent actors. Journalists, judges, human rights advocates and representatives of social movements were attacked due to their efforts to increase transparency and fight against impunity. The growing diffusion of drug money into the different spheres of Colombian society during the 1990s was another factor that undermined the impact of these reforms on peace.[14] As a consequence, the patterns of conflict became more diffuse or, in the words of French sociologist Daniel Pecaut (2001), a 'war against society'. Therefore, the short-term effects of the constitutional reforms on the war in Colombia were rather ambivalent.

### Strengthening the state and its armed forces

The election of Álvaro Uribe Velez in 2002 was the result of increasing violence and the perception of state collapse. Uribe, a former member of the Liberal Party, ran as an independent candidate. Following his electoral triumph, he sought to strengthen the state's coercive capacity. Colombia's armed forces had never had a monopoly on force, but as the dynamics of violence changed and the war spread to most parts of the country, increasing the state's military strength became a priority. Violence increased during the 1990s, most of all following the failure of the Pastrana administration's efforts in the peace process (1998–2002). The United States financed the modernization and professionalization of Colombia's armed forces through its drug-combating initiative, Plan Colombia. Uribe made the military increase a top priority and simultaneously tried to limit civil society advocacy and support for rights-based approaches and negotiated pathways to war termination. Profiting from international concern with the threat of 'terrorism' after 9/11, Uribe framed nonstate violence as 'terrorism' and targeted a military victory for the Colombian state (González *et al.* 2003; Arnson 2007; Grabendorff 2009).

The armed forces grew from 145,000 troops in 2000 to 275,000 in 2010 (IISS). The military expanded its presence in urban areas, in the major economic centres, around the transport infrastructure and in the conflict zones. Supported by US counterinsurgency intelligence, the Colombian military managed to limit the scope of action of the remaining guerrilla groups (the FARC and the ELN) with a series of military attacks in which senior members were killed and camps destroyed. Uribe also initiated a highly controversial demobilization programme for paramilitaries, who were offered preferential treatment in the courts if they cooperated. The programme led to the demobilization of around 32,000 paramilitary combatants (Gutiérrez and González 2012, 116).

The reform of the Colombian security sector may best be framed as a 'conversion' given that the measures implemented sought to strengthen the territorial presence and control of the Colombian state while the overall framework and internal rules remained in place. In addition to establishing a monopoly on force, Uribe also tried to reduce the influence of the new judicial institutions in order to stay in power. Furthermore, security sector reform led to an increase in the state's coercive capacity but only a partial gain in legitimacy. Alliances between old and new paramilitary groups and regional elites still exist, although Colombian courts send more than 60 congressmen to jail during the so-called para-political scandal on corruption and electoral finances (Gutiérrez and González 2012). The lack of democratic accountability and respect for human rights of the state's security institutions (military and police) seriously limits the scope of the reforms.[15]

Summarizing the different experiences with reforms in the midst of war, we may observe that the most used mechanism was layering; that is, attaching new rules to existing institutions. While there was some displacement, this was only related to partial reforms (e.g. the electoral system for the Senate), as more comprehensive reforms were obstructed by the traditional regional elites, who would have lost their power basis at the national level. The security sector reform represented a process of conversion, where new meanings were attached to existing institutions. The Colombian state was thus able to increase its coercive power but not its accountability. The following section will discuss the effects of these reforms on the war.

All reform initiatives were directed towards the 'political' side of the conflict, while the conflict over land access was not only not addressed but increased. The political reforms opened up some spaces for civil society participation and organization, though mostly in urban areas. In the rural areas violence increased to previously unseen levels. The control of municipalities became important for all actors. The nonstate armed groups (both the guerrillas and paramilitaries) were able to increase their presence through funds obtained via different illegal activities (production, trade and taxation of drugs; extortion; kidnapping; illegal mining, etc.). The strategy of territorial control resulted in the forced displacement of over six million people – the second highest number worldwide (Internal Displacement Monitoring Centre 2015). The impacts of reforms in the midst of war are ambivalent at best as they were characterized and limited by 'layering' or 'conversion'. Due to military power relations and a lack of political consensus or support, fundamental reforms were not viable.

## Institutional reforms: building blocks for peace? Perspectives for Colombia and beyond

Similar to many other war-torn societies, the reforms Colombia introduced in the midst of war tried to influence the armed conflict by either mitigating its main sources or by enhancing the state's military capacity. In the Colombian case these reforms did not follow a 'master plan' of strengthening state capacities and legitimacy but were rather the result of specific power constellations and windows of opportunity. The Betancur administration complemented its external peace policies towards Central America with an internal strategy of negotiation and decentralization. The 1991 Constitution was possible thanks to the overrepresentation of reform-oriented actors in the assembly (M-19 as well as parts of the Liberal and the Conservative Parties). The international debate on terrorism and the growing awareness of the guerrillas' military threat enabled the Uribe government to increase the state's coercive power.

Given their relevance within the broader debate on institutions for sustainable peace and peacebuilding, many of Colombia's reforms constitute part of the international 'toolkit' for war-torn societies. Colombian experiences provide empirical evidence on the interplay between political and military power relations and the viability and depth of the reforms.

Decentralization in the midst of war was relatively counterproductive in the Colombian case, as it further weakened the central state and decentralized violence by making the control of municipalities much more attractive to nonstate armed actors. Furthermore, it strengthened the role of regional elites in a state that already had weak central capacities. Antireform (and in many cases violent) elites were able to increase their role not only in the regions but also within national political institutions, such as Congress.[16]

The new constitution, particularly its protection of fundamental civil and political rights, helped increase the possibility of nonviolent political participation. However, it is far easier to make good use of these reforms in Colombia's urban centres than in its rural areas. Selective repression by all armed actors will remain a major hindrance until the Colombian judiciary is able to cope with the high levels of impunity.

The political reforms of municipality democratization and enhanced representation helped increase voter participation in the beginning, but participation levels declined to a historical low shortly thereafter (see Figure 4.1).

However, the role of rights and the rule of law remain highly contested issues. Advocates of civil conflict management have become the targets of political violence, and there have been various efforts to dismantle important reforms. Thus, a sustainable termination of the war depends on the continuity and deepening of these constitutional reforms as well as on the effective protection of reform-oriented actors.

Colombia's reform of the security sector increased the coercive capacities of the armed forces but not their democratic control and subordination. However, despite the state's strengthened military position vis-à-vis nonstate paramilitaries and guerrillas, it was militarily unable to bring an end to the armed conflict. The strengthening of the armed forces may be perceived as the Colombian state's first

*Figure 4.1* Participation in national elections.
Source: IDEA Global Database on Elections and Democracy.

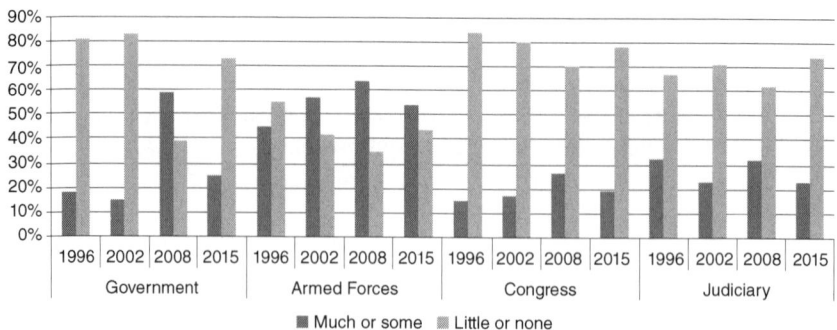

*Figure 4.2* Trust in political institutions (1996–2014).
Source: Latinobarómetro online.

attempt to develop a monopoly on force – something it has never possessed. The growing coercive capacity of the state during the presidency of Alvaro Uribe (2002–2010) appeared to increase trust in the government and the armed forces; though trust in Congress and the judiciary continues to be extremely low (see Figure 4.2).

Overall, Colombia's experience provides some evidence that reforms may pave the way for re-embedding conflicts, which is in line with other research on reducing violence through reforms.[17] However, there are three factors that should be taken into account by policy makers advocating reforms in the midst of war: (1) military and political power relations shape the design and implementation of institutional reforms; (2) widespread, organized collective violence can invalidate reforms as mechanisms of conflict mitigation, and (3) the experience of widespread violence can impact upon reforms that have even been initiated after the formal termination of war. Ultimately, the direct and indirect threat of renewed violence can shape postwar societies for decades.

## Notes

1   Analysis of war termination has not systematically included institutional reforms but has rather concentrated on the content of peace agreements (primarily power sharing; see e.g. Hartzell and Hoddie 2003), the role of external and internal mediation, or on the properties and consequences of war, such as war weariness or hurting stalemates (Zartman 1995).
2   See Skocpol and Pierson (2002) for an overview of historical institutionalism.
3   In the current debate on peacebuilding this relationship is largely reduced to the interaction between external and local actors. Only Newman (2013) has introduced a more historical perspective to the debate.
4   Widespread violence can also shape the handling of conflicts even if they have nothing to do with the 'master cleavage' (Kalyvas 2006).
5   North *et al.* (2009, 258) claim that 'the structure of all social institutions is deeply conditioned by the methods to address the problem of violence'. However, their main focus follows rather traditional modernization theory claiming differences in the role of violence in 'natural states' and 'open access orders', but they do not discuss the role of violence in the transition.

6   The Colombian establishment claims to have one of the most long-standing democratic systems in Latin America given its history of holding regular elections. However, restrictions in participation and the lack of rule of law make Colombia a highly defective electoral democracy.

7   For Colombia's violent history, see Berquist *et al.* (2001), González et al. (2003) and Kurtenbach (1991, 1999).

8   Data on the Colombian Armed Forces and estimations on the FARC come from different years of the IISS Military Balance. Data on paramilitary self-defence come from Romero (2003, 24).

9   Up until then, representatives of the state at the subnational level (governors, mayors) were not elected but rather named by the central state administration.

10  The peace process with the other armed groups had already broken down by November 1985 when members of the M-19 occupied the National Justice Palace and took the country's most senior judges as hostages. The military stormed the building without presidential consent, leaving a death-toll of over 100, including 12 magistrates and five senior guerilla commanders.

11  See the ODECOFI publications (Controversia 2009; Restrepo and Aponte 2009, Vasquéz *et al.* 2011; García and Aramburu 2011), which have an explicit focus on regional variation.

12  See IDEA data on voter turnout in Colombia.

13  In 1993 Law 70 extended some of these rights to Afro-Colombian communities and nonethnic municipalities (Gray 2008).

14  A major scandal illustrating the depth of involvement was the so-called *proceso 8000* during the Samper administration (1994–1998). Over 100 politicians had been receiving money from the drug cartels. The most prominent politician was the defence secretary, Fernando Botero Zea (son of the famous painter and sculptor). Despite various negotiations attempts (in Tlaxcala, Venezuela and Himmelspforten, Germany), these ultimately failed and violence increased. The Colombian state and its armed forces were unable to contain the violence, which resulted in the domestic and international perception of 'state collapse' (González 2003)

15  A major case is the 'false positives' scandal, in which the armed forces abducted young men in remote areas, shot them, put them in guerrilla uniforms and then claimed a military victory. A recent report by Human Rights Watch (2015) links senior military commanders to these crimes.

16  Former president Álvaro Uribe organized these elites at the national level. The relation to violent actors became evident in the parapolitics scandal; see Arcanos (2007) and López (2010).

17  Also with a focus on Colombia, Albertus and Kaplan (2012) find that land reform can be effective in undercutting support for non-state armed actors but that large scale land-owners impeded profound reform. Another important aspect – timing – is highlighted by Cederman *et al.* (2015) regarding territorial reforms. They argue that reforms following the outbreak of organized violence are mostly 'too little, too late'.

# References

Albertus, Michael and Oliver Kaplan. 2012. 'Land Reform as a Counterinsurgency Policy: Evidence from Colombia'. *Journal of Conflict Resolution* 57(2): 198–231.

Arcanos. 2007. *Paramilitares y Política*. Bogotá: Corporación Nuevo Arco Iris, No. 13.

Arcanos. 2012. *Las Bacrim retan a Santos*. Bogotá: Corporación Nuevo Arcoiris, No. 17.

Arjona, Ana. 2014. 'Wartime Institutions: A Research Agenda'. *Journal of Conflict Resolution* 58(6): 1360–1389.

Arnson, Cynthia J. 2007. 'The Peace Process in Colombia and U.S. Policy'. In Christopher Wellna and Gustavo Gallón (eds), *Peace, Democracy, and Human Rights in Colombia*. Notre Dame: University of Notre Dame Press, 132–164.

Berquist, Charles. 1996. *Coffee and Conflict in Colombia, 1886–1910*. Durham, NC: Duke University Press.

Berquist, Charles, Ricardo Peñaranda and Gonzalo Sánchez (eds). 1992. *Violence in Colombia. The Contemporary Crisis in Historical Perspective*. Wilmington, Delaware: Scholarly Resources Inc.

Berquist, Charles, Ricardo Peñaranda and Gonzalo Sánchez (eds). 2001. *Violence in Colombia 1990–2000. Waging War and Negotiating Peace*. Wilmington, Delaware: Scholarly Resources Inc.

Cederman, Lars-Erik, Simon Hug, Andreas Schädel and Julian Wucherpfennig. 2015. 'Territorial Autonomy in the Shadow of Conflict: Too Little, Too Late?' *American Political Science Review* 109(2): 354–370.

Chernick, Mark. 2001. 'The Dynamics of Colombia's Three Dimensional War. *Conflict, Security and Development* 1: 93–100.

Controversia. 2009. *Nación y Region. ¿Entre la Guerra y la Paz?* Bogotá: CINEP No. 192.

Dix, Robert H. 1980. 'Consociational Democracy: The Case of Colombia'. *Comparative Politics* 12(3): 303–321.

Duncan, Gustavo. 2005. 'Del Campo a la Ciudad en Colombia. La Infiltración Urbana de los Señores de la Guerra'. Documento CEDE No. 2 enero, available at: http://economia.uniandes.edu.co/~economia/archivos/temporal/d2005-02.pdf.

Elwert, Georg. 2004. 'Anthropologische Perspektiven auf Konflikte'. In Julia Eckert (ed.), *Anthropologie der Konflikte. Georg Elwert konflikttheoretische Thesen in der Diskussion*. Bielfeld: transcript, 26–38.

García, Clara Inés and Clara Inés Aramburu (eds). 2011. *Geografías de la guerra y la resistencia: Oriente y Urabá antioqueños 1990–2008*. Bogotá: CINEP-ODECOFI.

González, Fernán E. 2003. '¿Colapso parcial o presencia diferenciada del estado en Colombia? Una mirada desde la historia'. *Colombia Internacional* 58: 124–157.

González, Fernán E. 2014. *Poder y Violencia en Colombia*. Bogotá: ODECOFI-CINEP.

González, Fernán E., Ingrid J. Bolívar and Teófilo Vázquez. 2003. *Violencia política en Colombia. De la nación fragmentada a la construcción del Estado*. Bogotá: Centro de Investigación y Educación Popular CINEP.

Grabendorff, Wolff. 2009. 'Security Sector Reform in Challenging Environments'.. In Hans Born and Abrecht Schnabel (eds), *Security Sector Reform in Challenging Environments*. Geneva: Geneva Centre for the Democratic Control of Armed Forces, pp. 69–86.

Gray, Vanessa Joan. 2008. 'The New Research on Civil Wars: Does it Help us Understand the Colombian Conflict?' *Latin American Politics and Society* 50(3): 63–91.

Grindle, Merilee S. 1986. *State and Countryside. Development Policy and Agrarian Politics in Latin America*. Baltimore, MD, and London: The Johns Hopkins University Press.

Gutiérrez Sanín, Francisco. 2007. ¿Lo que el viento se llevó? Los partidos políticos y la democracia en Colombia (1958–2002). Bogotá: Ed. Norma.

Gutiérrez Sanín, Francisco and Andrea González Peña. 2012. 'Colombia's Paramilitary DDR and its Limits.' In Antonio Giustozzi (ed.), *Post-conflict Disarmament, Demobilization and Reintegration. Bringing State-building Back in.*.Farnham: Ashgate, pp. 113–132.

Hartlyn, Jonathan. 1988. *The Politics of Coalition Rule in Colombia*. Cambridge: Cambridge University Press.

Hartzell, Caroline and Mathew Hoddie. 2003. 'Institutionalizing Peace: Power Sharing and Post-Civil War Conflict Management'. *American Journal of Political Science* 47(2): 318–332.

Human Rights Watch and Max Schoening. 2015. *On Their Watch: Evidence of Senior Army Officers' Responsibility for False Positive Killings in Colombia*. New York: HRW.

IDEA (Institute for Democracy and Electoral Assistance). www.idea.int/resources/databases.cfm.

Internal Displacement Monitoring Centre. 2015. *Global Overview 2015. People Internally Displaced by Conflict and Violence*. Geneva: Norwegian Refugee Council.

IISS (International Institute of Strategic Studies): Military Balance. (various years). London.

Kalyvas, Stathis N. 2006. *The Logics of Violence in Civil War*. Cambridge: Cambridge University Press.

Koehler, Jan and Christoph Zuercher. 2003. 'Institutions and the Organization of Stability and Violence'. In Christoph Zuercher and Jan Koehler (eds), *Potentials of Disorder. Explaining Conflict and Stability in the Caucasus and in the Former Yugoslavia*. Manchester: Manchester University Press, pp. 243–270.

Kurtenbach, Sabine. 1991. *Staatliche Organisation und Krieg in Lateinamerika*. Muenster: Lit.

Kurtenbach, Sabine. 1999. 'Kolumbien: Politische Gewaltkultur, der Staat und die Suche nach Frieden'. *Iberoamerikanisches Archiv*.

Kurtenbach, Sabine. 2006. 'Caminos para salir de la violencia. ¿Puede Colombia aprender de sus experiencias propias y de otros países?' In Linda Helfrich and Sabine Kurtenbach (eds), *Colombia. Caminos para salir de la violencia*. Madrid: Vervuert, pp. 493–524.

Latinobarómetro. Online analysis available at: www.latinobarometro.org/latOnline.jsp.

Lopez, Claudia (ed.). 2010. *Y refundaron la patria [.] : de cómo mafiosos y políticos reconfiguraron el Estado colombiano*. Bogotá: Corporación Nuevo Arco Iris.

MacGinty, Roger and Oliver Richmond. 2013. 'The Local Turn in Peace Building: A Critical Agenda for Peace'. *Third World Quarterly* 34(5): 763–783.

Mazzuca, Sebastián and James A. Robinson. 2009. 'Political Conflict and Power Sharing in the Origins of Modern Colombia'. *Hispanic American Historical Review* 89(2): 285–321.

Newman, Edward. 2013. 'The Violence of Statebuilding in Historical Perspective: Implications for Peacebuilding'. *Peacebuilding* 1(1): 141–157.

Nielson, Daniel L. and Matthew Soberg Shugart. 1999. 'Constitutional Change in Colombia. Policy Adjustment Through Institutional Reform'. *Comparative Political Studies* 32(3): 313- 341.

North, Douglass, John J. Wallis and Barry Weingast. 2009. *Violence and Social Orders: A Conceptual Framework for Interpreting Recorded Human History*. Cambridge: Cambridge University Press.

Oquist, Paul H. 1978. *Violencia, conflicto y política en Colombia*. Bogotá: Banco Popular.

Pecaut, Daniel. 2001. *Guerra contra la Sociedad*. Bogotá: Ed. Planeta.

Ramírez, Socorro and Luis Alberto Restrepo. 1989. *Actores en conflicto por la paz. El proceso de paz durante el gobierno de Belisario Betancur 1982–1986*. Bogotá.

Restrepo, Jorge and David Aponte (eds). 2009. *Guerra y violencias en Colombia: herramientas e interpretaciones*. Bogotá: Editorial Universidad Javeriana, CERAC-ODECOFI.

Richani, Nazih. 2002. *Systems of Violence: The Political Economy of War and Peace in Colombia*. Albany, NY: State University of New York Press.

Romero, Mauricio. 2003. *Paramilitares y autodefensas 1982–2003*. Bogotá: Editorial Planeta.

Safford, Frank and Marco Palacios. 2002. *Colombia. Fragmented Land, Divided Society*. New York and Oxford: Oxford University Press.

Shugart, Matthew Søberg, Erika Moreno and Luis E. Fajardo. 2007. 'Deepening Democracy by Renovating Political Practices: The Struggle for Electoral Reform in Colombia. In Christopher Wellna and Gustavo Gallón (eds), *Peace, Democracy, and Human Rights in Colombia*. Notre Dame: University of Notre Dame Press, pp. 202–266.

Sisk, Tim. 2013. *Statebuilding*. London: Polity Press.

Skocpol, Theda and Paul Pierson. 2002. Historical Institutionalism in Contemporary Political Science. In I. Katznelson and H.V. Milner, *Political Science: State of the Discipline*. New York: W.W. Norton, pp. 693–721.

Thelen, Kathleen and James Mahoney. 2010. 'A Theory of Gradual Institutional Change'. In James Mahoney and Kathleen Thelen (eds), *Explaining Institutional Change. Ambiguity, Agency, and Power*. Cambridge: Cambridge University Press, pp. 1–37.

Thoumi, Francisco E. 2003. *Illegal Drugs, Economy, and Society in the Andes*. Washington, DC: Woodrow Wilson Press; Baltimore, MD: The Johns Hopkins University Press.

Uprimny, Rodrigo. 2003. The Constitutional Court and Control of Presidential Extraordinary Powers in Colombia. *Democratization* 10(4): 46–69.

Vásquéz, Teófilo, Andrés Vargas and Jorge Restrepo. 2011. *Una Vieja Guerra en un nuevo Contexto*. Bogotá: Editorial Universidad Javeriana, CINEP-CERAC-ODECOFI.

Walter, Barbara. 2014. 'Why Bad Governance Leads to Repeat Civil War'. *Journal of Conflict Resolution*, online first

Zamosc, Leon. 1986. *The Agrarian Question and the Peasant Movement in Colombia*. Cambridge: Cambridge University Press.

Zartman, I. William (ed.). 1995. *Elusive Peace. Negotiating an End to Civil Wars*. Washington, DC: Brookings Institution Press.

Zuercher, Christoph. 2004. 'Einbettung und Entbettung: empirische institutionenzentrierte Konfliktanalyse'. In Julia Eckert (ed.), *Anthropologie der Konflikte. Georg Elwert konflikttheoretische Thesen in der Diskussion*. Bielfeld: transcript, pp. 26–38.

Zuercher, Christoph and Jan Koehler (eds). 2003. *Potentials of Disorder. Explaining Conflict and Stability in the Caucasus and in the Former Yugoslavia*. Manchester: Manchester University Press.

# 5 Introducing institutional reform

## The role of sunset clauses in postconflict power-sharing arrangements

*Roland Schmidt and Artak Galyan\**

## Introduction

The purpose of this chapter is to shed light on the role of sunset clauses in post-conflict power-sharing arrangements. Power sharing has become a dominant approach to ending civil wars (Rothchild and Roeder 2005, 5). By sharing the levers of power between the belligerents, it is hoped that the commitment problem that often plagues war-to-peace transitions can be overcome and that peaceful, mutually beneficial cooperation can be routinized. The institutional safeguards in post-conflict power-sharing arrangements are meant to provide sufficient assurances to all parties that their counterparts will not be able to politically marginalize or militarily defeat them. Despite the vast amount of scholarly output on the merits of power-sharing arrangements (e.g. Hartzell and Hoddie 2003, 2007; Jarstad 2009; Lijphart 1999, 2008), surprisingly little attention has been paid to those provisions that end power-sharing arrangements: sunset clauses.[1]

Sunset clauses are provisions in power-sharing agreements that stipulate when and how the arrangements will be terminated or modified. In this respect, sunset clauses are unique mechanisms of post-conflict institutional reform. They introduce a major change to the institutional framework governing postwar politics and constitute a crucial milestone in the war-to-peace transition. This chapter is a first step to theoretically mapping and systematizing the role of sunset clauses in power-sharing arrangements and to highlighting their contribution to the transition process.

Based on a review of the texts of all peace agreements in the Uppsala Conflict Data Program (UCDP) Peace Agreement Dataset (Högbladh 2012) and the Peace Accords Matrix (Joshi and Darby 2013), we identified nine post-conflict power-sharing arrangements with sunset clauses.[2] Of the numerous possible aspects to focus on, this chapter pays special attention to the triggers of sunset clauses. These mechanisms define when to start bringing an end to a power-sharing arrangement or significantly changing it. With this in mind, we distinguish between conditional and unconditional sunset triggers and show how these two types are associated with the timely or delayed implementation of sunset clauses. Those sunset clauses that are dependent on the implementation of reforms are overwhelmingly triggered later than originally stipulated. Or, to put it differently, interim power-sharing arrangements that have sunset clauses tied to the fulfilment of specific conditions last longer than planned. They are characterized by a delayed fulfilment of the conditions necessary to trigger the sunset clause.

This chapter is structured as follows. After this introduction, the second section discusses the contribution of power-sharing arrangements to ending civil wars. The third section examines sunset clauses in depth and provides a conceptual mapping. The fourth section introduces the distinction between conditional and unconditional sunset triggers and presents our main finding on the relationship between sunset-trigger type and the length of transitional power-sharing arrangements. In order to more closely investigate this relationship, the fifth section presents a within-case study of the Comprehensive Peace Agreement in Sudan and Southern Sudan, which features a conditional as well as an unconditional sunset trigger. The final section discusses those aspects that deserve particular attention in further research.

## Power sharing as a means to end civil wars

Armed conflict in 'divided societies' is generally described to be particularly difficult to end (see e.g. Toft 2009; Walter 1997). In comparison to wars between states, armed conflicts within states last longer, and the agreements meant to end them also collapse earlier (see Elbadawi and Sambanis 2002; Licklider 1995; Walter 2002) and more often (Walter 2009, 244). Furthermore, countries coming out of a civil war are more likely to re-experience violence than those countries that have previously been able to avoid war (Walter 2009, 256).

The literature provides a variety of explanations for the persistence of such conflicts, but particularly emphasizes the difficulty warring parties have in credibly signalling and committing to peace (Fearon 1995, 1998; Lake and Rothchild 1996, 1998; Mattes and Savun 2009, 2010; Snyder and Jervis 1999; Walter 1997, 2002). In contrast to interstate conflicts - and with the exception of the extreme cases of genocide, ethnic cleansing, mass expulsions – or secession – the belligerents of a civil war are bound to live together in the same state once the fighting has ceased. They are thus prone to perceive each other as permanent threats given the previous bloodshed and destruction they witnessed (Chapman and Roeder 2007). Rather than taking the risk of being deceived by potentially false assurances and becoming vulnerable to an attack with devastating consequences, all sides appear to deem it more prudent to strike first or continue fighting (Posen 1993). This dilemma is further aggravated in deeply 'divided societies', where minorities fear state capture and 'tyranny of the majority', and are unwilling to take any risks that may put their communities in danger.

The most prominent approach to overcoming the above-outlined commitment problem is power sharing. Embarking from the seminal work of Lijphart on consociational democracy (Lijphart 1968, 1977, 1999, 2002, 2004) and building upon an entire stream in the literature (e.g. Cammett and Malesky 2012; Hartzell and Hoddie 2003, 2007; Mattes and Savun 2009, 2010; Norris 2008; Saideman *et al.* 2002), power-sharing arrangements are argued to diffuse the security dilemma by guaranteeing belligerents inclusion in the post-conflict state structures. By institutionalizing the representation of different groups and by making the passing of laws that directly affect the situation of a group contingent upon that group's consent, the proponents of power-sharing arrangements are confident that agreements can help groups overcome their commitment issues, bring hostilities to an end, and ensure a peaceful coexistence despite the presence of societal cleavages.

Power-sharing arrangements have obtained 'almost universal prominence in peace accords' (de Varennes 2003, 155) since the end of the Cold War. The Dayton Agreement in Bosnia, the Good Friday Agreement in Northern Ireland and the Interim Constitution in South Africa are just some examples of the 'wave of power-sharing democracy' (Lijphart 2002) that emerged in the early 1990s. Empirically, there is considerable support for the proposition that power-sharing institutions offer 'a viable strategy to build peace, states and democracy' (Wolff 2011, 1796; for a counterview see Selway and Templeman 2011) and are not mere 'scraps of paper' (Fortna 2003; Mattes and Savun 2009, 2010). Hoddie and Hartzell conclude that at the end of civil wars no alternative set of rules can provide the reassurances necessary to initiate the transition to peace and democratic practices (Hoddie and Hartzell 2005). Walter (2002, 80) finds that warring parties are 38 per cent more likely to sign a peace agreement if the deal contains a power-sharing provision. As for the durability of peace, there is the general proposition that more comprehensive power-sharing arrangements are more conducive to the long-term stability of peace (see Hartzell and Hoddie 2007). Pospieszna and Schneider (2011) find evidence that peace agreements are less likely to break down within five years if the agreement contains at least two power-sharing arenas.

## Sunset clauses: an understudied aspect of power-sharing arrangements

Traditionally, power-sharing arrangements have been conceptualized as permanent settlements. Only gradual social change that erodes the underlying cleavage has been considered able to render the arrangement obsolete. In contrast to this conventional understanding, the new wave of post-conflict power sharing since the early 1990s brought about several arrangements that were designed to be transitional. A distinct institutional element of these transitional power-sharing arrangements is the sunset clause.

Sunset clauses are provisions included in power-sharing arrangements that establish a temporal limit on these agreements. In their most comprehensive form, sunset clauses end a period of shared rule by completely removing the institutional safeguards that were effective during the transitional period. Pre-sunset power-sharing arrangements facilitate an incremental transformation whereby parties go from relying on their own capacity for violence to relying on a state vested with the monopoly on the use of force. By deferring the final settlement, the institutional framework regulating the pre-sunset period aims at defusing the inherent tension between peacebuilding, on the one hand, and state building and democratization, on the other. In this context sunset clauses assume a critical role when it comes to balancing the positive short-term and negative long-term consequences of power sharing. By dismantling the safeguards available to the parties, a sunset clause transforms the configuration of institutional constraints upon belligerents' behaviour. When the clause is triggered, space for a more competitive, less group-accommodating political contest becomes available.

### Rationale and contribution of power-sharing arrangements with sunset clauses

To a certain extent, the adoption of a post-conflict arrangement with an expiry date is a paradox. Why do conflict parties conclude an agreement that is going to eventually expose their vulnerabilities and potentially bring them back to the security dilemma they faced before the agreement? In this context it is crucial to understand the circumstances under which temporally constrained power-sharing arrangements become an acceptable institutional solution for warring factions. The role and contribution of pre-sunset institutional safeguards deserves a particular mention in this regard.

Peace agreements are prone to be concluded on a transitory basis. Over time the underlying consensus may disappear as the value of spoils and the belligerents' coercive capacities change. Consequently, it is possible that a peace agreement will have been built on shaky ground and will require renegotiation. The inclusion of a sunset clause can provide the opportunity for such updating. Once a society has sufficiently stabilized, post-settlement negotiations are more likely to result in a more robust and rooted agreement (see also Du Toit 2003, 116). Rather than limiting war-to-peace transitions to a single negotiation process that results in an unmodifiable agreement, Sisk (2008, 253) identifies the 'key to the long-term success of war-to-democracy transitions [in] the perpetuation of the bargaining process that led to the settlement long into the future' (see also Jarstad 2008). 'Peace settlements need to resolve the war with certainty, but they also need to be imbued with a set of provisions facilitating flexibility, continued bargaining and opportunity for amendment; (Sisk 2003, 149). In short, credible yet adaptable elite pacts are needed (Durant and Weintraub 2014).

We present two scenarios in which parties to a civil war opt for a temporally constrained power-sharing arrangement. In the first scenario, parties are driven by 'devious objectives' (Richmond 1998) rather than any genuine interest in making peace and sharing power. In such cases, parties sign up to power-sharing arrangements since the continuation of fighting would be harmful (for example, due to an impending military defeat, a costly military stalemate, or international pressure through sanctions or other means). They thus view an interim power-sharing arrangement as a way to win time, weather their temporary weakness and outmanoeuvre their opponents so that they can eventually resume fighting. In this context sunset clauses are a useful instrument to defer the final post-conflict arrangement.

In the second scenario, belligerents are genuinely interested in ending the conflict with a negotiated political settlement but fear being marginalized as a result of such a settlement. This is most often the case when there are considerable power differences between the parties (for instance, concerning military capabilities and electoral strength within a framework of unconstrained political competition) at the time of the agreement's conclusion. In such cases sunset clauses can help ease the concerns of the warring parties (particularly the less powerful) by adapting the power-sharing arrangement to the diverging interests of the belligerents.

By including an interim power-sharing arrangement, a peace deal becomes more acceptable to the dominant party that is constrained by the pre-sunset framework. The dominant party will eventually become stronger due to institutional changes and the removal of some of the constraints upon political competition introduced by the sunset clause. In turn, the pre-sunset power-sharing period may provide weaker parties with guaranteed, albeit temporary, access to the spoils. Measures such as the gradual integration of the armed forces or police and the development of a nonpartisan security sector are expected to reassure belligerents that their physical existence will not be endangered once the power-sharing arrangement ends. Economic power sharing, the creation of an integrated civil service and territorial devolution are meant to demonstrate to belligerents that their livelihoods and autonomy are secure. Therefore, groups will not need to capture the state through rigid group-accommodating institutions to ensure their well-being. The preplanned dismantling of safeguards is built on the premise that the factors that gave rise to the security dilemma will be sufficiently addressed in the pre-sunset stage, thus rendering power-sharing institutions obsolete.

Crucially, pre-sunset periods offer weaker parties the possibility to observe and test other parties' capabilities and true intentions. In the course of the implementation of pre-sunset power sharing, belligerents monitor each other's compliance with the arrangements and can build trust. Only if convinced of others' commitment to the agreement will parties respect and accommodate the interests of their former opponents after the power-sharing safeguards are removed by the sunset clause.

## *Difference in safeguards before and after sunset*

The institutional reform triggered by a sunset clause can take different forms. First, the post-sunset institutional framework may not feature any of the safeguards present in the pre-sunset period. In this case the whole protective corset that guaranteed the groups' security and spoils is dismantled. Parties would thus enter the post-sunset stage without any group accommodation. Second, the post-sunset framework may preserve some of the institutional safeguards that are considered essential. Previous research has found evidence of the particularly important contribution of power sharing in the military (Martin 2013) and territorial arenas

(DeRouen *et al.* 2009; Jarstad and Nilsson 2008). These two forms are empirically the most common.[3]

Since sunset clauses introduce a framework with fewer safeguards, they entail a risk of conflict relapse. Once triggered, sunset clauses launch a fundamental institutional change to the carefully calibrated agreement. Institutional safeguards that were necessary in obtaining the parties' consent to the agreement are reduced or entirely removed. Provisions that earlier made the opponents' commitment credible are no longer present. What follows is a heightened risk of peace breaking down. Sunset clauses are therefore at the heart of a delicate balancing process. They enable an institutional mechanism to move away from its rigid institutional framework but are required to do so without compromising the credibility of the parties' commitment.

The transition from the pre-sunset to the post-sunset stage is therefore one of the most fragile stages of the peace process. Safeguards that protected former belligerents and guaranteed a share of power are scheduled to be replaced by a framework with fewer constraints and guaranteed spoils. Given that the parties are not yet accustomed to the new post-sunset framework, they are likely to be uncertain of the capacity of the new institutions to protect their interests and whether other parties will respect their commitments. Thus, this transition creates new vulnerabilities and could evoke a return to the security dilemma that the pre-sunset power-sharing arrangement sought to address. In that sense, while pre-sunset periods of power-sharing arrangements are seen to 'tie the hands' of belligerents, sunset clauses essentially 'untie the hands' of belligerents. Whether this process indeed leads to renewed armed conflict depends considerably on the protection provided to the parties in the post-sunset period.

## Trigger types and timing of sunset

The timing of an arrangement's sunset clause plays a critical role in the war-to-peace transition. Early sunsets risk ending the interim arrangement prematurely and potentially triggering the breakdown of the peace process. During the pre-sunset period, former belligerents can build trust in each other and become certain of each other's commitment to establishing peace. New patterns of peaceful exchange can become routinized, and the acute polarization that dominated during the war can be replaced with contentious but peaceful political competition. These developments, however, need time, particularly against the backdrop of the recent fighting. If the sunset clause triggers the end of the power-sharing arrangement before intergroup relations have been attenuated, post-sunset politics will be confronted with the challenging combination of decreased power-sharing safeguards and high intergroup tensions – an environment that would give rise to the security dilemma and be conducive to the re-emergence of violence.

Conversely, long pre-sunset periods may also contain dangers. Power-sharing arrangements have been criticized for blocking civic or cleavage-transcending parties as well as facilitating the prevalence of intragroup patronage politics and the entrenchment of ethno-sectarian identification (see e.g. Darby and Mac Ginty

2003a; Sisk 2013; Younis 2013). The longer the pre-sunset power-sharing period lasts, the more likely it becomes that negative side effects will materialize and start to shape post-conflict politics. Experiences in post-conflict power-sharing countries provide ample examples of how elites purporting to represent their societal segments capture state institutions and use their privileged access to spoils to further their political agendas (a frequently cited example is Bosnia under the Dayton Agreement; see e.g. International Crisis Group 2012, 2014; Woodward 1999).

When evaluating the timing of sunset clauses in interim agreements, it is important to bear in mind that the timing may have different implications for different parties. Consequently, the former belligerents will have different views on it. Given the accommodation-decreasing consequence of a sunset clause, minority parties, which will see their position in relation to the majority weakened, are likely to favour longer pre-sunset periods. The later the sunset, the longer the interim arrangement provides the minority party with stronger safeguards and time to reap spoils. Longer pre-sunset periods make it more likely that the post-conflict institutions will become consolidated and be better able to shape the country's political dynamics. Intergroup tensions are also more likely to abate. Moreover, a later sunset will provide the minority party with more time to diligently examine the behaviour of the majority and more information from which to draw conclusions about how the other parties will behave in the post-sunset period.

### Sunset trigger types

In order to fully appreciate the delicate role of the timing of the end of interim power-sharing arrangements, it is instructive to take a closer look at the types of sunset triggers contained in the agreements. In broad terms, two distinct types may be identified: unconditional and conditional sunset triggers. Unconditional triggers stipulate the end of the pre-sunset period with a predefined date. The triggering of the clauses is not conditional on any other developments during the pre-sunset period. In contrast, conditional sunset clauses require the implementation of certain measures. Although conditional sunset triggers also include a specific time frame, the ending of the pre-sunset period depends on the fulfilment of stipulated conditions. As we will show below, the sunset trigger type has fundamental implications for the overall dynamics of the transition process. The following section proposes that the trigger type is associated with the timing of an agreement's sunset and, as a consequence, with the timing of the post-conflict institutional reform process. For instance, conditional triggers appear to delay the cessation of pre-sunset power-sharing arrangements and the launch of institutional reforms, while unconditional triggers appear to ensure the timely end of interim periods and the punctual launch of institutional reform.

Unconditional sunset clauses entail rigid specifications of an end date and thus provide parties with a clear schedule for the interim arrangement. The timing of the sunset is unambiguous and as such provides an element of certainty to the transition process – which would otherwise be characterized by mutual distrust and outguessing. However, this lack of flexibility could negatively impact upon the stability of the transition process in cases where the pre-sunset period is too short to alleviate the fears of the minority group about the looming post-sunset framework. In such instances minority parties may renege on their commitments and withdraw from the peace process.

Conditional sunset clauses are tied to specific reform measures that must be implemented before the post-sunset framework may be introduced. Without the implementation of these measures, the sunset clause will not be triggered. This linkage between reform measures and the removal of pre-sunset power-sharing safeguards provides parties with an additional guarantee before the more contestation-oriented post-sunset period commences. The flexibility of conditional sunset clauses is not without pitfalls. Making the implementation of reforms a precondition renders them vulnerable to tactical manipulation by parties that prefer to stretch out the safeguarded pre-sunset period. Such parties are able to exercise a veto-type power to delay the end of the interim power sharing by obstructing the fulfilment of the conditions necessary to trigger the sunset clause and initiate the post-sunset framework.

Elections are one of the most frequently used triggers to end interim power sharing (the Ivory Coast in 2010, Liberia in 2005 and South Africa in 1999). At first glance, the choice of elections as a sunset clause trigger seems to have its advantages, since elections can provide the new institutional framework with public legitimacy, fill any vacant positions and further democratic transition. Irrespective of the clear advantages, however, post-conflict elections are not without dangers.

Recent research has highlighted the double-edged nature of post-conflict elections and their potential to reignite violence. Cederman *et al.* (2013) reveal that civil wars along ethnic lines are more likely to erupt after competitive elections that follow periods of non-polling. Flores and Nooruddin (2012) highlight the positive effect of delayed elections upon peace stability. Brancati and Snyder (2013) find evidence that elections have a conflict-increasing effect, though they also identify power sharing as one favourable condition that can mitigate the risk of renewed violence. In the context of sunset clauses, however, it is exactly the favourable condition of power sharing that is at least partially removed. The uncertain outcome of competitive elections is already a source of uncertainty that in many instances leads to election-related violence. Thus ending an interim power-sharing arrangement and holding elections brings two sources of insecurity together, which could tip the fragile transition process back into armed confrontation. This obviously does not mean that elections which serve as sunset clause triggers are deterministically bound to prompt violence. In fact, there are several cases in which elections introduced a successful pre-sunset-to-post-sunset transition (e.g. Burundi's election in 2005, Liberia's election in 2005 and South Africa's election in 1999).

### Power-sharing arrangements with sunset clauses and different trigger types

This section proposes a link between the type of trigger and the timing of the end of the interim period. Based on a survey of all peace agreements in the UCDP Peace Agreement Dataset (Högbladh 2012) and the Peace Accords Matrix (Joshi and Darby 2013) we identified nine post-conflict power-sharing arrangements with sunset clauses. Table 5.3 in the Appendix provides an overview.

For the purpose of this chapter, power-sharing arrangements are understood as any peace agreements stipulating formal institutional safeguards that are meant to constrain the former belligerents of an intrastate conflict from dominating each other.[4] Our conceptualization of power sharing does not make any differentiation between the two major approaches to power sharing: consociationalism (Lijphart 1968, 1977, 1999, 2002, 2004) and centripetalism (Horowitz 1985, 1991, 1993, 2002, 2008). We only include power-sharing arrangements that were drafted with a view to regulating intrastate conflicts along ethno-religious lines in 'divided societies'. In those cases in which a conflict was ended by a sequence of agreements, we only considered the final, comprehensive one. Thus we did not consider the following: mere expressions of intent or aspirations, even if stipulated in the text of an agreement; pacts regulating the transition processes of a conflict without any communal dimension; transition process between an authoritarian regime and a democratic opposition; power-sharing arrangements following post-election violence (e.g. Kenya's 2008 National Accord and Reconciliation Act or Zimbabwe's 2008 agreement); power-sharing arrangements that were imposed or administered by a third party (e.g. Iraq 2004); or agreements that did not address any substantive issues but merely focused on procedural aspects of negotiations.

Table 5.1 provides an overview of the power-sharing arrangements we examined and the type of sunset trigger they used. Of the ten sunset clauses (in nine agreements), six entail conditional triggers and four contain unconditional triggers. Although the small number of observations cautions against making a sweeping generalization, Table 5.1 suggests that linking the end of pre-sunset power-sharing arrangements to specific conditions is a frequent phenomenon. Conditional sunset clauses feature a variety of requirements on which the pre-sunset-to-post-sunset period depends: creation of a new constitution (Burundi, Democratic Republic of Congo, South Africa), adoption of a new electoral law (Burundi), United Nations approval for elections to be held (Angola), reform of citizenship laws (Ivory Coast) and the holding of a census (Sudan and Southern Sudan). The implementation of these requirements serves two distinct though frequently overlapping purposes.

The first purpose is to address the underlying problems that have been driving the conflict. Only if those are taken care of can the conflict be genuinely resolved rather than simply managed. If this is achieved during the pre-sunset period, it is expected that there is a good chance that peace will be sustainable even after the institutional safeguards of the interim period have been removed. An example of tackling causal issues may be seen in the Ivory Coast's Ouagadougou Peace Agreement, which rectified the conflict-driving exclusion of the predominantly

Table 5.1 Sunset trigger types in power-sharing agreements

Conditional triggers

| Agreements | Description of trigger | Condition |
| --- | --- | --- |
| Lusaka Protocol (1994) (Angola) | Second round of presidential elections held in 1992; National Assembly to set date of elections in accordance with the law (Annex 7, section II, paras 1–2) | Declaration by the UN that the requisite conditions for the elections were met (Annex 7, section II, para 3) |
| Arusha Agreement (2000), Global Ceasefire Agreement (2003) (Burundi) | Election of new president by National Assembly and Senate (Protocol II, Chapter I, article 20, para 10) within 30 months (Chapter II, article 13, para 2) | Adoption of new electoral law, law on political parties, and postsunset constitution (Protocol II, Chapter II, articles 14–17) |
| Global and Inclusive Agreement on Transition in the DR Congo (2002), Inter-Congolese Dialogue: The Final Act (2003), Constitution of Transition (2003)[1] (DR Congo) | Election of president within 24 months following beginning of transitional period and possible extension by two times six months (Global and Inclusive Agreement on Transition in the DR Congo; Inter-Congolese Dialogue, article 4) | Implementation of measures linked to the organization of the elections (Constitution of Transition, Chapter VII, article 196); adoption of Post-transition Constitution (Constitution of Transition, Chapter VII, article 205)[2] |
| Ouagadougou Peace Agreement (2007) (Ivory Coast) | Elections within ten months, at the latest by 2008 (Third Complementary Agreement of the Ouagadougou Political Agreement, 2007, section 12) | Reform of citizenship law and enfranchisement of previously excluded Muslim population in the north (Ouagadougou Political Agreement, Chapter 1, article 1.1, 1.3.2; Chapter 2, articles 2.1–2.3) |
| Interim Constitution (1993) (South Africa) | Elections once the new constitution is in place. Five-year presunset period starting with first elections and ending with subsequent elections (Interim Constitution, Chapter 4, para 38); a new constitution within two years after start of presunset period (Chapter 5, para 73) | Adoption of the new constitution[3] |

## Conditional triggers

| Agreements | Description of trigger | Condition |
| --- | --- | --- |
| Comprehensive Peace Agreement (2005) (Sudan and Southern Sudan) | General elections at all levels should be completed by the end of the third year of the presunset period (CPA, Power sharing, Part 1, 1.8.3) | Organization of a nationwide census (CPA, Power sharing, Part 1, 1.8.3.) |

## Unconditional triggers

| Agreements | Description of trigger | Condition |
| --- | --- | --- |
| Accra Peace Agreement (2003) (Liberia) | Two-year presunset period followed by elections as sunset trigger (Accra Agreement, Part 8, article XXI. 2) | No conditions |
| Arusha Agreement (1993) (Rwanda) | Elections in 22 months after the establishment of Broad Based Transitional Government (BBTG); presunset period never started since war broke out before BBTG was set up (Arusha Agreement, Protocol of Agreement between the Government of the Republic of Rwanda and the Rwandese Patriotic Front on Miscellaneous Issues and Final Provisions, article 22) | No conditions |
| Lomé Peace Agreement (1999) (Sierra Leone) | Interim power sharing to end with next elections to be held in 2001 in correspondence with the Constitution (Lomé Agreement, article VI (10); article XI) | No conditions |
| Comprehensive Peace Agreement (2005) (Sudan and Southern Sudan) | Referendum six years after the start of the interim period (Comprehensive Peace Agreement, Machakos Protocol,[4] Part B, 2.5) | No conditions |

Muslim population of the North by reforming the citizenship law. The parties agreed that in order to end the interim power-sharing arrangement, a new citizenship law would have to be passed, one that would provide those rebelling against their exclusion with citizenship and voting rights.

The second purpose is to create new formal safeguards that will continue to be in effect during the post-sunset period. Unless new safeguards are established, the clause will not be triggered and the power-sharing arrangement will remain in place unaltered. Burundi's Arusha Agreement stipulated that a permanent constitution and a new electoral law be drafted during the pre-sunset period. The latter introduced a strict requirement for ethnically mixed electoral lists with a view to countering exclusively ethnically defined political parties and policies. This and other safeguards were considered by the minority Tutsi community to be sufficiently broad and robust to consent to the war-to-peace transition.

For conditional sunset clauses to function, the parties have to agree on the question of whether the condition has actually been fulfilled. In most cases this is a relatively straightforward matter undertaken by the parties to the agreement. In some cases, though, the answering of this question is transferred to a third party. For instance, the sunset clause in Angola's Lusaka Protocol stipulated that national elections be held on a date to be defined by the National Assembly. However, the decision on whether the 'requisite conditions' (Annex 7, section II, para 3) for these elections had indeed been fulfilled was a task transferred to the United Nations mission in the country. Similarly, in South Africa it was down to the Constitutional Court to decide whether the permanent constitution was indeed living up to the principles required by the National Party. By 'outsourcing' this critical decision to a third party considered by all parties to the agreement as an unbiased arbiter, the potential for conflict over the actual fulfilment of a sunset's condition is reduced.

### Effects of different trigger types

Table 5.2 provides a cross-tabulation of the types of sunset triggers with the actual timing of the sunset. The end of the interim period was not delayed in any of the arrangements with unconditional sunset clauses. The scheduled institutional changes from pre-sunset power sharing to post-sunset frameworks took place on the dates specified from the outset of the respective transition processes.

In contrast, conditional sunset clauses were strongly associated with a delay to post-sunset frameworks. Or, to put it differently, the conditions required to end pre-sunset power sharing were not deemed to have been fulfilled within the respective time periods that had initially been scheduled. Out of the six interim power-sharing arrangements with conditional sunset clauses, four were not ended according to schedule. The pattern presented by the tabulation in Table 5.2 suggests that there is an association between the type of sunset clause and the eventual duration of the pre-sunset period. Despite intending to provide an additional layer of security by tying the end of the interim period to the fulfilment of certain conditions, conditional sunset clauses ironically introduce a new

*Table 5.2* Type of sunset trigger and timing of sunset clause

| Timing of the sunset | Conditional triggers | Unconditional triggers |
|---|---|---|
| Sunset delay | Ouagadougou Political Agreement (Ivory Coast) Comprehensive Peace Agreement (trigger – elections) (Sudan and Southern Sudan) Arusha Agreement, Global Ceasefire Agreement (Burundi) Global and Inclusive Agreement on Transition in the DR Congo, Inter-Congolese Dialogue: The Final Act, Constitution of Transition (DR Congo) | |
| No sunset delay | Interim Constitution (South Africa) | Accra Peace Agreement (Liberia) Comprehensive Peace Agreement (trigger – referendum) (Sudan and Southern Sudan) |
| Breakdown before sunset | Lusaka Protocol (Angola) | Arusha Agreement (Rwanda) Lomé Agreement (Sierra Leone) |

source of insecurity by putting the schedule of the transition process into question. Nevertheless, the destabilizing influence of a doubtful schedule due to conditional sunset clauses seems to be limited. The fact that only one out of six agreements with conditional sunset clauses (the Ivory Coast's Ouagadougou Political Agreement) broke down during the pre-sunset period suggests that any newly introduced ambiguity in the schedule had no dominating grave consequences.

The reasons behind these delays may vary, but from a theoretical perspective the duration of the pre-sunset power-sharing arrangement has a direct bearing on the conflict parties' interests. To at least one party, a delay of the pending institutional change is of some benefit. With this incentive structure in place, the triggering of conditional sunset clauses is vulnerable to be delayed by tactical manoeuvring.

### Caveat

At this point it is important to highlight two important caveats that demand a more nuanced understanding of the mechanism linking types of sunset triggers to the delay of institutional reform. First, the proposed link between the type of sunset trigger and the delay in the start of the post-sunset framework across different cases warrants some qualification. Each sunset clause has to be understood in the context of the underlying conflict dynamics that led to the agreement, the inclusion of the sunset clause and any related conditionalities. It seems reasonable to assume that the type of sunset clause is to no small degree a function of the belligerents' respective bargaining power. The choice of the sunset trigger – whether conditional or unconditional – is to some degree a reflection of the realities on the battlefield and conflict outcome. This dependency has to be kept in mind when considering the implications of sunset trigger choices and requires tracing within the individual cases.

Second, when discussing the implementation of the reforms preceding sunset triggers, it is important to consider that most states covered in this chapter lacked the capacity to effectively implement ambitious reforms in a short time frame. As DeRouen *et al.* (2010) show, state capacity is an important indicator of whether peace agreements will indeed be implemented or not. With this caveat in mind it is important to emphasize that the delays in the implementation of conditional triggers in the cases presented here could also be the result of a combination of political manoeuvring and inadequate state capacity rather than only political tactics.

## Case study: Comprehensive Peace Agreement, Sudan and Southern Sudan

The following section builds on the above-presented tabulation of types of sunset clauses and the de facto timing of the pre-sunset period. It outlines the transition process from the pre-sunset period to the post-sunset period and the role of the sunset trigger type.

### *Unconditional trigger and timely sunset in Sudan and Southern Sudan*

The Comprehensive Peace Agreement (CPA) signed by the Sudanese government and the incumbent National Congress Party (NCP) and the leaders of the Sudan People's Liberation Movement (SPLM) from the South offers an instructive example of the dynamics of a conditional as well as an unconditional sunset clause. The agreement features two interrelated sunset dates: one is conditional on the holding of elections; the other – a referendum on secession – is unconditional and with a fixed date.

Signed in 2005, the agreement provided a framework for interim power sharing, which in principle offered the prospect of far-reaching reforms in the country. It was hoped that the arrangement would transform the country into a 'New Sudan', which would be sufficiently accommodating of all groups, and facilitate peaceful coexistence. Crucially, the pre-sunset period was limited from the outset to six years. At the end of this phase, the agreement provided for a referendum that gave the South Sudanese the opportunity to decide on whether to secede or to remain part of the country (Machakos Protocol, ch. I, part B, article 2.2). The timing of the referendum was unconditional. In January 2011, according to schedule, the South Sudanese voted overwhelmingly for secession, and South Sudan became an independent country a few months later.

An element in the pre-sunset period that was conditional, however, was the holding of elections. According to the agreement, general elections were scheduled to be held at the end of the third year of the pre-sunset period (article 1.8.3).

Technically, the holding of the elections was conditional upon the completion of a new census. The agreement stipulated that the census be completed by the end of the second year of the pre-sunset period (Machakos Protocol, ch.1, part B, article 1.8).

It is difficult to overestimate the potential consequences the census could have for the parties. In addition to being a precondition for holding elections, the census had further crucial implications. The demographic distribution of the country was the basis for the delimitation of electoral constituencies and the determination of the power-sharing balance at the national and subnational level in the pre-sunset period (Ahmed 2009). Demographic data acquired through the census were also the basis for the wealth-sharing part of the CPA and an important argument in the territorial disputes in the resource-rich border areas. Thus, the census had a direct bearing on the distribution of power between the two parties and constituted a potential threat to their standing. Expecting an unfavourable census outcome, the incumbent NCP party sought initially to delay the census and the subsequent elections for as long as possible and then tried to manipulate the results thereof.

The organization of the census and the elections depended on a number of interrelated and complex issues being resolved, such as demarcation of both the North–South boundary and the state borders. It was further complicated by security challenges along the North–South border, several insurgencies throughout the country, and the lack of an effective infrastructure. Of particular concern was the inclusion of approximately two million internally displaced persons from Darfur on the voter list (ICG 2009, 4). The incumbent NCP – and to a lesser degree the SPLM – exacerbated these difficulties as part of a deliberate stalling policy. The NCP and central government did not provide the necessary funds for the census for three years (ICG 2008). The central government also severely delayed the adoption of legislation essential for the organization of the census and elections. Furthermore, the NCP limited the participation of other parties in the development of the necessary legal basis and used its parliamentary majority to push through legislation that disadvantaged other parties (ICG 2009, 5). The required election legislation was eventually passed in 2009, just a few months before voting eventually took place. When the census was conducted and the results announced, the southern state legislatures passed rejection motions and the SPLM declared the results to be fraudulent. The SPLM argued that the census inflated populations in NCP strongholds and deflated those in other regions. As a result, the SPLM declared that it did not recognize the results of the census or any elections based on it (ICG 2009, 4).

The CPA envisioned that the general elections would be held by the end of the third year (2008) of the power-sharing arrangement at the latest. However, not even the census had been accomplished at that point. As a consequence, the elections could only be held in 2010, nine months prior to the referendum. While logistical challenges played a role, the incumbent NCP and the SPLM used their power to impede the overall process (Aalen 2013; ICG 2010). A welcome consequence of the delays was that the parties remained electorally uncontested for a longer period than initially scheduled, which enabled them to entrench their positions not only in anticipation of the eventual elections but especially in anticipation of a referendum result in favour of secession (Aalen 2013).

Given that it combines both an unconditional and conditional sunset trigger, the CPA in Sudan is an illustrative case of the consequences that trigger mechanisms can have. The CPA's unconditional trigger, which had a fixed date and was activated according to schedule, did not raise any distrust among the parties. This allowed both parties an exit option in the form of the secession of the South. The conditional trigger, on the other hand, was significantly delayed and – due to the interdependent conditions that had to be fulfilled in order to trigger the clause – created space for political manoeuvring, which was successfully utilized by the signatories to the agreement, especially the incumbent NCP. The delay in the implementation process led to a rise in mutual distrust and accusations of fraudulent behaviour.

## Conclusion and outlook

Despite the fact that the role of interim power sharing as a means to end violent intrastate conflict has grown since the early 1990s, sunset clauses have received surprisingly little attention. This chapter is a first step towards shedding some light on and providing a first analytical and conceptual mapping of this understudied mechanism.

In this chapter sunset clauses were presented as formal provisions in power-sharing arrangements that stipulate the end or a significant reduction of the group-accommodating system that governs intergroup relations in the pre-sunset period. Once triggered, sunset clauses introduce fundamental institutional changes and give way to more contestation-oriented rules. Intergroup relations that were previously bound by power-sharing regulations are unfettered, and intergroup contestation can take over. This critical location in the war-to-peace transition means that sunset clauses are of special importance and deserve further investigation.

We highlighted three aspects of sunset clauses from a theoretical perspective: (1) the difference between pre-sunset safeguards and post-sunset safeguards, and the implications that has for the return of the security dilemma; (2) the motivation behind including sunset clauses and their contribution to facilitating agreements and attenuating power imbalances, and (3) the conditional link between a sunset clause trigger and the timing of institutional change. To empirically ground the proposition that the trigger type has an influence on the timing of reform, we conducted a comprehensive review of peace agreements, identifying nine interim power-sharing agreements and ten sunset clauses. By comparing the type of sunset trigger used and the actual timing of sunsets, we showed that conditional sunset clauses are very frequently characterized by a delayed implementation. Only one agreement with a conditional sunset clause – the Interim Constitution in South Africa – was concluded on time.

This chapter by no means pretends to nor can it provide an exhaustive treatment of sunset clauses. Considerable gaps remain, and further research is needed. A particularly promising avenue of future research could be in-depth investigation of the relationship between the difference between pre-sunset and post-sunset safeguards, on the one hand, and the stability of an agreement, on the other. Such a line of inquiry could be guided by the question of under what conditions and to what extent a decrease of safeguards might facilitate a recurrence of violence or a transition from one institutional equilibrium to another. It is also worth examining, with regard to the implementation of the agreement, the interplay between parties' behaviour during the pre-sunset period and their expectations of the post-sunset framework. Another possibility could be to look at whether there are any safeguards that are necessary or sufficient for a successful transition into a post-sunset period. These are only a few of the questions that remain to be addressed.

The analysis of these and other remaining gaps on sunset clauses should not only strengthen our overall understanding of power sharing and war-to-peace transitions; they should also have direct policy implications. As we mentioned at the outset, power-sharing arrangements with sunset clauses have been increasingly used to end intrastate conflicts. If such engagements are to succeed, they have to be built on a solid understanding of the implications of sunset clauses.

## Notes

\*   Both authors contributed equally to this chapter. The position of authors' names alternates between joint publications. The authors thank Nadine Ansorg, Sabine Kurtenbach and their colleagues at GIGA for having provided them the opportunity to present preliminary research at the ISA 2014 conference, Toronto and the 3rd ISP Network Conference, Geneva. Previous versions benefited from comments by Matthijs Bogaards, Erin Jenne, Will Moore, Carsten Q. Schneider, Gerald Schneider, Timothy Sisk as well as the participants of the 2014 Annual Doctoral Conference and members of "Conflict and Security" research group at the Central European University (CEU), Budapest. The authors are grateful for their input.

1   Research on interim governments has provided important insights into interim power sharing and has strengthened our understanding of war-to-peace transitions. However, despite overlapping in some important aspects, the focus of this existing body of research is different from research on sunset clauses (e.g. Guttieri and Piombo 2007; Shain *et al.* 1995; Strasheim and Fjelde 2014).

2   Lusaka Protocol (1994) (Angola), Arusha Agreement (2000) and Global Ceasefire Agreement (2003) (Burundi), Inter-Congolese Dialogue (2003) (DR Congo), Ouagadougou Political Agreement (2007) (Ivory Coast), Accra Peace Agreement (2003) (Liberia), Arusha Agreement (1993) (Rwanda), Lomé Agreement (1999) (Sierra Leone), Interim Constitution (1993) (South Africa), and Comprehensive Peace Agreement (2005) (Sudan and Southern Sudan).

3   Burundi's Arusha Agreement (2000) and Global Ceasefire Agreement (2003) are exceptional cases, since their post-sunset safeguards eventually exceeded those of the pre-sunset period. This paradoxical development was the result of changes to both the pre-sunset and the post-sunset institutional framework, which were negotiated during the pre-sunset stage. The major rebel group, the CNDD-FDD, joined the peace process in 2003 with the signing of the Global Ceasefire Agreement and was provided with additional safeguards, which were later also reflected in the 2005 Constitution, which regulated the post-sunset period.

4   This conceptualization of power sharing is broad and (keeping in mind the chapter's focus on provisions that safeguard against intergroup conflict) also includes provisions

that other authors have categorized as power dividing. For example, whether an agreement provides for the existence of two separate armies (power dividing) or the integration of the belligerents into one army with joint command (power sharing) is irrelevant for our case selection.

# References

Aalen, L. 2013. 'Making Unity Unattractive: The Conflicting Aims of Sudan's Comprehensive Peace Agreement'. *Civil Wars* 15(2): 173–191. doi:10.1080/13698249.2013.817852.

Ahmed, E. 2009. 'The Comprehensive Peace Agreement and the Dynamics of Post-conflict Political Partnership in Sudan'. *Africa Spectrum* 44(3): 133–147.

Brancati, D. and Snyder, J.L. 2013. 'Time to Kill: The Impact of Election Timing on Postconflict Stability'. *Journal of Conflict Resolution* 57: 822–853. doi:10.1177/0022002712449328.

Cammett, M. and Malesky, E. 2012. Power Sharing in Postconflict Societies: Implications for Peace and Governance. *Journal of Conflict Resolution* 56(6): 982–1016. doi:10.1177/0022002711421593.

Cederman, L-E., Gleditsch, K.S. and Hug, S. 2013. 'Elections and Ethnic Civil War'. *Comparative Political Studies* 46: 387–417. doi:10.1177/0010414012453697.

Chapman, T. and Roeder, P.G. 2007. 'Partition as a Solution to Wars of Nationalism: The Importance of Institutions'. *American Political Science Review* 101: 677–691. doi:10.1017/S0003055407070438.

Darby, J. and Mac Ginty, R. 2003a (eds). *Contemporary Peacemaking: Conflict, Peace Processes and Post-war Reconstruction*, 2nd edn. New York: Palgrave Macmillan.

Darby, J. and Mac Ginty, R. 2003b. 'Introduction: What Peace? What Process?' In J. Darby and R. Mac Ginty (eds), *Contemporary Peacemaking: Conflict, Peace Processes and Post-war Reconstruction*. 2nd edn. New York: Palgrave Macmillan, pp. 1–6.

DeRouen, K., Lea, J. and Wallensteen, P. 2009. 'The Duration of Civil War Peace Agreements'. *Conflict Management and Peace Science* 26(4): 367–387. doi: 10.1177/0738894209106481.

DeRouen, K., Ferguson, M.J., Norton, S., Park, Y.H., Lea, J. and Streat-Bartlett, A. 2010. 'Civil War Peace Agreement Implementation and State Capacity'. *Journal of Peace Research* 47(3): 333–346. doi:10.1177/0022343310362169.

de Varennes, F. 2003. 'Peace Accords and Ethnic Conflicts: a Comparative Analysis of Content and Approaches'. In J. Darby and R. Mac Ginty (eds), *Contemporary Peacemaking: Conflict, Peace Processes and Post-war Reconstruction*. 2nd edn. New York: Palgrave Macmillan, pp. 151–160.

Durant, T.C. and Weintraub, M. 2014. 'How to Make Democracy Self-enforcing after Civil War: Enabling Credible yet Adaptable Elite Pacts'. *Conflict Management and Peace Science* 31: 521–540. doi:10.1177/0738894213520372.

Elbadawi, I. and Sambanis, N. 2002. 'How Much War Will We See? Explaining the Prevalence of Civil War'. *Journal of Conflict Resolution* 46: 307–334. doi:10.1177/0022002702046003001.

Fearon, J.D., 1995. 'Rationalist Explanations for War'. *International Organization* 49: 379–414.

Fearon, J.D. 1998. 'Bargaining, Enforcement, and International Cooperation'. *International Organization* 52: 269–305. doi:10.1162/002081898753162820.

Flores, T.E. and Nooruddin, I. 2012. 'The Effect of Elections on Postconflict Peace and Reconstruction'. *The Journal of Politics* 74: 558–570. doi:10.1017/S002238161 1001733.

Fortna, V.P. 2003. 'Scraps of Paper? Agreements and the Durability of Peace'. *International Organization* 57: 337–372. doi:10.1017/S0020818303572046.

Guttieri, K. and Piombo, J. (eds). 2007. *Interim Governments: Institutional Bridges to Peace and Democracy?* Washington, DC: United States Institute of Peace.

Hartzell, C. 2006. 'Structuring the Peace: Negotiated Settlements and the Construction of Conflict Management Institutions'. In T.D. Mason and J.D. Meernik (eds), *Conflict Prevention and Peacebuilding in Post-war Societies.* Abingdon: Routledge, pp. 31–52.

Hartzell, C. and Hoddie, M. 2003. 'Institutionalizing Peace: Power Sharing and Post-Civil War Conflict Management'. *American Journal of Political Science* 47: 318–332. doi:10.1111/1540-5907.00022.

Hartzell, C. and Hoddie, M. 2007. *Crafting Peace: Power-Sharing Institutions and the Negotiated Settlement of Civil Wars.* Philadelphia: Pennsylvania State University Press.

Hoddie, M. and Hartzell, C. 2005. 'Power Sharing in Peace Settlements: Initiating the Transition from Civil War'. In P.G. Roeder and D.S. Rothchild (eds), *Sustainable Peace: Power and Democracy After Civil Wars.* Ithaca, NY: Cornell University Press, pp. 83–106.

Högbladh, S. 2012. 'Peace Agreements 1975–2011 – Updating the UCDP Peace Agreement Dataset'. In T. Pettersson and L. Themnér (eds), *States in Armed Conflict, Research Report.* Uppsala University: Department of Peace and Conflict Research, pp. 39–56.

Horowitz, D.L. 1985. *Ethnic Groups in Conflict.* Berkeley: University of California Press

Horowitz, D.L. 1991. *Democratic South Africa? Constitutional Engineering in a Divided Society.* Berkeley: University of California Press.

Horowitz, D.L. 1993. 'Democracy in Divided Societies'. *Journal of Democracy* 4(4): 18–38. doi:10.1353/jod.1993.0056.

Horowitz, D.L. 2002. 'Constitutional Design: Proposals Versus Processes'. In A. Reynolds (ed.), *The Architecture of Democracy: Constitutional Design, Conflict Management, and Democracy.* Oxford: Oxford University Press, pp. 15–36.

Horowitz, D.L. 2008. 'Conciliatory Institutions and Constitutional Processes in Post-conflict States'. *William and Mary Law Review* 49(4): 1213–1248.

International Crisis Group (ICG). 2008. 'Sudan's Comprehensive Peace Agreement: Beyond the Crisis'. *Policy Briefing/Africa Briefing,* No. 50. Nairobi/Brussels.

International Crisis Group (ICG). 2009. 'Sudan: Preventing Implosion'. *Policy Briefing/Africa Briefing*, No. 68. Nairobi/Brussels.

International Crisis Group (ICG). 2010. 'Negotiating Sudan's North–South Future. *Update Briefing/Africa Briefing*, No. 76. Juba/Khartoum/Nairobi/Brussels.

International Crisis Group (ICG). 2012. 'Bosnia's Gordian Knot: Constitutional Reform'. *Policy Briefing/Europe Briefing*, No. 68. Sarajevo/Istanbul/Brussels.

International Crisis Group (ICG). 2014. 'Bosnia's Future'. *Europe Report*, No. 232. Sarajevo/Istanbul/Brussels.

Jarstad, A.K. 2008. 'Power Sharing: Former Enemies in Joint Government'. In A.K. Jarstad and T.D. Sisk (eds), *From War to Democracy. Dilemmas of Peacebuilding.* Cambridge: Cambridge University Press, pp. 105–133.

Jarstad, A.K. 2009. 'The Prevalence of Power-sharing: Exploring the Patterns of Post-election Peace'. *Africa Spectrum* 44: 41–62.

Jarstad, A.K. and Nilsson, D. 2008. 'From Words to Deeds: The Implementation of Power-sharing Pacts in Peace Accords'. *Conflict Management and Peace Science* 25(3): 206–223. doi: 10.1080/07388940802218945.

Joshi, M. and Darby, J. 2013. 'Introducing the Peace Accords Matrix (PAM): A Database of Comprehensive Peace Agreements and their Implementation, 1989–2007'. *Peacebuilding* 1: 256–274. doi:10.1080/21647259.2013.783259.

Lake, D.A. and Rothchild, D.S. 1996. 'Containing Fear: The Origins and Management of Ethnic Conflict'. *International Security* 21: 41–75.

Lake, D.A. and Rothchild, D.S. (eds). 1998. *The International Spread of Ethnic Conflict: Fear, Diffusion, and Escalation*. Princeton, NJ: Princeton University Press.

Licklider, R. 1995. 'The Consequences of Negotiated Settlements in Civil Wars, 1945–1993'. *American Political Science Review* 89: 681–690. doi:10.2307/2082982.

Lijphart, A. 1968. *The Politics of Accommodation: Pluralism and Democracy in the Netherlands*. Berkeley: University of California Press.

Lijphart, A. 1977. *Democracy in Plural Societies: A Comparative Exploration*. New Haven, CT: Yale University Press.

Lijphart, A. 1999. *Patterns of Democracy: Government Forms and Performance in Thirty-six Countries*. New Haven, CT: Yale University Press.

Lijphart, A. 2002. 'The Wave of Power-sharing Democracy'. In A. Reynolds (ed.), *The Architecture of Democracy. Constitutional Design, Conflict Management, and Democracy*. Oxford and New York: Oxford University Press, pp. 37–54.

Lijphart, A. 2004. 'Constitutional Design for Divided Societies'. *Journal of Democracy* 15: 96–109. doi:10.1353/jod.2004.0029.

Lijphart, A. 2008. *Thinking about Democracy: Power Sharing and Majority Rule in Theory and Practice*. New York: Routledge.

Martin, P. 2013. 'Coming Together: Power-sharing and the Durability of Negotiated Peace Settlements. *Civil Wars* 15(3): 332–358. doi:10.1080/13698249.2013.842747.

Mattes, M. and Savun, B. 2009. 'Fostering Peace After Civil War: Commitment Problems and Agreement Design'. *International Studies Quarterly* 53: 737–759. doi:10.1111/j.1468-2478.2009.00554.x.

Mattes, M. and Savun, B. 2010. 'Information, Agreement Design, and the Durability of Civil War Settlements'. *American Journal of Political Science* 54: 511–524. doi:10.1111/j.1540-5907.2010.00444.x.

Norris, P. 2008. *Driving Democracy: Do Power Sharing Institutions Work?* Cambridge: Cambridge University Press.

Posen, B.R. 1993. 'The Security Dilemma and Ethnic Conflict'. *Survival* 35: 27–47.

Pospieszna, P. and Schneider, G. 2011. 'Power Sharing Provisions and Long-term Success of Mediation in Internal Conflicts'. Paper prepared for presentation at the 2011 APSA Annual Meeting, 1-4 September, Seattle, WA.

Richmond, O. 1998. 'Devious Objectives and the Disputants' View of International Mediation: A Theoretical Framework'. *Journal of Peace Research* 35(6): 707–722. doi: 10.1177/0022343398035006004.

Rothchild, D. and Roeder, P.G. 2005. 'Dilemmas of State-building in Divided Societies'. In P.G. Roeder and D. Rothchild (eds), *Sustainable Peace: Power and Democracy after Civil Wars*. Ithaca, NY: Cornell University Press, pp. 1–26.

Saideman, S.M., Lanoue, D.J., Campenni, M. and Stanton S. 2002. 'Democratization, Political Institutions, and Ethnic Conflict: A Pooled Time-Series Analysis, 1985-1998'. *Comparative Political Studies* 35(1): 103–129. doi:10.1177/001041400203500108.

Selway, J. and Templeman, K. 2011. 'The Myth of Consociationalism? Conflict Reduction in Divided Societies'. *Comparative Political Studies* 45: 1542–1571. doi:10.1177/0010414011425341.

Shain, Y., Linz, J.J. and Berat, L. 1995. *Between States: Interim Governments in Democratic Transitions*. Cambridge: Cambridge University Press.

Sisk, T.D. 2003. 'Power-sharing after Civil Wars: Matching Problems to Solutions'. In J. Darby and R. Mac Ginty (eds), *Contemporary Peacemaking*. New York: Palgrave Macmillan, pp. 139–150.

Sisk, T.D. 2008. 'Peacebuilding as Democratization: Findings and Recommendations'. In A.K. Jarstad and T.D. Sisk (eds), *From War to Democracy: Dilemmas of Peacebuilding*. Cambridge: Cambridge University Press, pp. 239–259.

Sisk, T.D. 2013. 'Power-sharing in Civil War: Puzzles of Peacemaking and Peacebuilding'. *Civil Wars* 15: 7–20. doi:10.1080/13698249.2013.850873.

Snyder, J. and Jervis, R. 1999. 'Civil War and the Security Dilemma'. In B.F. Walter and J. Snyder (eds), *Civil War, Insecurity and Intervention*. New York: Columbia University Press, pp. 15–37.

Strasheim, J. and Fjelde, H. 2014. 'Pre-designing Democracy: Institutional Design of Interim Governments and Democratization in 15 Post-conflict Societies'. *Democratization* 21: 335–358. doi:10.1080/13510347.2012.729044.

Toft, M.D. 2009. *Securing the Peace: The Durable Settlement of Civil Wars*. Princeton, NJ: Princeton University Press.

Toit, P. Du. 2003. 'Why Post-settlement Settlements?' *Journal of Democracy* 14: 104–118. doi:10.1353/jod.2003.0065.

Wallensteen, P. and Sollenberg, M. 1997. 'Armed Conflicts, Conflict Termination and Peace Agreements, 1989–96'. *Journal of Peace Research* 34: 339–358. doi:10.1177/00 22343397034003011.

Walter, B.F. 1997. 'The Critical Barrier to Civil War Settlement'. *International Organization* 51: 335–364. doi:10.1162/002081897550384.

Walter, B.F. 2002. *Committing to Peace: The Successful Settlement of Civil Wars*. Princeton, NJ: Princeton University Press.

Walter, B.F. 2009. 'Bargaining Failures and Civil War'. *Annual Review of Political Science* 12: 243–261. doi:10.1146/annurev.polisci.10.101405.135301.

Walter, B.F. and Snyder, J. (eds). 1999. *Civil Wars, Insecurity, and Intervention*. New York: Columbia University Press.

Wolff, S. 2011. 'Post-conflict State Building: The Debate on Institutional Choice'. *Third World Quarterly* 32: 1777–1802. doi:10.1080/01436597.2011.610574.

Woodward, S. 1999. 'Bosnia and Herzegovina: How Not to End Civil War'. In B.F. Walter and J. Snyder (eds), *Civil Wars, Insecurity, and Intervention*. New York: Columbia University Press, pp. 73–115.

Younis, N. 2013. 'From Power-sharing to Majoritarianism: Iraq's Transitioning Political System'. In C. Spencer, J. Kinninmont and O. Sirri (eds), *Iraq Ten Years on*. London: Chatham House, pp. 19–21.

## Peace agreements

*Angola:*

Lusaka Protocol (1994), Lusaka, Zambia. http://peacemaker.un.org/sites/peacemaker. un.org/files/AO_941115_LusakaProtocol%28en%29.pdf .

*Burundi:*

Arusha Peace and Reconciliation Agreement for Burundi (2000), Arusha, Tanzania. www.
    ucdp.uu.se/gpdatabase/peace/Bur%2020000828a.pdf.
Global Ceasefire Agreement between the Transitional Government of Burundi and the
    National Council for the Defence of the Democracy-Forces for the Defence of
    Democracy (CNDD-FDD) (2003), Dar-es-Salaam, Tanzania. www.ucdp.uu.se/
    gpdatabase/peace/Bur%2020031116.pdf.
Pretoria Protocol on Political, Defence and Security Power Sharing in Burundi (2003),
    Pretoria, South Africa. www.ucdp.uu.se/gpdatabase/peace/Bur%2020031008.pdf.


*DR Congo:*

Political Negotiations on the Peace Process and on Transition in the DRC. Global and
    Inclusive Agreement on Transition in the Democratic Republic of the Congo (2002),
    Pretoria, South Africa. www.ucdp.uu.se/gpdatabase/peace/DRC%2020021216.pdf.
Inter-Congolese Political Negotiations: The Final Act (2003), Sun City, South Africa.
    www.ucdp.uu.se/gpdatabase/peace/DRC%2020030402.pdf.
Constitution of the Transition (2003), Democratic Republic of the Congo. www.issafrica.
    org/cdct/mainpages/pdf/Terrorism/Legislation/Democratic%20Republic%20of%20
    Congo/DRC%20Constitution%20in%20English.pdf.


*Ivory Coast:*

Ouagadougou Political Agreement (2007), Ouagadougou, Burkina Faso. www.
    securitycouncilreport.org/atf/cf/%7B65BFCF9B-6D27-4E9C-8CD3-CF6E4FF96
    FF9%7D/Cote%20d'Ivoire%20S2007144.pdf.
First Complementary Agreement of the Ouagadougou Political Agreement (2007),
    Ouagadougou, Burkina Faso. www.ucdp.uu.se/gpdatabase/peace/IVO%2020070327_
    fr.pdf.
Second Complementary Agreement of the Ouagadougou Political Agreement (2007),
    Ouagadougou, Burkina Faso. www.ucdp.uu.se/gpdatabase/peace/IVO%2020071128a.
    pdf.
Third Complementary Agreement of the Ouagadougou Political Agreement (2007),
    Ouagadougou, Burkina Faso. www.ucdp.uu.se/gpdatabase/peace/IVO%2020071128b.
    pdf.
Fourth Complementary Agreement of the Ouagadougou Political Agreement (2008),
    Ouagadougou, Burkina Faso. www.ucdp.uu.se/gpdatabase/peace/IVO%2020081222.
    pdf.


*Liberia:*

Peace Agreement between the Government of Liberia, the Liberians United for
    Reconciliation and Democracy (LURD), the Movement for Democracy in Liberia
    (MODEL) and the Political Parties (2003), Accra, Liberia. www.usip.org/sites/default/
    files/file/resources/collections/peace_agreements/liberia_08182003.pdf.

*Rwanda:*

Peace Agreement between the Government of the Republic of Rwanda and the Rwandese Patriotic Front (1993), Arusha, Tanzania. www.ucdp.uu.se/gpdatabase/peace/Rwa%20 19930804.pdf.

*Sierra Leone:*

Peace Agreement between the Government of Sierra Leone and the Revolutionary United Front (1999), Lomé, Togo. www.ucdp.uu.se/gpdatabase/peace/SiL%2019990707.pdf.

*South Africa:*

Constitution of the Republic of South Africa Act 200 of 1993 (Interim Constitution of 1994), South Africa. www.ucdp.uu.se/gpdatabase/peace/SyA%2019931118.pdf.

*Sudan and Southern Sudan:*

The Comprehensive Peace Agreement Between the Government of the Republic of the Sudan and the Sudan People's Liberation Movement/Sudan People's Liberation Army (2005), Nairobi, Kenya. www.ucdp.uu.se/gpdatabase/peace/Sud%2020050109.pdf.

# Appendix

*Table 5.3* Overview of post-conflict power-sharing agreements with sunset clauses

| Agreements | Trigger type | Length of presunset period, de jure | Length of presunset period, de facto |
|---|---|---|---|
| Lusaka Protocol (1994) (Angola) | Conditional | 11/1994 – until conditions for elections are reached | – |
| Arusha Agreement (2000), Global Ceasefire Agreement (2003) (Burundi) | Conditional | 2/2001–7/2003 | 11/2001 (11/2003)[5]–8/2005 |
| Global and Inclusive Agreement on Transition in the DR Congo (2002), Inter-Congolese Dialogue: The Final Act (2003), Constitution of Transition (2003) (DR Congo) | Conditional | 7/2003–7/2005 | 7/2003–7/2006 |
| Ouagadougou Political Agreement (2007) (Ivory Coast) | Conditional | 3/2007–6/2008[6] | 3/2007–11/2010 |
| Accra Peace Agreement (2003) (Liberia) | Unconditional | 10/2003–10/2005; two-year interim period ended by election | 10/2003–10/2005 |
| Arusha Agreement (1993) (Rwanda) | Unconditional | twenty-two months[7] 1999–2001 | |
| Lomé Agreement (1999) (Sierra Leone) | Unconditional | | |
| Comprehensive Peace Agreement (2005) (Sudan and Southern Sudan) | Conditional (elections); Conditional (referendum) | 1/2005–1/2008; 1/2005–1/2011 | 1/2005–4/2010; 1/2005–1/2011 |
| Interim Constitution (2003) (South Africa) | Conditional | 4/1994–2/6/1999 | 4/1994–2/6/1999 |

Notes

1 The presunset stage in the DR Congo was regulated by several documents that followed and complemented each other by establishing safeguards in the different power-sharing arenas: the Global and Inclusive Agreement on Transition in the DR Congo (December 2002), the Final Act of the Inter-Congolese Political Negotiations (April 2003) and the Constitution of Transition (April 2003).

2 The holding of elections was conditional on two issues, on one directly and on another one indirectly. Article 196 states that due to potential problems in the organization of elections, the transitional period could be extended twice for a period of six months each. Article 205 states that the transitional constitution would cease to have effect when the (permanent) constitution was adopted at the end of the transitional period. Elections trigger the end of the transitional period. Consequently, the passing of the (permanent) constitution is an indirect condition for the activation of the sunset trigger.

3 Although the interim constitution requires the adoption of the (postsunset) constitution within two years from the first sitting of the National Assembly under the interim constitution, there was no specific provision that tied the holding of the next general elections to the adoption of the new constitution. In practice, the passing of the new constitution, however, was a fundamental requirement for the National Party to pursue the transition process.

4 The Machakos Protocol forms part of the Comprehensive Peace Agreement.

5 Building upon the Arusha Agreement of 2000, the Global Ceasefire Agreement was signed in 2003.

6 Article 12 of the Third Complementary Agreement to the Ouagadougou Political Agreement stated that elections would take place by the end of the first half of 2008.

7 According to the Arusha Agreement, the interim period was supposed to commence on 10 October 1993 with the installation of the Broad Based Transitional Government (BBTG) and last for twenty-two months. However, this deadline was not met, and the agreement broke down with the start of the Rwandan Genocide on 7 April 1994 before the BBTG could be installed.

# 6 Business and institutional reform in hybrid political orders

*Brian Ganson and Achim Wennmann*

## Introduction

Business interest in postwar and otherwise fragile environments is increasing, driven by new discoveries of natural resources in many parts of Africa, Asia and Latin America as well as governments that promote ambitious national development plans. Many see the ensuing rising private investment in the agriculture, extractive and infrastructure sectors as a potential catalyst for ending poverty, fragility and cycles of violence (Gündüz and Vaillant 2006). Rather than delivering on the promise of inclusive growth, however, large-scale investments in post-conflict and other fragile environments often become an additional source of conflict. Projects are frequently designed in the absence of any meaningful local participation or strategic coordination between national and local development plans. These projects may clash with traditional ways of life and livelihoods, stress existing governance arrangements, and in many cases deepen economic inequalities and feelings of social injustice, fuelling conflict and undermining development (Ganson 2013).

Recognizing this dynamic, international donors fund a variety of good governance initiatives that aim to control irresponsible business practice and also enable a more predictable institutional framework to manage key economy sectors. The World Bank and the United Nations Environment Programme (UNEP), for example, have joined forces to work with conflict-affected and fragile states to consolidate all existing information on resource concession, infrastructure, land use and risk information into a single open-source platform (World Bank and UNEP 2013). The African Legal Support Facility, hosted by the African Development Bank, works to increase the capacity of African governments 'to negotiate and conclude fair and equitable arrangements for the management of Africa's natural resources and extractive industries' (ALSF 2008). Efforts such as these are typically rooted in the assumptions of a 'liberal' state. They are meant to help national governments better deal with the land, resource management and benefit-sharing questions that lie at the heart of conflicts over investments and address their impacts through better policy and regulation, institutions and human capacity within the government (Rodan 2007).

Drawing upon scholarly work on hybrid political orders and the dynamics of business investments in fragile states, this chapter explores the role that large-scale investments play in institutional reform in postwar contexts, and what unintended consequences they may trigger. It also examines the contributions businesses can make to strengthen the sustainability of institutional reform in postwar settings. The chapter finds that an international agenda which considers the state as the agent for the provision of security, welfare, justice and representation (Schwarz 2005; Call 2008; Ghani and Lockhart 2008) is out of sync with the de facto governance in postwar settings, putting them in conflict with one another. This leads to situations where the investments themselves, as well as international assistance programmes, intervene in a context with the wrong assumptions and inappropriate entry points. This often has perverse consequences, ranging from elite entrenchment to greater conflict risk and to the weakening of state and traditional institutions. However, we also find evidence that large-scale business investment can contribute to institutional reform, especially by supporting governance approaches using bottom-up and multi-stakeholder process designs that are more in tune with the de facto political orders. Thus, we provide a conceptual framework for understanding how such approaches, based on corporate self-interest in more predictability in an otherwise complex environment, can increase the sustainability of institutional reform and support the development of legitimate institutions that are more strongly rooted in the realities of the postwar context.

## Understanding hybrid political orders

The study of postwar institutional reform can draw on a recent wave of research regarding the evolution of governance arrangements in contexts that are often described as 'conflict-affected' or 'fragile' states (e.g. Menkhaus 2007; Call 2008; Reno 2008; North *et al.* 2009; Boege *et al.* 2009; Andrews 2014). Frequently based on years of field research, this literature underlines the importance of the de facto political orders in shaping development transitions. As part of this wave of research, the term 'hybrid political orders' has become a common reference for governance arrangements in conflict-affected and fragile states. In its policy guidance for statebuilding, the Organization for Economic Cooperation and Development (OECD) has even noted that 'the majority of states in the global South can [.] be described as hybrid political orders' (OECD 2011, 25). Yet the term sits uncomfortably with governments, international organizations and business because it implies an overlap of different forms of order competing with state or government power, and the existence of conflicting claims to legitimacy and economic resources. The term represents a departure from a focus on how states should be towards an emphasis on the de facto characteristics of governance systems (Wennmann 2010). Following this understanding, the state is considered not necessarily as the only provider of security, welfare and representation, but as one of multiple actors that provide authority, legitimacy and capacity, including transnational networks, strongmen or traditional institutions. The term 'hybrid' captures different nonstate forms of order and governance, including customary arrangements, and how they permeate each other in 'a different and genuine political order' (Boege *et al.* 2009, 606).

The logics of hybrid political orders may be illustrated by the historical experience of African states and work that has focused, for example, on 'closed-access orders', 'open-access orders', the 'political marketplace', the 'mediated state', 'pockets of effectiveness'; and 'ungoverned spaces'. The distinction between closed-access and open-access orders noted by North *et al.* (2009) is indicative of the difference between the working of institutions according to a liberal or hybrid framing of governance. According to their understanding, in closed-access orders, authorities limit access to valuable political and economic opportunities. Such barriers to entry enable authorities to create a credible commitment among elites not to fight each other because they are better off participating in a patrimonial network rather than violently challenging the authorities. Authorities also build relationships with a larger constituency of supporters through the provision of protection, welfare and justice. The concept is in contrast to open-access orders that structure access to political and economic opportunities in competitive terms through markets, elections and merit (North *et al.* 2009, 18–25).

Studies on hybrid political orders have cast new light on dynamics that are typically perceived as hostile to institutional reform through a liberal lens. Alex de Waal's writing on the 'political marketplace', for example, highlights the functions of patronage. He argues that 'a certain degree of patronage is normal and normative, but there is an excess amount that is considered unethical' (de Waal 2010, 12). Patronage may also be seen by a significant part of the population as a social fact of life and as legitimate. There may be an expectation in society that political leaders will use patronage to structure political power and reward followers. People living within the system may have more confidence in patronage politics (that they know) than formal state institutions (that they mistrust). Furthermore, patronage sometimes dispenses resources more rapidly and more fairly than international assistance or formal state services. Finally, patronage arrangements are far more resilient in times of crises and when formal systems fail (de Waal 2010, 2).

Similarly, drawing from experience in East Africa, Ken Menkhaus' work on the 'mediated state' emphasizes that 'the government relies on partnership (or at least coexistence) with a diverse range of local intermediaries and rival sources of authority to provide core functions of public security, justice, and conflict management' (Menkhaus 2007, 78). The 'mediated state' highlights that when a ruler or government has little capacity to impose control over a given territory – because it lacks either technical capacity or sufficient legitimacy – existing power realities foster governance arrangements based on deal making, co-option and subcontracting with whatever local nonstate authority is in power in a particular locality.

In other words, a state's inability or unwillingness to deliver justice or welfare services evenly to a population does not mean that these are not provided by someone else. In many contexts, state functions have been assumed by gangs, private networks, local militias, guerrilla armies or customary authorities, which can lead to countries being splintered into different zones of autonomy (Rapley 2006). Some of these actors may create their own insecurities and inefficiencies, but 'partly due to their success in providing security, these sub-state groups often become the most legitimate political authority in areas that they control' (Reno 2008, 143). In places where long-standing customary and traditional institutions generally enjoy higher confidence and loyalty than the national state, attempts to reinforce national structures may be perceived as steps towards less rather than more security by local populations that have been subject to generations of colonial and postcolonial predation.

Of course, state presence is not binary, even in a particular locality. The capacity of government in conflict-affected and fragile states is unequally distributed across the country, but also across spheres of government activity. This is underlined in public administration research on 'pockets of effectiveness'. These pockets are 'public organisations that are reasonably effective in carrying out their functions and in serving some conception of the public good despite operating in an environment in which most public organisations are ineffective and subject to serious predation [or] patronage' (Leonard 2008, 8). Such analysis reminds us that even though certain institutions may enjoy public confidence, those that relate more directly to the distribution of resources and the risks and benefits from them may not. Furthermore, contested control over the levers of government that control resources, their benefits and risks may undermine those functioning institutions that do exist.

Such an understanding of hybrid political orders requires us to take a step back from an image of so-called 'ungoverned' spaces:

> It is certainly the case that the broad stretches of real estate where tens of millions of people live beyond the effective reach of the state are dangerous and insecure places to live. But it is a serious misreading to label these areas as anarchic. In reality, communities are not passive victims in the face of state failure or collapse. They actively forge systems of security, law, deterrence of crime, conflict management and mutual support.
>
> (Menkhaus 2010, 181–182)

Since governance often occurs in ways that go undetected by outsiders and are very different from the expectations of Western observers, governance capacity often remains unrecognized or is simply labelled as 'chaos' (Duffield 2000, 82). Such perspectives do not adequately capture the mechanisms that order the political and social relations of fragile states and explain 'how things get done' despite the absence – from a Western perspective – of meaningful state legitimacy or institutional capacity. By contrast, taking into account the full landscape of power and authority helps us understand the perverse impacts of attempts to impose state structures upon existing hybrid political orders. We explore these impacts below.

## The dilemma of large-scale investment and institutional reform

The conceptual underpinnings of the literature on hybrid political orders represent an important reminder about the possible dynamics of institutional reforms in postwar contexts. Building on the record of development investments in fragile states, North *et al.* (2009) underlined how efforts to ensure positive development result in fragile states often failing to recognize hybrid political orders and the difference between 'closed-access' and 'open-access' orders. They also showed how interventions based on idealized liberal models tend to fail. They found that interveners try to transplant elements of the open-access order – such as competition, markets and democracy – directly into closed-access orders. The reforms threaten the rent creation that holds the society together and in many cases challenge the very logic upon which the society is organized. Not surprisingly, the elite and many nonelites resist, sabotage or subvert such reforms in closed-access societies that are not ready for them (North *et al.* 2007, 5).Therefore, exporting an open-access order into a closed-access order can have perverse effects that undermine the well-intentioned efforts of international donors or private investors.

The effects from transplanting open-access into closed-access orders have also been researched with respect to the political economy of statebuilding. A major comparative study on Afghanistan, the Democratic Republic of Congo, Guatemala, Kosovo and Pakistan underlined how political economy issues can 'freeze or reverse attempted reforms, create public insecurity and paralyse economic development' (Anten *et al.* 2012, 3). That study also found that

> institutional reforms that do not align with the prevailing interests and incentives of power-holders, or do not redirect these incentives so as to support the new formal arrangements, are liable to be subordinated to and incorporated within the logic of informal power and the political marketplace.
>
> (Anten *et al.* 2012, 4)

These political economy dynamics become especially virulent when multi-million-dollar investments hit conflict-affected and fragile states. Englebert and Portelance (2015) represent an exception to what is a relatively slim systematic evidence base. They found that by supporting elite agendas to exercise greater control over increased rents from large-scale commercial agriculture or other business activities, state-building that focuses on the areas of greatest interest to foreign investors may preserve rather than reform neopatrimonialism or government by patronage politics. Their quantitative analysis of GDP growth patterns in Africa noted that fast-growing economies do not score particularly well on governance measures (although they do score better than slow-growing ones); and that levels of foreign direct investment better explain differences between the groups (ibid.). Their qualitative analysis suggests that governments of these fast-growing economies focused on governance and institutional changes geared towards attracting large flows of investment – exactly the 'reforms' that are promoted by international institutions. However, such changes were made 'without any fundamental political restructuring' and avoided addressing broader domestic concerns over the distribution of benefits (ibid.). That analysis is echoed in critiques of institutional and governance reform in the agricultural sector. A primary focus of the G8 New Alliance for Food Security and Nutrition, launched in 2012 by 'African Heads of State and Government, corporate leaders and G8 members', is government policies 'that will facilitate responsible private investment in agriculture in support of smallholder farmers' (New Alliance for Food Security and Nutrition 2014), acting in particular 'to improve investment opportunities' (USAID 2012). However, human rights and development advocates have complained that the initiative simply 'aligns national policies to corporate interests' and 'disregards fundamental principles of transparency, participation and accountability'. For example, critics have questioned the complementarity of agricultural needs of smallholders and food security provisions of government action plans supported by the New Alliance, which focuses on investments in export crops grown on large plantations (Obenland 2014). Olivier de Schutter, former UN special rapporteur on the right to food, found that governments have been making promises to investors 'completely behind the screen', with 'no long-term view about the future of smallholder farmers' and without their participation (cf. Provost *et al.* 2014). To the extent that perceptions of unfairness in the economy underpin instability, such statebuilding efforts reinforce fragility.

Indeed, much statebuilding assistance appears to allow elites to further distance themselves economically from any need for popular support. It is too simple for entrenched elites to subvert the statebuilding agenda to their own ends. It has long been noted that even leaders of countries with no intention of effecting the changes promoted by international institutions become adept at the 'development speak' of liberal reform (Bayart 2000, 259). They may enact relatively minor measures that act 'as short-term signals that ensure developing countries attain and retain external support and legitimacy'. In fact, they are actually acting on the 'incentive to masquerade as the transformational leader needed to facilitate institutional reforms' provided by international assistance to 'further their own financial, political or administrative goals' (Andrews 2014, 2–3, 104). It is sometimes unclear whether international institutions are duped by their government counterparts or intentionally complicit in their actions. A global investigation led by the International Consortium of Investigative Journalists, involving over 50 journalists from 21 countries, estimated that 3.4 million people around the world were physically or economically displaced without respect for their human rights as part of World Bank-funded projects between 2004 and 2013; and that up to 30 per cent of projects the World Bank funded during that period were likely to cause resettlement (Chavkin *et al.* 2015). These projects included US$50 billion invested from 2009 to 2013 in projects with the highest risk rating for 'irreversible or unprecedented' social or environmental impact. However, the World Bank relied largely on promises from recipient governments to respect international guidelines to which they had agreed, with neither oversight nor enforcement mechanisms in place. A former lead specialist of the World Bank's Social Development

Department said, 'There was often no intent on the part of the governments to comply – and there was often no intent on the part of the bank's management to enforce' (Chavkin *et al.* 2015). The *Fundo Soberano de Angola* (Angolan Sovereign Wealth Fund) is a concrete example of how these dynamics play out in a postwar and oil-rich state. The fund stresses its 'commitment to Angola's social and economic development and capital preservation for its people' (Fundo Soberano de Angola 2015) and was described as 'a huge signal of discipline' (McGroarty 2013) by an economist of the World Bank, which had supported its establishment. However, with the Angolan president appointing his son as head of the fund and a business partner as the asset manager, it is hard to believe that the fund represents a meaningful shift in the country's economic regime towards more inclusive or peaceful development. As in many other fragile states, international statebuilding assistance helps ensure that Angolan 'institutions enabling and protecting rents extraction' are 'protected and buttressed', while the Angolan government itself ensures that 'institutions of power and revenue sharing' are 'side-lined and impaired', leading to 'monopolization, elite predation, and usurpation' (Amundsen 2014, 169).

There appears to be a broad and growing gap between the espoused purposes of liberal economic policy and institutions as supported by international statebuilding practice, and delivery on institutional reform by national governments. In many places this feeds growing disillusionment: 'When governments fail to deliver and there are allegations of corruption', concluded a study of conflict in the extractives industries, 'this increases the chances of populist movements or new governments calling for radical redistribution of wealth' (Stevens *et al.* 2013, 93). Recent work has documented over 90 significant political protests in the past decade in over 40 African countries (Branch and Mampilly 2015a), belying perceptions of populations that are 'too rural, too poor, and too trapped by tribalism to engage in popular, non-ethnic politics', and suggesting that the urban poor will be key drivers of political change (Branch and Mampilly 2015b). In Nicaragua, former Contra and Sandinista enemies have united to stop the construction of the Grand Interoceanic Canal that would displace them from their land, saying, 'We might go to war, not because we all want that, but because there is maybe no other option' (Stark 2015).

Importantly, these protests occur in countries characterized by democratic institutions as well as in nondemocratic states; the liberal political system is not delivering sufficient trust, cohesion or political consensus to reduce conflict risks. People on the ground appear to be responding to what the research is increasingly finding: even autocratic rulers with no intention of sharing power over the economy know that liberal institutions 'bestow onto their leaders a façade of democracy that enables them to maintain international and domestic legitimacy needed in today's day and age' (Kendall-Taylor and Frantz 2015, 78). These dynamics are well recognized in academic scholarship on 'quasi-states' and 'personal rule' in many African contexts (Jackson and Rosber 1982; Jackson 1990). Without the requisite political commitment, the façades of a liberal democracy do not lower overall repression levels, but instead enable autocrats to use repression in more targeted and less costly ways. Dictatorships with multiple parties and a legislature, for example, are more likely to use repression to target and punish specific opponents, but less likely to use it to indiscriminately restrict civil liberties. By increasing incentives to participate in the regime, these institutions provide dictators with an additional form of surgically-targeted political control.

(Kendall-Taylor and Frantz 2015, 78)

In fragile states, 'parties, legislatures, and elections' – typically supported by international statebuilding efforts – 'are enhancing the durability of autocracies' (ibid.).

Some international statebuilding aid tied to large-scale private investment has attempted to address this democratic deficit. Norway, for example, has supported an Angolan NGO to monitor public spending on education, health and agriculture, and to submit findings 'to the relevant parliamentary committees and ministries', as well as engage in other advocacy activities, with some signs of limited impact on government spending patterns (Tjonneland 2012, 6). However, the initiative can make no claim to addressing fundamental power dynamics or drivers of conflict. In Uganda, development organizations supported both the nonpartisan Parliamentary Forum on Oil and Gas as well as the Civil Society Coalition for Oil in Uganda to advocate for greater environmental and social safeguards, more robust financial oversight, and more limited ministerial powers. In addition, the Democratic Governance Facility – a basket fund of eight international development partners – funded public consultation processes to influence the institutional and regulatory framework (Ganson 2012). However, one may argue that these externally generated attempts to mimic democratic oversight have exacerbated rather than addressed conflict. The Ugandan executive has used its control through the ruling party over individual members to keep Parliament from significantly altering the government's legislative proposals, largely ignoring community and civil society concerns. During an address to Parliament in December 2012, President Museveni accused Members of Parliament and NGOs of 'acting on behalf of foreign interests' to 'cripple and disorient the development of Uganda's oil sector' (Oil in Uganda 2012). In April 2013, the National Resistance Movement – Uganda's ruling party – expelled four Members of Parliament for indiscipline, accusing two of them of belonging to the Parliamentary Forum on Oil and Gas, which it said was 'opposed to the National Resistance Movement's position on oil' (Mugerwa 2013). In 2014 the government renounced any civil society oversight of oil revenues earmarked for development priorities under the new public finance bill, and backpedalled on its commitments made in 2008 to join the Extractive Industries Transparency Initiative. The checks and balances of the liberal system, including political protests, are 'increasingly seen not as a basic form of democratic political action but rather as a threat that must be controlled' (Branch and Mampilly 2015b).

In sum, the research base and illustrative cases discussed above point to the multitude of unintended consequences – ranging from elite entrenchment and greater conflict risk to the weakening of state and traditional institutions – when international donors or private investors intervene to promote good governance based on incorrect assumptions about the nature of governance in a specific context. Anten *et al.* (2012, 11) emphasized that 'Who gains or loses from policies or political changes, or what common or contrasting material interests underlie political coalitions or competition, are among the most important questions to be asked in order to understand how a fragile state is governed'. Overall, this chapter suggests that scholarly work on hybrid political orders or political economy perspectives on statebuilding can help improve the understanding of the dynamics of large-scale investment and institutional reform. Despite this knowledge and the increasingly well-documented results of ill-fated interventions, 'there seems to be no viable alternative to some version of liberal peacebuilding' in contemporary international policy and practice (Paris 2012, 49). The imposition of economic models, laws and institutions upon societies in which there is no underlying consensus about their desirability or appropriate mechanisms for their implementation still often 'tests these institutions and the societies that depend on them, sometimes to breaking point' (Middlebrook 2012, 14).

## Institutional reform from the bottom up

Having reviewed the literature on hybrid political orders and revealed some of the complex dynamics of large-scale investment and institutional reform, one might question whether it is possible to think about large-scale investments as catalysts for constructive institutional reform. An answer may lie in changing the optics of how we understand the dynamics of reform processes. While liberal institutional reform has largely followed a top-down approach, the work on hybrid political order shows that it is possible to think about an alternative bottom-up approach. The lesson from our growing understanding of hybrid political orders for the governance of business and the economy may be a critique of the widespread conception of large-scale investment sites in conflict-affected and fragile states as contexts in which 'nothing works' and everything has to be built anew. The change of optic emphasizes existing governance capability as a potential connector and starting base for institutional reform in hybrid political orders. There may not be as great a need for fast construction of strong state institutions as for gradual, bottom-up change of 'the best of bad options' or imperfect governance arrangements. Such a process ideally nurtures the fusion of traditional and new state components through a progressive transformation process forged by means of transition pacts among multiple stakeholders (Wennmann 2010). Rather than relying on national authorities and structures, this process focuses on local stability premised on broad-based inclusion and legitimacy.

This bottom-up notion of governance transformations stands in contrast to the prevailing forms of international governance assistance that focuses on building state institutions from the top down, deliberately imposing a specific state model upon fragile states that performs certain functions and roles, particularly with regard to management of the economy. Traditionally, such an approach has been associated with the Washington Consensus, which focused on macroeconomic stabilization, trade liberalization, the opening of domestic markets to direct foreign investment and the privatization of state enterprises (Williamson 2008). Specific case experience makes such a record more concrete. In Uganda, for example, the UK's Department of International Development and the International Monetary Fund have primarily supported projects that develop the Ugandan government's capacity for revenue management with an increasing focus on oil. The government of Norway also offers the Ugandan government advice, funds various technical studies, and supports capacity building of the energy ministry and Petroleum Exploration and Production Department. This is part of Norway's broader Oil for Development Programme, which dispenses more than US$57 million annually to eight core countries and 11 noncore countries, primarily to strengthen state institutions (NORAD 2012). The UN Development Group's Guidance Note on Natural Resource Management in Transition Settings expresses what may be considered a typical mindset of such international development assistance, stating that 'Transition settings often provide unprecedented opportunities for transforming or building institutions anew', often on the basis of best practice examples (UNDG 2013, 8).

The prevailing model is usually understood as connecting the historical experience of European nations with Max Weber's classic definition of the state: 'a compulsory political organisation with continuous operations will be called a "state" insofar as its administrative staff successfully upholds the claim to the monopoly of the legitimate use of physical force in the enforcement of order' (Hay and Lister 2006, 8). From this perspective, state institutions manage state affairs and are distinct from civil society; they have their own interests, preferences and capacities. Weber's definition has rationalized the emphasis on the legitimacy of force used to constrain populations, state strategies to construct and sustain the use of force, the balance between coercion and consent of societies, and the mechanisms by which legitimacy may be established (Hay and Lister 2006).

The approaches of most international actors underline the continued application of Weber's understanding of the state, especially as they measure state capacity in terms of an absence of state attributes (institutions) and the delivery of state functions (security, welfare, justice and representation). This leads to language that classifies states, including postwar countries, as 'weak' or 'fragile' (see DFID 2005; USAID 2005; World Bank 2005). The Framework and Guidelines on Land Policy in Africa, for example, is a joint product of the African Union, the African Development Bank and the Economic Commission for Africa of the United Nations, and purports to be 'a consensus on land issues' in Africa (AUC-ECA-AfDB Consortium 2010, xi). However, it takes no cognizance of the hybrid nature of land governance in Africa or the centre–periphery, traditional–formal state conflicts that these de facto governance arrangements engender. International institutions sometimes attempt to take a more holistic view. For example, the United Nations Interagency Framework Team for Preventive Action Guidance on Strengthening Capacity for Conflict-Sensitive Natural Resource Management has identified the need to work with governments to build the capacity of and mediate among different stakeholders, and to assist civil society to participate in the natural resource management process at all levels (2012, 6–7). Nonetheless, even this approach to inclusion assumes a known and knowable nation state.

These perceptions mainly reflect what outsiders perceive that the state ought to be: the vision of strong state structures held accountable by parliamentary oversight and an engaged civil society supported by donors and development agencies. They do not necessarily reflect what the state or the system of governance actually is, as discussed in the previous section on hybrid political orders. In the context of contested governance surrounding large-scale investment sites, however, it is crucial to note that the role of the state may be in conflict among communities, various levels of government, and between formal government and traditional authorities. Official state authorities will depict some of their competitors for power and authority as 'illegitimate', questioning their patriotism and their motives. Yet the investment area for a mine, commercial farm or hydroelectric plant will often be in a region where the formally recognized government has the lowest level of legitimacy as perceived by local constituencies, which complicates questions about its governance. Statebuilding approaches – rather than the neutral, positive activity envisaged by donors and development actors – may constitute taking sides in an ongoing struggle over the nature of the state, the control of resources, and the distribution of risks and benefits.

The literature on hybrid political orders discussed above suggests that this top-down approach may not be the only or the most effective approach to the governance of large-scale investments in fragile environments. The OECD Policy Guidance states that even if 'various sources and forms of state legitimacy are unlikely to reinforce each other', it is only in extreme cases that such hybrid orders lead to sustained violence or state collapse (OECD 2011, 25). Outside this extreme, hybrid political orders are neither inevitably fragile nor ridden by violence and conflict:

> Societies continue to function, to form institutions, to negotiate politically, and to set and meet expectations. Traditional forms of authority are not necessarily inimical to the development of rules-based political systems. [.] In fact, the challenge is to understand how traditional and formal systems interact in any particular context, and to look for ways of constructively combining them.
>
> (OECD 2011, 25)

Such 'ways of constructive combination' may suggest the possibility of a bottom-up approach (Wennmann 2010, 19–20). Under such a construct, institutional reform would not prioritize the replacement of a particular hybrid political order with a more effective order of a national state, or a closed-access with an open-access order noted by North *et al.* (2009). It would also not concern the export of a specific governance model. Rather, it would prioritize coalition building in a specific location among local stakeholders and communities, central governments, domestic and multinational companies, and the international community that nurture a fusion of traditional, informal and new governance components through a progressive transformation process. This bottom-up approach connects to the strengths that exist in societies in contexts of weak states (Migdal 1988) and also to the research findings emphasizing the importance of 'problem-driven iterative adaptation' processes in explaining successful public sector reforms in developing countries (Andrews 2015). Anten *et al.* (2012) emphasize that bottom-up approaches locate the starting point for reform in the local political economy underlining the interests and incentives for change, as well as the benefits and losses from change, of existing power holders. A bottom-up approach focuses on existing capacities and what works at the municipal and district level, rather than what is lacking or failing at the national level. Such an approach recognizes that informal governance arrangements can provide classic state services such as protection, justice or welfare – sometimes even more effectively than the state itself – and realize the endurance of 'the underlying logic of informal power' in postwar situations (Anten *et al.* 2009, 4).

## Business and institutional reform in hybrid political orders

Few empirical studies have developed systematic case analyses regarding the interaction of large-scale investment projects with local hybrid political orders. The work by Hönke (2010) and Atanasijevic (2016) on the Democratic Republic of Congo are two notable exceptions. However, there is sufficient secondary literature available that allows for a better understanding of the relationship between hybrid political orders and large-scale investments. This is an issue that is usually beyond the reach of the public domain and one that few actors involved like to speak publicly about. Information often remains within the personal experience of company managers who are responsible for operating large-scale investment projects in fragile states, but can be usefully aggregated and drawn upon (Ganson 2013, 2014). Overall, there is meaningful (albeit largely anecdotal) evidence for the conceptual argument that bottom-up institutional reform can prove more effective than traditional liberal statebuilding efforts in the context of large-scale business activities in postwar and other fragile environments.

From the perspective of large-scale investors, the tension between the top-down governance reform promoted by international institutions and donors and the bottom-up approaches that may prove more effective raises several contentious issues. Most international legal mechanisms governing investment are informed by governance that takes a liberal, Weberian-type state model as a starting point (Carbonnier and Wennmann 2013). Companies often enter into the fray of fragile state conflict as allies of the most powerful elements of the national government that has provided, for example, the land for agricultural development or the concession agreement for a mine which is located in many cases far away from the national capital. International financing and political risk insurance may also require certain understandings with the national capital, sealed by bilateral or multilateral investment treaties among recognized state actors. Whether companies are intentionally or unintentionally supporting entrenched players, companies and their backers can feed existing conflict dynamics related to struggles for authority and legitimacy as they secure legal permission to operate. The resulting exacerbation of conflict with stakeholders who have different ideas about the social and political ordering should not be surprising.

Even if as a legal entity a business must align itself with the formal legal order, it must work as an operating entity within the specific political order present at a specific investment site. Representative of such experience is what a manager working in Mongolia said as part of a series of interviews about management in complex environments:

> While a legal framework must be negotiated with the national government, it is important not to confuse that with the agreement required from directly affected communities and their leaders. You should assume that customary law takes over 15 kilometres outside the capital and act accordingly.
> (Ganson 2013, 97)

Companies thereby find themselves connecting to different power relationships within the hybrid political order. Here, the international focus is often on the darker side of contests for power between an acknowledged (if imperfect) state and actors widely viewed as illegitimate; for example, warlords, gangs or local militias. Functional or pragmatic approaches to governance (Booth 2012; de Sardan 2008) may rationalize relationships in the Democratic Republic of Congo and elsewhere where de facto governance must be acknowledged in order to conduct business at all, even where such relationships legitimize unsavoury actors. But even where the local power is morally less problematic, such as a regional or traditional authority, companies and those concerned with business in fragile environments must acknowledge that they become a part of the hybrid political order and affect the (largely unwritten) rules and regimes governing business.

In addition, a business's presence and operations will surface and exacerbate latent conflicts that have at their core unresolved questions of ownership and governance among other actors in the system. These will be predictably pronounced where lands and livelihoods are implicated; for example, whose land the drilling rig is on and therefore who receives royalty payments, or whether in-migrants from neighbouring regions of the same country are considered 'local' for the purposes of company job preference or purchasing schemes. However, the imagined promises of large-scale investment and the fear of being left out can also have more generalized consequences; for example, among the fishermen who had coexisted across the Congo–Uganda border until oil was discovered, but who then found it necessary to defend their ill-defined border (Ganson 2012). In such cases the business is not the direct cause of conflicts nor particularly desirous of taking sides: it did not create the land conflict and it does not necessarily seek to avoid a royalty payment to someone. Nevertheless, it is caught up in the contest for the legitimacy and power to decide such issues.

Where large-scale business investments exacerbate poorly governed sociopolitical conflicts, the consequences can be disastrous for both companies and local populations. Newmont Mining has no access to attributive reserves of 6.5 million ounces of gold and 1,690 million pounds of copper from its US$4.8 billion Conga mine project in Peru because of local and regional political opposition. This is despite national government support for the project and declarations from the capital that communities 'unanimously' supported operations and that the opposition leader was 'no longer relevant' (Emery 2013). The project had 'become a lightning rod for larger debates about whether mining can benefit local communities without damaging the environment and whether or not national economic interests should trump local opposition to mining activities' (Trefis Team 2013), with serious implications for Newmont's production targets, revenues, reputation and share price, as well as for politics in Peru. The 2012 Marikana massacre in South Africa, in which government security forces killed dozens of striking platinum workers at a Lonmin mine, caused the company share price to drop 7 per cent overnight. The industry as well as the affected workers and communities remain in a protracted crisis punctuated by recurrent violence (Powell 2014).

Therefore, business calls for better governance of sociopolitical tensions, as well as their expression in initiatives such as the Extractive Industries Transparency Initiative (EITI), must be taken somewhat seriously as exercises in self-preservation. A company will focus on governance in the first instance because it directly benefits from a stable operating environment. Corporate discussions of 'political risk management' – that is, preventing possible negative impacts upon the business from geopolitics, sociopolitical developments, government action or stakeholder pressure – may seem foreign to government and NGO actors. But this may be largely a problem of lexicon. Increasingly international scrutiny of company behaviour by media, socially responsible investors, civil society actors and others also serves to keep governance issues on senior management agendas.

Nevertheless, many businesses approach the issue of institutional reform from a fundamentally government-centric perspective. In this sense, business reform efforts suffer from many of the same challenges as the approaches of the international donor and development community. Business frequently works on the premise that 'if only government would use tax money wisely, provide public services, or mediate policy conflicts, our business would be able to prosper and people would see the benefits'. The underlying premise of the business-supported EITI, for example, is to apply a global model to the challenges of government accountability for resource revenues and resulting conflicts. This draws upon the preference of business to work in well-regulated markets in which the rules of the game are spelled out in national laws or international standards. Such thinking also builds from the tendency to conflate the need for effective governance for post-conflict recovery with 'statebuilding' in the business and peace agenda (Bray 2006). However, for many companies working in the extractive, large-scale agriculture or construction sectors, prospective investment areas are simply far removed from contexts in which such conditions are the norm.

Consequently, some businesses are learning that 'colouring outside the lines' of formal government processes and institutions can achieve more positive results.

Corporate experience in this way to some extent mirrors the increasing focus on strong local networks and institutions as developed in the emerging literature on resilience (Jütersonke and Kartas 2012; Menkhaus 2013; Milliken 2013). Historically, company engagement with local communities has often been associated with paternalistic provision of services. However, more recent approaches have attempted to empower communities through shared ownership of the social investment process. For example, a company may enter into a memorandum of understanding that provides a multi-stakeholder forum controlled by the community itself with stable, multi-year financing to pursue its own agenda with its own partners of choice. Chevron's use of this approach in Nigeria, for example, has reduced violence and led to better development outcomes (Hoben *et al*. 2012). It may be difficult for companies to transition to local decision-making systems that they do not control, but results appear to be encouraging.

Corporate practice also underlines that governance challenges not only relate to contested land or water use, distribution of benefits, pollution or health and safety; they also relate to a struggle for control over the future vision for the community and the resources to implement it. The World Bank's 2003 Extractive Industries Review concluded that 'Many grievances from communities and especially from indigenous peoples living near extractive industries projects relate to their claims that their rights to participate in, influence, and share control over development initiatives, decisions, and resources are ignored' (EIR 2003, 18). Over the past decade, ensuring 'community consent' has become a formal requirement of multiple instruments such as by 'the broad community support standard' of the International Finance Corporation following the 2007 United Nations Declaration on the Rights of Indigenous Peoples, or as a more general condition of stable operations as characterized by the United Nations Global Compact launched in 1999. In this way, institutions and authorities outside of the state are recognized and legitimized.

Also congruent with a broader governance agenda is an evolving interest among businesses with operations in difficult markets to widen their vision from 'safe operations' to 'safe communities'. In practice, this means expanding the focus on the safety of people, assets and operations directly linked to the company to include broader investments in community capacities to respond to conflict and risk factors from whatever source. In South Africa, for example, conflict resolution mechanisms developed to settle labor–management disputes during the apartheid era expanded their remit to include political violence in the townships. In one case, this led to 'a total cessation of politically related deaths for six months in a community in which 300 people had died in political violence in only 18 months' (Hirschsohn 1996, 142). Elsewhere, as in South Africa, this shift may be partly attributed to the painful experiences of some companies in violent contexts, the costs and limitations of traditional security arrangements, and the quest for new strategies to make long-term investments in conflict-prone, but emerging, economies more sustainable.

At least implicitly, companies appear to be acknowledging their role as another source of power and authority in the hybrid political order. Where there is competition for legitimacy, the study of hybrid political orders teaches us that local power brokers can be particularly influential (Menkhaus 2014; Wennmann 2014). The company efforts discussed above may be understood at least partially as attempts to promote a new source of influence in a hybrid political order. While often imperfect, company efforts demonstrate the possibility for a more positive, or at least benign, role in support of institutional reform from the bottom up. Such contribution would be rooted in local frameworks that balance the company goal of operational stability with the imperatives of other stakeholders that matter for a specific investment location.

As underlined by this emerging corporate practice, some quarters have seen a 'paradigm shift from the "good governance" agenda of neo-liberal statebuilding to a focus on "arrangements that work"' (Meagher *et al.* 2014, 2). This may be partly a reflection of 'what matters is the function, rather than the form of institutions' – a principle that is broadly accepted by development practitioners (Centre for the Future State 2010, 21). In the context of large-scale investments, the emphasis on function rather than form underlines the importance that the legitimate needs of stakeholders are met even in the absence of a legitimate, uncontested state. Successful business-centric initiatives in postwar and other fragile states have frequently borrowed liberally from peacebuilding and development practices that similarly focus on function over form. These approaches may be described in general terms as a set of interconnected building blocks: institutionalized mechanisms or networks for monitoring the local context; the rallying of diverse and sometimes conflicting local stakeholders around higher quality data and more trustworthy analysis; dialogue that builds sufficient consensus for action; proactive conflict prevention and resolution interventions; and a backbone support organization that facilitates expert and neutral assistance (Ganson and Wennmann 2012). Unlike liberal international statebuilding, which appears to largely ignore the political economy of fragile states themselves, the above-mentioned approaches succeed despite conditions of social divisions, weak institutions, a lack of trust in government, legacies of grievance from the past, pressing socioeconomic challenges, or the presence of spoilers. They manage fragility by engaging parties on the basis of their partisan interests and desires to mitigate their own risks; creating vertical linkages from local conflicts to influential actors at regional, national or international levels; building from existing social and political capital and functioning institutions, whether formal or informal; and providing outside intervention in more acceptable forms of expertise and advice. These approaches are explored in more detail elsewhere (Ganson and Wennmann 2016).

When these elements come together, the emerging evidence suggests that stability and development can take hold even in postwar and other fragile environments. As an example of this thinking, Chevron in the Niger Delta organizes its community relations under General Memorandums of Understanding with eight Regional Development Councils representing clusters of communities. Each has a project review committee to identify, develop and implement community development projects; an accounts and audit committee to ensure transparency; and a peacebuilding committee. Chevron further supports initiatives that 'focus on engaging and empowering local actors in peace and conflict mitigation', explicitly contrasting 'the traditional donor-driven, top-down approach to peacebuilding implementation' with their 'local efforts that address the salient conflict risk factors' (Chevron 2015). Coordination of local, national and international interventions in the region is facilitated by comprehensive mapping of conflict risks and efforts to address them. These approaches, overall, have 'given community stakeholders a larger role in setting the terms of the conversation, and the process for interacting'. They provide a 'greater sense of fairness' that 'creates some of the key conditions for productive interaction and problem solving' (Hoben *et al.* 2012). This has notably contributed to a dramatic reduction in violence, both against company facilities and among communities that had previously considered themselves pitted against one another (ibid).

## Conclusion: the case for private approaches to public governance

To some extent, the dominant approach to business and institutional reform in hybrid political orders is one of attempting to 'eat the whole elephant' of good governance and good government at once. In many contexts, state institutions are created and developed, including their human resources, while at the same time efforts are made to empower civil society to play a counterbalancing role. The challenge of this approach is that it requires all parts of the system to work in harmony. It is a chain that is only as strong as its weakest link. Therefore, the agenda for institutional reform is easily undermined by patrimonial governance, rent seeking, competition for power and resources, or corruption – dynamics that we have discussed building on the literature on hybrid political orders and which are particularly starkly visible in the postwar political economy. The very factors that make a context fragile also frustrate well-meaning efforts to make the context less fragile. In addition, governments and institutions, both nationally and internationally, may not be able to change their optics and their actions within any reasonable time period to support more context-driven approaches to managing conflicts over authority and legitimacy of competing actors in the sociopolitical sphere. Given the scale and scope of business investment in fragile environments, this presents a crisis of governance.

   Connecting the literature on hybrid political orders and the dynamics of large-scale business in fragile environments to selected positive examples of intentional efforts by business to support multi-stakeholder governance processes, this chapter provides at least preliminary evidence that private efforts based on self-interest have perhaps a better chance of breaking the institutional reform deadlock in hybrid political orders. History, too, provides some hopeful examples of business creating schemes for private governance in ways that eventually led to legitimate and enduring state institutions. As far back as medieval Europe, merchants developed a system of private law and regulations, tribunals to administer them and means of enforcing judgments. This private *lex mercatoria* provided the foundation for the contemporary public law of international commerce (Héritier 2002). More recently, in pre-democratic South Africa, private companies in the 1980s worked with new black unions to create entirely private arrangements for worker dispute resolution, recognizing that workers could not acknowledge any authority of the apartheid regime or trust its institutions. The apartheid-era Independent Mediation Service of South Africa provided the blueprint for the Commission on Conciliation, Mediation and Arbitration in the new dispensation (Hirschsohn 1996). Combined with the conceptual framework developed in this chapter, such examples suggest the possibility of private actors leading institutional reform from the bottom up.

Promoting such bottom-up reforms, of course, requires an admission that business is part and parcel of the hybrid political order, and that its actions are therefore inherently political. This remains difficult to swallow for many actors, whether in the corporate boardroom, UN headquarters or civil society forums. However, at least at the level of corporate policy, most global companies that are active in fragile environments acknowledge that it is in their best interest to manage their own operations in ways that help strengthen dispute resolution and governance institutions. This is reflected in an ever-growing opus of voluntary and multi-stakeholder initiatives. Furthermore, company leaders increasingly recognize that they are stakeholders in broader efforts to promote long-term sociopolitical stability, and that this requires a capacity to work locally with both public officials and the communities impacted by their operations. In this sense, there is a nascent understanding of 'business in society' – even if that society is a postwar hybrid political order – rather than 'business and society'.

Still, there is a gap to close in terms of appreciation of the benefits of adopting a more positive appreciation of hybrid political orders. The dominant viewpoint still understands these orders as something deficient, undesirable and dangerous – which they surely are in some circumstances – and therefore to be extinguished with an emphasis on top-down statebuilding. Yet the encouraging practice examples described in this chapter suggest a contrary view. It is possible to find pragmatic solutions to advance institutional reform, despite the many constraints of conflict-affected and fragile contexts. One starting point is to acknowledge the richness of the sociopolitical landscape and the political power of business. It is then possible to see how they interact to create interests and incentives for institutional reform in the hybrid political orders that surround large-scale investment contexts. This chapter has highlighted the theoretical and evidentiary touchstones for bottom-up approaches that appear to increase the sustainability of institutional reform and support the development of legitimate government institutions that are more strongly rooted in their own context. In doing so, it aspires to open a window on new avenues for research and practice.

## References

ALSF (African Legal Support Facility) (2008) *Agreement for the Establishment of the African Legal Support Facility*, available at: www.afdb.org/en/topics-and-sectors/initiatives-partnerships/african-legal-support-facility/ (accessed 24 August 2015).

Amundsen, Inge (2014) 'Drowning in Oil: Angola's Institutions and the "Resource Curse".' *Comparative Politics* 46(2): 169–189.

Andrews, Matt (2014) *The Limits of Institutional Reform in Development: Changing Rules for Realistic Solutions.* Cambridge: Cambridge University Press.

Andrews, Matt (2015) 'Explaining Politive Deviance in Public Sector Reforms in Development'. *World Development* 74: 197–208.

Anten, Louise, Ivan Briscoe and Marco Mezzera (2012) *The Political Economy of State-building in Situations of Fragility and Conflict: From Analysis to Strategy.* The Hague: Netherlands Institute of International Relations 'Clingendael'.

Atanasijevic, Lara (2016) *Natural Resource Governance in Hybrid Political Orders: The Cases of North Kivu and Katanga.* CCDP Working Paper 12. Geneva: Graduate Institute of International and Development Studies.

AUC-ECA-AfDB, African Union Commission, Economic Commission on Africa, and African Development Bank Consortium (2010) *Framework and Guidelines on Land Policy in Africa.* Addis Ababa: AUC-ECA-AfDB Consortium.

Bayart, Jean-François (2000) 'Africa in the World: A History of Extraversion'. *African Affairs* 99(395): 217–267.

Boege, Volker, Anne Brown, Kevin Clements and Anna Nolan (2009) 'Building Peace and Political Community in Hybrid Political Orders'. *International Peacekeeping* 16(5): 599–615.

Booth, David (2012) *Development as a Collective Action Problem. Addressing the Real Challenges of African Governance. Synthesis Report of the Africa Power and Politics Programme.* London: Overseas Development Institute.

Branch, Adam and Zachariah Mampilly (2015a) *Africa Uprising: Popular Protest and Political Change.* London: Zed Books.

Branch, Adam and Zachariah Mampilly (2015b) 'Africa Uprising – Popular Protest and Political Change – Interview With the Authors'. *African Arguments*, 23 March, available at: http://allafrica.com/stories/201503241488.html (accessed 24 August 2015).

Bray, John (2006) *Public–Private Partnerships in State-building and Recovery from Conflict.* ISP BP 06/01. London: Chatham House International Security Programme.

Call, Charles T. (2008) 'Ending Wars, Building States'. In Charles T. Call with Vanessa Wyeth (eds), *Building States to Build Peace.* Boulder, CO: Lynne Rienner, pp. 1–22.

Carbonnier, Gilles and Achim Wennmann (2013) 'Natural Resource Governance and Hybrid Political Orders'. In David Chandler and Timothy D. Sisk (eds), *Routledge Handbook of International Statebuilding.* London: Routledge, pp. 208–218.

Centre for the Future State (2010) *An Upside Down View of Governance.* Brighton: Institute for Development Studies.

Chavkin, Sasha, Ben Hallman, Michael Hudson, Cécile Schilis-Gallego and Shane Sifflett (2015) *Evicted and Abandoned: How the World Bank Broke its Promise to Protect the Poor.* Washington, DC: International Consortium of Investigative Journalists and Huffington Post, available at: http://projects.huffingtonpost.com/worldbank-evicted-abandoned (accessed 24 August 2015).

Chevron (2015) *Partners for Peace in the Niger Delta.* Available at: http://p4p-nigerdelta. org/about (accessed 24 August 2015).

de Sardan, Jean-Pierre O. (2008) *Researching the Practical Norms of Real Governance in Africa.* Discussion Paper 5, Africa, Power and Politics Programme. London: Overseas Development Institute.

de Waal, A. (2010) 'Fixing the Political Marketplace: How Can We Make Peace without Functioning State Institutions? The Chr. Michelsen Lecture 2009, available at: www.cmi.no/news/?557=fixing-the-political-market-place (accessed 2 June 2011).

DFID (Department for International Development) (2005) *Why we Need to Work More Effectively in Fragile States*. London: DFID.

Duffield, Mark (2000) 'Globalisation, Transborder Trade, and War Economies'. In Mats Berdal and David M. Malone (eds), *Greed and Grievance: Economic Agendas in Civil Wars*. Boulder, CO: Lynne Rienner, pp. 69–90.

EIR (Extractive Industries Review) (2003) *Striking a Better Balance: The World Bank Groups and the Extractive Industries – Volume I*. Washington, DC: EIR.

Emery, Alex (2013) 'Newmont's Minas Conga Project Could Restart in 2014, Government Says'. *BN Americas*, 30 December, available at: www.bnamericas.com/news/mining/newmonts-minas-conga-project-could-restart-in-2014-government-says1 (accessed 14 May 2014).

Englebert, Pierre and Gailyn Portelance (2015) *The Growth–Governance Paradox in Africa. Africaplus*, available at: https://africaplus.wordpress.com/2015/01/06/the-growth-governance-paradox-in-africa (accessed 24 August 2015).

Fundo Soberano de Angola (2015) 'Fundo Soberano de Angola', available at: www.fundosoberano.ao/language/en/ (accessed 24 August 2015).

Ganson, Brian (2012). *Risk and Risk Mitigation in the Oil and Gas Sector in Uganda*. Research Report for the Geneva Peacebuilding Platform. Geneva: Geneva Peacebuilding Platform.

Ganson, Brian (ed.) (2013) *Management in Complex Environments: Questions for Leaders*. Stockholm: International Council of Swedish Industry.

Ganson, Brian (2014) 'Business in Fragile Environments: Capabilities for Conflict Prevention'. *Negotiation and Conflict Management Research* 7(2): 121–139.

Ganson, Brian and Achim Wennmann (2012) *Confronting Risk, Mobilizing Action: A Framework for Conflict Prevention in the Context of Large-scale Business Investments*. Berlin: FES International Policy Analysis.

Ganson, Brian and Achim Wennmann (2016) *Business and Conflict in Fragile States: The Case for Pragmatic Solutions*. London: Routledge for the International Institute for Strategic Studies.

Ghani, Ashraf and Clare Lockhart (2008) *Fixing Failed States: A Framework for Rebuilding a Fractured World*. Oxford: Oxford University Press.

Gündüz, Canan and Charlotte Vaillant (2006) *Addressing the Economic Dimensions of Peacebuilding through Trade and Support to Private Enterprise*. London: International Alert.

Hay, Colin and Michael Lister (2006) 'Introduction: Theories of the State'. In Colin Hay, Michel Lister and David Marsh (eds), *The State: Theories and Issues*. Basingstoke: Palgrave Macmillan, pp. 1–20.

Héritier, Adrienne (2002) *Common Goods: Reinventing European Integration Governance*. Boulder, CO: Rowman and Littlefield.

Hirschsohn, Philip (1996) 'Negotiating a Democratic Order in South Africa: Learning from Mediation and Industrial Relations. *Negotiation Journal* 12(2): 139–150.

Hoben, Merrick, David Kovick, David Plumb and Justin Wright (2012) *Corporate and Community Engagement in the Niger Delta: Lessons Learned from Chevron Nigeria Limited's GMOU Process*. Cambridge, MA: Consensus Building Institute.

Hönke, Jana (2010) 'New Political Topographies: Mining Companies and Indirect Discharge in Southern Katanga (DRC)'. *Politique Africaine* 120(4): 105–127.

Jackson, Robert H. (1990) *Quasi-states: Sovereignty, International Relations, and the Third World.* Cambridge: Cambridge University Press.

Jackson, Robert H. and Carl G. Rosberg (1982) *Personal Rule in Black Africa: Prince, Autocrat, Prophet, Tyrant.* Berkeley: University of California Press.

Jütersonke, Oliver and Moncef Kartas (2012) *Resilience: Conceptual Reflections.* Brief 6. Geneva: Geneva Peacebuilding Platform.

Kendall-Taylor, Andrea and Erica Frantz (2015) 'Mimicking Democracy to Prolong Autocracies. *The Washington Quarterly* 37(4): 71–84.

Leonard, David K. (2008) *Where are "Pockets" of Effective Agencies Likely in Weak Governance States and Why? A Propositional Inventory.* Working Paper 306. Brighton: Institute of Development Studies.

Mac Sweeny, Naomi (2008) *Private Sector Development in Post-conflict Countries: A Review of Current Literature and Practice.* London: Donor Committee for Economic Development.

McGroarty, Patrick (2013) 'Angola Wealth Fund is a Family Affair'. *The Wall Street Journal*, 26 February, available at: www.wsj.com/articles/SB10001424127887323864 3045783186833743 19560 (accessed 24 August 2015).

Meagher, Kate, Tom De Herdt and Kristof Titeca (2014) *Unraveling Public Authority Paths of Hybrid Governance in Africa.* London: IS Academy.

Menkhaus, Ken (2007) 'Governance without Government in Somalia: Spoilers, State Building, and the Politics of Coping. *International Security* 31(3): 74–106.

Menkhaus, Ken (2010) 'State Failure and Ungoverned Space'. In Mats Berdal and Achim Wennmann (eds), *Ending Wars, Consolidating Peace: Economic Perspectives.* London: Routledge for the International Institute for Strategic Studies, pp. 171–188.

Menkhaus, Ken (2013) *Making Sense of Resilience in Peacebuilding Contexts: Approaches, Applications, Implications.* Paper 6. Geneva: Geneva Peacebuilding Platform.

Menkhaus, Ken (2014) 'Local Governance and Peacebuilding'. In Alexander Ramsbotham and Achim Wennmann (eds), *Legitimacy and Peace Processes: From Coercion to Consent.* ACCORD 25. London: Conciliation Resources, pp. 74–77.

Middlebrook, Peter (2012) *Building a 'Fragile Consensus': Liberalisation and State Fragility.* Paris: OECD.

Migdal, Joel S. (1988) *Strong Societies and Weak States: State–Society Relations and State Capabilities in the Third World.* Princeton, NJ: Princeton University Press.

Milliken, Jennifer (2013) *Resilience: From Metaphor to an Action Plan for the Peacebuilding Field.* Paper 7. Geneva: Geneva Peacebuilding Platform.

Mugerwa, Yasiin (16 April 2013) 'Repeat of History as NRM Expels "Rebel" MPs'. *Daily Monitor* (Kampala), available at: http://mobile.monitor.co.ug/News/Repeat-of-history-as-NRM-expels--rebel--MPs/-/691252/1749452/-/format/xhtml/-/83ws7c/-/index.html (accessed 11 May 2016).

New Alliance for Food Security and Nutrition (2014) *Progress Report 2013–2014.* Washington, DC: USAID.

NORAD (2012) *Facing the Resource Curse: Norway's Oil for Development Program.* Report 6/2012. Oslo: NORAD.

North, Douglas C., John J. Wallis and Barry R. Weingast (2009) *Violence and Social Orders: A Conceptual Framework for Interpreting Recorded Human History.* Cambridge: Cambridge University Press.

North, Douglas C., John J. Wallis, Steven B. Webb and Barry R. Weingast (2007) *Limited Access Orders in the Developing World: A New Approach to the Problem of*

*Development*. Policy Research Working Paper No. 4359. Washington, DC: The World Bank.

Obenland, Wolfgang (2014) *Corporate Influence through the G8 New Alliance for Food Security and Nutrition in Africa*. Aachen, Berlin and Bonn: MISEREOR, Brot für die Welt and Global Policy Forum.

OECD (Organization for Economic Cooperation and Development) (2011) *Supporting Statebuilding in Situations of Conflict and Fragility: Policy Guidance*. Paris: OECD.

Oil in Uganda (14 Dec 2012). *Museveni Lashes Civic Critics and Foreigners, Praises Oil Scientists*. Available at: www.oilinuganda.org/features/civil-society/museveni-lashes-civic-critics-and-foreigners-praises-oil-scientists.html (accessed 11 May 2016).

Paris, Roland (2012) 'Saving Liberal Peacebuilding'. In David J. Francis (ed.), *When War Ends: Building Peace in Divided Communities*. Aldershot: Ashgate, pp. 27–58.

Powell, Anita (2014) 'Pressure, Tension Grow in South Africa Miners' Strike. *Voice of America*, 15 May, available at: www.voanews.com/content/pressure-tension-grow-in-south-africa-miners-strike/1915332.html (accessed 24 August 2015).

Provost, Claire, Liz Ford and Mark Tran (2014) 'G8 Alliance Condemned as New Wave of Colonialism in Africa'. *Guardian*, 18 February, available at: www.theguardian.com/global-development/2014/feb/18/g8-new-alliance-condemned-new-colonialism (accessed 24 August 2015).

Rapley, John (2006) 'The New Middle Ages'. *Foreign Affairs* 85(3): 95–105.

Reno, William (2008) 'Bottom-up Statebuilding?' In Charles T. Call with Vanessa Wyeth (eds), *Building States to Build Peace*. Boulder, CO: Lynne Rienner, pp. 143–162.

Rodan, Jenick (2007) 'How to Negotiate an Oil Agreement'. In Macartan Humphreys, Jeffrey D. Sachs and Joseph E. Stiglitz (eds), *Escaping the Resource Curse*. New York: Columbia University Press, pp. 89–113.

Schwarz, Rolf (2005) 'Post-conflict Peacebuilding: The Challenges of Security, Welfare and Representation'. *Security Dialogue* 36(4): 429–446.

Stark, Nehemia (2015) 'In Pictures: Nicaraguan Farmers Resist Grand Canal, the World's Largest Construction Project'. *Guardian*, 4 April, available at: www.theguardian.com/world/2015/apr/04/nicaragua-farmers-contra-sandinista-resist-grand-canal-construction (accessed 24 August 2015).

Stevens, Paul, Jaakko Kooroshy, Glada Lahn and Bernice Lee (2013) *Conflict and Coexistence in the Extractives Industries*. Chatham House Report. London: Royal Institute of International Affairs.

Tjonneland, Elling (2012) *The Norwegian People's Aid, Oil and Development: A Review of Oil for the Common Good (2007–2011)*. CMI Report 2012: 5. Oslo: CMI.

Trefis Team (2013) *Newmont's Conga Project in Peru Faces Uncertain Fate*. *Forbes*, 12 April, available at: www.forbes.com/sites/greatspeculations/2013/04/12/newmonts-conga-project-in-peru-fates-uncertain-fate/ (accessed 24 August 2015).

UNDG (United Nations Development Group) (2013) *Natural Resource Management in Transition Settings*. Guidance note. New York: UNDG.

United Nations Interagency Framework Team for Preventive Action (2012) *Strengthening Capacity for Conflict-sensitive Natural Resource Management*. New York: UNDP.

USAID (United States Agency for International Development) (2005) *Fragile States Strategy*. Washington, DC: USAID.

USAID (2012) *The New Alliance for Food Security and Nutrition: Fact Sheet*. Washington: USAID.

Wennmann, Achim (2010) *Grasping the Strengths of Fragile States: Aid Effectiveness between 'Top-down' and 'Bottom-up' Statebuilding.* CCDP Working Paper 6. Geneva: Graduate Institute of International and Development Studies.

Wennmann, Achim (2014) 'Negotiated Exits from Organized Crime? Building Peace in Conflict and Crime-affected Contexts. *Negotiation Journal* 30(3): 255–273.

Williamson, John (2008) 'A Short History of the Washington Consensus'. In Narcís Serra and Joseph E. Stiglitz (eds), *The Washington Consensus Reconsidered: Towards a New Global Governance.* Oxford: Oxford University Press, pp. 14–30.

World Bank (2005) *Fragile States: Good Practice in Country Assistance Strategies.* Board Report 34790. Washington, DC: World Bank.

World Bank and UNEP (United Nations Environment Programme) (2013) *Expert Consultation: Geo-mapping Extractive Resources in G7+ Fragile States.* Washington, DC and Geneva: World Bank and UNEP.

# Part III

# The challenges of security sector reform in postwar societies

# 7 The international dimension of post-conflict police reform

*Felix Haaß, Julia Strasheim and Nadine Ansorg*[1]

## Introduction[2]

In September 2014 the European Council extended the mandate for the European Union mission for security sector reform (SSR) in the Democratic Republic of Congo, to further assist in building a more accountable police force that will be able to improve the safety and security of all Congolese citizens. The extension of the mandate came as the United Nations (UN) Joint Human Rights Office called to accelerate police and military reform in the Democratic Republic of Congo, where the Congolese security forces continue to carry out grave human rights abuses against civilians. Despite years of international engagement in police reform, the Congolese police force is one of the major sources of insecurity in the country, together with the Congolese military and the countless rebel groups. A UN report found that internationally trained Congolese police forces had engaged in the abduction and execution of a countless number of unarmed civilians, including children (Blair 2014).

The Democratic Republic of Congo is only one of many post-conflict societies in which international donors and domestic parties struggle to implement a reform of the police force (Brzoska 2006; Hänggi 2004; OECD 2007; Schroeder and Chappuis 2014). This is a noble goal, since scholars and policy makers have identified police reform as one of the most important steps in the process of peacebuilding. Police reform after the termination of a conflict is not only important for a functioning security sector; but, if we understand an institution as a formal mechanism or a set of rules that channels societal conflicts (cf. Ansorg and Kurtenbach, Introduction, this volume), a reformed police force is also a vital guarantor that social and political actors comply with the broader 'rules of the game', and that societal conflicts remain embedded within nonviolent institutional borders (Koehler and Zürcher 2003). Yet, this function of the police does not automatically follow from the establishment or reform of a police force following a conflict. Rather, the police force must be embedded in a system of democratically established checks and balances in order to fulfil its role as guarantor of a country's broader set of institutions. Multilateral institutions, such as the UN and bilateral donor agencies, have recognized the importance of functional police forces in postwar societies. With this ideal on their agenda, they have increasingly invested enormous resources in the implementation of police reform. This is the case, not only in the Democratic Republic of Congo, but also across the globe. Between 2005 and 2009, aid earmarked for SSR purposes has almost tripled, from US$300 million in 2005 to nearly US$900 million in 2009 (Pachon 2012). In addition, the UN has broadened the scope of its peacekeeping missions. Many of today's multidimensional peace operations also aim to strengthen local police forces.

Do international peacebuilders, by way of either SSR aid projects or by deploying peacekeeping troops, influence the successful implementation of police reform in the aftermath of violent conflict? While past research has dealt with this question in a series of case studies and evaluations of best practices, to our knowledge a systematic, quantitative answer to this question has not yet been given. In this chapter, therefore, we directly address this gap, and undertake a statistical analysis of the relationship between SSR aid, UN peace operations and the implementation of post-conflict police reform.

We define police reform as changes in the structure of the police force and the conduct of its personnel, often with norm-oriented goals such as transforming the force into an accountable institution that serves the needs of local communities (see Denham 2008, 1). In order to achieve such change in the police force, we argue that international peacebuilders can contribute in two ways. First, aid projects that directly finance SSR should increase the likelihood of the success of post-conflict police reform. The more aid money that is earmarked for SSR infrastructure, the more the necessary expertise, financial resources and equipment will arrive in the post-conflict country, and thus it will enable local actors to better implement steps in the reform. Second, if a peacekeeping mission is given a more robust and comprehensive mandate, the greater the chances for the success of post-conflict police reform. Robustly mandated operations better reduce the security stalemate between warring parties. This opens up the political space necessary for domestic political actors to deal with the issue of police reform.

We test these hypotheses for a subset of police reforms that are considered to be some of the most sensitive issues of police reform. Thus, because they touch upon the most delicate issues of reforming security actors, especially in the aftermath of conflict, they offer a 'hard' case for our theory. These are: reforms of political accountability of the police (that is, who *controls* the police politically), and reforms on the composition of the police force (that is, who is allowed to be a *member* of the police force). The latter especially is often highly sensitive in post-conflict countries, since it touches on the question of whether former opponents can and should form joint security forces. These types of reform also crucially determine the success of post-conflict peace, which links our chapter to the overall theoretical framework of the book (see Ansorg and Kurtenbach, Introduction, this volume). First, is there a correlation between the presence of international peacebuilders and the implementation of reform of prewar institutional settings of police? Second, can we find a correlation between the presence of international peacebuilders and the integration of societal rifts in the police force?

To test our hypotheses, we proceed as follows. We first provide a brief overview of past research on post-conflict police reform, and identify several challenges from previous studies. We then provide a theoretical argument concerning the factors that should be positively associated with implementation. We next discuss our research design, and present self-collected data on police reform implementation. This is followed by the results of several logistic regression models. We find that international SSR financing and peace operations are both linked to implementing reforms that tackle the political control of the police, but that they are not linked to the implementation of the composition of the police force. These findings point to the fact that the presence of international actors is vitally important for the implementation of postwar institutional reforms, since they are able to reduce the costs of implementation. Otherwise, they can pressurize domestic political actors into meeting criteria such as the legislative control of the police following the war. However, this impact is only limited to reforms on political control of the police force. The final section concludes the chapter.

## Previous research on post-conflict police reform

The police are typically regarded as the most visible arm of a government. The means by which they discharge their duties and interact with local communities has a direct impact upon the population's view of the state, and their acceptance of its authority (Wiatrowski and Goldstone 2010). As a result, scholars and practitioners alike see the police force as 'one of the most critical institutions of the state' (Downie 2013, 1), especially in societies that are emerging from armed conflict. Formal and effective security institutions have never existed outside the capital city, or are often destroyed during war (Besley and Persson 2010). Moreover, courtrooms, police stations and legal records are often damaged during conflict, meaning that police and judiciaries often need to be rebuilt from the ground up (Besley and Persson 2010). Furthermore, police training programmes as part of a wider post-conflict SSR process should have a positive impact on the job performance of officers, and prevent incidences of police brutality against civilians.

The academic literature identifies two perspectives on the study of post-conflict police reform. First, a number of studies advocate for the need to rebuild formal state security institutions following a war (Glassmyer and Sambanis 2008; Paris and Sisk 2009). This view on police reform builds on the notion that in a state of weakness following a civil war, formal police forces need to be rebuilt from scratch (Strohmeyer 2001). A key goal of police reform is thus to reestablish a state's monopoly on force, and the institutions necessary to uphold this monopoly. Thereby, this line of research on police reform relates closely to the focus of authority in the statebuilding literature. This holds that a vital component of reforming institutions such as police forces following a war, is to ensure that the governing regime has the capacity to enforce its power, and exercise its authority throughout the national territory (Holsti 1996; Paris and Sisk 2009; Tilly 1975).

Second, challenging the Western-centric model of security provision, the essential security perspective is to focus on the inclusion of domestic models of security governance, and on informal security institutions. Rejecting one-size-fits-all police reform based on the example of a Weberian state, this perspective calls for a better understanding of local approaches to security building in order to increase legitimacy and public acceptance. In post-conflict societies, this can mean creating hybrid models of security, shaped on a combination of international and domestic methods, or on combining formal and informal policing (Krause 2012; Mac Ginty 2011; Schroeder *et al.* 2014). Studies on the critical tradition hold that informal nonstate institutions, such as neighbourhood watches, can be more efficient providers of security than mistrusted police forces. Thus, informal provisions of security should be promoted, either as a transitional mechanism or a permanent one (Sedra 2010).

Both perspectives on post-conflict police reform suffer from a number of shortcomings. First, police reform is not just a practical exercise of training officers and building police stations, but a process that is deeply political in nature (Bernabéu 2007; Cawthra and Luckham 2003). O'Neill (2005, 9), for instance, holds that police reform needs 'heavy emphasis on police accountability', and the creation of democratic oversight bodies that can prosecute the misconduct of officers. Yet, a systematic and comparative analysis of political aspects of post-conflict police reform is missing. Most best practice guidelines focus on technical aspects of reform (such as the training of officers), and academic studies often centre on the role of international actors in police reform (Brzoska and Heinemann-Grüder 2004; Call and Barnett 2000; Call 2002; Cordone 2000; Muehlmann 2008). The lack of emphasis on political aspects is also due to the fact that studies on police reform are somewhat embedded in the broader debate on post-conflict institutional engineering as discussed in the Introduction to this book, and thus miss out on important explanatory factors of post-conflict political development. In general, institutional engineering means designing elements of a political system so that they contribute to nonviolent conflict management between antagonistic groups (Wolff 2011). A key argument in this line of research is that one of the main determinants for nonviolent politics is how antagonistic groups, such as warring parties or ethnic identity groups, control political institutions (e.g. Hartzell and Hoddie 2007; Roeder and Rothchild 2005; Sisk 2008; Walter 2002). However, the significance of the composition and control of police forces has often only been implicitly acknowledged in past research on police reform (Bastick 2007; Brzoska and Heinemann-Grüder 2004; Caplan 2005).

Second, past research recognizes that one of the most vital determinants on whether reforms of security governance following armed conflict contribute to peace is that such reforms are implemented accordingly. For instance, the integration of demobilized ex-combatants of warring parties into security forces has not necessarily been found to effectively contribute towards peace, mainly because it is often poorly executed (Glassmyer and Sambanis 2008). However, we still know little about the determinants for the implementation of reform; once warring parties have agreed on specific political aspects of police reform, such as the force's composition and its control by overseeing bodies, what factors determine why parties implement reforms in some cases but not in others?

Finally, previous research on post-conflict police reform also suffers from a methodological shortcoming. On the one hand, it is largely dominated by policy-oriented best practices guidelines (e.g. Bryden and Hänggi 2004; Cooper and Pugh 2002; Wulf 2004), and on the other hand by in-depth case studies (e.g. Downie 2013; Gross 2009; Muehlmann 2008; Simons and Zanker 2013). A lack of broader comparative analyses implies that few findings of past research on post-conflict police reform can be generalized across time, cases and regions. Thus, more comparative studies that analyse post-conflict police reform over time and in a variety of cases can contribute to our understanding of such reform.

## The international dimension of police reform after conflict

In line with previous research, we define police reform as changes in the structure and conduct of the police, often with norm-oriented goals such as transforming the force into an accountable institution that serves the needs of local communities (see Denham 2008, 1). While we are aware that police reform entails a technical component such as the training and equipment of police forces, as well as a political component, we deliberately focus on the political aspects of police reform. Political aspects of police reform, such as composition or accountability, are highly sensitive issues in post-conflict countries, and may therefore be considered as a particularly hard test of our theoretical propositions.

We focus on two main political dimensions of police reform addressed by domestic and international actors. The first is that police reform in the aftermath of war entails implementing or strengthening *accountability structures*. Typically, these structures are constructed or reconstructed in the image of Western-style institutions, by appointing independent and impartial civilian oversight committees to hold the state's security forces to account (O'Neill 2005). The second dimension is that many programmes aim to regulate the *representation* of socially or politically relevant groups in the police force. These include groups such as women, ethnic or religious identity groups and warring parties. For instance, including warring parties in the police reduces their perceived security stalemate, and may increase the chances of success of the newly built security institution (Walter 2002). Furthermore, particularly in conflicts over ethnic or identity issues, identity group representation in the security forces is the focus of reform efforts to 'achieve an ethnic composition reflecting the community they serve' (Caplan 2005, 45). Moreover, international donors, such as the UN and the Organization for Economic Cooperation and Development (OECD), increasingly stress the need for gender balancing and mainstreaming. This means that the number of female personnel in the police should be increased, and that consideration must be given to the impact of reforms upon women at every stage of the reform process (OECD 2007; Valasek 2008).

We argue that two characteristics of international peacebuilders are most likely to affect the implementation of political police reforms following war: the volume of resources they bring, and the scope of their mandate. War-torn countries rarely have the financial means to conduct large-scale reforms of their security forces; on the contrary, training, equipment, deployment and maintenance of police are all costly endeavours. This is especially so in the aftermath of war, when former rebels need to be disarmed and reintegrated into national security forces, while the government is hardly in a position to collect taxes (Nkurunziza 2010). The investments and technical expertise of international development organizations are supposed to fill this gap. At the same time, this SSR-earmarked aid often comes with certain demands and benchmarks for implementing democratic reform. In order to receive financial support in their reform efforts, countries are expected to meet certain political criteria such as the legislative control of security institutions, or the representation of all significant groups in the security bodies. Furthermore, there is significant variation in the amount of international resources available, which tends to be concentrated in a few high-profile countries such as Iraq and Afghanistan (Pachon 2012). Hence, SSR-earmarked aid is most likely to be allocated to post-conflict countries with particularly difficult situations. These are countries where multilateral and bilateral donors are most interested to see a move towards democratic accountability and representation of the police; but these countries must also be more willing to push towards substantial implementation of reform. The left panel in Figure 7.1 documents the annual average share of foreign aid commitments that have been earmarked for SSR-related projects.[3] The plot shows both a high annual variation and an increase in the share of SSR-earmarked aid since 1975.

The obvious hypothesis that follows from this line of reasoning is that we should expect higher volumes of development aid earmarked for SSR activities to be associated with a greater likelihood of implementing political police reform.

> Hypothesis 1: Countries that receive higher shares of SSR-earmarked development aid are more likely to implement police reform activities.

A second characteristic of international peacebuilders that is likely to facilitate post-conflict police reform is through the implementation of multilateral peace operations, and more precisely through the strength of their mandate. International peace operations are typically deployed in the form of UN peacekeeping missions, but also increasingly come under mandates from regional organizations such as the African Union or the European Union. While these missions carry out a wide variety of tasks, including election monitoring, facilitating political dialogue and humanitarian aid, police reform has become a key objective for the majority of these missions (Hänggi 2004; Perdomo 2007). The tasks assigned to peace operations differ vastly according to their mandates. Some missions, such as the UN Peacekeeping Force in Cyprus, merely monitor a ceasefire between two sides; whereas others, such as the UN Organization Stabilization Mission in the Democratic Republic of the Congo, have much more far-reaching goals, including monitoring local elections, disarming and reintegrating ex-combatants, and even actively fighting non-cooperative rebel groups. The number of these extensively and robustly mandated UN missions has increased over time. The lower panel in Figure 7.1 shows the annual count of peace operations with either a 'strong' or a 'multidimensional' mandate, and shows a marked increase in the number of robust peace operations deployed since 1975.

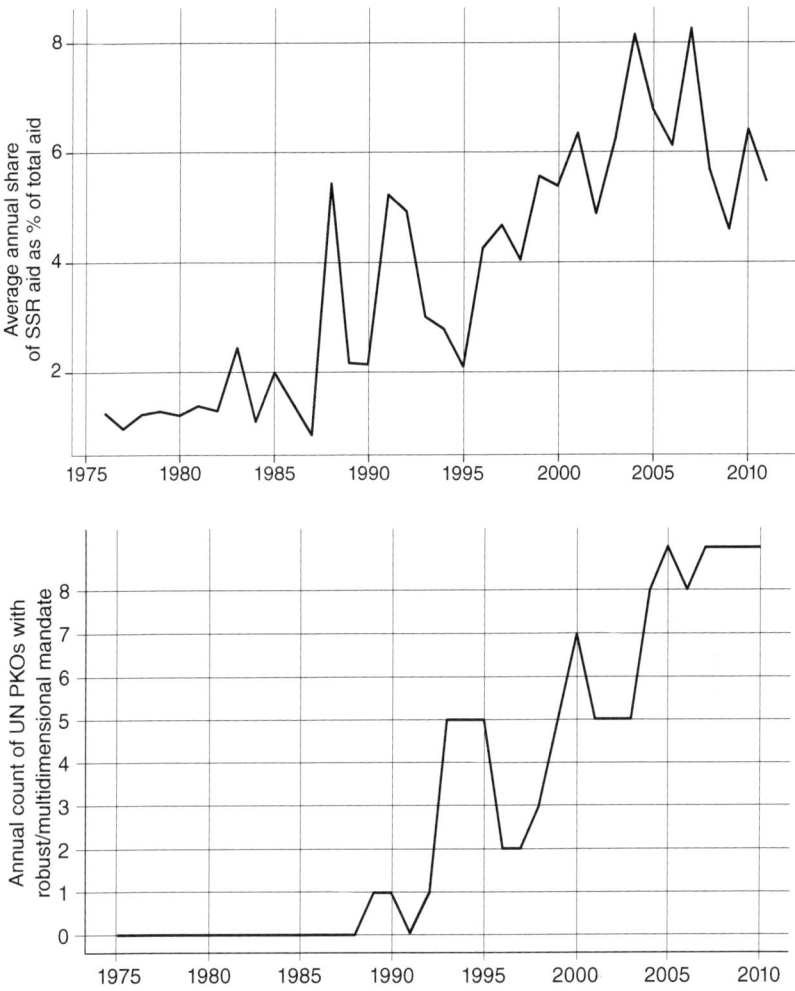

*Figure 7.1* Trends in international assistance to and peacekeeping operations in conflict-
affected and post-conflict countries
Source: Data on SSR aid from AidData 2.1 (Tierney et al. 2011) but based on own
calculations (see below). Peacekeeping data from Doyle and Sambanis (2006), updated
by Hegre et al. (2011).

Doyle and Sambanis offer evidence that the latter types of operations, so-called
peace enforcement missions, decrease the risk of conflict recurrence compared
with more moderately mandated missions (Doyle and Sambanis 2006).
Considering that more extensively mandated operations can provide for a better
security situation, they should also enable police reform to be implemented more
smoothly. In addition, SSR is often part of their core mandate, so they should
provide the required expertise to implement reforms in a post-conflict country.
Furthermore, and in line with our previous argument, missions with a stronger

mandate should be in a better position to push towards the implementation of political police reform than those with a weak mandate, such as those that only monitor a ceasefire between warring parties.

> Hypothesis 2: The more extensive a peace operation's mandate, the higher the likelihood of implementing police reforms.

International actors' resources and mandates do not affect all dimensions of police reform equally. Given the strong preference of international peacebuilders towards establishing peace through state building, we expect them to focus more strongly on the political control aspect of reform implementation, namely police accountability. Organizations in charge of peace operations, most notably the UN, and most donor agencies that finance SSR programmes, are influenced by the Weberian concept of the state holding the monopoly on violence, as well as the Western concept of dividing the powers of the state into various branches (Jackson 2011). Thus, the creation of independent police oversight bodies as part of a SSR programme should focus more on the efforts of international actors rather than on sociopolitical reforms that deal with the composition of security forces (for example, identity or gender groups), as well as whether or not to include representatives from warring parties.

> Hypothesis 3: The effect of SSR-earmarked development aid and peace operation mandates has a stronger effect on implementing political control aspects of police reform than on reforms altering the composition of the security forces.

## Research design: predicting the implementation of police reform

Do international peacebuilders, both in the form of SSR aid projects and in the deployment of peacekeeping troops, have an influence on the successful implementation of police reform in the aftermath of violent conflict? We tried to answer this research question, and tested our hypotheses, by considering all peace agreements made between 1975 and 2011 that conformed to two conditions: first, they followed at least one year of intrastate armed conflict; second, the warring parties consented to police reform provisions by signing a peace agreement.[4] We follow academic convention by defining intrastate armed conflict as 'a contested incompatibility [.] where the use of armed force between two parties, of which at least one is the government of a state, results in at least twenty-five battle-related deaths in one calendar year' (Themnér and Wallensteen 2013). We understand peace agreements to be pacts that deal with the resolution of the incompatibility issues that led to intrastate conflict, and that are signed by the key actors engaged in such conflict (see Kreutz 2010). Thus, the sample for our analysis only comprised cases where warring parties had agreed on police reform provisions in the first place, allowing us to trace the mechanisms that enable these parties to consequently implement these provisions. This strategy resulted in a sample of 79 peace agreements for investigation.[5]

In our analysis on determinants of implementation, we studied two binary dependent variables: the implementation of *political control* provisions of police reform, and the implementation of *composition* provisions of police reform. For both variables, we gathered information and coded it ourselves. Depending on the availability of the information for a particular case, we used a variety of sources, including the following: annual Country Reports on Human Rights Practices by the US State Department,[6] UN reports on peacebuilding missions in post-conflict countries, and case studies on police reform in individual post-conflict countries.

The first dependent variable concerns the implementation of provisions on political control of the police force through the strengthening of accountability structures. We favoured the state-building perspective to post-conflict police reform discussed in the second section, and only looked at formal institutional structures as being accountability provisions. Thus, we define provisions on accountability structures to be those terms that seek to regulate formal governmental control over police forces. Specifically, this definition refers to provisions that determine the authority to which the police force must answer and take responsibility for the police's actions. In terms of implementing such provisions, we coded *political control* implementation as 'fulfilled' and allocated it the value of '1' if, within five years after the peace agreement was signed, an institutional police oversight body had been created, or the legislature's role in police oversight had been strengthened. All other cases were coded as '0'. For instance, in South Africa, following the introduction of the 1993 Interim Constitution, it was reported that by 1996 a civilian secretariat had been formed 'to advise the minister, assure civilian oversight of the SAPS [South African Police Service], and monitor police performance' (Gastrow and Shaw 2001, 264). In contrast, following the 1997 Chittagong Hill Tracts Peace Accord in Bangladesh, '[victims] of police abuse were [.] reluctant to file cases against the police, as there was no independent body charged with investigation of criminal allegations against members of the police force' (USDS 2003).

The second dependent variable in our analysis of police reform concerns the implementation of provisions that regulate the composition of police forces. Composition refers to provisions in the peace agreement that regulate the mode of representation of groups, for which we focus on identity groups, women and the inclusion of former warring parties in the police. In terms of implementing provisions, we coded *composition* implementation as 'present' and allocated the value of '1' if sources indicated that police units which clearly represented different identity groups were active in the post-conflict country. All other cases were coded as '0'. For instance, following the 1998 Good Friday Agreement in Northern Ireland, it was reported that, whereas the police had traditionally been dominated by Protestants, an 'active recruitment of Catholics by the Northern Ireland Civil Service produced rough proportionality in overall numbers' (USDS 2001), although Catholics still remained significantly underrepresented in senior grades. After the accord, Parliament passed a policing bill, mandating that 'a 50:50 religious balance be maintained in new recruitment until the religious composition of the police reflects the mix in society at large" (USDS 2001). Thus, we considered this as the implementation of provisions that regulate the composition of the Northern Ireland police force.

We studied two main independent variables. First, we relied on the AidData 2.1 dataset to calculate *aid flows that are earmarked for SSR* (Tierney *et al.* 2011).[7] We aggregated the commitment amount in constant 2009 US dollars of all aid projects that were SSR-earmarked for the year in which the peace agreement was signed.[8] To account for the varying sizes of the economies and populations of recipient post-conflict states, we normalized the resulting value to a post-conflict country's gross domestic product (GDP) and its population size. We took data on GDP from the UN (2015) and data on population size from the World Bank. Since the variable is highly skewed, we had to log-transform it.

Second, we studied the *extensiveness of a peace operation's mandate*. We distinguished between different kinds of peacekeeping missions: observer missions, traditional peacekeeping missions, multidimensional peacekeeping missions and peace enforcement missions. Data were taken from an updated version of the original Doyle and Sambanis (2006) data on peace operations by Hegre *et al.* (2011). We followed the method of these authors by dummy coding each type of peacekeeping mission. Based on this information, we constructed an ordinal variable ranging from 0 to 2, indicating the extensiveness of a peacekeeping operation's mandate, ordered from least extensive (0) to most extensive (2).[9] To mitigate effects of endogeneity, our data included information on the peacekeeping mission present in the year prior to the peace agreement. As the extensiveness variable has only three levels, it entered our model as a categorical variable and two dummy variables that denote traditional observer missions and robust, multidimensional missions, with the reference category being 'no peace operation'. To test whether the peacekeeping effect is driven by troop size rather than by mandate, we also estimated a model that included the number of peacekeeping troops deployed in the year prior to the peace agreement.

Finally, we added several controls into our statistical analyses. First, we included the *presence of a power-sharing deal* between the conflict parties. We relied on data from the Uppsala Conflict Data Programme (UCDP) peace agreement dataset, which includes a variable on provisions for a shared government that is considered to be positive once '[t]he agreement included provisions for extensive power-sharing in new government' (see codebook of the UCDP peace agreement dataset, and Högbladh 2011). Second, we followed scholarly convention (see Hartzell *et al.* 2001, 205) to control for the level of *conflict intensity,* and constructed a measure of battle-related deaths per month. Those conflicts with higher conflict intensity could be the 'hard' cases in terms of implementation of police reform, where provisions are less implemented than in 'easier' cases. Data on battle-related deaths, and conflict start and end dates, were taken from the UCDP (UCDP 2013) for dates after 1989. For agreements prior to 1989, data were taken from the Peace Research Institute Oslo (PRIO) Battle-Deaths dataset 3.0 (Lacina and Gleditsch 2005). Third, we included a measure of *regime type*. Data were taken from Freedom House (2012), and ranged from 1 (free/fully democratic) to 7 (not free/fully autocratic).[10] It is to be expected that authoritarian regimes are less likely to implement provisions on police reform than democracies. Fourth, we captured the level of *post-conflict economic development* through a measure of GDP per capita, using data from the UN (United Nations 2015). Countries with higher economic development may be more likely to implement police reform provisions, since they may have more resources to do so.

## Results and discussion

We analysed the determinants of police reform implementation in the fields of political control and political composition of police forces. Tables 7.1 and 7.2 display the results of our logistic regression models that predict the implementation of *political control* properties of police reform (Table 7.1), and of *composition* aspects of police reform (Table 7.2). For all models, we clustered standard errors by conflict in order to account for correlated observations.

The results in Table 7.1 confirm Hypothesis 1, and show that SSR aid correlates positively and is statistically significant with the dependent variable of Table 7.1, the implementation of reforms on political control of police forces. This indicates

*Table 7.1* Logistic regression models for the implementation of political control aspects of police reform

|  | *Model 1* | *Model 2* | *Model 3* | *Model 4* |
|---|---|---|---|---|
| SSR aid as % of GDP | **0.58**\*\* |  | **0.46**\* |  |
|  | (0.19) |  | (0.19) |  |
| SSR aid per capita |  | **0.58**\*\* |  | **0.46**\* |
|  |  | (0.19) |  | (0.19) |
| UN PKO mandate: Traditional | **1.62**\* | **1.62**\* |  |  |
|  | (0.75) | (0.75) |  |  |
| UN PKO mandate: Robust | **1.64**\* | **1.64**\* |  |  |
|  | (0.79) | (0.79) |  |  |
| PKO troops |  |  | 0.07 | 0.07 |
|  |  |  | (0.06) | (0.06) |
| Power sharing | 0.06 | 0.06 | 0.03 | 0.03 |
|  | (1.18) | (1.18) | (0.94) | (0.94) |
| Conflict intensity | 0.01 | 0.01 | **0.01**† | **0.01**† |
|  | (0.01) | (0.01) | (0.00) | (0.00) |
| GDP per capita | 0.34 | -0.24 | 0.33 | -0.14 |
|  | (0.46) | (0.37) | (0.48) | (0.39) |
| Freedom House | **−0.92**\* | **−0.92**\* | **−0.82**\* | **−0.82**\* |
|  | (0.36) | (0.36) | (0.34) | (0.34) |
| AIC | 90.05 | 90.05 | 92.75 | 92.75 |
| BIC | 107.92 | 107.92 | 108.39 | 108.39 |
| Log likelihood | −37.03 | −37.03 | −39.37 | −39.37 |
| Deviance | 74.05 | 74.05 | 78.75 | 78.75 |
| Number observed | 69 | 69 | 69 | 69 |

Notes
\*\*\*$p < 0.001$, \*\*$p < 0.01$, \*$p < 0.05$, †$p < 0.1$, Standard errors in parentheses, clustered by conflict.

that more SSR aid in post-conflict countries is associated with an increased probability of implementing political control aspects of police reform. This finding is robust over all four models, and with different SSR aid measures; the results in models 1 and 3 that measure SSR aid as percentages of GDP are virtually identical with models 2 and 4 that measure SSR aid per capita.

The results of models 1 and 2 also provide support for Hypothesis 2, since the mandates of peace operations are positively associated with a higher likelihood of the implementation of political control aspects of police reform. However, this effect is not driven by troop size, as models 3 and 4 indicate that the coefficient of troop size of peacekeeping missions is small and statistically insignificant.

Both variables – *SSR aid* and *the mandate of the peacekeeping mission* – have substantially meaningful effects, as can be seen in the first and second panel of Figure 7.2. If we hold all other variables constant, and move from very low levels of SSR aid to very high levels, we detect that the probability of the implementation of political control aspects of police reform increases dramatically. For instance, a change of SSR aid from about 2 per cent of aid (e.g. Chittagong Hill Tracts Peace Accord, Bangladesh, 1997) to about 5 per cent (Comprehensive Peace Accord, Burundi, 2006) increases the probability of implementation from less than 1 per cent (confidence interval: 0 per cent, 2.8 per cent) to over 77 per cent (confidence interval: 38 per cent, 90 per cent). A similar effect accounts for the mandates of peace operations; that is, if we hold all other variables constant, and simulate a change from no peace operation whatsoever to traditional peacekeeping or robust peacekeeping, the probability of the implementation of political control aspects of police reform more than doubles, from 32 per cent (confidence interval: 16 per cent, 55 per cent) to 71 per cent (confidence interval: 37 per cent, 91 per cent). Notably, the effect of a peacekeeping mandate does *not* increase with more robust mandates. Rather, the effect of traditional peacekeeping is almost exactly the same as the effect of robust or multidimensional peacekeeping. This suggests that it is not the type of mandate, but rather the mere presence of peacekeepers, that is linked to a higher likelihood of the implementation of political control aspects of police reform.

Finally, higher Freedom House scores are negatively associated with the likelihood of implementing political control over the police force. Thus, there is a correlation between more autocratic post-conflict regimes and a less likely implementation of provisions on the political control of police forces. Substantially, if we compare a country with a Freedom House score of 1.5 (e.g. the United Kingdom of Great Britain and Northern Ireland) to a country with a Freedom House score of 7 (e.g. Sudan), the probability of successfully implementing reforms on political control over the police falls from 88 per cent (confidence interval: 57 per cent, 98 per cent) to 7 per cent (confidence interval: 1 per cent, 35 per cent) (again, if all other variables are held at their median or mode). This finding is in line with previous research, since political control of police forces by an independent oversight body or the legislature would counteract the repression exercised by the police in many authoritarian regimes (Davenport 2007).

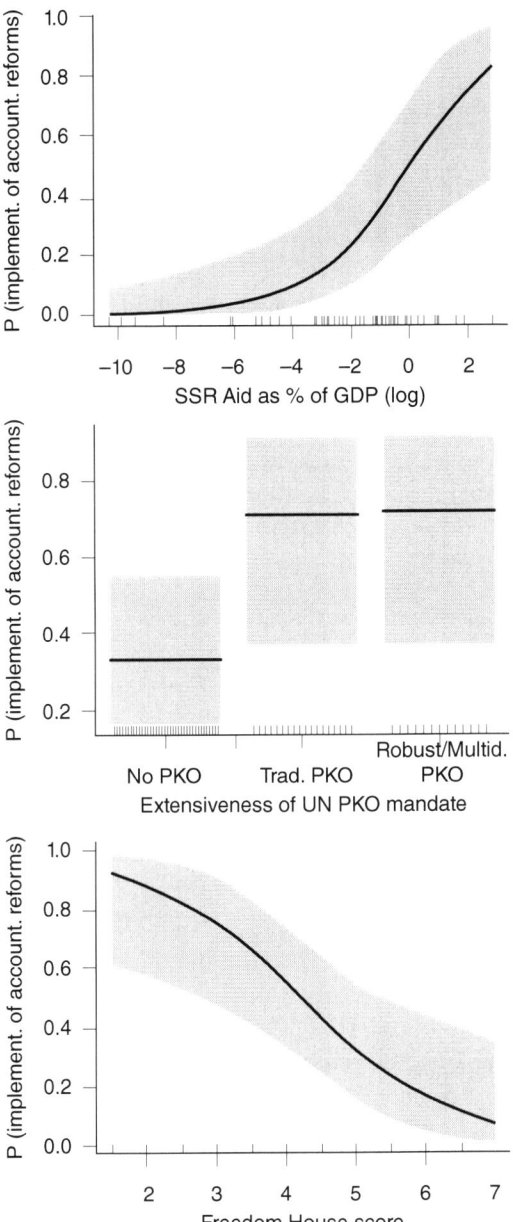

*Figure 7.2* Predicted probabilities of the effect of SSR aid, PKO mandate and regime type
on implementation of political control aspects of police reform.

Source: Predicted probabilities were calculated based on Model 1 in Table 7.1 and by
holding all quantitative variables at their median and all categorical variables at their
mode using the visreg package in R (Breheny and Burchett 2015).

Table 7.2 displays the results for the logistical regression on the implementation of reforms of the composition of a police force. Columns 1 to 4 record the results of logistic regression models that predict the implementation of different dimensions of reforms of police composition. 'General' is a catch-all category that is coded 1 if any one of the other three dimensions is implemented. The remaining three columns record the results of models that predict the implementation of reform by integrating warring parties into the police force (column 2), integrating identity groups into the police force (column 3) and gender composition of the police force (column 4). The results show that we found no effect of SSR aid on the implementation of any type of police force composition.[11]

The results on the relationship between UN peace operations and the implementation of reforms of police composition are somewhat inconclusive. We found a statistically significant effect for robustly mandated UN peace operations on the implementation of reform aspects of identity group integration and gender composition of the police force. These patterns are similar for the other dimensions of force composition reform, but the coefficients are not statistically significantly different from zero for the integration of warring parties into the police force, or the 'General' category.

*Table 7.2* Logistic regression models for the implementation of reform of police force composition

|  | (1) General | (2) Warring parties | (3) Identity groups | (4) Gender |
|---|---|---|---|---|
| SSR aid as % of GDP | 0.25 | 0.24 | 0.37 | 0.29 |
|  | (0.20) | (0.25) | (0.25) | (0.22) |
| UN PKO mandate: Traditional | 0.16 | −0.44 | −1.50 | −1.65 |
|  | (0.87) | (0.97) | (1.99) | (1.18) |
| UN PKO mandate: Robust | 2.33 | 2.47 | **4.79**\*\* | **2.70**\* |
|  | (1.49) | (1.94) | (1.76) | (1.11) |
| Power sharing | 0.75 | 1.37 | 0.74 | −0.73 |
|  | (0.91) | (0.84) | (1.33) | (0.71) |
| Conflict intensity | 0.00 | **0.01**\* | 0.00 | 0.00 |
|  | (0.00) | (0.01) | (0.01) | (0.01) |
| GDP per capita | **0.81**† | 0.06 | **2.13**\*\*\* | −0.28 |
|  | (0.47) | (0.71) | (0.57) | (0.50) |
| Freedom House | −0.40 | −0.34 | **−1.59**\*\* | −0.59 |
|  | (0.35) | (0.32) | (0.51) | (0.37) |
| AIC | 86.95 | 82.70 | 54.29 | 84.24 |
| BIC | 104.82 | 100.58 | 72.16 | 102.11 |
| Log likelihood | −35.47 | −33.35 | −19.15 | −34.12 |
| Deviance | 70.95 | 66.70 | 38.29 | 68.24 |
| Num. obs. | 69 | 69 | 69 | 69 |

Notes
\*\*\*p < 0.001, \*\*p < 0.01, \*p < 0.05, †p < 0.1, Standard errors in parentheses, clustered by conflict.

In Figure 7.3 we plotted the predicted probabilities of the effect of the mandate of a UN peace operation on the implementation of composition aspects of police reform. The effect of robust UN peace operations on the implementation of reform aspects on integration of identity groups into the police forces is visible in the lower left panel of Figure 7.3. If we simulate progress from no peacekeeping mission to a robust peacekeeping mission, holding all other variables constant at their medians or modes, the probability of implementing the reform of identity group integration into the police force increases from 2 per cent (confidence interval: 0.18 per cent, 25 per cent) to 75 per cent (confidence interval: 35 per cent, 94 per cent). A similar effect may be seen for the implementation of reforms on gender composition of the police force. Again, if we simulate progress from no peacekeeping mission to a robust peacekeeping mission when holding all other variables constant at their medians or modes, the probability of implementing the reform on gender composition of the police force increases from 38 per cent (confidence interval: 20 per cent, 59 per cent) to 90 per cent (confidence interval: 60 per cent, 98 per cent).

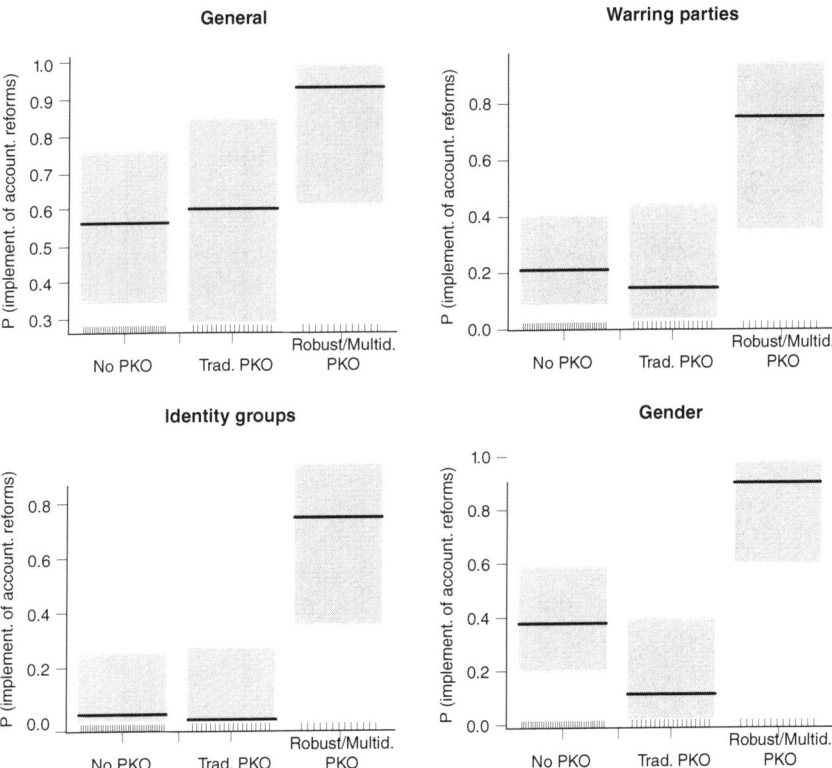

*Figure 7.3* Predicted probabilities of the effect of type of UN PKO mandate on implementing composition reforms of the police.
Source: Predicted probabilities were calculated based on the models in Table 7.2 and by holding all quantitative variables at their medians and all categorical variables at their modes using the visreg package in R (Breheny and Burchett, 2015).

Overall, the limited results of the models presented in Table 7.2 suggest tentative support for Hypothesis 3 in which we presumed that international assistance in the form of SSR aid and stronger peacekeeping mandates would be more strongly associated with a higher likelihood of implementing political control reforms than with composition reforms. Our data indicated that SSR aid is only associated with reforms towards political control, while we did not find evidence for a similar pattern for the relationship between SSR aid and the reform of police force composition. Our data do not indicate whether the latter finding is indeed due to the hypothesized stronger preference of international actors for rebuilding state structures following the Western model (of which an impartial police force under civilian control is an integral part). However, the fact that we did find such a relationship between SSR aid and the implementation of police reforms on political accountability, but not on composition, lends at least some credibility to this proposition.

We are careful not to place too much weight on the direction of causality in these statistical models, since the analysis suffers from at least two sources of endogeneity: reverse causality, and sample and treatment selection. Reverse causality is a potential problem in this analysis, since the successful implementation of the political control aspects of police reform, and the implementation of composition aspects of police reform, may both be drivers of the allocation of aid as well as the presence of peacekeepers. To put it differently, SSR aid and peace operations may only be sent to a post-conflict country because the local conflict parties request the international community to help them implement police reforms. In our models, we attempted to mitigate this problem by creating temporal lags of our main independent variables: *SRR aid* and *type of peace operation mandate*. Since our dependent variables are measured within the first five years after the peace agreement, independent variables that are lagged by one year prior to the signature of the peace agreement are unlikely to be caused by either the signature of a peace agreement or the implementation of police reforms. The downside of this strategy is that we only indirectly measured the effects of SSR aid and type of peace operation mandate, since both variables may subsequently change in response to the implementation of police reform.

The second source of endogeneity is selection bias. In fact, this problem consists of two interrelated problems. The first is the nonrandom selection of SSR aid and UN peace operations. Even though both SSR aid and peace operations may be driven by the implementation of police reform as described above, there may be other factors influencing SSR aid allocation and the deployment of a UN peace mission. These can be external drivers, such as strong diplomatic links of a post-conflict government to one of the major powers, or internal drivers, such as a major incidence of one-sided violence that necessitates a swift deployment of a peacekeeping operation. To the extent that these external factors systematically affect the implementation of police reform, our estimates for SSR aid and type of mandate of a UN peace operation are also systematically biased. The other source of selection bias may stem from the fact that provisions that regulate police reform are also not randomly allocated, but are most likely the result of strategic bargaining among conflicting parties.

The econometric 'fix' for both problems would be Heckman-style selection models (Heckman 1979) or, in the cases of SSR aid and UN peace operations, instrumental variable regressions (Wooldridge 2008). However, the small sample size makes it difficult to calculate estimates using such models. Furthermore, to our knowledge, no temporally valid instrumental variables for UN peacekeeping deployment exist. We encountered similar problems when looking for instrumental variables specifically for SSR aid. Our second-best fix for this problem, therefore, is that we control for the major variables that have been found to drive aid allocation, namely GDP per capita (since poorer countries typically receive more aid) (see Hoeffler and Outram 2011), higher levels of peacekeeping deployment and conflict intensity (since peacekeepers tend to go to deadlier conflicts) (see Fortna 2008). We acknowledge that this strategy cannot account for every potentially unobservable confounding variable, and are therefore cautious in applying a strict causal interpretation of these findings.

Despite these statistical shortcomings, our findings are valuable for at least three reasons. First, our study is the first that quantitatively links international assistance in the form of SSR aid and type of UN peace operation mandate to the implementation of police reform. For this purpose, the finding that higher volumes of SSR-earmarked aid and UN peace operation deployment tend to go together with the implementation of the political control aspects of police reform in post-conflict countries is good news for policy makers involved in post-conflict police reform. Second, our study contributes to the existing debate about post-conflict police reform by introducing unique data on the implementation of different dimensions of post-conflict police reform. We acknowledge that our data are limited, since they provide only a minimum of information on whether some kind of implementation of police reform took place, and not on how extensive or how successful such implementation of police reform was. Nevertheless, systematic and generalizable information on the implementation of police reform is rare to nonexistent. Therefore, our data make a unique quantitative contribution. Third, our findings offer new avenues for qualitative researchers looking for case selection strategies. Building on works that integrate quantitative and qualitative methods, such as Lieberman (2005), this chapter offers a starting point for selecting typical or atypical cases that may be explored qualitatively in order to shed light on the underlying mechanisms of our findings.

## Conclusion

Do international peacebuilders influence the successful implementation of police reform in the aftermath of violent conflict? In this chapter, we have focused on the implementation of political aspects of police reform, such as improved accountability structures or composition of the police force. We analysed our research question by applying a theoretical model that built on the international dimensions of police reform implementation. We argued that in particular two characteristics of external peacebuilders are associated with the implementation of police reform following war: the volume of resources they bring, and the extensiveness of their mandate. We hypothesized that higher shares of SSR-earmarked development aid, and more extensively mandated peace operations, are correlated with a greater likelihood of police reform implementation.

To test our hypotheses, we applied several logistical regression models. For our dependent variables, we used newly coded information on the implementation of *political control* provisions of police reform, and the implementation of *political composition* provisions of police reform in post-conflict countries. For our independent variables, we relied on the AidData 2.1 dataset (Tierney *et al.* 2011) and data on mandates for peace operations (Doyle and Sambanis 2006; Hegre *et al.* 2011).

We found that international SSR financing is more highly correlated with implementing political control reforms than with implementing reforms that alter a police force's composition. The effect is similar for the mandates of peace operations. While the mandates of peace operations are positively associated with a higher likelihood of the implementation of political control aspects of police reform, they only have a minor effect on the implementation of composition aspects of police reform.

Our results contribute to the broader institutional reform literature, and the overall focus of this volume, in two key ways. First, our findings demonstrate more generally the vital importance of international actors in implementing postwar institutional reforms. While the role of international agencies in postwar institutional reform has often been subject to critical assessment, our results indicate that international actors can reduce the costs of implementation, or put pressure on domestic political actors to meet criteria such as the legislative control of the police following war. Second, however, our diverse findings on the two dependent variables *political control* and *composition* show that the impact of international actors varies according to the type of institutional reform. While the presence of peacekeepers, and more SSR aid, both increase the chances of reforming political control of the police, we did not observe a similarly strong relationship between aid and composition reforms of the police. Only robust peacekeeping presence seems to be associated with increased chances of reforming police force composition.

These results offer several avenues for further research. First, we were unable to conclusively answer the question of whether a stronger international preference for state building based on a Western model is the reason why we found a stronger relationship between SSR aid and political police reforms than between SSR aid and composition reforms of the police. Further qualitative studies will be needed in order to explore this relationship. Second, scholars building on these findings should further disaggregate our implementation variables. More fine-grained measures of the extent and success of police reform implementation are necessary in order to clarify the precise mechanisms that link SSR assistance, peace operations and police reform. Third, these more fine-grained measures (ideally in a time-varying format) should also address the endogeneity problems pointed out above, and should adequately control for selection bias and reverse causality. Finally, future work should investigate whether the implementation of police reform has any impact on post-conflict peace, and a reduction of violence executed by state and nonstate security actors.

## Notes

1  Equal authorship applies.
2  Previous versions of this chapter were presented at the third ISP Conference on 'Institutional Reforms in Post-war and Divided Societies – Part of the Problem or Part of the Solution?' on 27–28 May 2014 in Geneva, and at the 2015 Annual Convention of ISA on 18–21 February 2015 in New Orleans. We thank Keith Krause, Govinda Clayton and the participants of the third ISP Conference for their valuable comments on previous versions of this chapter. In addition, we thank Miriam Bach and John Preuss for their excellent research assistance in collecting the data on the implementation of police reform.
3  We included all countries from our peace agreement sample (see below) in calculating the annual averages.
4  For more information please see the dataset on provisions for police reform in peace agreements (PRPA) in Ansorg *et al.* (2016).
5  Our sample contains full, partial and process agreements (see Högbladh 2011). We reran the tests with the individual subsets of our sample. The results remained robust with full agreements alone, as well as with full and partial agreements. Only the sample size for process agreements is too small to achieve any meaningful results.
6  They are available online at: www.state.gov/j/drl/rls/hrrpt/ (last accessed 10 February 2015)
7  We used specific sector codes to distinguish between SSR aid and non-SSR aid. For instance, aid that is aimed at *Security System Management and Reform* or *Land mine clearance* can be clearly considered SSR-earmarked, whereas aid aiming at primary education or basic healthcare is clearly non-SSR aid. The data and codes are available at: <http://aiddata.org/sites/default/files/aiddata_coding_scheme_0.pdf>.
8  In robustness checks, we also lagged this value by one year in order to account for possible reverse causality between the signing of a peace agreement and aid flows. This does not alter our results.
9  The range is the following: 0 = no peace operation, 1 = observer mission and/or traditional peacekeeping, 2 = multidimensional peacekeeping and/or peace enforcement mission.
10  We chose Freedom House over the more commonly used Polity Index (Marshall and Jaggers 2002) because Polity is coded for several of our cases as an 'interregnum' period, which falls outside its -10 to +10 index, and would lead to too many missing values.
11  We re-estimated the models using SSR aid per capita as the SSR variable, which did not substantially change the results, and is thus not reported here.

## References

Ansorg, Nadine, Felix Haass and Julia Strasheim. 2016. 'Police Reforms in Peace Agreements, 1975–2011: Introducing the PRPA Dataset'. *Journal of Peace Research*, doi: 10.1177/0022343316628932.

Bastick, Megan. 2007. 'Integrating Gender in Post-conflict Security Sector Reform'. Policy Paper No. 29. Geneva: Geneva Centre for the Democratic Control of the Armed Forces (DCAF).

Bernabéu, Irene. 2007. 'Laying the Foundations of Democracy? Reconsidering Security Sector Reform Under UN Auspices in Kosovo'. *Security Dialogue* 38(1): 71–92. doi:10.1177/0967010607075973.

Besley, Timothy and Torsten Persson. 2010. 'State Capacity, Conflict, and Development'. *Econometrica* 78(1): 1–34. doi:10.3982/ECTA8073.

Blair, David. 2014. 'British Aid Funded African Police Force That "Executed" Children'. *Telegraph*, 27 November, available at:www.telegraph.co.uk/news/worldnews/africaandindianocean/democraticrepublicofcongo/11259137/British-aid-funded-African-police-force-that-executed-children.html.

Bryden, Alan and Heiner Hänggi. 2004. *Reform And Reconstruction of the Security Sector.* Münster: LIT Verlag.

Brzoska, Michael. 2006. 'Introduction: Criteria for Evaluating Post-conflict Reconstruction and Security Sector Reform in Peace Support Operations'. *International Peacekeeping* 13(1): 1–13. doi:10.1080/13533310500424603.

Brzoska, Michael and Andreas Heinemann-Grüder. 2004. 'Security Sector Reform and Post-conflict Reconstruction under International Auspices'. In *Reform and Reconstruction of the Security Sector*, edited by Alan Bryden and Heiner Hänggi, pp. 121–142. Münster: LIT Verlag.

Call, Charles T. 2002. 'Competing Donor Approaches to Post-conflict Police Reform'. *Conflict, Security and Development* 2(1): 99–120. doi:10.1080/14678800200590599.

Call, Chuck and Michael Barnett. 2000. 'Looking for a Few Good Cops: Peacekeeping, Peacebuilding and CIVPOL'. In *Peacebuilding and Police Reform*, edited by Espen Barth Eide and Tor Tanke Holm, pp. 43–68. London: Frank Cass.

Caplan, Richard. 2005. *International Governance of War-torn Territories:Rule and Reconstruction.* Oxford: Oxford University Press.

Cawthra, Gawin and Robin Luckham. 2003. *Governing Insecurity: Democratic Control of Military and Secuirty Establishments in Transitional Democracies.* London: Zed Books.

Cooper, Neil and Michael Pugh. 2002. 'Security-sector Transformation in Post-conflict Societies. The Conflict, Security and Development Group Working Papers'. London: Centre for Defence Studies, King's College London, available at: http://securityanddevelopment.org/pdf/work5.pdf.

Cordone, Claudio. 2000. 'Police Reform and Human Rights Investigations: The Experience of the UN Mission in Bosnia and Herzegovina'. In *Peacebuilding and Police Reform*, edited by Tor Tanke Holm and Espen Barth Eide, pp. 191–209. London: Frank Cass.

Davenport, Christian. 2007. 'State Repression and Political Order'. *Annual Review of Political Science* 10: 1–23. doi: 10.1146/annurev.polisci.10.101405.143216.

Denham, Tara. 2008. 'Police Reform and Gender'. Gender and Security Sector Reform Toolkit. Geneva: DCAF, OSCE/ODIHR, UN-INSTRAW.

Downie, Richard. 2013. 'Building Police Institutions in Fragile States. Case Studies from Africa'. A Report of the CSIS Africa Program. Washington, DC: Center for Strategic and International Studies.

Doyle, Michael W. and Nicholas Sambanis. 2006. *Making War and Building Peace. United Nations Peace Operations.* Princeton, NJ, and Oxford: Princeton University Press.

Fortna, Virginia Page. 2008. *Does Peacekeeping Work? Shaping Belligerents' Choices After Civil War.* Princeton, NJ: Princeton University Press.

Freedom House. 2012. Available at: www.freedomhouse.org/.

Gastrow, Peter and Mark Shaw. 2001. 'In Search of Safety: Police Transformation and Public Responses in South Africa'. *Daedalus* 130(1): 259–275.

Glassmyer, Katherine and Nicholas Sambanis. 2008. 'Rebel–Military Integration and Civil War Termination'. *Journal of Peace Research* 45(3): 365–384. doi:10.1177/0022343308088816.

Gross, Eva. 2009. *Security Sector Reform in Afghanistan: The EU's Contribution.* Occasional Paper, No.78 , 1 April 2009. Brussels: European Union Institute for Security Studies.

Hänggi, Heiner. 2004. 'Conceptualising Security Sector Reform and Reconstruction'. In *Reform and Reconstruction of the Security Sector*, edited by Alan Bryden and Heiner Hänggi, pp. 3–20. Münster: LIT Verlag.

Hartzell, Caroline and Matthew Hoddie. 2007. *Crafting Peace: Power-sharing Institutions and the Negotiated Settlement of Civil Wars.* University Park: The Pennsylvania State University Press.

Hartzell, Caroline, Matthew Hoddie and Donald Rothchild. 2001. 'Stabilizing the Peace After Civil War: An Investigation of Some Key Variables'. *International Organization* 55 (1): 183–208. doi:10.1162/002081801551450.

Heckman, James J. 1979. 'Sample Selection Bias as a Specification Error'. *Econometrica* 47(1): 153–161. doi:10.2307/1912352.

Hegre, Håvard, Lisa Hultman and Havard Mokleiv Nygard. 2011. 'Simulating the Effect of Peacekeeping Operations 2010–2035'. In *Social Computing, Behavioral-cultural Modeling and Prediction*, edited by John Salerno, Shanchieh Jay Yang, Dana Nau and Sun-Ki Chai, pp. 325–332. New York: Springer.

Hoeffler, Anke and Verity Outram. 2011. 'Need, Merit, or Self-Interest – What Determines the Allocation of Aid?' *Review of Development Economics* 15(2): 237–250. doi:10.1111/j.1467-9361.2011.00605.x.

Högbladh, Stina. 2011. 'Peace Agreements 1975–2011 – Updating the UCDP Peace Agreement Dataset'. In *States in Armed Conflict 2011*, edited by Thérése Pettersson and Lotta Themnér, pp. 39–56. Uppsala: Uppsala University, Department of Peace and Conflict Research.

Holsti, Kalevi J. 1996. *The State, War, and the State of War.* Cambridge: Cambridge University Press.

Jackson, Paul. 2011. 'Security Sector Reform and State Building'. *Third World Quarterly* 32(10): 1803–1822. doi:10.1080/01436597.2011.610577.

Koehler, Jan and Christoph Zürcher. 2003. 'Institutions and the Organization of Stability and Violence'. In *Potentials of Disorder*, edited by Jan Koehler and Christoph Zürcher, pp. 243–270. New Approaches to Conflict Analysis. Manchester: Manchester University Press.

Krause, K. 2012. 'Hybrid Violence: Locating the Use of Force in Postconflict Settings'. *Global Governance* 18(1): 39–56.

Kreutz, Joakim. 2010. 'How and When Armed Conflicts End: Introducing the UCDP Conflict Termination Dataset'. *Journal of Peace Research* 47(2): 243–250.

Lacina, Bethany and Nils Petter Gleditsch. 2005. 'Monitoring Trends in Global Combat: A New Dataset of Battle Deaths'. *European Journal of Population/Revue Européenne de Démographie* 21(2–3): 145–166. doi:10.1007/s10680-005-6851-6.

Lieberman, Evan. S. 2005. 'Nested Analysis as a Mixed-method Strategy for Comparative Research'. *American Political Science Review* 99(3): 435–452.

Mac Ginty, Roger. 2011. *International Peacebuilding and Local Resistance: Hybrid Forms of Peace.* New York: Palgrave Macmillan.

Marshall, Monty and Keith Jaggers. 2002. 'Political Regime Characteristics and Transitions, 1800–2000: Dataset Users' Manual'. Polity IV Project, University of Maryland, available at: www.cidcm.umd.edu/inscr/polity.

Muehlmann, Thomas. 2008. 'Police Restructuring in Bosnia-Herzegovina: Problems of Internationally-led Security Sector Reform'. *Journal of Intervention and Statebuilding* 2(1): 1–22. doi:10.1080/17502970701810856.

Nkurunziza, J. 2010. 'Civil War and Post-conflict Physical Capital Reconstruction in Africa'. In *Globalisation, Institutions and African Economic Development – Proceedings of the African Economic Conference 2008*, pp. 337–365.

OECD. 2007. 'OECD DAC Handbook on Security System Reform. Supporting Security and Justice'. Paris: Organisation for Economic Co-Operation and Development, available at: www.oecd.org/development/incaf/38406485.pdf.

O'Neill, William G. 2005. 'Police Reform in Post-conflict Societies: What We Know and What We Still Need to Know'. Policy Paper, The Security–Development Nexus Program. New York: International Peace Academy, available at: www.ipinst.org/~ipinst/media/pdf/publications/polreferpt.pdf.

Pachon, Alejandro. 2012. 'Financing Security Sector Reform: A Review of Official Development Asisstance Data'. *CIGI SSR Issue Papers* 4.

Paris, Roland and Timothy D. Sisk, eds. 2009. *The Dilemmas of Statebuilding: Confronting the Contradictions of Postwar Peace Operations*. London: Routledge.

Perdomo, Catalina. 2007. 'International Assistance for Security Sector Reform'. *OASIS* 12: 77–117.

Roeder, Philip G. and Donald Rothchild. 2005. 'Power Sharing as an Impediment to Peace and Democracy'. In *Sustainable Peace: Power and Democracy after Civil Wars*, edited by Philip G. Roeder and Donald Rothchild, pp. 29–50. Ithaca, NY: Cornell University Press.

Schroeder, Ursula C. and Fairlie Chappuis. 2014. 'New Perspectives on Security Sector Reform: The Role of Local Agency and Domestic Politics'. *International Peacekeeping* 21(2): 133–148. doi:10.1080/13533312.2014.910401.

Schroeder, Ursula C., Fairlie Chappuis and Deniz Kocak. 2014. 'Security Sector Reform and the Emergence of Hybrid Security Governance'. *International Peacekeeping* 21(2): 214–230. doi:10.1080/13533312.2014.910405.

Sedra, Mark. 2010. 'Security Sector Reform 101: Understanding the Concept, Charting Trends and Identifying Challenges'. Waterloo, Ontario, Canada: The Centre for International Governance Innovation, available at: https://www.cigionline.org/sites/default/files/ssr_101_final_april_27.pdf.

Simons, Claudia and Franzisca Zanker. 2013. 'Die Polizeireform in Den Postkonfliktstaaten Burundi Und Liberia [Police Reform in Post-conflict Burundi and Liberia]'. 5. GIGA Focus Afrika. Hamburg: GIGA German Institute of Global and Area Studies.

Sisk, Timothy D. 2008. 'Power Sharing after Civil Wars: Matching Problems to Solutions'. In *Contemporary Peacemaking. Conflict, Peace Processes and Post-war Reconstruction*, edited by John Darby and Roger Mac Ginty, pp. 195–209. New York: Palgrave Macmillan.

Strohmeyer, Hansjörg. 2001. 'Collapse and Reconstruction of a Judicial System: The United Nations Missions in Kosovo and East Timor'. *The American Journal of International Law* 95(1): 46–63. doi:10.2307/2642036.

Themnér, Lotta and Peter Wallensteen. 2013. 'Armed Conflicts, 1946–2012'. *Journal of Peace Research* 50(4): 509–521. doi:10.1177/0022343313494396.

Tierney, Michael J., Daniel L. Nielson, Darren G. Hawkins, J. Timmons Roberts, Michael G. Findley, Ryan M. Powers, Bradley Parks, Sven E. Wilson and Robert L. Hicks. 2011. 'More Dollars than Sense: Refining Our Knowledge of Development Finance Using AidData'. *World Development* 39(11): 1891–1906.

Tilly, Charles. 1975. 'Western-state Making and Theories of Political Transformation'. In *The Formation of National States in Western Europe*, pp. 601–686. Princeton, NJ: Princeton University Press.

UCDP. 2013. 'UCDP Battle-related Deaths Dataset v.5-2013'. Uppsala: Uppsala University.

United Nations. 2015. 'Per Capita GDP at Current Prices – US Dollars'. UN Data, available at: https://data.un.org/Data.aspx?d=SNAAMA&f=grID%3A101%3BcurrID%3AUSD %3BpcFlag%3A1.

USDS. 2001. '"United Kingdom". Independent States '. United Kingdom Country Reports on Human Rights Practices. Washington, DC: U.S. Department of State, Bureau of Democracy, Human Rights, and Labor, available at: www.state.gov/j/drl/rls/hrrpt/2000/ eur/856.htm.

USDS. 2003. 'Bangladesh'. Country Reports on Human Rights Practices. Washington, DC: U.S. Department of State, Bureau of Democracy, Human Rights, and Labor, available at: www.state.gov/j/drl/rls/hrrpt/2002/18309.htm.

Valasek, Kristin. 2008. 'Security Sector Reform and Gender'. In *Gender and Security Sector Reform Toolkit*, edited by Megan Bastick and Kristin Valasek. Geneva: DCAF, OSCE/ODIHR, UN-INSTRAW.

Walter, Barbara F. 2002. *Committing to Peace: The Successful Settlement of Civil Wars*. Princeton, NJ: Princeton University Press.

Wiatrowski, Michael D. and Jack A. Goldstone. 2010. 'The Ballot and the Badge: Democratic Policing'. *Journal of Democracy* 21(2): 79–92. doi:10.1353/jod.0.0168.

Wolff, Stefan. 2011. 'Managing Ethno-national Conflict: Towards an Analytical Framework'. *Commonwealth and Comparative Politics* 49(2): 162–195.

Wooldridge, Jeffrey M. 2008. *Introductory Econometrics: A Modern Approach*. Australia: South Western.

Wulf, Herberg. 2004. *Security Sector Reform in Developing and Transitional Countries*. Berlin: Berghof Research Center for Constructive Conflict Management.

**Appendix**

Table 7.3 List of cases

| Number | Country | Peace agreement | Agreement date | Were police accountability reforms implemented? |
|---|---|---|---|---|
| 1 | Angola | The Bicesse Agreement | 31 May 1991 | No |
| 2 | Angola | The Lusaka Protocol | 20 November 1994 | No |
| 3 | Angola | Memorandum of Understanding or Memorandum of Intent | 4 April 2002 | Yes |
| 4 | Angola | Memorandum of Understanding on Peace and National Reconciliation in Cabinda Province | 1 August 2006 | No |
| 5 | Bangladesh | Chittagong Hill Tracts Peace Accord | 2 December 1997 | No |
| 6 | Bosnia and Herzegovina | The Washington Agreement | 1 March 1994 | Yes |
| 7 | Bosnia and Herzegovina | The General Framework Agreement for Peace in Bosnia and Herzegovina (the Dayton Agreement) | 14 December 1995 | Yes |
| 8 | Burundi | Arusha Peace and Reconciliation Agreement for Burundi | 28 August 2000 | Yes |
| 9 | Burundi | Ceasefire Agreement between the Transitional Government of Burundi and the Conseil national pour la défense de ladémocratie-Forces pour la défense de la démocratie | 2 December 2002 | Yes |
| 10 | Burundi | The Pretoria Protocol on Political, Defence and Security Power Sharing in Burundi | 8 October 2003 | Yes |
| 11 | Burundi | The Pretoria Protocol on Outstanding Political, Defence and Security Power Sharing Issues in Burundi | 2 November 2003 | Yes |
| 12 | Burundi | Agreement of Principles Towards Lasting Peace, Security and Stability | 18 June 2006 | Yes |
| 13 | Burundi | Comprehensive Ceasefire Agreement between the Government of Burundi and the Palipehutu-FNL | 7 September 2006 | Yes |
| 14 | Cambodia | Agreement on a Comprehensive Political Settlement of the Cambodia Conflict 'The Paris Agreement' | 23 October 1991 | No |

| | | | | |
|---|---|---|---|---|
| 15 | Colombia | Acuerdo final Gobierno Nacional-Ejército Popular De Liberación | 15 February 1991 | Yes |
| 16 | Comoros | Agreement on the transitional arrangements in the Comoros | 20 December 2003 | No |
| 17 | Congo | Accord de Cessez-le-Feu et de Cessation des Hostilités | 29 December 1999 | Yes |
| 18 | Croatia | The Erdut Agreement | 12 November 1995 | Yes |
| 19 | Democratic Republic of Congo | Political agreement on consensual management of the transition in the Democratic Republic of the Congo | 16 April 2002 | No |
| 20 | Democratic Republic of Congo | Global and Inclusive Agreement on the Transition in the Democratic Republic of Congo | 16 December 2002 | Yes |
| 21 | Democratic Republic of Congo | Inter-Congolese Political Negotiations – The Final Act | 2 April 2003 | Yes |
| 22 | Democratic Republic of Congo | 23 March 2009 Agreement | 23 March 2009 | Yes |
| 23 | Djibouti | Accord de reforme et concorde civile | 12 May 2001 | No |
| 24 | El Salvador | New York Agreement | 25 September 1991 | Yes |
| 25 | El Salvador | Mexico Agreements | 27 April 1991 | Yes |
| 26 | El Salvador | The Compressed Negotiations | 25 September 1991 | Yes |
| 27 | El Salvador | The Chapultepec Peace Agreement | 16 January 1992 | Yes |
| 28 | Guatemala | The Agreement on Constitutional Reforms and the Electoral Regime | 7 December 1996 | Yes |
| 29 | Guatemala | The Agreement on the Implementation, Compliance and Verification Timetable for the Peace Agreements | 29 December 1996 | Yes |
| 30 | Guatemala | The Agreement on the Strengthening of Civilian Power and the Role of the Armed Forces in a Democratic Society | 19 September 1996 | Yes |
| 31 | Haiti | The Governor's Island agreement | 3 July 1993 | Yes |
| 32 | India | Memorandum of Understanding with TNV | 12 August 1988 | No |
| 33 | India | Memorandum of Settlement | 23 August 1993 | No |

Table 7.3 continued

| Number | Country | Peace agreement | Agreement date | Were police accountability reforms implemented? |
|---|---|---|---|---|
| 34 | Indonesia | Cessation of Hostilities Framework Agreement | 9 December 2002 | Yes |
| 35 | Indonesia | Memorandum of Understanding between the Government of the Republic of Indonesia and the Free Aceh Movement | 15 August 2005 | Yes |
| 36 | Israel | Declaration of Principles on Interim Self-Government Arrangements/Oslo Agreement | 13 September 1993 | No |
| 37 | Israel | Agreement on the Gaza Strip and the Jericho Area | 4 May 1994 | No |
| 38 | Israel | Israeli–Palestinian Interim Agreement on the West Bank and the Gaza Strip/Oslo B | 28 September 1995 | Yes |
| 39 | Israel | Protocol on Redeployment in Hebron | 15 January 1997 | Yes |
| 40 | Israel | The Wye River Memorandum | 23 October 1998 | No data |
| 41 | Israel | The Sharm el-Sheik Memorandum Wye II | September 04, 1999 | Yes |
| 42 | Ivory Coast | Linas–Marcoussis Peace Accords | 23 January 2003 | Yes |
| 43 | Ivory Coast | Pretoria Agreement on the Peace Process in Côte d'Ivoire | 6 April 2005 | No |
| 44 | Ivory Coast | Ouagadougou Political Agreement | 4 March 2007 | No |
| 45 | Ivory Coast | Fourth Complementary Agreement to the Ouagadougou Political Agreement | 22 December 2008 | No |
| 46 | Liberia | Akosombo Peace Agreement | 12 September 1994 | No |
| 47 | Liberia | Accra Ceasefire Agreement | 17 June 2003 | Yes |
| 48 | Liberia | Accra Peace Agreement | 18 August 2003 | Yes |
| 49 | Macedonia | The Ohrid Agreement | 13 August 2001 | Yes |
| 50 | Mali | Pacte National | 11 April 1992 | No |
| 51 | Mozambique | The Protocol on the Agreed Agenda | 28 May 1991 | No |
| 52 | Mozambique | The Acordo Geral de Paz (AGP) | 4 October 1992 | No |
| 53 | Nepal | Comprehensive Peace Agreement, 2006 | 21 November 2006 | No |
| 54 | Niger | Accord e tablissant une paix définitive entre le gouvernement de la republique du Niger et lórganisation de la résistance armée | 15 April 1995 | No |

| No. | Country | Agreement | Date | Implemented |
|---|---|---|---|---|
| 55 | Papua New Guinea | Bougainville Peace Agreement | 30 August 2001 | Yes |
| 56 | Philippines | GRP-RAM/SFP/YOU General Agreement for Peace | 13 October 1995 | No |
| 57 | Philippines | Mindanao Final Agreement | 2 September 1996 | No |
| 58 | Rwanda | The Protocols of Agreement between the Government of the Republic of Rwanda and the Rwandese Patriotic Front on Power Sharing within the Framework of a Broad-Based Transitional Government, | 9 January 1993 | No |
| 59 | Rwanda | The Protocol Agreement between the Government of the Republic of Rwanda and the Rwandese Patriotic Front on the Integration of Armed Forces and The Protocol of Agreement between the Government of the Republic of Rwanda and the Rwandese Patriotic Front on Miscellaneous Issues and Final Provisions | 3 August 1993 | No |
| 60 | Rwanda | The Protocol of Agreement between the Government of the Republic of Rwanda and the Rwandese Patriotic Front on the Repatriation of Refugees and the Resettlement of Displaced Persons, | 9 June 1993 | No |
| 61 | Rwanda | Arusha Accords | 4 August 1993 | No |
| 62 | Sierra Leone | Abidjan Peace Agreement | 30 November 1996 | No |
| 63 | Sierra Leone | Lomé Peace Agreement | 7 July 1999 | Yes |
| 64 | Somalia | Addis Ababa Agreement | 27 March 1993 | No Data |
| 65 | Somalia | Nairobi Declaration on National Reconciliation | 24 March 1994 | No |
| 66 | South Africa | Interim Constitution | 18 November 1993 | Yes |
| 67 | South Africa | Western Contact Group (WCG) Settlement Proposal | 12 July 1978 | No |
| 68 | Sudan | Agreement on Security Arrangements During the Interim Period | 25 September 2003 | No |
| 69 | Sudan | Protocol Between the GOS and SPLM on Power Sharing | 26 May 2004 | No |
| 70 | Sudan | The Protocol Between the GOS and SPLM on the Resolution of Conflict in Southern Kordofan/Nuba Mountains and Blue Nile States | 26 May 2004 | No |
| 71 | Sudan | Sudan Comprehensive Peace Agreement | 9 January 2005 | No |

*Table 7.3* continued

| Number | Country | Peace agreement | Agreement date | Were police accountability reforms implemented? |
|---|---|---|---|---|
| 72 | Sudan | Darfur Peace Agreement | 5 May 2006 | No |
| 73 | Sudan | Doha Agreement | 23 February 2010 | Yes |
| 74 | Uganda | Nairobi Peace Agreement | 17 December 1985 | No data |
| 75 | Uganda | Agreement on Comprehensive Solutions between the Government of the Republic of Uganda and Lord's Resistance Army/Movement | 2 May 2007 | No |
| 76 | Uganda | Implementation protocol to the Agreement on Comprehensive Solutions | 22 February 2008 | No |
| 77 | United Kingdom | The Good Friday Agreement | 10 April 1998 | Yes |
| 78 | Zimbabwe | Lancaster House Agreement | 21 December 1979 | Yes |

# 8 Armed disorder after peace

## Armed actors, conflict and reform in nineteenth-century Mexico, *c.* 1820 to 1870

### Esteban Ramírez González

> The main foundations of every state [.] are good laws and good arms; and because you cannot have good laws without good arms, and where there are good arms, good laws inevitably follow, I shall not discuss laws but give my attention to arms.
>
> —Niccolò Machiavelli, *The Prince*, XII

## Introduction

This chapter addresses post-conflict reform from a historical perspective, moving beyond a dichotomous distinction between conflict and peace in order to focus instead on the transformation of concatenated forms of armed disorder in the aftermath of violent conflict. As an alternative to the conventional emphasis on path dependence and critical junctures at the macro level, this chapter focuses on competing models for the organization of armed force as well as their transformation over time. The following sections provide empirical evidence from large-scale reforms that attempted to transform the organization of armed force in nineteenth-century Mexico, as a point of departure from which to probe the counterintuitive mix of continuity and discontinuity that accompanies transitions between periods of conflict and reform (from violent conflict to 'armed disorder'). On this basis, I stress two sets of mechanisms shaping post-conflict settings: (1) institutional learning and emulation, and (2) *ad hoc* adaptation and improvisation.

The relevance of these questions is patent in contemporary debates about 'hybrid' violence and statebuilding in the developing world (Krause 2009, 2012). Mexico, for example, still faces blurred boundaries between violent conflict and armed disorder and between political violence and criminal violence, and which were common in the nineteenth century (Felbab-Brown 2015). In parts of both Latin America and the developing world at large, locally organized armed actors openly compete for power and resources, and closely interact, through varying levels of conflict or cooperation, with state institutions (Krause 2010; Schlichte 2009; Staniland 2012, 2015). In some cases, in present-day Latin America, criminal organizations have taken the 'functionally equivalent role of mini-states by monopolizing the means of violence and providing protection in exchange for loyalty and territorial dominion' (Davis 2010: 30; see also Lupsha 1996), as did rogue military commanders and local militias in the nineteenth century.

A considerable body of literature has already addressed some of these puzzles independently, including the contributions to this volume that are concerned with power-sharing agreements, conflict cleavages, and the properties of institutional reforms that increase likelihood of a sustainable peace in the aftermath of conflict. Similarly, scholars have relied on the notions of path dependency and critical junctures in order to address the seemingly dichotomous nature of long-term institutional change.[1] In the following sections I make the case for bringing the organizational and historical dimensions of armed actor dynamics to the centre of questions about post-conflict reform. On this basis, the chapter concludes with some reflections regarding the paradoxical patterns of institutional change driven by armed actors in those settings – such as present-day Latin America – where, rather than peace or outright conflict, armed disorder and low-intensity violence remain the norm.

## Armed disorder after peace: three interrelated puzzles

From a historical perspective, post-conflict reform poses three interrelated puzzles that are relevant in contemporary debates about political violence and state building: (1) the persistence of violence in the aftermath of formal peace; (2) the resilience of wartime organizations and local governance mechanisms (in particular, armed actors and traditional authority structures) in post-conflict settings, and (3) the dependence on wartime actors and governance mechanisms for the implementation and success of post-conflict reforms. These puzzles (and practical challenges for peacebuilders) may be summarized as the problem of 'armed disorder' after peace.

The persistence of different forms of armed disorder – in the guise of the 'low-intensity' conflict or 'hybrid' violence occurring after peace settlements have been reached, or of latent conflict cleavages – is striking in both contemporary and historical instances of armed conflict. Recently, scholars have identified 'the continuing salience of economic and political violence' (Berdal and Zaum 2013: 3) in post-conflict economies, as well as the existence of 'chaotic governance and security configurations' (Meagher 2012: 1074) based on informal systems and the agency of local communities.[2] In many post-conflict settings, governance configurations usually entail the coexistence of state structures and autonomous armed actors rather than effective 'monopolies of legitimate coercion' and the rule of law (Davis 2008: 4).

Such continuity often reflects governments' lack of autonomy and capacity as much as wartime actors' adaptation to emerging state institutions and governance configurations in post-conflict settings (Boege *et al.* 2009: 22). Wartime actors become incorporated into formal government structures by serving as intermediaries, placing strategic resources at the service of the state, or through the formation of new identities or alliances with government, business, and criminal interests. In recent post-conflict settings, for example, wartime actors have re-emerged 'as commercial organizations, as community-based NGOs, and in quasi-administrative roles [.] while remaining able to exploit wartime commercial expertise and connections' (Reno 2010: 135).

Furthermore, when the state or third parties lack the institutional autonomy and infrastructural capacity to control the implementation of post-conflict reforms, wartime actors and local governance mechanisms often 'capture' (privatizing, adapting or neutralizing) top-down initiatives such as disarmament, demobilization and reintegration (DDR) efforts and power-sharing agreements. Modern-day Afghanistan, for example, illustrates the type of post-conflict disorder in which the state has waived 'the goal of maintaining a monopoly of violence [because of] the persistence of warlords or militia commanders [with autonomous armed forces]' (Mac Ginty 2013: 23).

## Armed disorder and post-conflict reform in nineteenth-century Mexico

Nineteenth-century Mexico provides an ideal scenario in which to examine questions about the interaction between armed disorder and post-conflict reform over time. In the aftermath of Independence (1821), social and political actors equipped with their own armed organizations actively participated in conflict dynamics and helped shape post-conflict institutional reforms. In the 1830s conflicts between regular army and provincial militia units led to the first large-scale reorganization of force in the country. In the following decades centralist (and, subsequently, pro-military) governments endeavoured to strengthen and reform the regular army in order to impose their authority upon provincial elites, rural communities, and on their autonomous armed forces. Federalist and, subsequently, liberal governments pursued a similar centralizing agenda, but did so instead on the basis of alliances formed among provincial governments, politicians and their autonomous forces (Costeloe 1975, 2000; Medina 2007; Sinkin 1979).

However, in the long term, the lack of institutional capacity and infrastructural power at the national level – compounded by frequent rebellions, fiscal crises and foreign interventions – frustrated both of these efforts. One disillusioned observer characterized armed disorder in nineteenth-century Mexico in the following terms:

> In Mexico, the mistaken view that governments cannot enforce their authority without soldiers has multiplied military organizations [.]. Auxiliary troops, gendarmes, public security guards, and civic militias are all the same thing under different guises, but have not contributed to the security which governments hoped to achieve through their creation.
>
> (Mora 1986 [1836]: I: 407–458)

Armed actor dynamics, moreover, spanned conflict and post-conflict periods. During times of conflict, armed actors secured territorial control, appointed local authorities, regulated trade, levied taxes, and acquired control over foreign trade and custom houses. In the aftermath of conflict, wartime actors endured and played a key role by mediating in the adaptation of national-level reforms and institutions in local contexts (Escalante 1992, 1999). In short, in nineteenth-century Mexico the persistence of armed disorder and the resilience of wartime actors constituted the main challenges confronted by state-building reformers. But who were the main wartime actors perpetuating armed disorder in post-conflict settings, and what was their relationship to local governance mechanisms and macro-level disputes over emerging state institutions?

## Organizational models and governance mechanisms

The heterogeneity displayed by the armed units emerging from periods of violent conflict, the lack of available systematic data and the current gaps in the secondary literature pose significant challenges for the study of armed actor dynamics in nineteenth-century Mexico. Drawing from primary and secondary sources documenting armed political mobilizations, as well as of a systematic study of legislation and ministerial reports, this chapter is able to reconstruct the prevalent organizational models of armed force active during this period (1820–1870), namely the national army, local militias and the National Guard. On this basis, the following sections trace their interactions during periods of both conflict and reform.[3]

### Regular army

The regular army was established in 1821 as an amalgam of 'regular' and 'auxiliary' royalist militias with irregular insurgent guerrillas. The army displayed a remarkable symbolic continuity and remained the dominant model during the period, which has led many historians to include all types of armed actors under this label: the army of the time lacked, however, infrastructural capacity and institutional continuity, and cannot be treated as a unitary actor. First, despite considerable military spending by the national government, commanders often had to improvise their own units, securing funds and conscripts through private means during periods of armed conflict (DePalo 1997: 19, 25, 27). Frontier garrisons (*presidios*) and detachments (*guarniciones*) deployed to distant rural areas, reportedly degenerated into lawlessness, or were recurrently left destitute by the predatory practices of their commanding officers (DePalo 1997: 19, 25; Escalante 1992; Fowler 1996: 4; Kahle 1997: 174–175).

Historians have, echoing nineteenth-century polemics against militarism, tended to describe the army as a monolithic entity, one subservient to corporate interests and conservative politics (Kahle 1997). More recent accounts have in contrast emphasized the army's heterogeneity and internal divisions, in particular how different interests and conflicts present within society at large were reproduced within the army itself (DePalo 1997: 25; Fowler 1996; Hernández López 2001: 16). While regular army units did indeed coalesce in the defence of common interests (for example, pro-military policies and the demands for judicial and fiscal privileges (*fueros*)), such instances of collective action were ultimately rare, short-lived and ideologically inconsistent. Large-scale coalitions were particularly dependent on negotiations between military commanders and politicians, as much as they were on the commanders' capacity to maintain the loyalty of their (forcefully recruited) troops (DePalo 1997; Fowler 2000a, 2000b: 25–26, 46).

For this reason, even when ideological divides turned into decisive conflict cleavages at the national level, different armed units followed divergent strategies for the fulfilment of their agendas: those directly controlled by popular military commanders or national politicians tended to adopt their patrons' ideology (Stevens 1991: 34), while detachments in rural areas were more likely to negotiate with local actors – municipal or provincial governments and their militias – in order to reconcile their grievances and ideological preferences with the chance of backing the winning party (Costeloe 1975, 2000; DePalo 1997: 81; Medina 2007).

Disputes at the national level, such as the contest between federalism and centralism, were often appropriated by armed actors involved in different local conflicts. Pro-centralist rebellions, for instance, provided an (armed) outlet for municipal grievances against the 'tyranny' of provincial capitals (Hernández Chávez 1989; Katz 1988: 91–100, 266, 463–470; Reina 1998: 30–35). Conversely, private conflicts between economic elites, such as those over free trade versus protectionist policies, could also escalate into national-level rifts. In 1841, for example, General Paredes toppled the protectionist government of General Bustamante with support from provincial merchants interested in securing lower import tariffs. Despite the contradictory economic interests of their sponsors, both governments advocated for a similar pro-military and conservative centralism (Córdova 1976: 12; DePalo 1997: 41).

## *Local militias: provincial and civic*

I use the term 'local militias' to designate an intermediate form of armed organization – between the extremes set by the professional regular army and irregular guerrilla units. During this period (1820–1870), locally organized armed forces were characterized by their close connection with local governance arrangements, which they tended to reproduce as much in their command and fiscal structures as they did in their social outlook and ideological affinities. An important distinction must be made here between 'provincial' and 'civic' militias – the former funded and organized by provincial governments as autonomous armed forces and the latter by municipal governments or rural communities for the purposes of self-defence and the promotion of public order (DePalo 1997: 19; Kahle 1997: 111–147, 183–189).

Traditional historiography identifies a clear-cut alignment between different ideologies and armed organizations; that is, between liberal politicians and local militias (and subsequently National Guard units) and between conservatives and the regular army. However, a detailed analysis of War Ministry reports (*Memorias de Guerra*) submitted to Congress suggests that there was a long-standing tension between professional soldiers' disregard for irregular forces (and outright fear of popular mass mobilization) and the progressive realization that locally funded forces constituted a necessary alternative to the costly ranks of rebellious officers and ever-deserting conscripts that made up the regular army.[4]

While both the regular army and militia units of the time may be justifiably characterized as a 'collection of provincial constabularies more concerned with preserving regional autonomy than defending national interests' (DePalo 1997: 25). However, there were significant differences in the kinds of intermediate actors and meso-level governance mechanisms that these models privileged. The army strengthened the influence of 'national' military and political leaders (*caudillos*) and of a network of regional military commands (*comandancias militares*) with fiscal and political attributions. On the other hand, local militias empowered a rising generation of provincial governors, regional politicians and military commanders, supported by nascent administrative structures. There was also considerable fluidity among them: militias and other locally organized forces were occasionally incorporated into regular or auxiliary army units as a reward for supporting successful rebellions in their specific regions or as a desperate measure to compensate for mass desertions (*Memoria [.] 1850*: 28).

### The National Guard

The National Guard (NG) was established in the wake of the insufficiency of regular army units during the US–Mexican War (1846–1848). Local units were organized by municipal and provincial authorities, with the help of material and financial assistance from the national government.[5] In a deliberate attempt to avoid the negative features of decentralized militias that had raised their heads between the 1820s and 1830s, national legislation introduced some key institutional changes: while NG units remained dependent on local governance configurations and previous experiences of administering an armed force, the new institutional design placed these decentralized units under a common regulatory framework and made them subject to *dual* (provincial and national) control and ownership structures (Dublán and Lozano 1876–1912: 5: 162–169, 414–421).

In the same way that previous models of decentralized armed force had privileged a particular set of intermediate actors and governance mechanisms, the establishment of the NG contributed to the emergence of a network of provincial governors, local politicians and NG commanders in the years between the 1860s and 1870s which historians have identified as forming the basis for an emerging 'political machine' (Medina 2007: 273–330; Perry 1978; Sinkin 1979: 75–91).

### Irregular groups: heterogeneity and fluidity

Irregular armed groups consisting of bandits, private guards, demobilized military units and smugglers were also active throughout this period (Vanderwood 2009, 2014). Endemic violence and rural insecurity incentivized the decentralization of coercive resources: indigenous communities, estates (*haciendas*) and small rural communities (*pueblos*) formed their own armed units for the purpose of private protection (Hernández Chávez 1989; Kahle 1997; Vanderwood 2009). These parochial units were also drawn into large-scale political conflicts by their sponsors, and, during periods of violent conflict and their aftermath, irregular units displayed high levels of fluidity to and from ad hoc militias and security guards (*guardias de seguridad*) set up by the government.[6] Transitions between different models of organized force often displayed a degree of symmetry. For instance, disbanded *caudillo* armies and bands of deserters infested the countryside in the aftermath of armed conflicts, while bandits and rebel guerrillas were patronized by parties to conflict during times of civil and international strife, in order to subject their opponents and their civilian supporters to low-intensity warfare (Tamayo 1972: 327; Vanderwood 2009:63–73).

### *Armed political mobilization and institutional reform*

Heterogeneity and fluidity in the organization of armed force made for incredibly complex political dynamics and counterintuitive alliances. This interaction, occurring throughout periods of both conflict and reform, provides a valuable point of reference by which to bridge the study of these violent statebuilding conflicts – resulting from 'context-specific social conflict, historically contingent processes and institutional learning and adaptation' (Egnell and Haldén 2013: 1) – and contemporary inquiries into post-conflict reform.

In particular, armed political mobilization in the form of *pronunciamientos* – declarations of rebellion or allegiance by a variety of different (armed) political actors – were common practice in nineteenth-century Mexico. *Pronunciamientos* were formalized by the official acts or memoranda stating grievances and making proposals for their resolution, which were signed by military commanders, representatives of different armed units, and municipal and provincial officials.[7] These documents allow us to map the participation of different armed organizations in the armed politics of the period.

Figure 8.1 presents a summary of armed units' participation in *pronunciamientos* between 1821 and 1862. It illustrates the three major trends that are assessed over the course of this chapter: the predominance of the regular army (*c.* 1820–1860), the rise and eventual demise of local militias (*c.*1820–1840), and the ascent of the NG (*c.*1840–1860).

Figure 8.1 also illustrates the considerable increase in legislative output concerned with military organization and reform during this time period. This sample comprises laws, decrees, memoranda and ministerial directives, and evidences the strong commitment to legal and institutional reform displayed by contemporary political and military leaders (DePalo 1997: 23–24, 39, 47–48; Fowler 1996).

Over the years, organizational models and regulatory blueprints became increasingly sophisticated, combining clear signs of innovation and learning with self-reference and short-term adaptation. Pre-Independence legislation, for example, continued to be invoked well into the 1850s, while throughout this period reformers reinstated legislation and regulations that had been drafted by their ideological predecessors.[8] These ambitious attempts to control and normalize

*Figure 8.1* Armed mobilization and legislative output on military organization (c.1820–1860).

Notes

*Legislation, decrees and government memoranda addressing the organization of armed force, including those regarding the regular army ('permanent' and 'active') units, militias ('provincial' and 'civic'), as well as other security forces (e.g. National Guard).

Source: Data compiled from Dublán and Lozano (1876–1877, vols I–IX).

** Participation of regular army units, National Guard and local militias in *pronunciamientos* (rebellions or counter-rebellions).

Source: Data compiled from Fowler *et al.*, 'El Pronunciamiento in Independent Mexico' database, University of St Andrews.

| | 1820–30 | 1830–40 | 1840–50 | 1850–60 |
|---|---|---|---|---|
| Legislative output [right-hand scale]* | 12 | 82 | 187 | 348 |
| Regular army** | 27 | 139 | 177 | 74 |
| Local militia [freq.]** | 6 | 139 | 177 | 8 |
| National Guard [freq.]** | | | 8 | 38 |

through a nascent legal-bureaucratic apparatus the multiple forms of organized coercion that existed are often dismissed as naive and unrealistic. Yet a key dimension of this apparent failure – namely the resilience of wartime actors and the continued dependence of post-conflict reforms on local governance mechanisms – has thus far not received sufficient attention in the historiography.

### Key mechanisms and structural constraints

In the aftermath of conflict, wartime actors succeeded in shaping post-conflict settings, 'capturing' emerging state institutions, and adapting top-down reforms in order to reinforce their authority and autonomy on the ground. In this context, key structural factors shaped the role played by predominant armed forces' organizational models in the long-term iteration of conflict and reform.

#### Local concentration of authority and the decentralization of armed force

The local concentration of resources and political power in the hands of *caudillos*, municipalities, landowners, and indigenous villages following Independence made it easier for local elites to organize armed units on the basis of traditional authority and governance structures (Hamnett 1986; Medina 2007: 173–189; Ortíz Escamilla 2014). Given the lack of infrastructural capacity and the significant costs involved in running large-scale organizations, national and provincial governments effectively operated through informal arrangements, with local and meso-level actors serving as intermediaries (Escalante 1992; Katz 1988; Wiarda 1998: 35–36).

   Local actors thus contributed private authority and resources in exchange for legitimacy and autonomy, or for incorporation into formal government structures. In particular, during periods of conflict, the capacity to mobilize locally organized armed forces increased these actors' bargaining power and direct control over local resources and governance structures. In post-conflict settings moreover, reforms offered such local (armed) actors the opportunity to reinforce existing local governance mechanisms and traditional structures. When national governments' dictates were incompatible with their own interests, rebellion remained a privileged exit strategy available to actors with armed forces at their disposal (Katz 1998; Reina 1998).

#### Decentralized armed forces and the political economy of rebellion

In this context the predominant organizational models had a strong impact on the nature of decentralized armed units, as much as they also did on their capacity to successfully interact with the contemporary political system through the mediums of rebellion and armed mobilization. Given that nineteenth-century rebellions disrupted the fragile flow of fiscal resources – through their targeting of custom houses, mints and profitable state monopolies, or by paralysing taxable economic activities – governments were often toppled by rebellion-induced insolvency rather than by outright military defeat (Tenenbaum 1986). Military units were well aware that orchestrating a critical mass of rebellions in strategic locations was enough to deprive the national government of essential resources for its survival (Kahle 1997: 111–139; Perry 1978: 205–208). Given the costs of scaling up military and political operations beyond local environments, however, rebellions and parochial armed units rarely ventured beyond their comfort zones without the support of external sponsors, which constrained the bargaining power and political possibilities of local armed groups (Reina 1998).

In 1857 an overwhelmed War Minister personally complained to the Interior Minister about the constant demands for military interventions made by provincial governors and district prefects so as to combat disorder and rural insecurity: 'If [on every request] it becomes necessary to deploy the army [.] no armed force will ever suffice and the available troops will be distracted from their true purpose.'[9] Rather than requesting the deployment of troops, the War Minister further argued, local authorities should instead endeavour to re-establish order with the support of (armed) members of their own local community.[10]

The decentralization of armed resources and the prevalence of local armed mobilization shaped national governments' counterintuitive decision to tolerate and even promote the development of autonomous armed units by local actors, in the context of a *zeitgeist* of ongoing general rebellion and political instability. Once such a system of decentralized coercion had been established, both formal and informal arrangements conceded a privileged role to armed intermediaries.

*Intermediaries, organizational models and reform*

Despite considerable efforts to create centralized organizations and autonomous agents, the national government generally failed to achieve overall control over local and intermediate actors during this period. In this context, therefore, prevalent organizational models help us specify some of the meso-level mechanisms shaping the reproduction of wartime actors in post-conflict settings. In particular, efforts aimed at post-conflict reform also allowed wartime actors, such as different types of armed units, a significant measure of control over the implementation of reforms, and empowered intermediaries who were thus capable of adapting new frameworks to their own needs while exacerbating existing tensions between decentralized wartime actors and the national governments dependent on their support (Carmagnani 1983: 287–289; Hernández Chávez 1989: 266).

## Unpacking post-conflict reforms

The following sections unpack three key periods of conflict and reform in order to illustrate the influence that adaptation and short-term improvisation on the ground had on top-down efforts for the reorganization of armed force. The significant continuity between violent conflict and post-conflict disorder – from a historical perspective – challenges the dichotomous interpretation of conflict and peace, and furthermore raises questions about the mechanisms through which wartime actors shape the implementation of post-conflict reforms.

## Conflicts and the demise of provincial militias, 1821–1835

Mexico's independence resulted from an agreement between the key factions – the royalist army and militias on the one side, insurgent guerrillas on the other – involved in a violent War of Independence (1810–1821). However, the settlement was ultimately short-lived, as the new imperial (1822–1823) and republican (1824–1827) governments were unable to address the underlying tensions that existed between formal government institutions and the de facto governance (and armed) configurations that had emerged during a decade of insurgency and civil war (Escalante 1992: 162; Hamnett 1986; Ortíz Escamilla 2014: 11–18).

In this context, ideological undertones and political interests resonated with the alternatives for arranging armed force. Local militias, for example, were often presented as a resurrection of the patriotic citizen corps – raised across Spanish America in the eighteenth century in defence of their communities – and, at least theoretically, they stood in opposition to the patrimonial armies of *caudillo* warlords that emerged during the insurgency (1810–1821). However, it was clear that provincial militias also reflected regional elites' attempts to consolidate their nascent political autonomy under a federalist system (DePalo 1997: 6–18). Centralist politicians and former colonial elites resented the loss of central authority and privileges that had been previously enjoyed by metropolitan centres; senior military commanders, meanwhile, questioned the fiscal and military capacity of a federal republic to secure Mexico's sovereignty and territorial integrity amid the threat posed by Spain's active plans for invasion (Costeloe 1975: 327–350, 371–412; DePalo 1997: 19–20, 24–25).

At the local and regional levels federalism also faced its discontents: Rural populations often distrusted the increasing power of provincial capitals and their governments. The rise of these new provincial governments – armed with their own militias, bureaucracies and legislatures – radically increased the costs of provincial administration, as well as the fiscal burden imposed upon a rural economy now exhausted by decades of armed conflict (Carmagnani 1984; Medina 2007: 265; Tenenbaum 1986). The wide variation in *local* governance structures – ranging from the austere municipalities and military colonies in the northern frontier to the patrimonial communities and indigenous settlements in the south – meant that enormous diversity also existed in the types of militia active during the period. In some cases, local militias resembled private guards operating in the service of provincial governors, landowners or rebellious rural communities (Medina 2015; Santoni 1988; Suárez and Jiménez 2000).

As Figure 8.2 illustrates, regular army and local militia units became increasingly involved in the conflicts between centralist and federalist factions. As war broke out between a coalition of provincial governments on the one side and the national

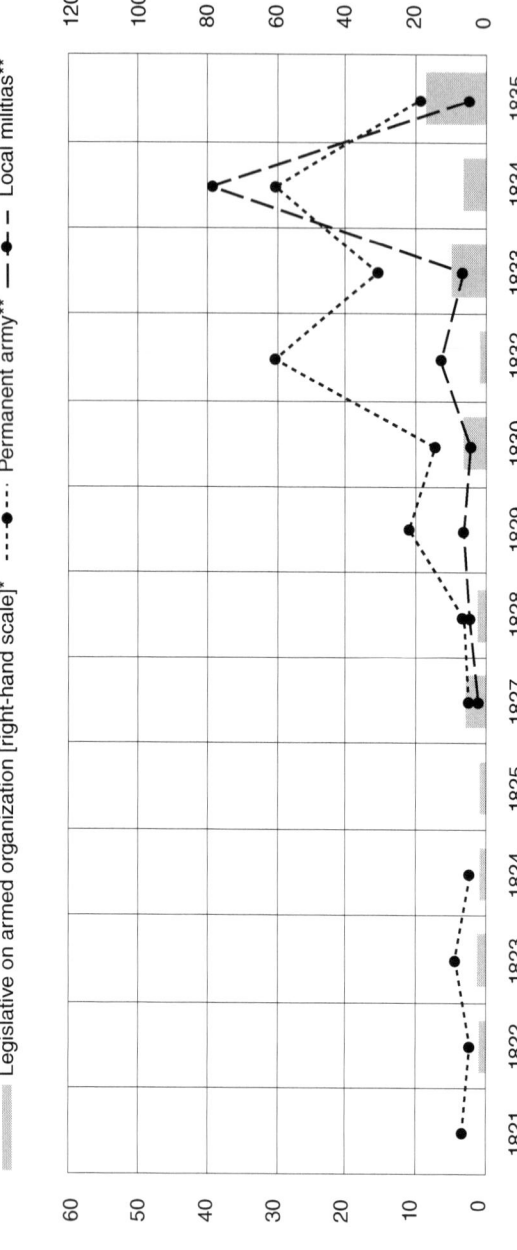

Legislative on armed organization [right-hand scale]*  ----●---- Permanent army**  —●— Local militias**

*Figure 8.2* Federalism versus centralism conflict and the demise of provincial militias (1821–1835).

Notes

\* Legislation, decrees and government memoranda addressing the organization of armed force, including those regarding the regular army ('permanent' and 'active' units), local militias ('provincial' and 'civic'), as well as other security forces (e.g. National Guard).

Source: Data compiled from Dublán and Lozano (1876–1877, vols I–IX).

\*\* Participation of regular army units, National Guard and local militias in *pronunciamientos* (rebellions or counter-rebellions).

Source: Data compiled from Fowler *et al.*, 'El Pronunciamiento in Independent Mexico' database, University of St Andrews.

government on the other in 1832, the question of whether provincial governments – instituted as federal states under the 1824 Constitution – should be allowed to maintain autonomous armed forces remained one of the *casus belli* (DePalo 1997: 19–23). The centralist government of General Bustamante – accompanied by pro-government army units between March and November 1832 – defeated a coalition of federal states and their provincial militias in four conventional battles that 'exacted a particularly ruinous toll on both the permanent army and the active militia' (DePalo 1997: 23; see also Fowler 2000a: 67–68). In 1835 the defeat of a second revolt, led by the Governor of Zacatecas, marked the definitive imposition of centralism and the implementation of a first wave of national reforms (Costeloe 1975, 2000).

Provincial militias were proscribed and the regular army strengthened – deployed as an instrument of territorial and political control. New military commandancies were established and empowered with extensive political and administrative duties in order to control the provincial governments, as well as combating rural unrest (DePalo 1997: 19–23). As tax auditors, regional military commanders also acquired both fiscal authority over provincial governments and control over strategic rents, such as certain monopolies, mints and customs houses (Córdova 1976). Additional measures were taken in order to restrict popular participation in national politics and to undermine the autonomy of provincial and local administrations, such as reducing the number of municipalities and introducing voting rights and rules in favour of official appointments that benefited proprietors (Arroyo García 2011; Warren 1996).

## International conflict, military rebellion and the creation of the National Guard 1835–1849

The centralist reaction privileged a military solution to the 'fragmented sovereignty' posed by provincial governments and their autonomous militias; however, the regular army lacked the institutional capacity to see it through to completion. Rather than achieving the centralization of political authority under military command, the regular army instead became overstrained and politicized. In the 1840s and 1850s, as the government grew increasingly dependent on regular army units and their commanders, military spending on salaries and pensions rocketed, leading to a permanent fiscal deficit and additional challenges to sustaining political stability (DePalo 1997: 42–43; Medina 2007: 263; Tenenbaum 1986). At the same time, rebellions by rogue military commanders thrived: between 1834 and 1853, for example, six regime changes at the national level were achieved by way of military rebellion (Fowler 2000a; Kahle 1997: 195–198).

Figure 8.3 illustrates the predominance of regular army units, as well as their participation in the multiple rebellions occurring during this period. Ironically, internal conflict and the political instability brought about by endemic rebellion soon invited one of centralists' and the military's greatest fears: foreign intervention. First, Texan colonists reacted to centralist policies by declaring

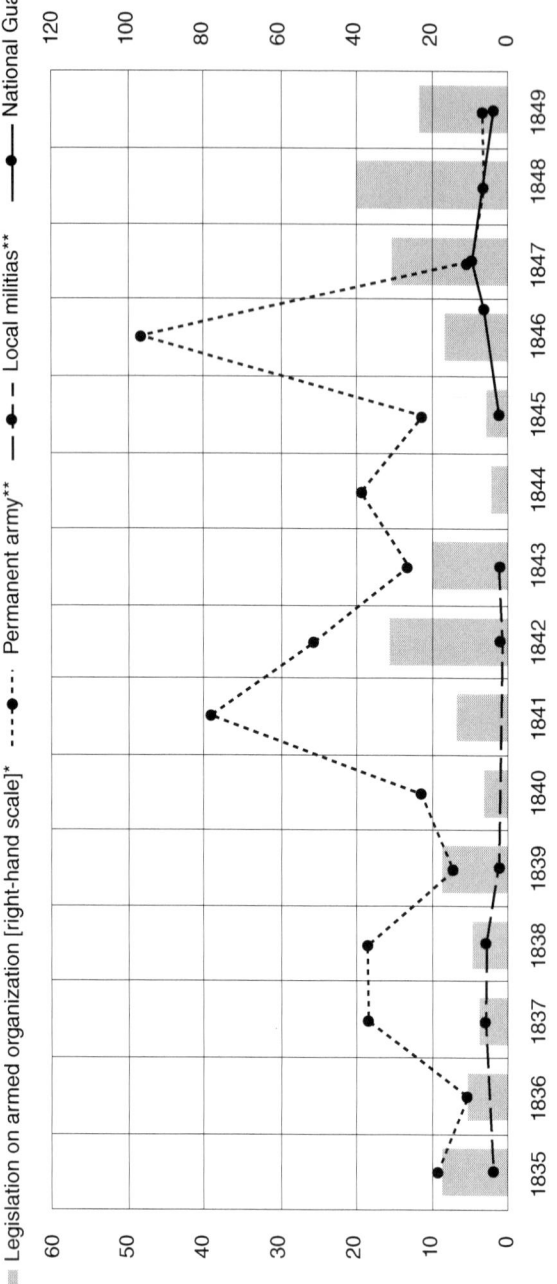

— Legislation on armed organization [right-hand scale]*    ---●--- Permanent army**    ---●--- Local militias**    ——●—— National Guard**

*Figure 8.3* International conflict, military rebellion and the creation of the National Guard (1835–1849).

Notes

* Legislation, decrees and government memoranda addressing the organization of armed force, including those regarding the regular army ('permanent' and 'active' units), local militias ('provincial' and 'civic'), as well as other security forces (e.g. National Guard).

Source: Data compiled from Dublán and Lozano (1876–1877, vols I–IX).

** Participation of regular army units, National Guard and local militias in *pronunciamientos* (rebellions or counter-rebellions).

Source: Data compiled from Fowler *et al.*, 'El Pronunciamiento in Independent Mexico' database, University of St Andrews.

independence – which they subsequently gained after an improvised *caudillo* army failed to subdue their equally improvised militia forces (DePalo 1997: 27–35). Second, France launched an invasion in 1838 to demand reparations for damages suffered by their nationals during previous conflicts and to secure better conditions for French trade. Finally, US expansionism benefited in 1846 from the ongoing Texan conflict – as well as Mexico's belligerent rejection of its annexation by the US – by using it to justify a predatory intervention (DePalo 1997: 35).

Amid the failure to contain the advance of US troops during the ensuing US–Mexican War (1846–1848), a desperate Mexican national government called for the deployment of patriotic militias across the country. This newly formed NG had, however, a negligible impact on the outcome of the war – and furthermore, as Figure 8.3 shows, its influence on armed political mobilization was slight between 1847 and 1849. However, pressured by the US invasion, the government issued patents authorizing a variety of local actors to create their own armed units (Kahle 1997: 143). As such the NG revived a powerful precedent of regional and communal armed mobilization and incorporated pre-existing armed formations – organized by veterans of previous conflicts and regional strongmen – under a new institutional framework. In some cases these well-known regional *caudillos* were the very political entrepreneurs and communal leaders who had been behind the continuous rebellions of the 1840s. In some troubled rural regions, for example, new NG units joined peasant rebellions rather than contributing to the fight against the US: in Morelos, for example, guardsmen were so actively supportive of rural rebellions that the government eventually disbanded all local units (Reina 1998: 157–159, 164).

Eventually, the NG introduced a system of dual ownership and authority that tasked provincial governments with recruiting, training and commanding armed units in times of peace – albeit one that required national governments to confirm the appointment of commanders. With Congressional approval, the national government was also allowed to deploy guardsmen as auxiliary units of the regular army. At the macro level this dual system offered an institutional framework, however feeble, to promote cooperation between regional and national authorities and their support bases – making it easier to coordinate large-scale operations, the supply of weapons and ammunition, and political cooperation. By recognizing the de facto autonomy and power of local politicians and provincial governments in exchange for cooperation and nominal submission to the national government, this framework set the basis to overcome the anarchic system of 'petty sovereigns' – regional strongmen and military commanders – faced between the 1820s and 1840s (Medina 2007: 264–272, 2015; Merino 1998: 85–88).

### Armed (dis)organization amid political polarization: From a conservative national army to the liberal National Guard 1850–1862

During the 1850s and 1860s the regular army and the NG became the armed instruments deployed in the ideological confrontation between emergent radical liberal and conservative factions. While the NG did introduce an innovative regulatory framework for locally organized armed forces, in order to be effective several conditions still needed to be fulfilled: increasing coordination among provincial governors, commanders and the national government; the development of local administrative capacities; and the emergence of a new type of 'local politician (effective at 'governing' as well as mobilizing armed force) NG-commander'. While it is not possible to address each of these conditions at length here, it is necessary to stress how some of them were achieved through a combination of learning and short-term adaptation over the course of a decade of violent conflict (Roeder 2010: 247–292).

Figure 8.4 shows the increasing participation of NG units in national politics in the early 1850s, a period marked by political instability and armed mobilization. Amid the conservative rebellions against the federal government and rural uprisings in central Mexico, the NG played an ambiguous role. An incumbent authoritarian government increased the size of the national army and military spending between 1853 and 1855, while also stirring regional elites' resentment at arbitrary policies and unwelcome interventions in provincial affairs (Toral *et al.* 1979; Sinkin 1979: 75–99).

In August 1855 a revolution brought a heterogeneous group of (radical and moderate) liberal politicians and NG commanders to power, with the support of local armed units. Taking advantage of the political crisis, radical politicians pushed for a comprehensive set of reforms at the expense of traditional elites. In 1857, as these reforms became enshrined in a new constitution, military commanders and conservative politicians led a series of rebellions that escalated into a full-fledged civil war from 1857 to 1861 (Merino 1998: 88–95; Sinkin 1979: 101–102; Toral *et al.* 1979: 198–212).

In the aftermath of these consecutive periods of armed conflict, the regular army was proscribed and substituted by a select cluster of victorious guardsmen and army units loyal to the liberal government. Evidently, many of these troops had been quite literally 'improvised' during the conflict by NG commanders and provincial governors as irregular units, brought together on the basis of local experience in the organization of armed force (Medina 2007; Merino 1998; Toral *et al.* 1979).

In the north of the country units were formed as civic militias staffed by farmers and small proprietors – and managed by relatively efficient municipal and provincial administrations (Medina 2015). In many densely populated rural areas in the south, meanwhile, peasant armies were assembled by regional politicians seeking to harness the support of indigenous communities (Thomson and LaFrance 1999). In the south and the southeast of the country, NG units often took the form of armed retainers funded by landowners or local political leaders (Hart 2004: 240). The NG thus became the foundation for an emerging network of regional politicians and commanders, who developed more expansive personal connections and regional influence as their forces moved and fought across national territory.[11]

This nascent liberal national army moulded during the conflicts of 1854 to 1855 and 1857 to 1860 was, however, subsequently defeated in open combat by French expeditionary troops during the course of a second French intervention seeking to

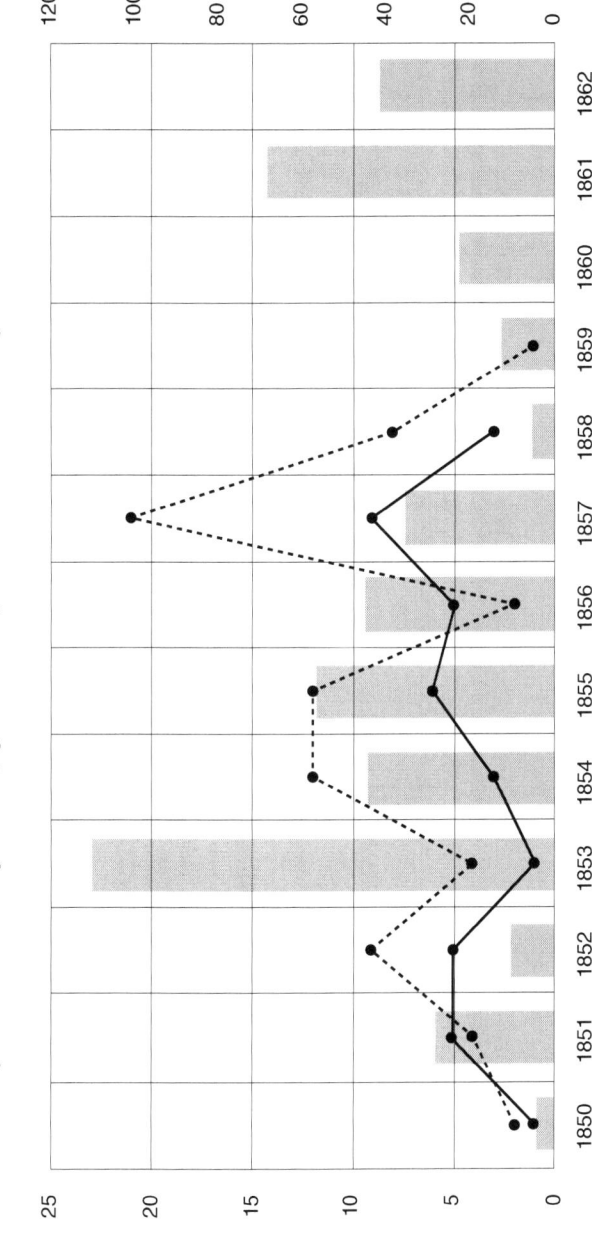

*Figure 8.4* From a conservative national army to the liberal National Guard (1850–1862)

Notes

* Legislation, decrees and government memoranda addressing the organization of armed force, including those regarding the regular army ('permanent' and 'active' units), local militias ('provincial' and 'civic'), as well as other security forces (e.g. National Guard).

Source: Data compiled from Dublán and Lozano (1876–1877, vols I–IX).

** Participation of regular army units, National Guard and local militias in *pronunciamientos* (rebellions or counter-rebellions).

Source: Data compiled from Fowler et al., 'El Pronunciamiento in Independent Mexico' database, University of St Andrews.

establish a 'Mexican Empire'. When the Republican government abandoned Mexico City in 1863, the financial and organizational burden of military mobilization thus once again fell on provincial governors and their modest administrative apparatus. Republican resistance became dependent on troops raised through the framework of the NG – who were, according to President Juárez, continuously improvising during the war – with the support of local communities and provincial governments loyal to the Republican cause.

Between 1863 and the Republican victory in 1867, despite the initial setbacks in open battles against the French, the NG underwent impressive development, but nevertheless remained a set of essentially decentralized forces. In 1867 the four regional armies of the victorious Republic were commanded by the regional leaders who had raised them originally out of small armed bands and guerrilla forces: Corona, Escobedo, Díaz and González Ortega (Medina 2007: 266–267; Tamayo 1972: 326–391; Toral *et al.* 1979: 246).[12]

At the micro level, the NG provided new forms of political mobilization and the enfranchisement of popular groups under the control of provincial and local politicians. As 'citizens-at-arms', guardsmen made demands that had no parallel among the forced conscripts of regular army units, such as the right to elect their own officers. Provincial governors and local politicians doubled up as NG commanders, and in the process of building local bureaucracies to support their military endeavours, they became increasingly dependent on local governmental capacity. Conversely, NG units became a powerful instrument to intervene in local politics: fixing elections, enforcing political and social order, and legitimizing the *illiberal* practices of local political bosses under the trappings of patriotic republicanism (Medina 2007: 267–272; Perry 1978).

The permanent armed mobilization during the *Reforma* civil war (1859–1861), French military occupation and the short-lived 'Mexican Empire' (1862–1867), however, had made the national government dependent on the goodwill and armed resources of provincial governors and regional military commanders that had remained loyal to the Republican cause. These 'chiefs, who had ruled their territories for four years almost unmolested, expected to have the situation continue' after 1867 (Sinkin 1979: 104). After 1867 the national government instituted an ambitious programme of demobilization, and therein used the NG as a repository for former combatants. However, the deployment of irregular attacks against French and imperial troops had also left behind a large number armed bands and rural communities schooled in the art of violent resistance. Therefore, in the same way that the decentralized forces of provincial governors coming together with NG commanders had coalesced into a proto-national army during the years of civil war and foreign intervention, in the aftermath of these conflicts NG units quickly split into personalistic conflicts led by aspiring politicians.

In addition to endemic banditry and low-intensity violence in rural areas, between 1867 and 1876 the government confronted no less than 37 major rebellions, many of them instigated by former NG commanders and local politicians disappointed with the national government (Perry 1978: 353–354). This nine-year period was therefore marked by an internecine 'war of the winners' between dissatisfied NG commanders and provincial politicians on the one hand, and the low-intensity violence to which the remains of conservative armed factions subjected rural communities on the other.

During the 1870s the national government made important efforts to institutionalize its interactions with governors, irregular armed units and armed rural communities on the basis of legal and extra-constitutional measures: including electoral manipulation, fiscal centralization and outright repression. Between 1879 and 1893 loyal NG units were gradually transferred to auxiliary or permanent army units; however, up until the late 1880s the fragile political stability in place remained dependent for its survival on the president's capacity to cultivate the acquiescence of regional strongmen, provincial governors and NG commanders (Carmagnani 1983: 296; Hernández Chavez 1989; Medina 2007: 266–268; Perry 1979: 261–269). Thus infused with a hybrid mix of Republican values and traditional political practices – and increasingly intertwined with local political machines, making them more efficient than the *ad hoc* militias had been – the NG became the school of the military leaders and politicians who achieved the first period of political stability in Independent Mexico *c.* 1880 to 1910.

## Institutional learning or contingent adaptation?

The armed disorder Mexico experienced during the nineteenth century illustrates the long-term challenges to the effective implementation of post-conflict reforms, as well as the influence that pervasive organizational models for armed force have in post-conflict settings. While traditional accounts often treat reform outcomes as the result of rational design at the macro level, or alternatively as the product of individual choices made at the micro level, this chapter instead highlights the impact that models operating at a ' "meso level" that links national-level cleavages with individual-level motivations' (Christia 2012: 5) had on the outcome of post-conflict reforms. Before concluding, I will briefly outline some reflections on the paradoxical patterns of institutional change driven by the seemingly disparate mechanisms shaping the implementation of post-conflict reforms: (1) institutional learning and emulation, and (2) *ad hoc* adaptation and improvisation.

### *Institutional learning and emulation*

Formal learning and emulation are clearly present in the efforts to reform the organization of armed force in nineteenth-century Mexico. First of all, key models for reform were adapted from the experience of both foreign countries and of previous governments (Dublán and Lozano 1876–1912: I–IX). As such, the first decades of independence displayed explicit efforts to reproduce legal-institutional models that would be recognized as successful and legitimate by different social actors. Historians have documented the polemics around the adoption of legal and constitutional models from Europe and the United States (Palti 2005, 2006); however, nineteenth-century reformers were also equally interested in the different forms of military organization alive in foreign countries (as well as in previous periods of armed conflict in Mexico).

War Ministry reports contained brief genealogies of the national armed forces and their performance in previous instances of armed conflict and succinct narratives of recent military operations, as well as commentaries about the latest organizational developments overseas. Similarly, legislative projects often built on the explicit analysis of foreign models: in 1857, for example, the interior minister presented a draft proposal for the formation of a rural police force (*Guardia de Seguridad*) based on his research on the recently created Spanish *Guardia Nacional* (Verján 2006: 70).

The focus on organizational models highlights moreover the different contexts in which formal models interacted with the contingency and *ad hoc* adaptation driven by conflict dynamics. While giving a detailed account of these processes is beyond the limits of this chapter, one additional dimension of grounded institutional learning is patent in the way in which predominant armed configurations influenced the reproduction of identities and the transmission of *knowledge* during periods of conflict in Mexico.

Figure 8.5 illustrates the contribution of alternative models for the organization of armed force to the formation and training received by the Mexican military elites that were active during the great 'civil war' of 1857 to 1867. On the basis of biographical data, the graph indicates the time period of enrolment and type of armed unit wherein these leaders first served.

While the national army trained the vast majority of military leaders, significant differences eventually emerged between those serving within regular and auxiliary units. Local militias and the NG account for a small number of military leaders; however, variation in those numbers corroborates *pronunciamiento* data and anecdotal evidence regarding their increasing impact on armed political mobilization during this period (1820–1860). The overlap between the clear

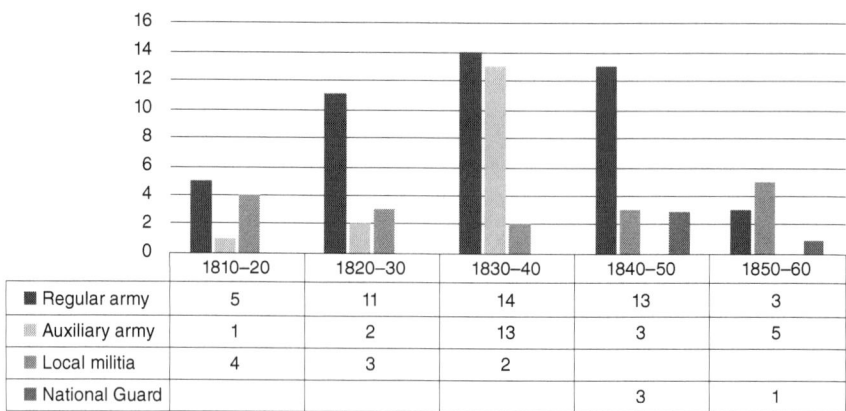

| | 1810–20 | 1820–30 | 1830–40 | 1840–50 | 1850–60 |
|---|---|---|---|---|---|
| ■ Regular army | 5 | 11 | 14 | 13 | 3 |
| ▨ Auxiliary army | 1 | 2 | 13 | 3 | 5 |
| ■ Local militia | 4 | 3 | 2 | | |
| ■ National Guard | | | | 3 | 1 |

*Figure 8.5* When and where did military leaders (active during the conflicts of 1857–1867) begin their careers?

Source: Hernández López (2001: 368–369).

'generational relay' experienced during this period and the appearance of different organizational models is also suggestive of the ways in which organizational models influence the interaction between institutional learning and *ad hoc* adaptation in the context of conflict and reform. Even though further research and detailed data are necessary to adequately assess these insights, some tentative hypotheses regarding the mechanisms linking organizational models for armed force and their impact on post-conflict reform may be advanced on the basis of this evidence.

If we emphasize institutional continuity, one possible interpretation is that these organizational models were strongly dependent on their capacity to reproduce identities and operating procedures specifically through the formation and training of cadres, even while these models themselves were being displaced by reforms or evolutionary pressures. In cases of a rupture or radical departure from a predominant model, local actors may still preserve certain organizational forms in order to derive short-term legitimacy or symbolic benefits from maintaining traditional organizational semblance as they interacted with peers or with competing organizations.

Such a line of reasoning may explain the continued predominance of the regular army during this period – as a model adopted by a number of heterogeneous actors rather than as a unitary organization – despite the suitability of locally organized forces for fighting the type of low-intensity conflict prevailing at the time, as well as capable of effectively incorporating local political support and material resources.

## Ad hoc adaptation and improvisation

On the other hand, if we emphasize contingent adaptation, an alternative explanation may contend that organizational models for armed force also served as 'laboratories' in which to evaluate and preserve successful forms of *ad hoc* adaptation and improvisation experienced during times of armed conflict. One could argue that evolutionary responses arising in the midst of war contribute to the resilience of these armed organizations, but only if such innovations were subsequently effectively institutionalized in post-conflict settings.

These examples illustrate the complex mechanisms involved in the transformation and adaptation of institutional post-conflict reforms, and furthermore the difficulty of explaining why some arrangements persist and find sustainable equilibria in the long term. Contemporary discussions about hybridity in peacebuilding and post-conflict settings may benefit from the incorporation of historical evidence regarding contingency and context-specific changes (Egnell and Haldén 2013). However, the resilience displayed by local actors over long periods of conflict and armed disorder – including through the continued adaptation of models for the organization of armed force – also contains a cautionary tale about the prospects for successful reform implementation in contemporary post-conflict settings.

## Conclusion

In nineteenth-century Mexico, armed actors contributed to the development of formal state institutions while also reproducing pre-existing governance mechanisms throughout the periods of conflict and reform. As drivers of violent disorder, wartime actors often derived significant benefits – both as intermediaries and from their adaptation of post-conflict reforms – to the detriment of civilian authority, the rule of law and civilian populations. Post-conflict institutional reforms were, for the most part, dependent on the processes through which wartime actors became integrated into post-conflict frameworks in exchange for short-term gains. For these reasons, efforts to overcome the persistence of governmental weakness through institutional reform contributed to the legitimatizing of privileged intermediaries – such as regional military and NG commanders – and resilient local governance mechanisms, despite the fact that these were often predatory and patrimonial in nature.

This chapter has made the case for assessing the long-term dimensions of conflict and the organization of armed force – including the persistence of violence, the resilience of wartime actors and the local adaptation of national-level changes – in order to account for the variation that exists in the outcomes of post-conflict reform. The mechanisms that explain such variation in the long term. Historical and micro-level comparative analysis along these lines may help further illuminate the paradoxical institutional choices faced by those developing societies that are confronted with violence and armed disorder today.

## Notes

1   Jeremy Adelman, for example, distinguishes between those 'pivotal moments' when societies lay down solid foundations for shifting landscapes that last over the centuries and the evolutionary change that unfolds 'over centuries of adaptation to local and global forces' (2004: 224). Cf. Mahoney and Villegas (2009) and Thelen (1999).

2   Alternative accounts refer to 'governance without government' (Raeymaekers *et al.* 2008), 'negotiated' or 'mediated states' (Hagmann and Péclard 2010), and 'hybrid political orders' (Boege *et al.* 2008). Regarding the notion of hybrid violence and for a critique thereof, see Krause (2012).

3   This typology is based on an analysis of War Ministry reports (*Memorias de Guerra*) and Dublán and Lozano's (1876–1912) compilation of key legislative promulgations. The use of equivocal terminology by nineteenth-century sources facilitates confusion: *milicia* was used as a generic term for armed forces and distinctions between the *milicia activa* (auxiliary units of the regular army) and local militias (including civic and provincial units) were not often explicitly made.

4   In 1825 *milicia activa* units were raised by provincial governments in those territories required by pre-Independence vice-regal legislation to contribute forces. The 1825 report praised the contribution of irregular militias to combating banditry in exchange for judicial privileges (*fueros*) (*Memoria [.] 1825*: 15–16, 17–18). In 1833 the war minister reported that civic militias at the service of provincial governments were deployed to ensure public tranquility, allowing the government to demobilize active militia units and to reduce expenses (*Memoria [.] 1833*: 8). In 1835 the report questioned the utility of 'masses of untrained volunteers' who lacked weapons, discipline and the willingness to obey officers, but concluded that a combination of

*professional* troops and volunteers might be useful (*Memoria [.] 1835*: 5–7). In 1839 the war minister noted the readiness to raise up to 50,000 civic militiamen against a foreign invasion, but warned against mass mobilization (*Memoria [.] 1839*: 16). The 1847 report commended the NG, but also urged commanders to prevent disorder and to protect private property (*Memoria [.] 1847*, n.p.).

5 Contributions reached significant levels during times of conflict; in addition to authorizing NG units to take weapons and ammunition from regular army depots, between October 1855 and August 1857, for example, the war minister reported the delivery of 31,485 fusils, 6,558 carbines, 671 pistols, as well as of ammunition and other materials (*Memoria [.] 1857*).

6 In fact, some of the regulations introduced in 1847 to 1848 constituted an attempt to constrain irregular armed groups incorporated into the NG, in order to prevent attacks against civil authorities and private property. Cf. Kahle (1997); see also *Memoria [.] 1847*.

7 Fowler (2000a) provides a detailed account of internal conflict in early independent Mexico. This chapter builds on that author's extensive research and publicly available collection of *pronunciamientos*: see "El Pronunciamiento in Independent Mexico" database (http://arts.st-andrews.ac.uk/pronunciamientos/).

8 For example, in 1842 *fueros* were reinstated on the basis of Spanish legislation from 1793 and 1817; cf. Dublán and Lozano (1876–1912: IV: 283). In 1853 the War Ministry issued a circular calling for the observance of militia regulations dating from 1767; cf. Dublán and Lozano (1876–1912: VI: 322).

9 Correspondence between the minister of war, the minister of the interior and the governor of San Luis Potosí regarding the role of local political authorities and the use of force in May 1857 (AGN/Gobernacion/Rurales/Sin Seccion/Caja 460/E4/18).

10 Ibid.

11 NG commanders, for example, imposed extraordinary taxes in order to finance their activities and simply informed the president for the sake of *post hoc* approval. The president was constantly requesting provincial governors not to retain rents that belonged to the national government. Finally, in an extreme case of armed politics, in 1863 the governor of Nuevo León invaded the neighbouring state of Tamaulipas. See President Juárez's correspondence in Tamayo (1972: 341, 348 and 378).

12 According to Medina (2007), this transition was achieved on the basis of key institutional reforms: universal conscription, the imposition of taxes on those exempted from military service and the promotion of a patriotic ideology. Thomson (1990) and Thomson and LaFrance (1999) suggest that the development of 'popular' – that is, local adaptations of – patriotic discourse contributed to the effectiveness of the NG as the basis for a nascent political machine.

# References

## Archives

Archivo General de la Nación (AGN), Mexico

## Primary sources

1825. *Memoria del Secretario de Estado y del Despacho de la Guerra, presentada a las Cámaras en enero de 1826*. Mexico City: Imprenta del Supremo Gobierno de los Estados unidos mexicanos.

1833. *Memoria del Secretario de Estado y del Despacho de la Guerra, presentada a las Cámaras el día 26 de abril de 1833*. Mexico City: Imprenta del Águila.

1835. *Memoria del Secretario de Estado y del Despacho de Guerra y Marina, leída en la Cámara de Representantes en la sesión del día 23 de marzo y en la de Senadores en la del 24 de marzo del mismo mes y año de 1835.* Mexico City: Imprenta de Ignacio Cumplido.

1839. *Memoria de la Secretaría de Estado y del Despacho de la Guerra y Marina, leída por el Escmo. Sr. General D. José María Tornel, en la Cámara de Diputados el 7 de enero de 1839, y en la de Senadores el 8 del mismo.* Mexico City: Imprenta de Ignacio Cumplido.

1847. *Memoria presentada por el Ministerio de la guerra á Junta de los Gobernadores de los Estados reunida en Querétaro en Noviembre de 1847.* Manuscript, 19 December 1847.

1850. *Memoria del Secretario de Estado y del Despacho de Guerra y Marina, leída en la Cámara de Diputados el 26, y en la de Senadores el 28 de Enero de 1850.* Mexico City: Tipografía de Vicente G. Torres.

1857. *Memoria del Ministerio de Guerra y Marina, presentada al Primer Congreso Constitucional de 1857, por el Ministro del Ramo, General Juan Soto.* Mexico City: Imprenta de Juan R. Navarro.

Dublán, M. and J.M. Lozano. 1876–1912. *Legislación Mexicana, 1687–1912.* 42 vols. Mexico City.

Mora, J.M.L. 1986 [1836]. *Méjico y sus revoluciones. Vol 1.* Mexico City: Fondo de Cultura Económica.

### Secondary sources

Adelman, J. 2004. 'Latin American *Longues Durees.*' *Latin American Research Review*, 39(1): 223–237.

Arroyo Garcia, I. 2011. *La arquitectura del Estado Mexicano: formas de gobierno, representación política y ciudadanía, 1821–1857.* Mexico City/Puebla, Mexico: Instituto Mora, Universidad Autónoma de Puebla.

Berdal, M. and D. Zaum. 2013. 'Power after Peace.' In M. Berdal and D. Zaum (eds) *Political Economy of Statebuilding. Power after Peace.* Abingdon, Oxford: Routledge.

Boege, V., A. Brown, K. Clements and A. Nolan. 2008. *On Hybrid Political Orders and Emerging States: State Formation in the Context of 'Fragility'.* Berlin, Germany: Berghof Research Centre.

Boege, V., A. Brown, K. Clements and A. Nolan. 2009. 'Undressing the Emperor: A Reply to our Discussants.' In M. Fisher and B. Schmelze (eds) *Building Peace in the Absence of States: Challenging the Discourse on State Failure.* Berlin, Germany: Berghof Research Centre.

Carmagnani, M.1983. 'Finanzas y Estado en México, 1820–1880.' *Ibero-Amerikanisches Archiv*, 9): 287–289.

Carmagnani, M.1984. 'Territorialidad y federalismo en la formación del Estado mexicano.' In I. Buisson, G. Kahle, H.J. König and H. Pietschmann (eds) *Problemas de la Formación del Estado y de la Nación en Hispanoamérica.* Cologne, Germany: Böhlau Verlag.

Christia, F. 2012. *Alliance Formation in Civil Wars.* Cambridge: Cambridge University Press.

Cordova, L. (ed.) 1976. *Del Centralismo Proteccionista al Régimen Liberal (1837–1872). Colección de Documentos para la Historia del Comercio Exterior de México. Vol. 7.* Mexico City: Banco Nacional de Comercio Exterior.

Costeloe, M. 1975. *La primera república federal de México (1824–1835). Un estudio de los partidos políticos en el México independiente.* Mexico City: Fondo de Cultura Económica.

Costeloe, M. 2000. *La República central en México, 1835–1846. 'Hombres de bien' en la época de Santa Anna.* Mexico City: Fondo de Cultura Económica.

Davis, D.E. 2008. 'Contemporary Challenges and Historical Reflections on the Study of Militaries, States, and Politics.' In D.E. Davis and A. Pereira (eds) *Irregular Armed Forces and Their Role in Politics and State Formation.* Cambridge: Cambridge University Press.

Davis, D.E. 2010. 'Non-state Armed Actors, New Imagined Communities, and Shifting Patterns of Sovereignty and Insecurity in the Modern World.' In K. Krause (ed.) *Armed Groups and Contemporary Conflicts: Challenging the Weberian State.* London: Routledge.

Depalo, W.A. 1997. *The Mexican Army, 1822–1852.* College Station,: Texas A&M University Press.

Egnell R. and P. Haldén. 2013. *New Agendas in Statebuilding. Hybridity, Contingency and History.* London: Routledge Studies in Intervention and Statebuilding.

Escalante, F. 1992. *Ciudadanos imaginarios. Memorial de los afanes y desventuras de la virtud y apología del vicio triunfante en la República Mexicana: tratado de moral pública.* Mexico City: El Colegio de México.

Escalante, F. 1999. 'El orden de la extorsión. Las formas del conflicto político en México.' In P. Waldmann and F. Reinares (eds) *Sociedades en guerra civil.* Barcelona: Paidós.

Felbab-Brown, V. 2015. 'The Rise of Militias in Mexico: Citizens' Security or Further Conflict Escalation?' *PRISM*, 5(4): 173–186.

Fowler, W. 1996. *Military Political Identity and Reformism in Independent Mexico. An Analysis of the Memorias De Guerra (1821–1855).* London: Institute of Latin American Studies.

Fowler, W. 2000a. 'Civil Conflict in Independent Mexico, 1821–57. An Overview.' In R. Earle (ed.) *Rumours of Wars: Civil Conflict in Nineteenth-century Latin America.* London: Institute of Latin American Studies.

Fowler, W (ed.) 2000b. *Forceful Negotiations: The Origins of the Pronunciamiento in Nineteenth Century Mexico.* Lincoln, NE: University of Nebraska Press.

Garner, P. 2001. *Porfirio Díaz.* London: Pearson.

Hagmann, T. and D. Péclard. 2010. 'Negotiating Statehood: Dynamics of Power and Domination in Africa.' *Development and Change*, 41(4): 539–562.

Hamnett, B. 1986. *Roots Of Insurgency: Mexican Regions, 1750–1824.* Cambridge: Cambridge University Press.

Hart, J.M. 2004. 'La Guerra de los campesinos del suroeste mexicano en los años 1840: Conflicto en una sociedad transicional.' In F. Katz (ed.) *Revuelta, rebelión y revolución. La lucha rural en México del siglo XVI al siglo XX* (2nd edn). Mexico City: Era.

Hernandez Chavez, A. 1989. 'Origen y ocaso del ejercito porfiriano.' *Historia Mexicana*, 39(1): 257–296.

Hernandez Chavez, A. 1992. 'La Guardia Nacional y movilización política de los pueblos.' In J.E. Rodríguez (ed.) *Patterns of Contention in Mexican History.* Wilmington, DE: Scholarly Resources.

Hernandez Lopez, C. 2001. 'Militares conservadores en la reforma y el segundo imperio, 1857–1867.' Unpublished Ph.D. dissertation. Mexico City: El Colegio de México.

Kahle, G. 1997. *El ejército y la formación del Estado en los comienzos de la independencia de México.* Mexico City: Fondo de Cultura Económica.

Katz, F. (ed.) 1988. *Riot, Rebellion, and Revolution: Rural Social Conflict in Mexico.* Princeton, NJ: Princeton University Press.

Krause, K. 2009. 'Beyond Definition: Violence in a Global Perspective.' *Global Crime,* 10(4): 337–355.

Krause, K. (ed.) 2010. *Armed Groups and Contemporary Conflicts: Challenging the Weberian State.* London: Routledge.

Krause, K. 2012. 'Hybrid Violence: Locating the Use of Force in Postconflict Settings.' *Global Governance: A Review of Multilateralism and International Organisations,* 18(1): 39–56.

Lupshsa, P.A. 1996. 'Transnational Organized Crime versus the Nation-State.' *Transnational Organized Crime,* 2(1): 21–48.

Mac Ginty, R. 2013. 'Hybrid Statebuilding.' In R. Egnell and P. Haldén (eds) *New Agendas in Statebuilding. Hybridity, Contingency and History.* London: Routledge Studies in Intervention and Statebuilding.

Mahoney, J. and C. Villegas. 2009. 'Historical Enquiry and Comparative Politics.' In C. Boix and S. C. Stokes (eds) *Oxford Handbook of Comparative Politics.* Oxford: Oxford University Press.

Meagher, K. 2012. 'The Strength of Weak States? Non-state Security Forces and Hybrid Governance in Africa.' *Development and Change,* 43(5): 1073–1101.

Medina, L. 2007. *Invención del sistema político mexicano. Forma de gobierno y gobernabilidad en México en el siglo XIX.* Mexico City: Fondo de Cultura Económica.

Medina, L. 2015. *Los bárbaros del Norte. Guardia Nacional y política en Nuevo León, siglo XIX.* Mexico City: Fondo de Cultura Económica, Centro de Investigación y Docencia Económicas.

Merino, M. 1998. *Gobierno local, poder nacional. La contienda por la formación del Estado mexicano.* Mexico City: El Colegio de México.

Milliken, J. and K. Krause. 2002. 'State Failure, State Collapse, and State Reconstruction: Concepts, Lessons and Strategies.' *Development and Change,* 33(5): 753–774.

Ortiz Escamilla, J. 2014. *Guerra y gobierno. Los pueblos y la independencia de México, 1808–1825.* Mexico City: El Colegio de México/Instituto de Investigaciones Dr. José María Luis Mora.

Palti, E.J. 2005. *La invención de una legitimidad. Razón y retórica en el pensamiento mexicano del siglo XIX (Un estudio sobre las formas del discurso político).* Mexico City: Fondo de Cultura Económica.

Palti, E.J. 2006. 'The Problem of "Misplaced Ideas" Revisited: Beyond the "History of Ideas" in Latin America.' *Journal of the History of Ideas,* 67(1): 149–179.

Perry, L.B. 1978. *Juarez and Diaz: Machine Politics in Mexico.* DeKalb, IL: Northern Illinois University Press.

Raeymaekers, T., K. Menkhaus and K. Vlassenroot. 2008. 'State and Non-state Regulation in African Protracted Crises: Governance without Government?' *Afrika focus,* 21(2): 7–21.

Reina, L. 1998. *Las rebeliones campesinas en México (1819–1906)* (5th edn). Mexico City: Siglo XXI.

Reno, W. 2010. 'Transforming West African Militia Networks for Postwar Recovery.' In K.B. Harpviken (ed.) *Troubled Regions and Failing States: The Clustering and Contagion of Armed Conflict.* Bingley: Emerald Books.

Roeder, R. 2010. *Juárez y su México.* Mexico City: Fondo de Cultura Económica.

Santoni, P. 1988. 'A Fear of the People: The Civic Militia of Mexico in 1845.' *Hispanic American Historical Review,* 68(2): 269–288.

Schlichte, K. 2009. *In the Shadow of Violence. The Politics of Armed Groups*. Chicago, IL: University of Chicago Press.

Shultz, R.H. and A.J. Dew. 2006. *Insurgents, Terrorists, and Militias. The Warriors of Contemporary Combat*. New York: Columbia University Press.

Sinkin, R.N. 1979. *The Mexican Reform, 1855–1876. A Study in Liberal Nation-building*. Austin: University of Texas Press.

Staniland, P. 2012. 'Organizing Insurgency: Networks, Resources, and Rebellion in South Asia.' *International Security*, 37(1):. 142–177.

Staniland, P. 2015. 'Militias, Ideology, and the State.' *Journal of Conflict Resolution*: 1–24.

Stevens, D.F. 1991. *Origins of Instability in Early Republican Mexico*. Durham, NC: Duke University Press.

Suárez, M. and J.R. Jiménez. 2000. *Constitución y sociedad en la formación del estado de Querétaro, 1825–1929*. Mexico City: Fondo de Cultura Económica.

Tamayo, J.L. 1972. *Epistolario de Benito Juárez*. Mexico City: Fondo de Cultura Económica.

Tenenbaum, B. 1986. *The Politics of Penury. Debts and Taxes in Mexico 1821–1856*. Albuquerque, NM: University of New Mexico Press.

Thelen, K. 1999. 'Historical Institutionalism in Comparative Politics.' *Annual Review of Political Science*, 2:.369–404.

Thomson, G.P. 1990. 'Bulwarks of Patriotic Liberalism: The NG, Philharmonic Corps and Patriotic Juntas in Mexico, 1847–88.' *Journal of Latin American Studies*, 22(1–2): 31–68.

Thomson, G.P. and D.G. Lafrance. 1999. *Patriotism, Politics, and Popular Liberalism in Nineteenth-century Mexico: Juan Francisco Lucas and the Puebla Sierra*. Wilmington, DE: Scholarly Resources.

Toral, J.L., M.A. Sanchez, G. Mendoza, L. Garfias and L. Martinez. 1979. *El ejército y fuerza aérea mexicanos*. Vol. 1. Mexico City: Secretaría de la Defensa Nacional (SEDENA).

Vanderwood, P.J. 2009. *Disorder and Progress. Bandits, Police and Mexican Development*. Lanham, MD: Scholarly Resources.

Vanderwood, P.J. 2014. *Los rurales mexicanos*. Mexico City: Fondo de Cultura Económica.

Vázquez, J.Z. 1984. 'El Ejército: Un dilema del Gobierno Mexicano (1842–64).' In I. Buisson, G. Kahle, H.J. König and H. Pietschmann (eds) *Problemas de la Formación del Estado y de la Nación en Hispanoamérica*. Cologne, Germany: Böhlau Verlag.

Vázquez, J.Z. 1994. 'De la difícil constitución de un Estado: México, 1821–1854.' In J.Z. Vázquez (ed.) *La fundación del Estado Mexicano 1821–1855*. Mexico City: Editorial Patria.

Verján, Y. 2006. 'Policías rurales y suspención de garantías. Mecanismos de coacción y represión en el proceso de formación del Estado Mexicano: 1861–1896.' Unpublished MA dissertation. Mexico City: Universidad Autónoma Metropolitana.

Warren, R. 1996. 'Elections and Popular Political Participation in Mexico, 1808–1836.' In V.C. Peloso and B.A. Tenenbaum (eds) *Liberals, Politics and Power. State Formation in Nineteenth-century Latin America*. Athens, GE: The University of Georgia Press.

Wiarda, H.J.. 1998. 'Historical Determinants of the Latin American State.' In M. Vellinga, *The Changing Role of the State in Latin America*. Oxford: Westview Press.

# 9 Looking beyond institutional reform

Engaging with the hybridization of peace and political order. Two cases from Oceania and West Africa

*Volker Boege*

## Introduction

Over the past two decades, international peacebuilding has followed the liberal peace approach.[1] Liberal peacebuilding is closely linked to statebuilding because state fragility has been seen as a major cause of violent conflict. Hence, liberal peacebuilding has embarked on an ambitious project of state reconstruction, including the reform of the state's security sector, building the capacities of the central machinery of government and fostering the effectiveness of the various branches of the state apparatus. The underlying assumption is that a 'proper' state – that is, a state of the Western liberal ideal type – is the best guarantor of sustainable peace. A liberal market economy and a liberal democratic civil society are seen as necessary underpinnings of such a liberal state; it is therefore part of the current peacebuilding philosophy to support the institutions of the market economy and civil society. However, this paradigm of 'peace building as state building' (Richmond 2011) has largely failed to achieve its goals.

As a response to this failure, local, hybrid and relational turns in peacebuilding have emerged which, it has to be said, have so far been turns more in the academic discourse and at the conceptual level rather than in actual peacebuilding policies and practice (Mac Ginty 2015; Mac Ginty and Richmond 2015; Mac Ginty and Richmond 2013; Brigg 2016; Randazzo 2016). The local is now acknowledged as the core arena of peacebuilding. It is the site of ongoing processes of interchange, entanglement, permeation, reassemblage and reconfiguration (Mac Ginty and Richmond 2013; Albrecht and Moe 2014).[2] In this understanding, the local

> becomes a verb as well as a noun or a simple descriptor of place. It is interpreted in its own right, and not as a mere adjunct to the somehow more important levels of analysis such as the state, the region or the metropolis.
>
> (Mac Ginty 2015: 848)[3]

Local nonstate societal actors are seen to impact upon the implementation of internationally predetermined peacebuilding agendas through various forms of agency, including obstruction, resistance, capture, reappropriation, co-optation, adoption, adaptation, mimicry and redirection. They are also deemed capable of appropriating international agendas and resources for their own purposes and according to their own functional logic and political economy (Richmond 2011; Richmond and Mitchell 2011; Mac Ginty and Richmond 2013; Richmond and Mac Ginty 2014). Accordingly, this shifts the focus of attention to relations and interactions and thus foregrounds a relational understanding of peacebuilding and statebuilding, or, better, peace formation and state formation (Richmond 2013).[4] In this context 'the state' is conceptualized as 'a relational setting' (Thelen *et al.* 2014: 7). Following on from this 'relational rather than objectivist way of conceptualising the state' (Froedin 2012: 272), hybridity and the hybridization of political order, peace and security have become concepts that help us grasp the realities of post-conflict situations (Boege *et al.* 2009; Richmond and Mitchell 2011; Mac Ginty 2011; Mac Ginty and Richmond 2015).

Focusing on the local, thinking in relational terms and using hybridity as an analytical lens for understanding institutional arrangements in post-conflict countries allow us to overcome the state-centric, fixed and dichotomous concepts that have so far informed liberal peacebuilding and statebuilding and encourage 'concentration on fluidity and leaching of identities, institutions and ideas' (Mac Ginty and Richmond 2015: 6).

In this chapter I will explore the fluidity and complexity of institutional arrangements by investigating the post-conflict cases of Liberia in West Africa and Bougainville, Papua New Guinea in Oceania. I will focus on the hybridization of security governance (Schroeder *et al.* 2014) as a core dimension of peace formation in postwar societies.

Peacebuilding in Liberia, which commenced in 2003, is a long-term and comprehensive international endeavour; it is the biggest peace mission in the United Nations' (UN) history so far. International interveners have been very closely following a liberal 'peacebuilding-as-statebuilding' approach. In fact, it could be considered a textbook case. Moreover, it is a case in which the chances for the implementation of a liberal peace are exceptionally good given the determination and commitment of international peacebuilders and the availability of huge resources (finances, manpower, expertise, time and political attention). The perceived success of peacebuilding in Liberia means that international interveners have something to show for their engagement. Nevertheless, there are concerns regarding the sustainability of this success – particularly with regard to what might happen when the relevant international actors, who have now been in the country for 13 years, finally withdraw. Although their long-term commitment is unquestionably laudable, the repeated extensions of the mandate – albeit in constantly reduced form – points to an unease about what has been accomplished so far and how sustainable these accomplishments will be in the absence of international interveners. As I will argue here, these doubts are warranted because the international peacebuilders have (1) focused on state institutions at the expense of the hybridization of the political order and security provision on the ground, and (2) ignored (the potential for) hybrid forms of peace on the ground. International actors have dominated the peacebuilding process in Liberia. As a consequence, local approaches have been sidelined, which has put the sustainability of peace, order and security at risk.

In comparison with the international peacebuilding intervention in Liberia, the one in Bougainville was short and very modest. In fact, it is the smallest peace mission in the history of the UN so far. After the security situation was stabilized, a number of UN agencies and international organizations, as well as aid agencies from neighbouring states and international nongovernmental organizations, arrived in Bougainville to support reconstruction, rehabilitation and peacebuilding. Even though international engagement is once again increasing, this is linked to the upcoming referendum on the future political status of Bougainville and, hence, a final political settlement of the conflict. Like Liberia, Bougainville is also seen as a peacebuilding success. Its ingredients, however, are different. In Bougainville local actors were in control of peace formation and state formation at all times; international interveners were not in a position to dominate local–international interactions. Thus, peace and state in Bougainville are emerging as local–liberal hybrids that have a clear preponderance of local agency and reflect a deliberate attempt to work with the hybridity of peace, order and security rather than ignore or fight it.

In the following two sections of this chapter I provide an overview of the current institutional arrangements of the provision of peace and security in Liberia and Bougainville, paying special attention to local nonstate institutions and actors and to their relations and interactions with state institutions. Then, I employ the concept of hybridization to make sense of the institutional arrangements of the provision of peace and security. I close the chapter with some conclusions and general recommendations. My line of argument is guided by an 'end-user approach' to peacebuilding (Denney 2014), which considers the people on the ground as of the greatest importance.[5]

## Liberia

Liberia was the theatre of extremely bloody and protracted large-scale violent conflicts from the end of the 1980s until 2003, when a comprehensive peace agreement (CPA) was signed. The CPA provided for the deployment of the United Nations Mission in Liberia (UNMIL).

UNMIL is currently the biggest peace mission in the history of the UN. At the beginning, around 15,000 military personnel, 1,100 United Nations Police and hundreds of international civilian personnel (from around 40 UN member states) were deployed to Liberia. UNMIL has a very comprehensive mandate that covers the implementation of the CPA; humanitarian aid; human rights protection; security sector reform (SSR); and disarmament, demobilization, rehabilitation and reintegration. Over the past 13 years, the UN and its various branches and programmes have exerted massive influence in Liberia. Since 2007 UNMIL's presence has been gradually reduced and is scheduled to come to an end by mid-2016.

Since 2003 considerable progress has been made with regard to security, democracy and human rights, public service reform, and the development of state institutions' capacities. On this basis, peacebuilding in Liberia is deemed a success story. However, improvements in the core areas of health, education and the economy have been slow. Furthermore, the Ebola epidemic in 2014/2015 was a major setback for overall development. The current security situation in the country is somewhat contradictorily described by the UN as 'stable but fragile' (United Nations Security Council 2015: 4). There is concern about what might happen when the UNMIL eventually leave Liberia and hand over full security responsibilities to the government. This may be attributed to the fact that the UNMIL's liberal approach of using peacebuilding as statebuilding is confronted with unwieldy local realities.

## State security institutions

The Liberian state, founded in 1847 by freed slaves from the United States and the Caribbean, 'has never functioned as a state as that term is understood in the West' (Boas 2005: 88). The state apparatus was long controlled by the Americo-Liberian elite (approximately 5 per cent of the population), who never delivered meaningful services to the vast majority of the population. At that time, the political system was based on neo-patrimonial clientelism, with the president at the top of an extremely centralized apparatus of control and oppression. Even after the Americo-Liberian elite was toppled in a bloody coup in 1980, this did not change. Therefore, a central task of the post-CPA peace process has been to fundamentally rearrange state–society relations. However, in so doing, international peacebuilders have narrowly focused on (re)building the central machinery of government and the main state institutions (i.e. the army, the police, the judiciary, finances and the constitution). Enormous effort has been put into SSR, which has seen the army, the police and other security services virtually rebuilt from scratch (Boas and Stig 2010; Karim and Gorman 2016). SSR was characterized by a 'lack of transparency, accountability and participation of local actors' (Boas and Stig 2010: 286). Even today, the Liberian army and police are still seen as being largely dependent on the UNMIL and other international support.

Moreover, most Liberians are sceptical about the capacities, effectiveness and legitimacy of these institutions.[6] Police capacities remain limited and are constrained by logistical shortcomings. In large rural areas there is no police presence at all, with nearly 80 per cent of police officers serving in the capital city and its surrounds in Montserrado County (United Nations Security Council 2015: 9; Karim and Gorman 2016: 184). In Liberia, it is commonplace for people to complain about police inefficiency, corruption, mismanagement, brutality, human rights violations, low morale and discipline (Zanker 2015).

The judiciary, the court system and the correctional system are plagued by similar problems. There is a widespread lack of trust in the state justice institutions

(Zanker 2015: 7), with courts being seen as 'inaccessible and unaffordable' by ordinary people (Tubmanburg Women Focus Group 2014) and 'usually for the rich' (Quoipa Men's Focus Group 2014). In fact, 'Many felt that justice in the formal system has a price tag: it was generally held that without affluence and influence your chances of getting justice are between slim and none' (Quoipa Men's Focus Group 2014).

### Nonstate security institutions

Under these conditions, people have more trust in nonstate security institutions that are embedded in community life. A recent conflict analysis of Liberia found that 'social networks and community dispute settlement have been key sources for peace' (Herbert 2014: 2). In this context, customary institutions, particularly chieftaincy, figure prominently.

In the course of the quasi colonization of the Liberian hinterland, a wide variety of traditional community leadership types were subsumed under the category of 'chief'. Chiefs have their roots in precolonial and prestate social structures but were incorporated into the colonial and state structures, which were formalized through the 1912 Rules and Regulations Governing the Hinterland (R&R). The R&R established a state-sanctioned system of 'traditional' – de facto indirect – rule, which confirmed the chiefs' right to govern their communities and, at the same time, made them quasi-state institutions under the control of the president in Monrovia. Today's system of chiefs, which goes back to the R&R, is a hybrid, with legitimate authority stemming from the communities and the state. Although chiefs are seen and present themselves as traditional authorities, they 'quite clearly think of themselves as the local extension of the authority of the Liberian state' (Isser *et al.* 2009: 33).

Although many chiefs and elders were forced to flee or were killed during the civil wars, local governance structures were re-established relatively quickly in the post-conflict period. Quarter chiefs and town chiefs, clan chiefs and paramount chiefs, and councils of elders and advisers have again taken over local governance. They are responsible for keeping the peace and order locally, often in cooperation with religious actors and institutions. In Liberia secret societies – along with Christian leaders, Muslim leaders, so-called witch doctors and other representatives of indigenous spirituality – are of major importance (Ellis 2007). The Poro (for men) and Sande (for women) societies, as well as others, are usually grouped under the 'African traditional religion' classification, but their realm of responsibility and the influence of their priests (*zoes*) reach well beyond the narrowly defined religious sphere. Poro and Sande priests are in charge of the sociocultural, mental and spiritual well-being of communities and the relationships between social groups. They are also hybrid authorities in that they draw their legitimacy from the invisible world of the spirits and from the state: they come under the assistant minister for cultural affairs within the Ministry of Internal Affairs.[7]

Local leaders, such as chiefs and priests, refer to customary law in order to regulate everyday community life. Liberians, particularly those in rural areas, prefer customary law to state law. They find it easier to understand, more accessible, fairer, cheaper, more transparent, faster and more efficient, as well as more legitimate because it is embedded in local culture. 'For the most part, customary justice institutions garner considerably more local legitimacy and are regarded as fairer arbiters of justice than the formal alternatives' (Isser *et al.* 2009: 87). Therefore, Liberians tend to turn to community leaders to apply customary law when they are involved in disputes or are the victims of antisocial ('criminal') behaviour. Chiefs can decide to hand such cases over to the state courts, from where they may even return to the customary system. In fact, cases can move back and forth several times.

Community self-help organizations (such as Neighbourhood Watch or Community Watch forums and other forms of self-organized security groups) often collaborate with or under the control of chiefs and religious leaders. They play a much more important role in community life than do the state police. As one female interviewee explains, 'we don't have any state security like the police. We have the community watch forum that helps protect us. We are therefore our own security most of the time' (Female interviewee from Quiopa 2014). Even where there is some police presence, people tend to turn to these groups first – not least because the state police charges fees for their services. In addition to self-help organizations, there are multiple vigilante groups which engage in a range of activities; for example, outright crime, community protection, commercial enterprise, and the provision of services to private businesses and individuals (Kantor and Persson 2010).[8]

### Linkages and interactions

State and nonstate security institutions do not merely coexist; they overlap, link and interact. This is evidenced by disputes that move from the customary law system to statutory law system (and back), police tacitly letting chiefs or Neighbourhood Watch groups deal with issues that are actually police matters, and chiefs (bestowed with traditional and state legitimacy) solving disputes as community leaders. However, there has not been much effort to bring these various institutions together in a systematic, transparent collaboration. Any collaboration that has occurred has been largely *ad hoc*, informal and tacit. In this regard, international peacebuilders seem to have missed the boat. By focusing on state institutions, they have neglected to build links between the various providers of peace and order. There is, however, one significant exception: community policing.

Attempts to institutionalize community policing are entangled in the complex network of security institutions on the ground. As part of SSR, there have been considerable efforts to implement community policing at the local level. But there are different understandings about what it is, what its purpose is and what it can legitimately do (Zanker 2014). Community policing groups were established in 2004 (funded by the United Nations Development Programme) as formal institutions that seek to forge better links between communities and the state police. After funding was withdrawn in 2010, these groups also stopped working. They were relaunched by the Ministry of Justice in 2011 as community watch forums (CWFs), albeit with limited funding. However, state institutions seem to have lost control of these groups in many places, with communities organizing them independently and often under the leadership of quarter chiefs or town chiefs (who had not been included in the previous formal community policing programme). The result is that there are no clear lines of distinction between state-sanctioned community policing and informal or illicit vigilantism (Zanker 2014: 13). Meanwhile, the relationship between the state police and the CWF is ambiguous given that there is support and collaboration in some areas and none in others.

Community policing is generally seen as a positive by local end users, be it in its more formal state-controlled or informal autonomous form (Zanker 2014: 16). By contrast, international peacebuilders differentiate between good community policing (formal, state-controlled, top-down) and problematic community policing (informal, community-controlled, bottom-up), which is questionable with regard to accountability as well as compliance with human rights and state law. This, however, does not affect the legitimacy of informal community policing or vigilantism in the eyes of locals. They see vigilante groups as part of community policing or as an alternative to it in those places where formal community policing does not work. International peacebuilders, on the other hand, see such groups as a challenge to formal community policing.

The example of community policing demonstrates the limitations of internationals interveners' engagement with nonstate security institutions. This is not surprising given that the UN 'has little understanding of the traditional customary system' (Schia and de Carvalho 2010: 11). The UN and international donors

> have invested considerable effort and funds into the formal system, but widely neglected the customary system. [.] Customary institutions and secret societies are seen as a root cause of the war that would best be abolished, and democracy continues to be touted as the solution to Liberia's problems by the international community.
>
> (Neumann 2013: 261)

However, 'The rural population has a different view. They remember the abusive practices committed in the name of the state. [.] Many complain that the international community is applying double standards, devaluating customary approaches and overestimating formal democracy' (Neumann 2013: 261).

To summarize, peace and security in Liberia is currently built on an uneasy mix of formal state institutions (supported internationally), formalized customary institutions (sanctioned by the state) and informal local arrangements (which combine various customary and civil society elements in different and flexible ways, dependent on local circumstances and often in flux).[9] The boundaries between these are blurred. Although state representatives and nonstate security providers try to distance themselves from each other, they are actually 'both part of the same system' (Kantor and Persson 2010: 29). For example, vigilantes and

Community Watch groups are in some cases doing the work the police cannot or would not do, 'sometimes with formal approval and sometimes without' (Kantor and Persson 2010: 29). Altogether, this constitutes a complex system of hybrid security governance that contains a plethora of institutions and their relations and interactions.

## Bougainville

For almost ten years (1989 to 1998), the island of Bougainville, which is part of the independent state of Papua New Guinea, was the theatre of a war of secession between the security forces of the national government of Papua New Guinea (and Bougainville auxiliaries) and the Bougainville Revolutionary Army. The war was the longest and bloodiest violent conflict in the South Pacific since the end of the Second World War. Starting with a ceasefire agreement in 1998 and a peace agreement in 2001, Bougainville has undergone a comprehensive process of post-conflict peacebuilding over the past 15 years. Peacebuilding has been relatively successful so far. Currently, Bougainville is an autonomous region within Papua New Guinea and has its own constitution and its own autonomous government, the Autonomous Bougainville Government (ABG). A referendum on independence is scheduled for some time between 2015 and 2020, as provided for in the 2001 Bougainville Peace Agreement (BPA). Hence, Bougainville will either become a completely independent state in the future (with autonomy as a transitional phase to independence) or remain a widely autonomous political entity within Papua New Guinea.

### Locally driven, internationally supported peace building

In Bougainville the time of war was a time of statelessness. The Papua New Guinean state and its institutions were forced to withdraw from the island, and the secessionist movement was unable to establish new state structures. This opened the space for the resurgence of nonstate local customary institutions that had been sidelined, but had not completely disappeared, during colonial times and in the independent state of Papua New Guinea after 1975. The fact that customary institutions were able to assume control during this stateless time is an indication of their resilience.

Traditional authorities, such as elders and chiefs, were responsible for regulating conflicts and organizing community life. In doing so, they referred to customary norms and ways of operating, to the satisfaction of their communities according to most accounts (Regan 2000). They were also widely successful in achieving war-related reconciliation at the intra-communal and inter-communal levels by utilizing customary methods of conflict resolution. It was only on the basis of local customary peacebuilding that negotiations at the 'higher' political level led to a comprehensive, sustainable peace settlement. Moreover, customary institutions and local nonstate actors also played an important role in the high-level political process (Boege 2011, 2014).

Although post-conflict peacebuilding is rooted locally, it is important to mention that external support made a small but nevertheless indispensable contribution. Peacebuilding in Bougainville was supported in particular by New Zealand and Australia, a United Nations observer mission, and a regional peace mission (Regan 2010).

The small, but highly effective, observer mission sent by the UN (from 1998 to 2005) was of major importance not only for its symbolic value (since it demonstrated the international community's commitment) but also for its contribution to post-conflict disarmament. Furthermore, the UN mission gave the external interveners international legitimacy (Regan 2008). Neighbouring Australia, New Zealand, Fiji, and Vanuatu provided the personnel for, first, a truce monitoring group (1997–1998) and, later, a peace monitoring group (1998–2003) (Adams 2001; Wehner and Denoon 2001).

The Bougainvilleans managed to control the extent and content of the activities of the international peacebuilders at all times, mainly due to the fact that they successfully insisted on an unarmed intervention. This arrangement meant that the interveners were dependent on locals for their security and protection and not in a position to enforce anything against the locals' wishes. It also saw locals develop a strong sense of responsibility for the safety of their international 'guests'.

International interveners played an important role in initiating and facilitating conversations between the conflict parties. Their presence provided a secure space for former enemies to come together. This facilitation, as well as the assistance with disarmament and demobilization and with the political negotiations, made the international mission an indispensable element of peacebuilding in Bougainville (Regan 2010).

### 'Marrying' state and nonstate security institutions

Peacebuilding in Bougainville has now been going on for more than 15 years. Given the provisions of the BPA, Bougainville will either become an independent state in the future or a widely autonomous political entity within Papua New Guinea. Both options necessitate the establishment of new state institutions. As local customary institutions have proven to be effective in peacebuilding, there is a case for their utilization in the current process of state formation as well – especially as many Bougainvilleans have a deep distrust of Western-style centralized government institutions given their negative experiences. They would prefer a system of governance that acknowledges their own indigenous institutions. In fact, political order in Bougainville today comprises elements of the Western model of statehood and elements of customary governance. To a certain degree, these domains merely coexist; though there are efforts to integrate them. People in Bougainville talk about the need to 'marry' local customary institutions and liberal institutions for the purposes of state formation (Boege 2008). This would have particular implications for the maintenance of peace, order and security. In Bougainville, peace, order and security are presently based on the efforts of a combination of state, customary and other societal actors and institutions and their relations and interactions.[10] This means that a core dimension of statehood – that is, maintaining law and order, controlling violence, providing security for citizens and developing a framework for the nonviolent conduct of conflicts – is organized in a way that decisively differs from the Western Weberian notion of statehood (Braithwaite *et al.* 2010).

The Autonomous Region of Bougainville has its own police force, which operates somewhat uncomfortably between the national Papua New Guinea and ABG systems. In the peace negotiations with the Papua New Guinean government, establishing an independent Bougainville police force was one of the most crucial concerns for the Bougainvilleans. The BPA provides for such a force, the Bougainville Police Service (BPA, clauses 211–241, and Bougainville Constitution, clauses 148–150), which is envisioned to become 'an integral part of a Bougainville system of justice based on our customary practices of restorative justice' (BCC 2004). Members of the police service are constitutionally obliged to cooperate closely with councils of elders[11] and traditional leaders in the communities (Bougainville Constitution, clause 148). The emphasis on community-oriented policing is a consequence of the terrible experiences the Bougainvilleans had with the Papua New Guinean police force before and during the war (Dinnen and Peake 2015).

Today, throughout most of Bougainville the police can only function relatively effectively if they work together with the communities' chiefs and elders. In some areas there is competition; in other areas there is smooth-running cooperation, with the chiefs as the dominant authority. Police can only gain access to a village with an invitation from a chief (although this is not a legal provision, it is the reality on the ground). Chiefs seem to make use of the regular police only under exceptional circumstances and instead prefer to police their communities using their own means.

There have also been complaints that the regular police lack discipline, are inadequately trained, have poor leadership and are isolated from the community (Dinnen and Peake 2015). In general, people do not place much trust in the regular police as an institution. By contrast, the second component of the police system in Bougainville, the Community Auxiliary Police (CAP), have a far better reputation and are more important for community life. The CAP falls under the auspices of the ABG and may be seen as a state programme designed to build the capacity of the state's security sector. However, the CAP is also legally obliged to work closely with chiefs and elders; that is, nonstate actors to whom they are accountable (Dinnen and Peake 2015). The arrangement of Bougainville community policing transcends the state–nonstate divide; it is a 'practical example of hybrid policing, linking the authority of state with that of local social orders' (Dinnen and Peake 2013: 572). Hence the CAPs are 'potentially critical intermediaries between different social orders, with a foot in both camps' (Dinnen and Peake 2015: 35).

Interestingly, CAPs are trained by New Zealand police in the context of New Zealand aid to Bougainville statebuilding. The New Zealand police officers who run the CAP training programme as part of the Bougainville Community Policing Project acknowledge the de facto legitimacy of nonstate chiefs and contribute to their legitimization; their work would not be possible without closely liaising with the communities' chiefs and elders. This, however, is done in the interest of stabilizing and maintaining law and order – which is not narrowly understood as the law and order of the state.

As in Liberia, the rule of law cannot be limited to the rule of state law: customary law is strong in Bougainville and enjoys high legitimacy. This is in no small part due to the positive experiences with customary law during the transition from war to peace. Despite there being 'no effective policing, almost no courts and no prisons' at that time, 'Bougainville [remained] one of the safest communities in Papua New Guinea', which was 'largely a credit to traditional chiefs and other traditional leaders who accepted the burden of maintaining a community based justice system during [and after] the conflict' (BCC Report 2004: 182).

In the opinion of the chiefs and elders, custom comes first; the law of the state second (if accepted at all). The formal justice system, by contrast, is weak. It is also viewed with considerable suspicion given that most Bougainvilleans find it difficult to access, costly, highly formalistic, time-consuming, confusing and unpredictable. Although the BPA allows for the establishment of a genuine Bougainville court system and the Bougainville Constitution includes provisions for such a system, little progress has been made. One reason for this is the substantial cost of such an undertaking. Another reason is that the ABG has made a strategic decision not to rely primarily on state institutions but to also allow space for customary law and customary institutions.

Finally, it should be noted that the distinctions between the two spheres are blurred. For instance, village courts are officially state institutions but often apply customary law – and when doing so they often go well beyond the limits of their formal competencies. Community leaders who act as village court magistrates are often not aware of the fact that they are working in the context of a formal state institution. Similar to the CAP, village courts are thus an expression of Bougainville's hybrid institutional arrangements.

To sum up, peace, order and security in Bougainville are based on the relations, the complementarity and the collaboration of a variety of actors and institutions that represent the interests of the state, custom and civil society; however, the boundaries between these spheres are blurred and in flux. What is generally seen as a *sine qua non* of statehood – namely the capacity of state institutions to implement and enforce the rule of (state) law – is lacking in Bougainville (and Liberia). This deficiency, though, has not hindered post-conflict peacebuilding or the maintenance of order. Bougainville state institution builders have astutely abstained from trying to implement a monopoly on the legitimate use of force as the means to maintain order and security. The ABG recognizes that state security institutions are rather weak and lack efficiency and legitimacy, while customary institutions are well established, are relatively effective and have a high degree of legitimacy. The government is of course working on improving the capacities, effectiveness and legitimacy of state institutions (with some very modest support from international statebuilders from Australia and New Zealand), but does not see this as the only means to secure peace and order. Even in this classic field of state responsibility, the Bougainvillean government has taken a course of action that puts the role of state institutions into perspective and is open to collaboration with nonstate institutions. The positive mutual accommodation of Western-style state and local customary institutions can indeed provide an orderly and safe environment for the people. Bougainville's successes in peace and state formation are due to this positive mutual accommodation, which has led to a unique Bougainvillean form of political community and the emergence of peace and order (Wallis 2014).

## Hybridization of institutional security arrangements

The institutional arrangements in Liberia and Bougainville may be understood as consisting of hybrid political orders and emerging hybrid security governance (Boege *et al.* 2010; Schroeder *et al.* 2014).[12] For instance, the domains of the liberal state and local custom not only coexist (with complementarities and synergies, as well as frictions and incompatibilities) but are also entangled. The emerging webs of institutional arrangements are of course context-specific in Liberia differs from that in Bougainville and other post-conflict states in the Global South. Nevertheless, certain similar patterns may be found. For example, in both Liberia and Bougainville illiberal local actors and institutions (such as chiefs, healers, elders and religious leaders, and customary law and traditional dispute resolution) are of major significance for peace and order. They are not only temporarily filling in gaps left by the limited presence or complete absence of state institutions until such a time when state institutions can take over; they are here to stay. In contrast to familiar civil society actors like nongovernmental organizations or community-based organizations, these actors and institutions are often overlooked or misunderstood by international peacebuilders. This has negative consequences for peacebuilding, as opportunities are missed or potentially benign local peace actors are marginalized and alienated.

International interveners' focus on building state institutions in Liberia misses, first, the reality of the presence of a wide variety of nonstate providers of peace, security and order, and, second, the reality of the illiberal or non-Western nature of Liberian state institutions, which are enmeshed with nonstate institutions, actors, norms and values. This blend of institutions facilitates the emergence of complex and fluid constellations of governance that transcend the realm of the Western liberal state (and of civil society in the Western liberal sense) familiar to and preferred by international interveners. It is in these constellations, however, that peace emerges, with state institutions and international peacebuilders playing their roles, but only as elements in a complex web of relationships and interactions. Efforts to harmonize these interactions in Liberia seem to consist primarily of attempts by state institutions (and their international supporters) to control them rather than engage in genuine reflective exchange and dialogue. By contrast, Bougainvilleans had much more space to develop their own homegrown institutional arrangements. This allowed them to 'marry' the local and the liberal, which was also possible because of the modest size of international peacebuilding support and the preparedness of international peacebuilders to go with the local flow, be it voluntarily or involuntarily.

The provision of peace and security solely by state institutions is not a viable option in Bougainville or Liberia. The hybridization of security governance renders obsolete the Western concept of the state as the central overarching entity with the monopoly on the legitimate use of physical violence. Although governments may claim or pretend that such an arrangement does exist, in reality they have no central dominance over the variety of providers of peace and security or their relationships and interactions.

In reality, security actors and institutions straddle the state–nonstate boundary, which thus calls into question the state–nonstate dichotomy. First, it must not be forgotten that the individuals who represent and enact the various institutions live in and move between the spheres of state and custom. For example, 'while police officers and court staff may represent "modern" organizations, they are also staffed by individuals who are woven into cultural fabrics' (Denney 2014: 263). Second, while there are some institutions and actors that at first sight appear to be state (the police, the army, the courts) or nonstate (priests, vigilantes, chiefs), a closer look reveals blurred boundaries and intersections, such as chiefs, who are both state and nonstate due to their double relational embeddedness (Thelen *et al.* 2014: 8), and community police, which are also state and nonstate, though they can be more of one than the other depending on the context. It also exposes intense interactions and relationships which further blur the boundaries between entities such as the police and Community Watch groups or the state justice system and customary law.

The customary law–state law interface illustrates this point. Customary law in many post-conflict countries is strong and vital, whereas the state judicial system is weak. People in both Liberia and Bougainville generally find customary law easier to understand, more accessible, fairer, cheaper, more efficient and more legitimate. The interface between customary law and state law is often uneasy, characterized by (partial) contestation, (partial) complementarity and (partial) incompatibility. Customary law has a specific relationship to the state: it is distinct from the laws of the state but, at the same time, it is accepted by the state as a source of law in its own right. Formally, customary law is inferior to state law and confined to certain areas of jurisdiction, with serious crimes such as murder or rape being punished under state law. In de facto terms, however, such boundaries are fluid in both Liberia and Bougainville, and customary law often reaches beyond the restrictions imposed upon it by state regulation. Moreover, customary law also covers areas which are not and cannot be covered by state law but are nonetheless of major importance for conflicts in community life (e.g. sorcery or witchcraft). At the same time, customary law is open to change and adapts to new challenges as it engages with statutory law and rights discourses introduced into the communities by civil society organizations (e.g. discourses on women's and children's rights). In other words, customary law is far from fixed and static. However, changes to customary law cannot be imposed from the outside (e.g. by state institutions or human rights nongovernmental organizations); rather, they are a matter of debate and contestation for people in the communities.

For locals, the end users, their everyday reality is shaped by a complex web of interacting and overlapping institutions and actors – a context wherein relations are more important than institutions (Kantor and Persson 2010: 11). People show formidable pragmatism and adaptability when it comes to combining the indigenous and the exogenous, merging the formal and the informal, and exploring what works in their circumstances and incorporating it into their culture and customs – which are fluid, interculturally adaptive and hybridizing all the time.

## Conclusion

In this chapter I have espoused an understanding of institutional security arrangements that 'foregrounds relations over entities, becoming over being, and dynamism over fixity' (Brigg 2014: 7). In other words, what really matters are processes, relationships and interactions rather than distinct entities. Relationships and interactions are complex and fluid. Hybridization – an ongoing process of mixing, reconverting, leaching and blending – is the main feature of the provision of peace and security, not the centrally orchestrated and controlled building of a uniform institutional system. State security institutions and institutional reform programmes of governments and their international supporters (e.g. security sector reform, constitutional reform, decentralization, democratization, justice sector reform, etc.) are nothing but elements in a web of relationships and interactions, and of a much broader mix of processes of state and peace formation.

Consequently, it has to be acknowledged that the actual processes of peace and state formation cannot be planned for or implemented by international peacebuilders and statebuilders. Liberia and Bougainville provide ample evidence that societies, which in the view of international interveners are to be the recipients of international liberal post-conflict institution building, are not just blank pages on which the international peacebuilders' agenda may be written.

Local populations are not just passive recipients of peace- and statebuilding; they have agency of their own. Instead of the mere delivery of liberal templates of peace and state by benevolent outsiders to passive (and grateful) local recipients, what is really occurring in places like Bougainville and Liberia is a meeting of profoundly different life worlds and worldviews; that is, the collision, interaction, negotiation, entanglement and enmeshment of different understandings of and approaches to political order and peace – and the ensuing emergence of hybrid forms of peace and security governance. Although these forms may differ considerably from the Western liberal state, they can also efficiently and legitimately control violence and provide a framework for the nonviolent conduct of conflict. Bougainville and Liberia confirm the observation that there is a 'wide gulf between international reform discourses and the realities of domestic security governance in many areas of the world' (Schroeder *et al.* 2014: 228).

It is hard to imagine that in a place like Liberia or Bougainville a state monopoly on force will be achieved in the foreseeable future; nor is it necessary or desirable. Hybrid forms of peace and order need not be second-best options; rather, they can provide effective and legitimate alternatives. There are ways of securing peace and order beyond relying on the institutions of the state. There is potential for improved, more conscious and planned integration and collaboration, as pursued in Bougainville. This requires deliberate attempts to bridge the divides and to engage in (cross-cultural) dialogue and positive mutual accommodation.

Such a relational and dialogue-based approach necessitates a fundamental change in attitudes and approaches on the part of international actors with regard to institutional engineering, using peacebuilding as statebuilding, and acknowledging and engaging with the hybridity of political order and security on the ground. This means supporting and pursuing 'link-building as opposed to state-building' (Baker 2010: 613).

In other words, international support for state institutions has to take into account those institutions' embeddedness in and their relations with broader societal networks of peace and security provision. International actors will have to learn to appreciate local perceptions of what constitutes legitimate security institutions, to widen their understanding of legitimate institutions accordingly, and to engage with local institutions beyond the realm of the state (and the comfort zone of a civil society forged in their own image) irrespective of whether those institutions' practices conform to Western liberal standards or not. For this to happen, international peacebuilders will need to demonstrate much more modesty and a far greater willingness to learn.

## Notes

1   For more on the 'liberal peace' and its critique, see Paris and Sisk (2009); Newman *et al.* (2009); Paris (2010); Richmond (2011); Tadjbakhsh (2011); Campbell *et al.* (2011); Mac Ginty (2013).

2   This local turn and the associated relational and hybrid turns have bureaucratic, ideological and epistemological confines, as well as constraints grounded in power relations and power politics (Chandler 2013). Furthermore, these turns can lead to practices that are highly questionable from a peacebuilding perspective; for example, the evasion of responsibility and accountability on the part of international interveners or the modernization of counterinsurgency strategies (Moe 2013, 2014; Albrecht and Moe 2015). Criticism of the local turn as pursued 'mainly for instrumental or rhetorical reasons' (Mac Ginty and Richmond 2013: 771) is also valid. At the same time, however, these turns can open avenues for new approaches in the scholarly discourse and for innovative peacebuilding practices.

3   'The local is a sphere of activity that is constantly being made and remade, sometimes with replication and sometimes with change. It is made, remade and negotiated through the everyday actions of inhabitants, as well as those of exogenous and institutional actors. In this way the widened concept of the local has the potential to liberate us from the confines of International Relations as a discipline and related conceptual straitjackets of the state and institutions' (Mac Ginty 2015: 851).

4   For different types of relational approaches in (the study of) peacebuilding, see Brigg (2016). Brigg opts for a 'thick relationality' approach, which 'reverses the prevailing priority of entity over relation in mainstream social science to focus attention on how entities continually arise or emerge through relations and processes' (2016: 61). In this chapter I follow the more modest path of 'thin relationality', which 'draws attention to underappreciated relations among entities' and 'reaffirms the centrality of relationships of all types to peacebuilding' (Brigg 2016: 66).

5    Denney criticizes donor approaches to SSR that are usually led 'by a provider approach
     – taking *who the provider is* as the starting point – rather than by an end user approach
     – taking *how those who use security and justice services experience security and
     justice* as the starting point' (Denney 2014: 259; italics in original).

6    The following is based on field research conducted in Liberia in 2013 and 2014 by the
     Liberian team members of a joint research project conducted by the Kofi Annan
     International Peacekeeping Training Centre, Accra, and the University of Queensland,
     Brisbane,entitled 'Understanding and Working with Local Sources of Peace, Security
     and Justice in West Africa'. If not otherwise indicated, quotes in the text are from
     fieldwork reports.

7    In the past, several presidents were members of secret societies. Today, high-ranking
     state representatives are also members and are thus bound to the societies' norms,
     rules and decisions.

8    There is also a relatively large commercial security sector with private security
     companies and private police forces. However, they do not play a role in the everyday
     security of ordinary Liberians; rather, they provide services to big business and the
     Liberian elite. For more on this commercial security sector, see von Boemcken (2011).

9    In the best case scenario this can lead to a pragmatic arrangement of security
     governance in which town chiefs, youth leaders, women leaders and their assistants,
     together with councils of elders, form the local governing body – a body that would
     consist of balanced ethnic and religious representation and assign positions through a
     combination of (informal) elections and appointment by the different groups of the
     community. For an example, see Neumann (2013: 266–267).

10   The following is based on field research conducted by the author in the context of
     various research projects carried out between 2007 and 2016.

11   Councils of Elders are the lowest level of formal government in Bougainville. They
     are institutions within the state structure but also have significant legitimacy within
     communities given their adherence to local custom. Elders are selected by the leaders
     of all the clans (this includes chiefs, religious leaders, women and youth representatives)
     in areas containing councils.

12   The concept of hybrid political orders challenges the conventional state-fragility and
     statebuilding discourse, which evaluates states according to a Weberian ideal type
     (which is hardly a reality even in the most developedWestern states) and focuses on
     what is lacking (namely statehood in the Western sense) instead of on what is actually
     present. By contrast, the hybrid political orders approach draws attention to what is
     the case on the ground. It acknowledges the coexistence, competition and entanglement
     of different types of legitimate institutions, thus clarifying that the liberal state and
     customary nonstate realms and their institutions and practices do not exist in isolation
     from each other, but rather intersect and permeate each other (Boege *et al.* 2009,
     2010). It is this shift away from binaries (such as traditional and modern, formal and
     informal, state and nonstate) that is 'the primary appeal of hybridity and hybridization'
     (Peterson 2012: 12); it allows us to question the fixity of categories and boundaries
     (Richmond and Mac Ginty 2015) by taking note of the traditional within the modern,
     the modern within the traditional, the formal within the informal, the informal within
     the formal and so forth.

# References

Adams, Rebecca (ed.). 2001. *Peace on Bougainville – Truce Monitoring Group. Gudpela
    Nius Bilong Peace*. Wellington: Victoria University Press.
Albrecht, Peter and Louise Wiuff Moe. 2014. 'The Simultaneity of Authority in Hybrid
    Orders'. *Peacebuilding* 3(1): 1–16.

Baker, Bruce. 2010. 'Linking State and Non-state Security and Justice'. *Development Policy Review* 28(5): 597–616.

BCC. 2004. *Report of the Bougainville Constitutional Commission.* Report on the third and final draft of the Bougainville Constitution, prepared by the Bougainville Constitutional Commission. Arawa and Buka.

Boas, Morten. 2005. 'The Liberian Civil War: New War/Old War?' *Global Society* 19(1): 73–88.

Boas, Morten and Karianne Stig. 2010. 'Security Sector Reform in Liberia: An Uneven Partnership without Local Ownership'. *Journal of Intervention and Statebuilding* 4(3): 285–303.

Boege, Volker. 2008. *A Promising Liaison: kastom and State in Bougainville.* ACPACS Occasional Papers Series 12. Brisbane: The Australian Centre for Peace and Conflict Studies (ACPACS).

Boege, Volker. 2011. 'Hybrid Forms of Peace and Order on a South Sea Island: Experiences from Bougainville (Papua New Guinea)'. In Oliver Richmond and Audra Mitchell (eds), *Hybrid Forms of Peace: From Everyday Agency to Post-liberalism.* New York: Palgrave Macmillan, pp. 88–106.

Boege, Volker et al. 2009. 'On Hybrid Political Orders and Emerging States: What is Failing – States in the Global South or Research and Politics in the West?' In Martina Fischerand Beatrix Schmelzle (eds), *Building Peace in the Absence of States: Challenging the Discourse on State Failure.* Berghof Handbook Dialogue Series 8, pp. 15–35.

Boege, Volker et al. 2010. 'Challenging Statebuilding as Peacebuilding – Working with Hybrid Political Orders to Build Peace'. In Oliver P. Richmond (ed.), *Palgrave Advances in Peacebuilding: Critical Developments and Approaches.* New York: Palgrave Macmillan, pp. 99–115.

Bougainville Constitution. 2004. *The Constitution of the Autonomous Region of Bougainville.* Adopted by the Bougainville Constituent Assembly at Buin on 12 November.

BPA. 2001. 'Bougainville Peace Agreement, 30 August 2001'. In Andy Carl and Lorraine Garasu (eds), *Weaving Consensus – The Papua New Guinea–Bougainville Peace Process* (Conciliation Resources Accord Issue 12/2002). London: Conciliation Resources, pp. 67–85.

Braithwaite, John, Hilary Charlesworth, Peter Reddy and Leah Dunn. 2010. *Reconciliation and Architectures of Commitment. Sequencing Peace in Bougainville.* Canberra: ANU ePress.

Brigg, Morgan. 2014. *Culture, 'Relationality', and Global Cooperation.* Global Cooperation Research Papers 6. Duisburg: Centre for Global Cooperation Research.

Brigg, Morgan. 2016. 'Relational Peacebuilding'. In Tobias Debiel Thomas Held and Ulrich Schneckener (eds), *Peacebuilding in Crisis: Rethinking Paradigms and Practices of Transnational Cooperation.* London and New York: Routledge, pp. 56–69.

Campbell, Susanna, David Chandler and Meera Sabaratnam (eds). 2011. *A Liberal Peace? The Problems and Practices of Peacebuilding.* London: Zed Books.

Chandler, David. 2013. 'Relational Sensibilities: The End of the Road for "Liberal Peace"'. *Global Dialogues* 2. Duisburg: Centre for Global Cooperation Research, pp. 19–26.

Denney, Lisa. 2014. 'Overcoming the State/Non-state Divide: An End User Approach to Security and Justice Reform'. *International Peacekeeping* 21(2): 251–268.

Dinnen, Sinclair and Gordon Peake. 2015. 'Experimentation and Innovation in Police Reform: Timor-Leste, Solomon Islands and Bougainville'. *Political Science* 67(1): 21–37.

Dinnen, Sinclair and Gordon Peake. 2013. 'More Than Just Policing: Police Reform in Post-conflict Bougainville'. *International Peacekeeping* 20(5): 570–584.

Ellis, Stephen. 2007. *The Mask of Anarchy. The Destruction of Liberia and the Religious Dimension of an African Civil War.* New York: New York University Press.

Froedin, Olle Jonas. 2012. 'Dissecting the State: Towards a Relational Conceptualization of States and State Failure'. *Journal of International Development* 24: 271–286.

Herbert, Sian. 2014. *Conflict Analysis of Liberia.* Birmingham: GSDRC, University of Birmingham.

Isser, Deborah H., Stephen C. Lubkemann and Saah N'Tow. 2009. *Looking for Justice. Liberian Experiences with and Perceptions of Local Justice Options.* Peaceworks No. 63. Washington, DC: United States Institute of Peace.

Kantor, Ana and Mariam Persson. 2010. *Understanding Vigilantism. Informal Security Providers and Security Sector Reform in Liberia.* Stockholm: Folke Bernadotte Academy.

Karim, Sabrina and Ryan Gorman. 2016. 'Building a More Competent Security Sector: The Case of UNMIL and the Liberian National Police'. *International Peacekeeping* 23(1): 158–191.

Mac Ginty, Roger. 2011. *International Peacebuilding and Local Resistance: Hybrid Forms of Peace.* New York: Palgrave Macmillan.

Mac Ginty, Roger (ed.). 2013. *Routledge Handbook of Peacebuilding.* London and New York: Routledge.

Mac Ginty, Roger. 2015. 'Where is the Local? Critical Localism and Peacebuilding'. *Third World Quarterly* 36(5): 840–856.

Mac Ginty, Roger and Oliver P. Richmond. 2013. 'The Local Turn in Peace Building: A Critical Agenda for Peace'. *Third World Quarterly* 34(5): 763–783.

Mac Ginty, Roger and Oliver Richmond. 2015. 'The Fallacy of Constructing Hybrid Political Orders: A Reappraisal of the Hybrid Turn in Peacebuilding'. *International Peacekeeping,* DOI: 10.1080/13533312.2015.1099440.

Moe, Louise Wiuff. 2013. 'Relationality and Pragmatism in Peacebuilding. Reflections on Somaliland'. *Global Dialogues* 2. Duisburg: Centre for Global Cooperation Research, pp. 44–53.

Moe, Louise Wiuff. 2014. *The Strange Wars of Liberal Peace. The 'Local', Hybridity, and the Governing Rationalities of Counterinsurgent Warfare in Somalia.* Paper presented at ISA Annual Convention, Toronto.

Neumann, Hannah. 2013. *Through the Eyes of the Locals: Two Post-war Communities and their Struggles from War to Peace.* Berlin: Diss.Phil., Freie Universität Berlin.

Newman, Edward, Roland Paris and Oliver Richmond (eds). 2009. *New Perspectives on Liberal Peacebuilding.* Tokyo: United Nations University Press.

Paris, Roland. 2010. 'Saving Liberal Peacebuilding'. *Review of International Studies* 36(2): 337–365.

Paris, Roland and Timothy Sisk (eds). 2009. *The Dilemmas of Statebuilding. Confronting the Contradictions of Postwar Peace Operations.* London: Routledge.

Peterson, Jenny H. 2012. 'A Conceptual Unpacking of Hybridity: Accounting for Notions of Power, Politics and Progress in Analyses of Aid-driven Interfaces'. *Journal of Peacebuilding and Development* 7(2): 9–22.

Randazzo, Elisa. 2016. 'The Paradoxes of the "Everyday": Scrutinising the Local Turn in Peace Building'. *Third World Quarterly,* DOI: 10.1080/01436597.2015.1120154.

Regan, Anthony J. 2000. ' "Traditional" Leaders and Conflict Resolution in Bougainville: Reforming the Present by Re-writing the Past?', In Sinclair Dinnen and Allison Ley (eds), *Reflections on Violence in Melanesia.* Annandale, Canberra: Hawkins Press – Asia Pacific Press, pp. 290–304.

Regan, Anthony J. 2008. 'The Bougainville Intervention: Political Legitimacy and Sustainable Peace-building'. In Greg Fry and Tarcisius Tara Kabutaulaka (eds), *Intervention and State-building in the Pacific. The Legitimacy of 'Cooperative' Intervention.* Manchester: Manchester University Press, pp. 184–208.

Regan, Anthony J. 2010. *Light Intervention. Lessons from Bougainville.* Washington, DC: United States Institute of Peace.

Richmond, Oliver P. 2011. *A Post-liberal Peace.* London and New York: Routledge.

Richmond, Oliver. 2013. 'Failed Statebuilding versus Peace Formation'. In David Chandler and Timothy D. Sisk (eds), *Routledge Handbook of International Statebuilding.* London and New York: Routledge, pp. 130–140.

Richmond, Oliver and Audra Mitchell (eds). 2011. *Hybrid Forms of Peace: From Everyday Agency to Post-liberalism.* New York: Palgrave Macmillan.

Richmond, Oliver P. and Roger Mac Ginty. 2015. 'Where Now for the Critique of the Liberal Peace?' *Cooperation and Conflict* 50(2): 171–189.

Schia, Niels Nagelhus and Benjamin de Carvalho. 2010. *Peacebuilding in Liberia and the Case for a Perspective from Below.* NUPI Working Paper 778 Security in Practice 8 – 2010. Oslo: NUPI.

Schia, Niels Nagelhus and John Karlsrud. 2013. ' "Where the Rubber meets the Road": Friction Sites and Local-level Peacebuilding in Haiti, Liberia and South Sudan'. *International Peacekeeping* 20(2): 233–248.

Schroeder, Ursula, Fairlie Chappuis and Deniz Kocak. 2014. 'Security Sector Reform and the Emergence of Hybrid Security Governance'. *International Peacekeeping* 21(2): 214–230.

Tadjbakhsh, Shahrbanou (ed.). 2011. *Rethinking the Liberal Peace: External Models and Local Alternatives.* London: Routledge.

Thelen, Tatjana, Larissa Vetters and Keebet von Benda-Beckmann. 2014. 'Introduction to Stategraphy. Toward a Relational Anthropology of the State'. *Social Analysis* 58(3): 1–19.

United Nations Security Council. 2015. *Thirteenth Progress Report of the Secretary-General on the United Nations Mission in Liberia.* S/2015/620.

von Boemcken, Marc (ed.). 2011. *Commercial Security and Development. Findings from Timor-Leste, Liberia and Peru.* BICC Brief 45. Bonn: Bonn International Center of Conversion.

Wallis, Joanne. 2014. *Constitution Making during State Building.* New York: Cambridge University Press.

Wehner, Monica and Donald Denoon (eds). 2001. *Without a Gun. Australians' Experiences Monitoring Peace in Bougainville, 1997–2001.* Canberra: Pandanus Books.

Zanker, Franzisca. 2014. *Mixed Messages: Efforts at Community Policing in Post-war Liberia.* Paper presented at ISA Annual Convention, Toronto.

Zanker, Franzisca. 2015. *A Decade of Police Reform in Liberia: Perceptions, Challenges and Ways Ahead.* SSR 2.0 Brief Issue No. 4. Centre for Security Governance.

# Conclusion

## Institutional reform and peacebuilding

*Nadine Ansorg and Sabine Kurtenbach*

How can we stop violence in the aftermath of war? And how can we prevent the recurrence of large-scale conflict? There is no shortage of examples of past or current crises in which these questions have been the most urgent but also the most difficult to answer. The 1990s were characterized by concerns over the Balkans, Northern Ireland, Rwanda and South Africa, while the first decade of the twenty-first century witnessed conflicts in Liberia, Sri Lanka and Burundi. Today, we are seeing large-scale conflicts in Syria, Afghanistan and Iraq. Apart from all requiring significant engagement by local actors and international donors alike, there is no definitive answer on how to establish peace in such countries.

Institutional reform is one nonviolent way to manage and prevent conflict. This may include promoting democratization and statebuilding (e.g. via interim governments, power sharing, increasing political participation among the population, and developing an accountable and democratically controlled security sector). While the peace-enhancing role of institutions in the aftermath of war is generally recognized, the specific features of institutions, their formal or informal character and their relation to state and society are highly contested both in research and practice.

The contributions of this edited volume provide further insights into what does and does not work with regard to institutional reform and peacebuilding in post-conflict settings. The chapters provide little evidence of successful institutional reform in postwar contexts, but rather call for a much more nuanced approach. The international strategy to find an institutional reform short cut to 'Denmark' rarely works, if at all.[1] The contributions here stress two key relationships: that between institutional reforms and prewar institutions, and that between institutional designs and societal divisions.

### The relationship between prewar institutions and postwar institutional reform

When engaging in prewar or postwar institutional reform, the 'shadow of the past', as Schneider puts it in his contribution to this edited volume (Chapter 2), is often stronger than expected and should certainly not be underestimated. One thing we can be certain of: there is no blueprint for institutional reform in the aftermath of war. Or, as Boege argues in Chapter 9, we have to acknowledge 'actual processes of peace and state formation cannot be planned for or implemented by international peace builders and state builders'. Institutional reforms are highly dependent on the prewar institutional settings and follow the logic of path dependency; that is, prewar institutions often do not cease to exist following the outbreak of violence, but rather continue to function during and after conflict. New institutional arrangements are thus complementary or link to former institutional experiences. Even after a military victory and the displacement of prewar institutions, prewar customs or habits will permeate new institutions and have an impact on their ability to mitigate conflict. This points to the necessity and the added value of systematically including the link between prewar institutions, how they change during war and armed conflict, and postwar reform. Hence, while there is an increased need to change prewar institutional settings, particularly in postwar countries, peacebuilders must account for the path dependency of institutional reform when attempting large-scale reform.

Schneider, for instance, finds that a country's colonial past in the form of its legal tradition also hinders countries from embarking on a more inclusive path. States with British legal origins are less likely to adopt proportional representation, but slightly more likely to engage in horizontal power sharing. In addition, ethnic fractionalization and the discrimination of relevant ethnic groups reduce the chance that a country adopts formal power-sharing rules.

In Chapter 4 on the implementation of institutional reforms in the midst of war, Kurtenbach makes a similar case about the influence of war and violence, pointing out that ongoing violence limits the scope of reform. The displacement of prewar institutions is rarely possible, while layering and drift may enhance the space of action for nonviolent actors. At the same time, these reforms are at high risk of being undermined or captured by armed actors.

In Chapter 5, Schmidt and Galyan show that new and integrative institutions such as power sharing can be introduced in the aftermath of war to prevent a security dilemma. However, they highlight that such arrangements often rely on the inclusion of so-called sunset clauses, which prevent future frustration in a society. Thus, after a period of safeguard, institutional reforms that do not completely break with prewar institutions could be likely to prevent rigid and inflexible institutional designs.

The ambiguity of many reforms in the context of war is a major factor behind the 'hybridity' of many postwar orders. All contributions on security sector reform in the third part of this book provide overwhelming evidence of the important relationship between prewar institutions and postwar reform.

In Chapter 8, Ramírez González argues that path dependency does not always lead to the status quo, but rather to changing patterns of violence and disorder and a fluid state of nonstability. He shows that post-conflict institutional reforms in Mexico were, for the most part, dependent on the processes through which wartime actors became integrated in post-conflict frameworks in exchange for short-term gains. For these reasons, efforts to overcome the persistence of governmental weakness through institutional reform helped legitimize privileged intermediaries – such as regional military commanders – and resilient local governance mechanisms despite the fact that these were often predatory and patrimonial in nature. On this basis, historical and micro-level comparative analysis along these lines may help illuminate the paradoxical institutional choices faced by developing societies confronted with violence and armed disorder today.

In Chapter 9, Boege's comparison of security sector reform in Bougainville and Liberia offers a greater understanding of the persistence of informal, customary institutions and their relevance for peace and stability. The influence of external actors and their 'liberal reform agenda' may have rather destabilizing effects. Therefore, local populations are not just passive recipients of peace building and state building; they are active agents in their own right. Their perceptions, ideas and actions may differ considerably from those typically found in Western liberal states, but they can become efficient and legitimate in controlling violence and providing a framework for the nonviolent conduct of conflict. Boege thus argues that international actors will have to learn to understand local perceptions of what constitutes legitimate security institutions in order to broaden their understanding of legitimate institutions and to engage with local institutions beyond the realm of the state.

Ganson and Wennmann make a similar argument in Chapter 6, emphasizing that bottom-up reforms in the economy of postwar situations are much more sustainable than top-down approaches. Promoting bottom-up reforms, of course, requires an admission that business is part and parcel of the hybrid political order and that its actions are therefore inherently political. However, this may be difficult to swallow for many actors, whether representing the corporate sector, the United Nations or civil society.

In their quantitative contribution in Chapter 7, Haaß, Strasheim and Ansorg highlight the potential of international aid to facilitate the implementation of police reforms. They argue that international actors can sometimes reduce the costs of implementation or pressure domestic political actors into meeting criteria such as postwar control by the police. However, the impact of international actors varies according to the type of institutional reform. For instance, while the presence of peacekeepers and more aid for security sector reform increase the chances of reforming political control of the police, aid does not have a similarly strong effect on police composition reforms.

## The relationship between institutional designs and societal divisions

A major finding of this edited volume is that the success of institutional reform is highly dependent on societal cleavages. Because postwar societies are always characterized by major divisions between societal groups (e.g. ethnic or religious groups), it is imperative that these cleavages are addressed and that conflicts are re-embedded into nonviolent institutional settings. Thus one major task of local and international actors is to foster cohesion between formerly warring parties, as the continued absence of social cohesion may be a condition of the recurrence of violence.

In Chapter 1, Basedau shows that the success of institutional ethnic conflict management depends on the depth of divisions. In his analysis of institutional reform in 34 African countries, he finds that inclusiveness has the potential to reduce the likelihood of conflict in more deeply divided societies. However, absent divisions make institutions largely irrelevant. Furthermore, Schneider points to the fact that institutional designs aimed at conflict mitigation seem to be more viable if they are established prior to armed conflict. Establishing integrative institutions after conflict onset does not seem to have such a peace-enhancing effect. Galyan's study on Sri Lanka provides evidence of recurring cycles of violence when there is incongruence between institutional designs and societal divisions.

Kurtenbach's examination of Colombia in Chapter 4 shows that the ambiguous outcome of reforms can be explained by the fact that political reforms only addressed the political system but not the underlying social divisions. The lack of political participation was at least partially overcome with political decentralization and constitutional reform in 1991. The related social problems – high levels of inequality and a lack of land access in the rural areas – remained unaddressed. The current peace process is the first attempt to deal with rural underdevelopment as a major driver of armed conflict and violence.

## Avenues for future research

The contributions to this edited volume identify four main avenues of future research regarding postwar institutional reform and the relationship of such reform to path dependency, prewar institutions and societal divisions.

First, more work needs to be done to understand the potential and pitfalls of path dependency. As the contributions of this edited volume show, the path dependency of institutions and institutional reform can rarely be avoided. At the same time, local and international peace builders see an urgent need for reform that addresses the deepest cleavages in a society. Following an extensive period of violent conflict, it is essential that the underlying causes of the conflict are mitigated. However, the trick is to find theoretically reasonable patterns of path dependency that not only manage the causes of conflict but can also link to existing and efficient local or informal institutional structures. Future endeavours need to engage in more theoretically founded and empirical work on the right degree and level of path dependency of institutional reform.

Second, future studies on institutional reform need to find theoretically sound explanations of patterns or categories of how societal divisions and cleavages may best be addressed by institutional reform. We learned from the contributions to this edited volume that to be successful, institutional reform has to account for divisions in a society. Moreover, as Basedau shows, integrative institutions have huge potential to address particularly deep societal divisions. What needs to be studied further is whether there are patterns of institutional reform that work better for certain structures of society than others. For instance, executive power sharing may work particularly well in societies with two strong groups, while community-level integrative solutions are likely to be a better option in societies with many small, regionally concentrated groups.

Third, while taking into account prewar institutional arrangements and societal divisions, research and practice should be aware of the potential interaction effects between different institutional reforms, which could at times mitigate conflict or enhance it. For instance, if we only look at the very particular area of security sector reform, we will find dozens of examples of incoherent programmes that triggered continued postwar violence instead of creating stable and trustworthy environments. In most cases the amount of aid (all forms) invested in a postwar country can be verified. However, most of the effort invested is devoted neither to coordination between different donors nor to coordination between different sector programmes. Afghanistan is a case in point (Sedra 2007: 10): security sector reform was divided into five pillars, each to be overseen by a lead donor nation. Military reform was led by the United States; police reform, by Germany; judicial reform, by Italy; the disarmament, demobilization and reintegration of ex-combatants, by Japan; and counter-narcotics, by the United Kingdom. As Sedra 2007: 10 points out, 'the Afghan process was hindered by capacity deficits, coordination breakdowns and a precarious security environment'. There was neither coordination between the different donor nations nor coordination between different sectors, due to the specific structure of the Afghan security sector reform programme. On top of that, the judiciary was the sector that got the least amount of attention, as reform was to be advanced in earnest once the security situation had stabilized; unfortunately, this never really happened. Similar problems may be said to be true in many other cases. Hence, researchers need to study the interaction effects between different aspects of institutional reform that can be either beneficial or destructive to the unstable postwar environment.

Fourth, many of the chapters here underline the necessity to include timing and sequencing in peacebuilding programmes. Nonetheless, this debate is generally limited to the question of sequencing between stabilizing and liberalizing. However, timing – that is, the position of an event in a temporal timeline (Grzymala-Busse 2011)—is only part of the problem. Time is a much more complex concept. In her analysis of institutional reform in post-communist countries, Grzymala-Busse (2011) distinguishes between duration (temporal length of an event), tempo (amount of change per unit of time), acceleration (derivate of velocity with respect to time) and timing (position of a temporal timeline). Hence, a more nuanced approach to the question of time in postwar institutional reforms would help us develop a better understanding of the important factors.

Translating this into the challenges of institutional reform in the context of war and including the path-dependency perspective, prewar institutions and societal divisions, we can point to two new research avenues. Regarding duration, the length and intensity of war may play an important role for the prospects of reform. Institutions depend on a certain level of trust that may be difficult to achieve after long and violent wars, which may lead existing institutions to be considered as more trustworthy than new ones. The widespread uncertainty in the aftermath of war not only shapes the decisions of former combatants due to a 'security dilemma' (Walter 1997) but also affects large parts of the population. This may be one reason for path dependency. Boege's narrative of the provision of security through customary institutions provides empirical evidence of this uncertainty and the consequences of it. The same problem of ill-conceived solutions for long-term problems may be relevant for tempo and acceleration, as external actors in postwar contexts have limited time due to other urgent crises, inadequate funds and exit options. Timing is also crucial with regard to two aspects:

1   *Local structures, history and prewar institutions.* Some prewar institutions can be matched more easily to external standards than others. Prior experience with institutions such as elections or accountability mechanisms can be helpful for related postwar reforms.
2   *International context.* During the 1990s, there were high hopes that early liberalization would bring peace, which led to peacebuilding approaches with an emphasis on elections and political participation. A decade later – most of all after 9/11 – the quest for stability became the international priority.

Taking these different aspects of time seriously, future research could provide systematic insights into and across postwar contexts. The inclusion of history and the dynamics of change could also bring forward the debate on hybridity. As Ramirez shows in his chapter on Mexico, hybridity is not a new development; rather it is the common outcome of complex reform processes and helps us include informal institutions and everyday practices.

## Policy implications

The different chapters of this volume also provide practical implications for peacebuilding approaches in postwar societies beyond a mere 'context matters' argument.

First, historical and cultural institutions should always be taken into account when designing reforms or new institutions. Reformers should first ask what institutions can mitigate or embed conflicts and how they need to be changed. The shape and dynamic of a process will then depend on the existing institution and the reform design. Depending on the reform process, the group of actors involved will be different, as will the related timing and time frame. Regarding the security sector, for example, external and internal actors should ask themselves the following questions: Who provides security on the ground? How did these institutions change due to war and violence? Are they compatible with the reform process or new designs? What actors do reform processes need to include? Similar questions should be asked about other institutional changes that are part of the liberal peacebuilding menu, such as decentralization and electoral politics.

Second, different reforms cannot be singled out, as they will directly or indirectly relate to each other. Where electoral politics change, the importance of or the access to executive power at the national level, regional and local elites might see themselves as losers of the reform. At the same time, decentralization may strengthen the relative position of local elites. External actors should be very aware of the changing power relations influenced by reforms and not only transfer best practices or hope that institutions function as they were designed to do.

Third, reform processes need to be executed with a high level of conflict sensitivity. In recent years a lot of evidence has been gathered on election-related violence. The problems go much deeper than the riots or protests following contested elections, such as in Kenya. Selective political violence against independent journalists and human rights defenders is as harmful to the meaning of elections as armed conflict. Postwar state repression does not need to be widespread to renew fear.

Fourth, institutional reform is a long-term process that requires more than a decade. The renewed outbreak of violence in Burundi points to the underlying conflict factors, which may persist for decades after the war. Elites may accept institutional reform at the beginning of a postwar reform process (e.g. term limits for the executive), but they may also change their stance in a certain context (for example, after an international mission leaves the country or when power relations change in their favour).

Fifth, the systematic inclusion of time as an important factor could help identify short-term possibilities and their long-term implications. Power-sharing arrangements are an important case in point: while they may serve to stabilize postwar peace during the initial years, the introduction of sunset clauses (see Schmidt and Gaylan, Chapter 5, this volume) may substantially change actors' perceptions either in favour of or against subsequent reforms.

The main message provided here to policy makers is simple: there is no short cut to achieving postwar peace; rather, it is a continuous struggle of nonviolent conflict transformation.

## Note

1   'Denmark' does not refer to the country but rather to 'the common core of the structure of the workings of the public sector in countries usually called "developed" (including new arrivals like Singapore)' (Pritchett and Woolcock 2004: 192).

## References

Grzymala-Busse, A. 2011. 'Time Will Tell? Temporality and the Analysis of Causal Mechanisms and Processes'. *Comparative Political Studies* 44(9): 1267–1297. doi:10.1177/0010414010390653.

Pritchett, Lant and Michael Woolcock. 2004. 'Solutions When the Solution Is the Problem: Arraying the Disarray in Development'. *World Development* 32(2): 191–212. doi:10.1016/j.worlddev.2003.08.009.

Sedra, Mark. 2007. 'Security Sector Reform in Afghanistan and Iraq: Exposing a Concept in Crisis'. *Journal of Peacebuilding and Development* 3(2): 7–23. doi:10.1080/154231 66.2007.486990145914.

Walter, Barbara F. 1997. 'The Critical Barrier to Civil War Settlement'. *International Organization* 51(3): 335–364.

# Index